Greetings
from *Cool Breezes*

A Family's Year Aboard

by Jeananne Kathol Kirwin

Fair winds!
Jeananne Kathol Kirwin

To PDK
who is, despite his protests,
the hero of this story.

For yesterday is but a dream,
And tomorrow is only a vision:
But today well-lived makes
Every yesterday a dream of happiness,
And every tomorrow a vision of hope.
Look well therefore to this day!
Such is the salutation to the dawn.

– *Salutation to the Dawn* from the Sanskrit

Canadä

*The Publishers acknowledge the financial assistance of the
Government of Canada through the Book Publishing Industry
Development Program (BPIDP) for our publishing activities.*

National Library of Canada Cataloguing in Publication

Kirwin, Jeananne Kathol, 1958-
Greetings from cool breezes: a family's year aboard / Jeananne
Kathol Kirwin.

ISBN 0-88887-309-3

1. Kirwin, Jeananne Kathol, 1958—Travel—Bahamas. 2. Boats
and boating—Bahamas. 3. Bahamas—Description and travel.
4. Kirwin, Jeananne Kathol, 1958—Travel—Cuba. 5. Boats and
boating—Cuba. 6. Cuba—Description and travel. I. Title.

G475.K47A3 2006   917.296   C2005-905870-6

*Cover design by Bull's Eye Design, Ottawa.
Printed and bound in Canada on acid free paper.*

Greetings
from *Cool Breezes*

A Family's Year Aboard

by Jeananne Kathol Kirwin

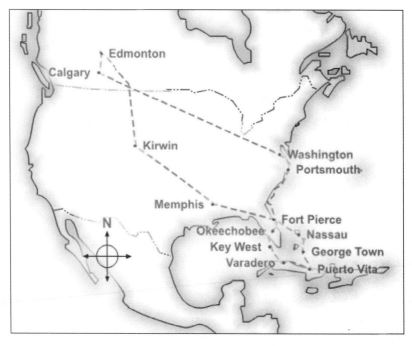

Borealis Press
Ottawa
2005

Table of Contents

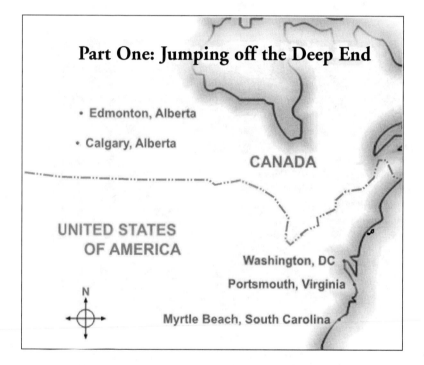

Part One: Jumping off the Deep End

- Edmonton, Alberta
- Calgary, Alberta

CANADA

UNITED STATES
OF AMERICA

Washington, DC

Portsmouth, Virginia

N

Myrtle Beach, South Carolina

June 2000.
The Kirwin family, front row from left to right:
Ben, Meara, Liam, Jeananne, and Erin. Back row, Pat.
These landlubbers are sailor wannabes.

Chapter 1
The Ten-Year Plan

Twenty years from now you will be more disappointed by the things you didn't do than by the ones you did. So throw off the bowlines. Sail away from the safe harbour. Catch the trade winds in your sails. Explore. Dream. Discover.

– Mark Twain

The alluring sea beckons sailors from every corner of the earth. They ply the seven seas and traverse the world's great lakes and waterways. They meander along rivers and canals, and tuck into safe harbours. A motley crew, these sailors are. A few are single-handers, sailing solo wherever the wind takes them. Many are retired couples, living a long-held dream. A handful are adventurers, risk-takers who race in regattas and circumnavigate the globe. And some of these travellers are parents with children, cruising in the slow lane.

For one year, my family and I jumped off the Canadian prairie and into the deep end, and joined them.

There were six hands – and four paws – aboard our boat. My husband Pat was forty-three years old when we embarked, a tall, lanky man with silver hair and engaging blue eyes; a litigation lawyer with a wry sense of humour and a congenital deafness in his left ear. Our eldest, Erin, had just turned twelve. She was a tall, strong, graceful girl with long blond hair, a lovely singing voice, an excellent eye for detail, and loads of social skills. Ben was ten years old. Tall and intellectual, he was artistic and sensitive, unfailingly cheerful and eager to help. Liam was nine years old. He was a very physical and affectionate boy with a large, athletic body, a musical streak, and a keen mind. Meara had just turned four, a sweet, cheerful wisp of a girl with dimpled cheeks and big blue eyes, who chattered constantly. Our red dog, Jasper, a Labrador retriever, was five in human years. And I was forty-two years old, a lawyer with a part-time practice and an over-time career as wife, mother and volunteer; a typical harried and many-hatted North American woman. I was also a wannabe writer, with plenty of story ideas but never enough time to write.

Our decision to take a year off in the middle of our lives wasn't made on a sudden whim. Far from being a half-baked idea, our plan was, if anything, overcooked. One fall evening in 1990, when Ben and Erin were one and two years old, Pat and I took a night off. We became immersed in one of those blue-sky conversations young couples seem able to enjoy only when they leave the confines of home.

"Hey, Jake, you know what I'd like to do next?" Pat asked.

"What's that?" I said, thinking he referred to the next segment of our date night.

Then he dropped the bomb.

"I'd like to take our family on a long sailing trip!"

I was stunned. This conversation was not just far-reaching: it was far-fetched. We were born and raised landlubbers. We had two toddlers, a baby on the way, two fledgling law careers, and no family money or independent income. Some years, the Valentine's Day gift budget had been two loonies – one for each of us.

Yet Pat's idea caught my imagination. Taking a mid-life break was a good idea, given our family history. Pat's dad died as a very young man, and I was grieving my own father, who had passed away just the year before on the verge of his own retirement. Our fathers taught us we couldn't afford to delay our dreams. Then there was the practical aspect: boat travel offered not only an adventurous means of locomotion but also built-in accommodations for the whole family.

Apart from these logical reasons, the lure of the sea and the romantic concept of sailing off into the sunset appealed to us prairie-dwellers. Pat had taken up sailing when we lived in Toronto. He'd learned the ropes (or should I say the lines) on the Great Lakes, and discovered he was born to sail. I too had gloried in those gusty, often exhilarating days on the water, but unlike Pat, I was by no means a natural. Mechanically inept, physically uncoordinated, and prone to motion sickness, my participation on several of those sailing jaunts had been confined to mixing evening cocktails and passing bungee cords to the guys as they wrapped the lowered sails.

We spent the entire weekend of that momentous date, and many months following, talking out different variations on the boat trip concept. At last we settled upon what we called "the five-year plan." When our new baby turned five, we'd embark on our adventure. That would be the summer of 1996. We'd travel for one year, experiencing the full round of the seasons on the water. In order to finance the acquisition of our boat, we'd sell our small house in Edmonton, Alberta, which would soon be mortgage-free. And although we'd thought of having four children, we'd complete our family with three.

As the saying goes, life is what happens while you are busy making other plans. Instead of living mortgage-free, we moved into a bigger house in 1994. We rationalized that instead of selling it, we could rent it out while we were away. In the spring of 1995, we acquired a puppy. Labs love water, we told ourselves, and so Jasper would fit right in on board. Changes at Pat's law firm affected our departure date, but mostly it was the fulfillment of an original plan that delayed the realization of the second. In the fall of 1995, we discovered that instead of setting sail the next summer, we'd be welcoming the birth of our fourth child.

"I was a surprise," young Meara often told her admirers, with a smile and a shrug of her shoulders. "I didn't know I was going to be born!"

The five-year plan thus stretched to almost ten. Even so, we remained constantly focused on our major goal, the boat trip. Financial decisions, such as the term of our mortgage renewals and whether we could drive our old cars another year, were made bearing in mind our projected departure date of summer 2000.

Even our choice of reading materials was affected. Pat subscribed to a few sailing magazines, including a periodical about multihulls. By then he'd decided a sailing catamaran would be the boat for us. Lacking a several-ton keel, catamarans are tough to sink. Theoretically they might flip in a hurricane, but even then, their crews can hang on. As well, multihulls give a flat ride; unlike monohulls, they don't heel in high winds. Exciting on a short run, heeling is not a long haul cruising advantage. Last but not least, a catamaran provides substantially more living space than a monohull of equal length.

Meanwhile, I read every book I could find about family adventures at sea. I wondered how cruising children were schooled, how family dynamics impacted daily life, and how quotidian chores like laundry, cooking and provisioning were accomplished. I'd always pay close attention to the mother/wife figure in each story, and noticed that unlike me, most had a wealth of sailing experience.

Vacations, too, became goal-oriented. I'd have to be much more than the "bungee-girl" on an extended cruise with a crew of four children and a dog, so Pat and I took two week-long Canadian Yachting Association courses in Vancouver. Pat went on to take another course in San Francisco, and chartered boats on the Great Lakes and the San Juan Islands with his brothers to gain more experience.

Our family's only test as a crew arose the summer of 1999, when Pat and I took the older three children on a chartered boat on the Bras d'Or Lakes of Nova Scotia. Although we ran aground on an uncharted sandbar and sailed in fog, we best remembered jaunts in the dinghy, exquisite harbours, and a beach with a swinging rope where the kids spent hours flinging themselves into the chill blue water.

"I love boat trips!" Liam roared.

Pat and I felt not just delight but also relief to witness the kids revelling in the sailing experience, and to learn that as a large crew in small quarters, we could cope. We'd come to realize yet another good reason for the mid-life timing of this journey: the opportunity it would give us to spend time with the children while they still liked spending time with us.

From that point forward, we sailed full-tilt toward our departure date of August 2000. The year before we left, I researched alternatives for the kids' schooling, took first aid and Spanish courses, and brushed up on my *français* to better teach the kids. I investigated excess health insurance and visa requirements at our projected destinations. I set up the months-long course of travel immunizations for the whole family, including Jasper, acquired a year's worth of prescriptions, and found tenants to rent our home.

Another project that consumed the months leading up to our departure, related to the boat trip yet more tangibly creative, was the creation of five duvet covers, one for each of the four children and a fifth for Pat and me. In 1998, I designed a sailboat motif and began piecing the quilt-like squares, fashioning the sails of each pieced square from scraps of favourite clothes and blankets. Each duvet cover had twenty unique squares set in a sea of blue piecework, and each bore its owner's name spelled out in the international alphabet of sailing pennants. These duvet covers were gifts to my husband and children, links to home and reminders of their roots.

Designing and sewing sailboat squares was imaginative work, but what I longed to do was create a book. There was no official to-do list for what I hoped to accomplish during our boat trip, but what I privately hoped was that I might write a novel. I had a loose premise and plotline worked out, and mental images of several key characters. Little did I know that the book I would write would have its genesis in the fortnightly emails I composed for our kith and kin, family and friends back home, each one bearing the subject line *Greetings from Cool Breezes*.

In the spring of 2000, we cleared the rooms of our personal belongings. Some of these we gave away. Some we set aside to accompany us on our year's travels. The balance, an embarrassingly large accumulation of material wealth, we crammed into the basement rec room. The sheer magnitude of our task, packing up our lives, was daunting. More than that, it was instructional. I'd have many opportunities to recollect the burden of our excess in the year to come, when we'd meet many happy people with far less baggage than we had.

Perhaps the most symbolic gesture of shedding the trappings of our modern urban life came the day I stored my jewellery in the bank safety deposit box. I replaced my fancy watch with a much more utilitarian model. It was water-resistant, of course, with an alarm to wake us in time to meet the tide, and a glow-in-the-dark face for reading during night watches at sea. My two diamond rings were more difficult to remove, both emotionally and physically. Fixtures on my fingers for over a dozen years, they'd literally worn grooves in my skin.

Erin watched as I prised these treasures from my hands. "Look, Mom, your fingers have scars," she exclaimed.

She was right, but I didn't mind. My hands now felt lighter and nimbler, more ready for a jump off the deep end.

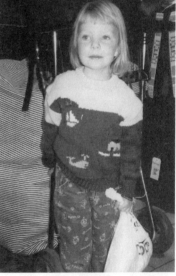

August 2000. Ben takes the helm on the trip from Myrtle Beach, South Carolina to Portsmouth, Virginia, while Meara checks in at the airport for a flight to Washington, D.C.

Chapter 2
Beyond our Comfort Zone

A journey of a thousand miles begins with a single step.
  — Chinese proverb

The air was fragrant with the purple bloom of lilacs and the pungent smoulder of barbeque smoke. Our broad Alberta skies were full of light, even at supper hour; approaching summer solstice, we'd enjoy sunlight another four hours. With the long dark winter, slushy fickle spring, and ravenous mosquito season behind us, our prairie world was in its prime. And yet, I grumbled.

"I can't wait to get on a boat and escape!" I said, passing plates of food to my assembled children, gathered to say grace.

"Why do you say that, Mom?" asked Ben.

"Tonight we're not just triple-booked, but quadruple-booked," I sighed.

This was a typical June evening for many young urban families: kids in community league sports, one parent coaching and the other chauffeuring. Our situation was slightly more complicated because we had three athletes with overlapping game times, as well as a pre-schooler in tow. But tonight was impossible. Ben was due in two places at one time: his baseball playoff game and his school spring play.

"Go to your baseball game," said my husband Pat. "When you join a team, you gotta show up."

"But I'm the narrator in my school play," Ben pointed out.

"Is there an understudy?" I asked.

Ben shook his head.

In the end, I phoned Ben's coach to explain his absence, dropped off Erin at her soccer game, and took Ben to his school. Meara tagged along as usual, buckled into the car seat that had since infancy become as familiar to her as her own bed. In the meantime, Pat and Liam roared off to their own soccer game.

Dishes undone, dog unfed, door unlocked, Pat and I reconnected at home later that evening to compare notes. In this case the good news was also the bad news: both Liam's and Erin's teams had won their games.

"It's great when the kids' teams do well," Pat sighed, collapsing in bed beside me. "But wouldn't our time pressures ease up if they hadn't made playoffs?"

Time was in short supply the spring of 2000. We were counting down toward the day we'd leave on our long-awaited boat trip. Disentangling ourselves from our hectic North American lifestyle was proving much more time-consuming than we expected. Besides his ongoing legal work, Pat was immersed in negotiations on yet another offer to purchase a sailing catamaran. I was in the midst of transferring my part-time law practice to another lawyer and packing up the house, and had just discovered carpenter ants. The tension from overdrive multi-tasking was palpable in my veins. After only four or five hours' sleep, I'd awaken with a start before dawn each day, my head spinning with new chores to add to my never-ending, ever-scrolling to-do list. Unable to fall back asleep, I'd get up and begin chipping away at it.

"Just think, next spring we'll avoid all this – we'll be on a boat!" I replied, half-asleep already. I'd begun to perceive our sailing sabbatical as an escape hatch from the multi-tasking merry-go-round.

The couple who agreed to rent our house needed it in July, more than a month sooner than we'd be ready to leave. We were so confident that the retired professor and practising psychologist would take good care of our home that we made it happen. My mother Eldean would host my four children and me in Calgary, Alberta. Since she was allergic to animal dander, and Pat had work left to finish at the office, Pat and Jasper would stay in Edmonton at my aunt and uncle's vacant half-duplex. This compulsory separation was less than ideal, but the compromise it entailed prepared us for adapting to other domestic alterations in the months ahead.

To say goodbye was another source of stress. Pat and I were flattered yet frazzled by all the farewell parties we attended. Pat found it particularly frustrating to repeatedly describe our incomplete plans in successive social contexts.

"I feel like we should just hand out a question-and-answer sheet," he quipped.

By the end of June, school was out and the house was packed. We were ready for our sailing trip, except for one small detail: we lacked a boat.

"The boat inspector says the cat we put an offer on has dry rot," Pat announced as he scrolled down a screen on a catamaran resale website. This was our third offer to fall through due to boat defects.

I found it difficult to accept that this very basic requirement of our journey was still a big question mark. Most sailors purchase, outfit, refit, provision and test run their vessels months or even years before embarking on an extended sailboat trip. We were taking a leap of faith, pulling up stakes in the belief that our boat – a reliable, affordable, roomy sailing catamaran – was out there somewhere. I felt we were living an oxymoron: unwillingly spontaneous.

"Maybe this is a sign," I mused aloud.

"A sign of what?" Pat asked, looking up from the computer monitor.

"A sign we shouldn't be taking this trip."

"That's ridiculous," Pat retorted, turning back to the monitor. "When the going gets tough, the tough get going. They don't just say 'It's a sign,' and give up!"

He was right, of course. We persevered and made the boat trip happen. That's why we'd smile, bemused, whenever an acquaintance, on hearing of our travel plans, would sigh, "Aren't you lucky!" Yes, we were blessed, I'd think, but it was prairie-style persistence and optimism that got us off the land and onto a boat.

On July 13, 2000, Pat locked the door to our house. The rest of us watched, aware this would be our last look at our home for over a year. Then we climbed into our old minivan and headed south.

Our year's travels thus began not with the fanfare of farewell on a seaside dock, but with a three-hour drive from Edmonton to Calgary. We were moving beyond our comfort zone in increments. The first segment of our year's journey wasn't so much about travel, sailing or adventure so much as it was about transition and acclimatizing to a new way of living. Of course, we didn't know that then.

Enroute to Calgary, the children chattered with excitement, but Pat and I were exhausted, sagging much like our vehicle as it rolled down the highway under its unaccustomed weight. Unloading the van at my mother's doorstep was like unpacking Mary Poppin's magic carpetbag.

"I can't believe all the stuff that came out of there!" Eldean exclaimed.

Pat's aptitude for spatial relationships would serve us well in the small confines of a boat.

Among our duffel bags and boxes, I'd squeezed in the five almost finished duvet covers, along with all the materials required to complete them. During our stay at Eldean's, while the children took swimming lessons and played with their cousins, I attached the pieced tops to flat sheets, creating envelopes into which the duvets could be inserted on cold nights. When the duvet covers were done, I laid them out for my children to admire.

"I see a piece of my favourite party dress," Erin observed.

"And look, there's a bit of my old race car pyjamas!" Liam pointed.

Meanwhile, Pat found two boats on the Internet website that looked promising, and put a conditional offer on one of them, a cat called *Cool Breeze*.

"It's time for me and Ben to head to South Carolina and check her out," Pat said, on one of his weekend visits.

Pat and I had already decided that Ben would accompany Pat on this adventure for several good reasons, none of which Liam appreciated. His behaviour reflected his unhappiness. There were many tense moments and churning emotions over the next several weeks as I single-parented a boy who clearly craved his father, leading me to wonder how our crew would fare on a small boat, spending "twenty-four/seven," as Erin would say, for a whole year. Togetherness, one of the points of our journey, had become a source of apprehension.

On August 10 our advance party flew to Washington, D.C. to buy a boat. Pat and Ben phoned us nightly, reporting on their quest. The boat surveyor they hired to inspect *Cool Breeze* deemed her to be in good condition. Made of solid Fiberglas, she was sound and strong; measuring thirty-seven feet long and seventeen feet at the beam, she was roomy enough for our large crew. And she was affordable. Within a week, she was ours.

Finding and buying our boat – our future home – felt like a milestone moment. Pat phoned me mid-day to share the good news.

"The only hitch is we have to rename her," Pat reported. "A boat called *Cool Breeze* is already registered in Canada, and the regulations require each boat to have a unique name."

We tossed around several new monikers, like *Alberta Rose, Jasper, Prairie Schooner,* and *Carpe Diem.* In the end, though, out of respect for the sailors' superstition that it's bad luck to rename a boat, we tacked on an *s* and registered her as *Cool Breezes.* The name was destined to become a source of amusement to fellow sailors as we travelled the American eastern seaboard that unseasonably cold autumn, flying the Canadian ensign: "I see you brought *Cool Breezes* from Canada!" they'd tease.

On August 19, Pat and Ben loosened *Cool Breezes'* docklines from her berth in Myrtle Beach, South Carolina, and pointed her twin bows north toward Portsmouth, Virginia. The rest of us were due to fly on August 24 from Calgary to Washington, D.C. From there the three children and I would make our way to Portsmouth, planning a rendezvous with *Cool Breezes* and her two-man crew at a certain marina a few days later. Meanwhile Jasper would stay at "Club Heather," the home of my running friend, until Pat returned to Edmonton in September to wrap up one last file. He'd bring her back to the boat when he returned ten days later.

To have made plans, concrete if convoluted, was exciting. At the same time, the four of us in Calgary felt
stir-crazy, impatient to embark.

"Let's take our kids on a road trip," suggested my sister Barbara, who also lived in Calgary. "It'll help pass the
time before your flight."

We drove to Sylvan Lake, a tourist destination set in
the Alberta parklands. Barb's son Shelby played with Erin,
Liam and Meara in an outdoor water park. The next day,
we explored a nearby farmer's cornfield labyrinth. The children delighted in the "maze of maize," but my main
recollection of that trip is of a rare moment of suspended
awareness along the drive. Allowing myself to live in the
moment, I blurred my vision and absorbed a prototypical
prairie vista from my passenger window. The impression
created by distance over time, passing field after constant
field along the country road, was of a single striped mural.
A broad band of blithely waving blond wheat and undulating yellow canola streamed by, flecked with the occasional
spot of leafy green. Above it stretched an endless stripe of
bleached cerulean. Imprinted in my memory since childhood, this landscape would often appear in my mind's eye
over the next year, even as we gazed at the seascape.

Before dawn on August 24, Eldean and Barb drove us
to the airport. With three young kids, four carry-on backpacks filled with schoolbooks, Liam's guitar, five duffel
bags stuffed with clothes and a huge drawstring bag full of
duvets, I looked like a single mother running across the
border with her kidnapped children.

"What if the American immigration authorities turn
you back?" my mother worried.

The airport officials didn't bat an eye. The only negative comment we received was from a fellow passenger as
we loaded bag after bag on the conveyor belt.

"It's amazing what some people need to take on a two-week vacation!" she sneered to her companion, at a volume clearly intended for my hearing. I was tempted to respond that these were the trappings of six people and a dog on a sailboat for a year.

Our flight to Washington, D.C. was blessedly uneventful. After our hot wet airport goodbyes, I felt deflated, yet relieved. Whatever remained undone would never get done, and there was a perverse peace in that. Like a pilgrim who sheds the trappings of secular life and embarks on a markedly different path, I could now focus on what lay ahead. I pressed open my brand new diary to a blank white page, and began to reflect. *We've extricated ourselves from the web of our hectic urban lifestyle,* I wrote. *That frees us to explore or even reinvent ourselves this year.*

Later that evening, I tucked Meara into the bed we shared in our Washington, D.C. hotel room.

"Thank-you, God, for keeping us safe," Meara whispered.

I breathed my own prayer of thanks, grateful to have successfully completed the first leg of our journey with all my luggage and children intact. I snapped off the bedside lamp and laid down my head. But it was far too soon to relax, I discovered: that very first night of our adventure, I found a lump in my breast.

I lay there pondering the repercussions of this find. Armed with enough vaccinations to resist every disease, supplied with antibiotics to last our lifetime, bolstered against injury with first aid training, we were nevertheless unprepared for cancer. Back in Alberta, I would have scurried to my doctor the very next morning, but here I had no medical relationships whatsoever. Besides, I was now on a journey; my itinerary could no longer be adjusted so easily to accommodate medical appointments. Smaller than a marble, that lump seemed larger than life.

I awoke refreshed the morning. Then, like a cloud passing over the sun, awareness of my newfound problem drifted into my consciousness, shadowing my anticipation. There's no point to worrying, I told myself. I couldn't do anything about it that day. Perhaps if I ignored it, the lump would disappear.

We had reservations that day on a train to Newport News, Virginia, the closest railway stop to Portsmouth. I called ahead to inquire about transporting our unusually large quantity of luggage and oversized bag of duvets.

"Come to the station early, and we'll check it all into the baggage car for you," the clerk said. When we arrived at the station, though, the clerk informed me that the train on which we had booked seats had no baggage car.

"No worries," said the friendly porter who'd appointed himself our guardian angel. "They'll still let you on board with all this stuff."

Our train was late, very late, and it was hot. We waited, wilted, on the dimly lit platform, engulfed in train fumes and wails. Finally our train arrived with a shriek. Pressed by a huge crowd of commuters, we lurched toward the train doors. Our adoptive porter had just begun to help us board, when a station attendant confronted us.

"You can't take all of this with you in a passenger car," she announced gruffly, arms akimbo on her matronly hips.

"But there's no baggage car on this train," our porter argued.

My face must have revealed my distress; even the children looked dismayed. The Amtrak attendant relented enough to allow us to board with all the regular bags and the guitar, but insisted we part with the "big bag," the one filled with our precious duvets. My heart drooped. I glanced at our porter, but he just shrugged.

"Tell you what, I'll check your big bag with the baggage clerk for you," he promised. "It'll arrive in a cuppla days at Newport News."

Knowing I must entrust two years' labour and considerable sentimental value with this man, I studied his kind dark face and made a mental note of the name on his badge. Pressing some cash in his hand, I nodded.

When the train reached Newport News, it was late and dark, but the bus to Norfolk, Virginia was waiting. Compared to the train, the bus was a breeze to board. Clutching her favourite stuffed toy, Meara cuddled into my lap. Soon we both fell asleep.

We awoke startled when the bus lurched to a stop in Norfolk. The movie title *Planes, Trains and Automobiles* sprang to mind as I announced to the kids, "Now we get to take a cab across the river to Portsmouth!"

We clambered into our last set of wheels that day and, soon after that, into our hotel beds, right next door to the marina where *Cool Breezes* would dock. That's when Meara discovered she'd lost her favourite toy on the bus.

"I can't sleep without my Sealie!" she sobbed. Leaving Sealie behind was as much a loss to Meara as abandoning my duvets had been to me. No sooner had my exhausted little girl dropped off, than the hotel room phone rang.

"Pat!" I exclaimed, overjoyed to hear his voice. "We're here!" I added, stating the obvious.

"Well, Jake, we're nowhere close," he said, and went on to describe *Cool Breezes'* delay: the malfunction of the port diesel engine, the drama of being caught in a lightning storm, and the rudder repair occasioned by running into an unmarked sandbar. I could hear the frustration in his voice. This was no time to tell him about the precious things we'd lost, or the worrisome thing I'd found.

The four of us stayed in Portsmouth two more days.

We whiled away the time wading through the muggy air in the hot sun, exploring the picturesque historical quarter, and swimming in the hotel pool. Each evening, Pat would call to report on *Cool Breezes'* northward progress.

On Sunday the 27th, we attended Mass. As if in answer to my prayers, we received word that afternoon that our big bag of duvets had been delivered to Newport News.

"Let's grab a cab and go get it!" I shouted to the kids. An hour later, as I hoisted that precious bundle over my shoulder, I felt jolly as Santa Claus with his big bag of toys.

Back at the hotel room, we received another wished-for message: that Pat and Ben would arrive in Portsmouth the next day.

Does absence make the heart grow fonder, or does out of sight mean out of mind? I had no doubt as to which truism held the truth, as I took a long and leisurely soak in the hotel tub that night, and surveyed my naked self in the mirror. It somehow surprised me that the reflection of my breast revealed no lump.

Only twenty days had passed since I'd last seen my man, but it seemed a lifetime ago.

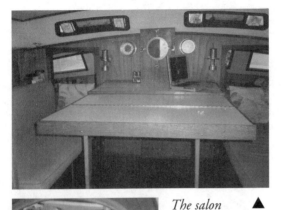

The salon ▲

◀ *Erin's stateroom*

The boys' stateroom ▼

The galley ▼

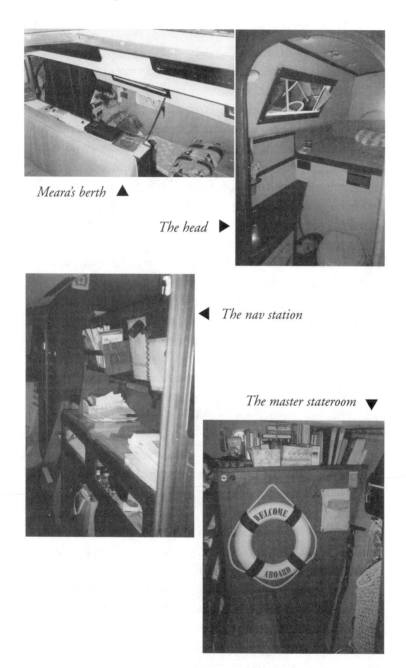

Meara's berth ▲

The head ▶

◀ *The nav station*

The master stateroom ▼

From: The Kirwin crew
To: Kith and Kin
Subject: **Greetings from *Cool Breezes*:
All Aboard!**

It's August 28 and we're in Portsmouth. Today we reunite with our family's advance party, and meet our new home: an auspicious day to begin sending group email!

After a hearty buffet breakfast, Erin, Liam, Meara and I check out of our hotel room. We stash our luggage with the desk clerk, and cross the street to the marina where we've arranged to meet Pat and Ben.

"We're expecting *Cool Breezes* to arrive later this afternoon," I advise the dockmaster. "If she arrives earlier, could you please tell my husband we'll be back around three o'clock?"

The young fellow stares, incredulous. He might have muttered, "As if I care."

"Doesn't this guy realize how momentous our reunion is?" I wonder aloud.

"He just doesn't get it, Mom," Erin replies, with a nonchalant shrug.

The four of us have a day to kill. We slake our impatience by means of distraction; we ferry to Norfolk, across the Elizabeth River from Portsmouth. Portsmouth is prettier, but Norfolk is bigger, and boasts an attractive wharf-side development. Later, standing on the high banks above the Norfolk ferry docks, eagle-eyed Liam points down to a boat on the river.

"That's her, that's them, that's gotta be *Cool Breezes!*"

Indeed, there she is, a handsome, bosomy kind of grand lady, with cream-coloured decks and wine-coloured canvas. We jump up and down, shouting and waving to the crew, but we're too far away to be heard.

Our standpoint affords us a wonderful first perspective of *Cool Breezes*, yet at that particular moment, we feel every inch of the gap between our boat and ourselves. We hurry down the hill to the ferry docks, but it feels like the sluggish and impatient run of dreams, as if our ankles are tangled in sheets. The ferry seems purposely slow as it inches toward us on the Norfolk docks and crosses the unbearably wide Elizabeth River. When at long last the ferry touches the Portsmouth docks, we spring off and sprint to the marina.

"Mommy, carry me!" Meara pleads.

"You two run on ahead!" I call to Erin and Liam. I hoist my four-year-old on my hip, sling my knapsack on my other shoulder, and trot along behind them. What a sight we are, running breathlessly, laughing through the streets of the Olde Towne! We don't care a whit; we know no one. Anonymity is one of travel's great advantages.

Our reunion on the docks of the Portsmouth marina is unforgettable. We're jumping, we're hugging, we're embracing each other with our very eyes. The sheer gladness isn't just in togetherness, but in our togetherness here, on a dock, with a boat, and long-awaited adventures before us. We relish the reality of Erin's declaration: "It's really happening!"

It's hard to say who's more eager: Pat and Ben to show off the boat, or the rest of us to see it. Everyone clambers into the cockpit for the official first tour. Off the roomy cockpit at the stern of the boat are two inboard diesel engines and a pair of davits, the structure that hoists and suspends our inflatable rubber dinghy. Overhead is a canvas covering called a dodger. The helm, including the steering wheel and engine controls, is in the front of the cockpit, on the starboard, or right-hand side. Next to the helm in the centre of the cockpit is the companionway, leading to the boat's interior.

The first interior room is the salon. Its floor is flush
with the cockpit. Like a restaurant booth, it has two upholstered bench seats, each flanking a foldaway table. We six
try it on for size, and yes, three of us fit on each bench. The
table is set into a handsome teak wall called the bulkhead.
On the bulkhead, a brass clock, mirror and barometer are
mounted between two square windows. Each window
looks into one of the two forward staterooms.

"Look, I can get to my bed through my window!"
Liam laughs, demonstrating. There is, of course, a more
dignified way to enter the staterooms. To each side of the
salon a set of three steps descends into one of the cat's twin
hulls. The boys' queen stateroom, Erin's single stateroom,
and the galley, or kitchen, are located in the left or port
hull. In the right or starboard hull are the navigation station, the master stateroom with a queen berth, the head,
our miniscule bathroom, and a narrow countertop that
with the addition of a foam mattress and a stretch of netting to hold her in, becomes Meara's new berth.

I'm impressed with the abundance of teak on the walls
and floors, Pat with the abundance of spare parts. I admire
the wealth of windows lining the hulls, admitting the sun
and the sparkle of sea; Pat admires their design. He eagerly
shows us how the Plexiglas and screen coverings can be
interchanged to suit the weather, and the clever way they
can be "chinked" closed against rain and mosquitoes. The
kids are especially pleased with the trampoline, that large
netted area between the twin bows.

"And look, Jake," Pat says, pointing to a blue medallion fastened over the nav station.

"St. Christopher!" I exclaim.

The patron saint of travellers is likely a mere legend.
Nevertheless, his name and figure embody the desire for
divine protection felt by many sailors, Catholic or not,

including the previous owners of our boat. We're pleased to have St. Christopher aboard.

We newcomers are eager to stow our gear in the boat's myriad cubbies and lockers; that would mean we belong. We load our baggage into the wheelbarrows supplied by the marina, and haul them across the street from the hotel and down the marina ramps. The trundling sound of barrow wheels along wooden docks is uneven but cheerful. Ben unclips the lifeline surrounding the deck, the boys hoist the bags into the cockpit, and we begin to unpack. Tucking each item away in its own small niche, and knowing that all things aboard are compact, requisite, or both, is satisfying. I feel proud and competent when I spread our sailboat duvet covers on the berths, then alarmed and incompetent when I survey the narrow galley with its miniature appliances. Perhaps we'll sleep well on board, but how well will we eat?

That irksome question is neatly avoided this first night. We treat ourselves to a celebratory Chinese dinner in the Olde Towne of Portsmouth. Brimming with stories at the table, and filled with a sense of well being in this world, our family strolls to our new home. We couldn't feel happier, like kids at Christmas. Our cup runneth over!

The children nestle happily into their new berths. Sitting on the docks, Pat and I let our feet swing over the dark water. Sipping our glasses of wine, we drink each other in.

That was yesterday. The marina office where I'm polishing off this email closes in seven minutes, and the dockmaster is glaring. Will send another email as soon as I can.

Till then, God bless and fair winds,
Love PJ+crew

September 2000, Great Bridge, Virginia.
Meara and Hannah aboard Clover.

Chapter
Carpe Diem

Envious time is fleeing; seize the day.
  — Horace, Odes

The pressing problem of the failed port engine loomed large over the next few stifling days. A quick decision was in order, since Pat was due to fly to Edmonton on September 3 and would be away for ten days working on that one last file. After two days standing up at phone booths, making inquiries, Pat decided the best place to repair our engine would be at a facility twelve miles down the inland waterway from Portsmouth. On August 31, we loosened the docklines and pointed our bows southward.

To leave that particular marina was liberating. An upper crust kind of facility, it forbade the "unsightly presence" of towels and clothing left on lifelines to dry. Rows upon rows of sparkling white and spanking new powerboats lined the docks, some equipped with their own hot tubs, helicopters and hired crew in uniform. The only sailboat in a sea of powerboats, our vessel was also among the smallest and oldest. And except for one exquisitely dressed six-year-old princess, our kids were the only children in the marina. I felt the constant, ridiculous need to shush them as they splashed in the marina swimming pool, to the disdain of the deeply tanned and well-coifed matrons sipping their white wine spritzers.

Of course, the kids paid no notice. Leaving that marina was not so much a relief for them as a source of excitement. This was another momentous occasion: the family's very first excursion aboard *Cool Breezes*!

"What should we do, Dad, what should we do?" they peppered Pat, as we prepared to leave the marina.

Pat did his best to instruct his rookie crew, but our docking skills weren't smooth. Nor did we shine when we encountered our first lock enroute. Our captain nearly burst a blood vessel as we fumbled about with our docklines. Even the lock keeper scowled. Then, when we pulled away from the repair facility's fuel docks, we discovered we'd failed to detach all our lines from the dock cleats, to the amusement of the dockmaster and several observant fellow sailors, and to the mortification of our skipper. Despite our crew of six, we hadn't enough hands on deck. Our first outing as a family crew may have been memorable, but not in the way we wished.

Nor were environs at the repair facility quite what we envisioned. This part of Virginia was called "the swamp," and for good reason. The air was hot and sticky. The water was still, dark and dirty. From across the yard, and around the clock, we could hear drills boring the steel hull of an immense boat. The dockmaster invited us to move to a more secluded basin, where the incessant grind of metal on metal would be tempered. But we couldn't risk it. A buzzing horde of wasps had nested in the basin, and Liam was severely allergic to wasp stings. That fancy-pants marina in Portsmouth began to seem attractive.

Meanwhile, Pat and I weren't sleeping well, cooped up in the close quarters of our stateroom those clammy nights. Each night I'd clamber over Pat from my place beside the wall and fall asleep on the salon floor. Every morning, I'd awaken covered with a shroud of apprehension, worried about the lump in my breast, yet paralyzed to do anything about it. I couldn't tell Pat, I told myself. He had that one lingering file back home to worry about, and now engine repairs. Sleep-deprived, worried about single-parenting four children aboard a boat in this strange locale, and reluctant to part with Pat for ten days, I let my old enemy anxiety creep up on me.

On the eve of Pat's flight to Edmonton, three events combined to improve my outlook on the next stage of our adventures. First, the repair facility got rid of the wasp nest, so we moved *Cool Breezes* to the more private basin. Then Pat signed out one of the marina's courtesy cars for a few hours and took all four of the children shopping. Their outing allowed me to soothe my nerves with an afternoon nap, and enabled them to buy me a variety of treats, like a few mellow CDs, some herbal teas, and a stack of Hershey milk chocolate bars. And finally, we indulged ourselves in a very pleasant dinner out with the kids at an air-conditioned restaurant, followed by red wine and adult conversation in the cockpit of *Cool Breezes* with some fellow cruisers.

Pat rose at 3:00 a.m. September 3 and set out in a rental car for the Washington, D.C. airport. As I stood in our cockpit, waving goodbye at that wee dark hour, I felt a prickle of recognition. This sense of incredulous helplessness, this distinct sensation of support crumbling beneath me, was familiar; I recalled feeling it the first time I'd been left alone with more than just one baby. This was a different situation, and I was an older, more experienced mother, yet my thought was the same: doesn't anyone realize how inept I am? It's all about attitude, I reminded myself. I shook my head at how slow I was to learn this life lesson. Brushing away a farewell tear, I crawled back into my sea berth. There was already a silver lining to the cloud of Pat's absence: I'd get the bed to myself!

"Boo!" Meara giggled from her countertop berth, only a few feet away from my head, as I struggled to the surface of my sleep later that morning. This greeting would become a regular feature of life aboard *Cool Breezes*. "Come snuggle with me," I beckoned. "My bed is so empty."

Seize the day, I told myself, watching that dear little soul pad her barefoot way on the teak floor to my stateroom. I began to envision this ten-day interlude of single parenting as a time of settling in. While Pat was away and the mechanics at the repair facility diagnosed the port engine problem, I'd become better acquainted with my galley and establish our school routine.

Like students across North America, my children began the new school year the morning after Labour Day. In the early years of our trip planning, we'd assumed the kids would take government correspondence courses during our travels. Upon further investigation, we discovered that the distance-learning curriculum hadn't been updated for a dozen years or more, and that we were geographically far beyond the boundaries of our school board's homeschooling alternative. The educators we consulted advised that since our children would be returning to "the system," the best course would be to study from the same texts as their peers in Alberta. Using books loaned by the kids' schools, I'd concentrate on Math, Language Arts, and French. Science was a discrete subject that the kids would grasp just reading the text, and we could skip Social Studies, since the kids would be living a year-long social studies field trip.

Although I sometimes struggled to exert the discipline required to maintain momentum, I thoroughly enjoyed my role as schoolmistress to my kids. Language Arts was naturally my favourite subject to teach. The experts said my kids would be fine as long as they read daily and wrote frequently. Labouring under the tutelage of their English major/aspiring writer mother, my pupils went far beyond that call of duty. Together we studied grammar, composed poems, recounted travel stories on the family website, wrote emails and letters, completed novel studies, and kept faithful daily journals.

"I'd say that's pretty frequent writing," Ben remarked dryly.

My greatest teaching satisfaction that year, though, came from extracurricular digressions. I seized the opportunity of becoming my children's teacher to include some lifestyle learning as well. Every school morning, right after ringing the brass bell, we'd read from a book of daily reflections. Each day's entry presented a scenario told from a kid's point of view, followed by questions for discussion. The daily reflection unfailingly provoked a lively discussion about morality. Later in the year, we read aloud a hilarious children's etiquette book, and worked through Ben's Grade Six drug awareness and resistance study unit. And since we'd heard many Bible passages read aloud but never read the Holy Book from Genesis to Revelation, we made Bible study a part of each day. I'd read aloud a passage, and then the children would retell it in their own words. It's hard to say who learned more, the teacher or the students.

Officially, I had only three students: Erin in Grade Seven, Ben in Grade Six, and Liam in Grade Four. I expected that Meara would colour or play during boat school, but she sat with us daily at the salon table, working on her own math workbook, doing puzzles, counting coins, drawing pictures and printing words in her journal, and listening attentively whenever we read aloud. She proved to be my most enthusiastic pupil.

"This is the best school ever!" Liam pronounced. I had to agree: that first week of boat school went very well. Liam's assessment was based partly on the fact that each school day was only three hours long, and partly on an appreciation for my book choice for our first novel study. To the children's delight on the first day of school, I pulled out a certain yearned-for novel: the latest instalment of J.K. Rowling's *Harry Potter*.

As we grew more settled into our new school routine, we felt the need to name it. Borrowing from the kids' Catholic school tradition back home, we decided to name our school after a saint. On a research field trip to the local library, we tried to find a patron saint named specifically for mariners. In the end, inspired by the blue medallion we'd found already fastened aboard *Cool Breezes*, we named our school St. Christopher's Boat School.

Those early days began to take on a familiar pattern: boat school in the morning, an outing in the afternoon, a phone call to Pat in the evening, then reading aloud in the weak light of the salon lamp. Even our nighttime prayers began to follow an outline. After each of us recounted the day's highlights and thanked God for our blessings, we'd conclude with childish voices reciting in unison, "And St. Christopher, keep us safe."

Once the children were tucked snug in their berths, I'd wind down with my own ritual. I'd brew a cup of herbal tea, and retrieve a bar of Jersey milk from my secret stash. I'd slip some mellow jazz or classical music into the CD player, and light a candle. Then, curling up delectably alone at the salon table with my emails or my diary, I'd revel almost trance-like in a keen awareness of the moment.

Life is becoming simpler, I wrote in my diary. *Although we're still in the middle of an urban area, my old hurrying habits are growing distant. I can see that living aboard means not knowing what comes next, that moving outside comfort zones tends to expand inner horizons, and that this kind of existence is invigorating.* Conspicuously absent from my diary was any mention of my big worry: the tiny breast lump. Although we were now detached from community commitments, we didn't become hermits. We couldn't have been reclusive even if we tried. The cruising community was extremely friendly, sometimes to a fault. A disparate group of people with a variety of personal backgrounds – a veritable motley crew – could be found in any marina or anchorage. Yet sailors had much in common: helpfulness, resourcefulness and conviviality. Perhaps this sociability arose in compensation for the long spells of solitude at sea, or perhaps the personality type that liked to travel also tended to be affable.

Meeting other cruisers was easy. We'd find each other in the laundry room, the skippers' lounge, or the bathhouse. More commonly, though, we'd meet in passing. Cockpits were the front porches of these nautical neighbourhoods; the docks were the sidewalks. The simple exchange of a greeting would quickly lead to an invitation aboard, and the foundation of a fast friendship. My year-long fascination with fellow sailors began during those early days in Virginia, awaiting Pat's return. Although our boat was docked, in a social sense our explorations had already begun.

At this particular marina, it was especially easy to befriend other cruisers. All of us were immobilized for weeks, waiting what we soon discovered to be a main feature of the cruising lifestyle: boat repairs. Our immediate point of connection was commiserating on the expense and unreliability of everything nautical. Trading tales of mechanical horrors made everyone feel better about his own predicament. Later that year, when I came upon the word *schadenfreude* to describe the perverse pleasure derived from others' misfortune, I immediately recalled our early days at the repair facility.

"As they say, misery loves company," said Liam in his gruff young voice.

The more seasoned sailors had their own proverbs.

"A boat is a bottomless hole in the water into which its owner throws money," quipped one old seadog.

"The happiest day of a sailor's life isn't the day he buys his boat, but the day he sells it," bantered another.

The kids and I were all ears. There was so much to learn, so much salt for our parched prairie skins to absorb! Our very first teachers were Tevi, Liz and Hannah. They were preparing their pretty thirty-foot sloop *Clover* for a long voyage, while mothballing another boat, their magnificent motorsailer *Tuppence*, in the massive covered storage sheds behind the docks.

"We're on a trip around the world," Hannah informed us. She was a comely and robust girl of six with long curly brown braids and lashes.

"Actually we're on a trip around *in* the world," her father corrected with a laugh.

Tevi was big-boned and hairy, handsome and ponytailed. Once a confirmed bachelor living aboard *Tuppence*, he was a mechanical engineer and occasional cruiser until the day his world turned upside down: the day he met Liz. The cause of his happy upheaval was lovely and briny, a wiry woman bearing the telltale smile lines and sun-bleached hair of one who has spent her life outdoors. Before she met Tevi, Liz earned her livelihood waitressing, childbirth coaching, giving massages, writing sailing articles, repairing sails, and organizing boating holidays, anything to fund her life of adventure, either on the seas or the ski slopes of the world. I admired her greatly. Unlike me, she caught on quickly, not just to life's lessons but also to its practical matters. While I was reduced to heating packaged meals in my struggle to adapt to my little galley, she rewired the entire electrical system and refinished all the teak aboard *Clover*. While I jogged the smoggy city streets for exercise, Liz began each day with a long walk in the woods with her dog and a yogic salute to the sun.

Hannah and Meara spent many happy hours playing together. Meara enjoyed the companionship of the kind-hearted older girl, and Hannah the role of big sister. At the end of one joyful afternoon aboard *Clover*, Meara skipped down the dock toward me, clutching a brand new cuddle toy.

"When I told Hannah I lost Sealie on the bus ride, she gave me this dolphin!" She named the new toy "Dolphy," and has shared her bed with him ever since. In the months ahead, she and the boys would create a whole imaginative realm using maps from the school atlas, some model boats, and Dolphy as the centre of the adventure. I can still hear the children's husky chant, a rhythmic invocation to begin the fantastical game: "It is Dolphin-land, it is Pony-land, it is Fairy-land, they are Magic-lands!"

Finding our husbands to be otherwise occupied – Pat at his Edmonton office and Tevi in the dungeon of his motorsailer's engine room – and eager for respite from the incessant metal drilling in the shipyard, Liz and I took family outings together almost every afternoon. On the unbearably muggy days, we'd visit an indoor playground, take in a movie, linger in the library, or even just shop for groceries – anywhere with air conditioning to cool off the profusely sweating landlubber crew of *Cool Breezes*.

One memorable afternoon, the two families rented a minivan and took a day trip to Virginia Beach. The weather that September day was glorious, the beach relatively uncrowded, and the pounding ocean a perfect playground for our bodysurfing children. Liam and Hannah especially relished the rush and the dash of the surf. After a picnic lunch, Ben and Meara became absorbed in their sandcastle construction, Erin in weaving friendship bracelets, Hannah and Liam in water-play, and I in Liz's childhood story.

Then without warning, the blissful serenity was shattered. A giant wave crashed ashore, sweeping up everything – our snacks, dry clothes, beach bags, shoes, blankets, towels, everything – and coating it in sand. Although we cleaned up as best we could at the freshwater pumps on the beach, we remained encrusted with salt and sand when we presented ourselves to the hostess of a restaurant on the strip.

"Just look at us," I muttered, glancing at our windswept, damp and tousled crew.

"Get used to it," Liz replied. "Typical cruisers, that's what we look like."

A half-day remained on our vehicle rental, so we mothers and children arose early and drove to Nauticus, a popular sealife museum in Norfolk. The St. Christopher's students were quick to point out that this constituted a school day for them, a combined field trip and science lesson. I didn't quibble; we had no time that day for regular boat school. Our afternoon would be filled with laundry, sweeping and otherwise eradicating our thirty-seven-foot dwelling of the Virginia Beach sand transported aboard via our clothes and bodies. We had extra incentive that day: Pat and Jasper were arriving at nightfall.

As our seafood chowder simmered on the stove late that afternoon, I took a moment to embellish the boat's interior. With a growing and glowing sense that *Cool Breezes* was becoming home, I strung a seascape-patterned curtain in Erin's doorway, hung lobster claw oven mitts above the stove, tacked prisms to the galley window frames, propped miniature Canadian flags in the nav station compartments, and stowed children's books in bins. My tasks were light but came loaded with symbolism. Each item had come from home, carefully set aside years ago for the long-awaited boat trip; each reminded me that once we had lived in the future, and now, at last, we could live in the present. The challenge would be to live fully in each moment.

After supper we sauntered to the nearby supermarket for party treats. Dusk fell. I lit a candle on the salon table and read aloud to the kids while we waited for Pat and Jasper. *Cool Breezes* shone. We were ready.

"Well, well, well," called a familiar voice.

"Daddy, Daddy, Daddy!" came the predictable refrain.

The crew jumped ship, spilling out onto the dock where Pat stood waiting, admiring his boat and his progeny from a distance. He appeared clearly pleased with what his eyes beheld and, a moment later, what his arms held. Then we turned to watch Jasper. This was her first time aboard our floating home. She stepped gingerly into the cockpit, gauging the shift beneath her paws. She walked along the decks, sniffing out her new digs, then explored the boat's interior.

"Look, she's trying to get down the steps to the hulls!" Erin laughed.

Jasper soon figured out she couldn't navigate the steep stairways and returned to the cockpit. Sensing immediately that Hannah's gift of a big beanbag was meant for her, she turned herself in a circle and collapsed in it, then fell asleep.

This was another joyful reunion, another exciting event in the family annals, another time to celebrate.

While the children fell all over themselves telling Pat every small detail of our lives, I set out the party treats, including a bottle of Cabernet Sauvignon.

"Cheers!" cried Liam, raising his glass of pop. "Finally, our whole family is together in one place!"

"Hmmm," I remarked to Pat, sipping my own libation. "This wine tastes so mild!"

Pat picked up the bottle for a closer look.

"'Alcohol removed'," he read.

So much for living life to the fullest.

Chapter 4
The Sailing Community

*Sailing: the fine art of getting wet and becoming ill
while slowly going nowhere at great expense.*
— Henry Beard and Roy McKie, Sailing:
A Lubber's Dictionary

We hoped that when Pat returned with Jasper in mid-September, our crew could finally liberate itself from life on land and follow the lure of the sea. We expected that the engine problem would be solved while the captain was away. Yet almost nothing had happened. The port engine languished on a workbench for a week, and was then diagnosed as irreparable. Watching our docklines tugging at their cleats, I distinctly felt the trickling loss of precious time from our long-awaited year away. The slap of water on the hulls teased me. Like the rub of our fenders against the rough dock planks, I chafed to leave.

In addition to our increasing frustration at the delay, we felt astounded at the inefficiency and sheer cost of engine replacement. The repair facility staff claimed it couldn't find a match for the functioning starboard engine. It would have to order and install not one but two new matching engines of a different make. Engines of a different make would also entail new sail drives. The cost of buying and installing a new pair of engines and sail drives ran to the tens of thousands of dollars.

September 2000, Great Bridge, Virginia.
The four children aboard Jasper J *with Jim and Edwina.*

"I'm not convinced that's our only option," Pat said. "Besides, I have a different financial incentive than the staff here to find a single matching engine."

Through a search of the Internet and after a few follow-up phone calls, Pat found a matching port engine within a day. He ordered express delivery of the engine to the repair facility. Noting our irritation, the boatyard manager promised not only immediate installation, but also free dockage for the entirety of our wait.

A week later, the engine arrived. The very next morning, Stan the friendly mechanic began the five-day task of installation. St. Christopher's boat school moved offsite during Stan's time aboard, partly to take all those young bodies out of the way, but mostly because the port engine compartment was accessed through the head, thereby putting it out of commission for us.

Backpacks slung over our shoulders, we'd troop down the long dock to the marina "salon." Despite its grand name, this was a modest room next to the bathhouse, furnished with mismatched tables and chairs, and equipped with a payphone. There, visiting cruisers – "transients" as the marinas called us – could enjoy respite from life on board. It was also the home of the marina's book exchange. The book swap was truly a miscellany, a collection of not just books, but also galley and boating tools, Christmas decorations, gift wrap, clothing and non-perishable food, all free for the taking to cruisers. The unwritten rule here and at every book swap on our travels was that if you took something, you must give something.

During our twenty-five days at the repair facility, we made good use of the book exchange. Besides reading material, we donated items leftover from the previous owners of our boat: deck shoes (good but too small) and bedding (good but too garish). In exchange, I rescued a miniature fake Christmas tree and tucked it away as a surprise for the kids.

After boat school was dismissed at noon each day, the kids and I met with Pat. Like Stan, he'd have spent the morning puttering aboard *Cool Breezes*, creating more storage space in the bilges and deck lockers.

"Ah, there's nothing half so much worth doing as simply messing about in a boat in the water," Pat sighed one noon hour, paraphrasing the Water Rat in Kenneth Grahame's classic, *The Wind in the Willows.*

"If the boat is our school, and Mom's the school-teacher, you must be the school custodian," Liam teased. "You're always tinkering with something."

Pat wasn't so sure of the analogy.

"Well if the boat is your school, Mom's the teacher and I'm the custodian, then what's Jasper?"

"She doesn't do anything," Ben said. "She must be the principal!"

Once Stan had trundled off whistling with his big metal lunch box, we'd grab a quick bite on board, and take off for the afternoon. Often, for relief from the heat and humidity, we'd walk to the air-conditioned library. Sometimes we'd borrow the marina car for a few hours. With wheels, we had more choices. We could make a provisioning trip to a nearby warehouse store, visit a museum, or while away a few hours at Pat's favourite store, West Marine, where all things nautical could be found. Hannah from *Clover* always tagged along.

Come evening, once the metal grinding in the boat-yard ceased, the marina social scene came to life.

"I'd like to break in my new barbeque," Pat said one day as he fastened his latest West Marine acquisition to the stern. "Let's have a dinner party."

By then I'd gained confidence as chief cook in our

miniature galley. I'd grown accustomed to baking in my tiny box of an oven, juggling pots on my two-burner stove, and using a foot pump to run water through the faucet of my twin toy sinks. I embraced a vision of myself unfolding my homemade seashell tablecloth and napkins, lighting my ocean-scented candles and the boat's brass oil lamps, and playing our Gipsy Kings CD. One evening, we fed our kids and shipped them off to play aboard *Clover* with Hannah, while Liz and Tevi joined us at an intimate table for four.

We sipped wine in the cockpit, then dined in the salon on barbequed kebabs, grilled Atlantic salmon and a tasty chocolate dessert. Mainly though, we feasted on hearty adult conversation. That's when Tevi, fortified with wine, revealed his true opinion of us.

"In all our years of sailing, we've never met anyone like you," he said.

"What do you mean?" Pat asked.

"Well, no one just comes off the prairies, buys a boat and sails away," Tevi laughed. "Most people buy their boats years in advance of their big trip. They fix up their boat just the way they like, and outfit it just right. They might even actually take the boat out on a few trial runs. But not you guys. You guys are audacious."

He stressed the label not only with conviction, but also pleasure. Kin to Mark Twain's innocents abroad, we were Tevi's innocents aboard.

"Yeah, he's right," Liz nodded. "Let's see your palms. I'd like to read them."

Pat and I eagerly stretched out our hands. Liz twisted our palms this way and that, screwing up her face as she scrutinized our lines. Finally she released our hands and said simply, "I'm amazed at how uncreative you both are."

I was amazed at her conclusion. She had no idea how much creative effort was required for us landlubbers to get just this far, I thought. But Pat merely shrugged, raised his glass of wine and proposed a toast: "Well then, here's to audacity!"

Walking along the dock each day towards the salon and bathhouse, we couldn't help but meet and greet the crew of *Jasper J,* a beamy and well-appointed sloop. Like us, Edwina and Jim had docked at the repair facility for a lengthy stay. Unlike us, they didn't appear particularly anxious to leave. Within hours of tying up, they became the social heart of the marina. Married with grown kids back in Nebraska, Jim and Edwina had cruised the same route for over a decade. They'd run down the U.S. eastern seaboard in the fall, winter in the Bahamas, and sail back north come spring. They were a casual couple, Jim nearly two heads taller than Edwina, both clad in lumberjack shirts, baggy shorts and well-worn T-shirts.

"They always look like they're trying to win a dressing-down contest," Pat said.

Jim was extremely gregarious, an incurable smoker of cigars and teaser of girls.

"What's that big red mark on your nose, Erin?" he shouted loudly as she passed by his cockpit one day. "Is that a zit?"

Erin glared, but she was mortified.

"I don't even have a zit, Mom!" she wailed.

But Pat was gleeful. In Jim, he found someone with the same wry wit, a guy like him who dreamed big and didn't mind taking a risk, a fellow prairie dog with a boat.

"You even look like him, Dad," Ben said, referring to Jim's height and silver hair. "He could be your father."

Edwina, on the other hand, was as sweet as she was cute. She was the cheerful, patient, quiet source of constancy from which her more flamboyant husband drew strength. She loaned me armloads of live-aboard cookbooks, and proffered much-needed advice in the subtle manner of the truly well-intentioned: so discretely that it came across as a casual remark rather than a preachy lecture. Edwina was not only motherly, but also grandmotherly. Keenly missing her grandkids living in the American mid-west, she gave my children countless little thoughtful gifts. She and Jim had a little game going with Meara.

"Why don't you move aboard our boat and live with us?" Edwina would ask. "That way you could be the only child, not just one of four."

"We'll give you brownies with chocolate ice cream for breakfast every day, and candy any time you want," Jim would add with a wink.

Some months later, listening to a certain sea shanty by Canadian folksinger Eileen Quinn, I thought of Jim and Edwina. That particular tune paints a poignant character sketch of the wife of a retired couple living aboard a sailboat. She yearns for her life on land, even as they live in fulfilment of the husband's dream: "He loves the sea/and the wide open space/and he's thinking he's lucky/he checked out of the race/She's thinking her grandchildren/won't recognize her face." Edwina told me that every fall, as they pointed their bow south, Jim would say this was their last trip to the Bahamas. She'd picture herself at home, surrounded by friends and family, taking her little ornaments from their boxes and returning them to her cabinets. And that's how I picture her now, in Lincoln, Nebraska: Jim and Edwina have buried the anchor.

So many times, sharing a pot of tea with Edwina, I knew she was just the person to tell about that lump in my breast. I longed for a confidante, yearned for the counsel and support of female companions. Although I'd challenge myself to speak up, I was tongue-tied. To give voice to my fear, to say the word "lump," would be to give it hard reality.

Neither silence nor denial diminished the lump. Everywhere I looked, I saw overt messages to act. October was breast cancer awareness month, proclaimed the omnipresent billboards, gnawing at my growing sore of worry. Even the American postage stamps shouted at me. The timing seemed unhappily synchronous.

Late one evening, keeping company with my diary, I recorded this observation. Then I stared, riveted. There it was on paper, a whispered admission. I began to scribble furiously, in profuse relief, as if recording a police station confession. *I found a lump in my breast over a month ago,* I divulged at last. *It's likely just a cyst but still, I must get it checked if only for peace of mind.* My diary had become both confessor and counsellor.

Mentioning the unmentionable empowered me. First thing next morning, I slipped away to the payphone in the marina salon and called our extended health-care provider. The clerk provided names of doctors in Washington, D.C., one of the cities we'd already planned to visit. I maintained my composure on the telephone, even when asked the nature of my medical problem. As soon as I hung up, though, I fell apart.

That's when Pat found me. That's how the poor fellow first learned my secret. Shocked, overwhelmed, he managed nonetheless to console me as we strolled hand-in-hand along the docks, flanked on each side by the brooding swamp.

"Why didn't you tell me, Jake?" Pat asked, his voice strained.

"I didn't want to add to your troubles," I said. Thoughts I'd never spoken aloud tumbled out unbidden. "You had enough to worry about. We've come this far with no small effort. After ten years, we're finally about to set sail on this dream-come-true boat trip. How can I let a lump in my breast sabotage everything? What if I have to go home for treatment? How can you and the kids do this thing without me? What if it's cancer?"

"It's not cancer," Pat replied firmly, as if convincing himself.

We ambled along the weathered wooden pier in silence, staring bleakly at the murky water, mired in private dark thoughts. Not until I'd blurted it out did I realize that uppermost in my mind was the prospect of ruining my family's long-awaited dream. Surgery, radiation, chemotherapy, even the possibility of death seemed remote. More tangible was the fear that after such a long wait, we'd have to abandon the boat and go home.

I returned to the salon payphone and made an appointment at a Washington clinic. I'd done all I could; the rest was up to God. That's what I told myself, but inwardly, that little lump niggled relentlessly.

Meanwhile Stan was nearly finished installing the new port engine.

"Looks as if we'll be able to take off tomorrow afternoon," I reported to Liz.

"But tomorrow is a Friday!"

"Yes," I answered, with uncertainty. "Is something happening that day?"

"Every sailor knows Friday is a very unlucky day to begin a voyage," Liz said, aghast. "You'll get storms or a mechanical breakdown or something bad for sure."

When I reported to Pat Liz's shock that we might venture forth on a Friday, he was incredulous. He couldn't believe that this logical woman, capable of re-wiring her boat and navigating an ocean, would adhere so tenaciously to an old salt's superstition.

Because Stan didn't finish the installation until late Friday afternoon, Pat and I were spared the decision whether to listen to Liz. Instead of leaving on Friday, we celebrated the autumn equinox with our "transient" neighbours. The dock party was Liz's idea. She dispatched Hannah and Meara to recruit all the cruisers to join in a potluck dinner at the dockside picnic tables. The two little girls proved irresistible. Everyone came, including a very young couple from Cape Cod. Robby and Evelyn had arrived at the marina a month earlier and ordered a new mast. The mast had arrived and been installed two weeks ago, yet the boat hadn't left.

"Turns out Evelyn's not so crazy about actually sailing," Jim confided to the small group of us. "In concept, the cruising life is grand, but now that she's been out on the water a few months, and then tied up at a marina a few weeks, she finds she's not actually so keen about cruising. She thinks life aboard is just fine, so long as the boat's docked."

"Meanwhile I bet Robby's eager to loosen the docklines and push off," Tevi speculated. "I've sure seen that scenario before."

"And I've seen a few marriages break up over the issue too," added Jim.

I glanced at Evelyn, a lithe young woman with a mane of white-blond curls. What if I turned out to be a darker, older version of her?

Another couple attending the dock party hadn't yet moved aboard their boat. While Brenda and Dave awaited the final coat of paint to dry on their brand new pontoon houseboat, they rented a room above the local bait shop. An odd and often tipsy pair, they'd fish every evening in the murky swamp.

"Do you think they eat the fish they catch?" Liam once asked, watching Dave reel in his catch.

"I wouldn't think so," Pat had replied. "Even the most naïve landlubber knows better than to eat fish caught in the polluted waters of a marina."

But Pat was wrong. "Look, Dad," Liam said, pointing at Brenda. She'd just sailed into the dock party, glass of wine in one hand and platter of "fresh-caught" fish in the other.

Other than the conspicuously untouched fish, the dockside potluck came together beautifully. Everyone contributed an appetizer or dessert, a beverage of choice, and cash for take-out pizza. Pat presented an Alberta specialty, barbequed roast beef sliced and served on buns, the undisputed highlight of the meal.

After dinner, we pressed the children into an impromptu talent show. Our kids sang songs from their choir days, Liam played a few guitar tunes, and Hannah delivered the star performance on her violin. Primed by the glow of the sunset, the warmth of camaraderie, and a drink or two, the audience was wildly receptive. The evening was a fitting conclusion to our long stay, an inkling that the cruising community bonds quickly and tightly.

"Tomorrow morning we'll test out the new engine," we told the kids as we tucked them into their berths. "If the sea trial goes well, we'll take off in the afternoon." They were excited. Frankly, so were Pat and I. We'd been live-aboards for a month already, but now we were about to become sailors.

Later that evening, we spread a chart of Chesapeake Bay on the salon table and began to plan our route north toward Washington, D.C.

"Knock, knock," called Liz and Tevi, rapping on our hull.

"Come aboard," Pat said.

Since *Clover* had navigated the great Chesapeake, Tevi and Liz had the wisdom of experience to pass along. We made loose plans to reunite with our friends at a certain point in time at a certain port in North Carolina, but in the end, we never did see the crew of *Clover* again. Last we heard, after making their way all the way down to the Virgin Islands, Tevi and Liz enrolled Hannah in regular school. Although there they enjoy the amenities of life on land, I imagine them gazing wistfully at the lovely little *Clover* as she dances on a mooring in the sparkling turquoise waters, longing to launch her on the deep blue sea.

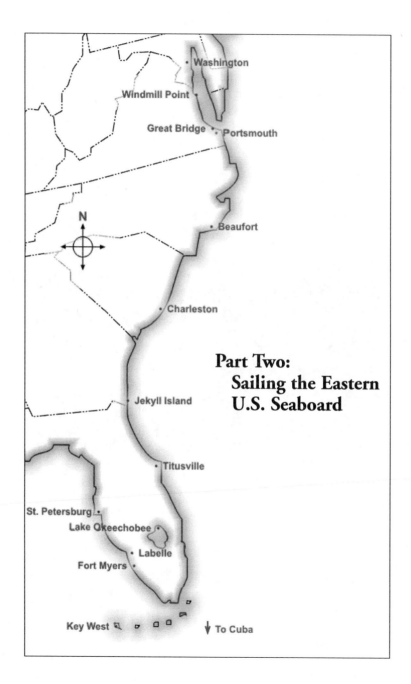

N

Washington

Windmill Point

Great Bridge • Portsmouth

Beaufort

Charleston

**Part Two:
Sailing the Eastern
U.S. Seaboard**

Jekyll Island

Titusville

St. Petersburg

Lake Okeechobee

Labelle

Fort Myers

Key West   ↓ To Cuba

September 2000, Great Bridge, Virginia.
Adventures await the crew of Cool Breezes!

From: The Kirwin crew
To: Kith and Kin
Subject: **Greetings from *Cool Breezes*: Underway at Last**

Today is September 24, the day we set sail. We'll leave the Virginia repair facility where *Cool Breezes* has been docked, and head north to Washington, D.C. The feeling is grand!

Fellow cruisers gather on the dock. Hannah and Meara share a tender goodbye. Meara climbs aboard, clutching Dolphy, a surrogate for Hannah herself. As we pull away – with all our lines untied this time – we exchange heartfelt farewells. We've got our new friends' email addresses, and they ours. All of us will be heading south by November, so perhaps we'll reconnect. Then again, we may not. An edge of melancholy tinges our exhilaration.

"I wonder whether we'll ever see these people again," Erin wonders aloud, daring to voice everyone's thoughts. Her eyes glisten, but Meara's overflow.

Sadness gives way to elation an hour later when we emerge from the lock – our captain's nerves intact this time – and face the bracing wind on the broad Elizabeth River. Even Jasper seems invigorated. Her long tongue whips in the breeze and her brown nails click rhythmically on the Fiberglas deck as she ventures out of the cockpit and along the narrow corridor beside the lifelines toward the foredecks. There she joins the boys, who love to stand on the trampoline at the bows, holding the jib stay for balance.

"Remember, one hand is for you, one hand is for the boat," Captain Pat admonishes the kids each time they leave the cockpit. In calm weather, the older three are permitted to leave the cockpit without their life vests, unless they forget

Pat's rule. If they let go the boat while underway, they must return to the cockpit and do push-ups. As for Meara, no rules seem necessary. She's as likely to shed her life vest or leave the cockpit as she is to jump overboard.

After four weeks tied to a dock, we revel in our liberation. Liam's grin is etched on his face. Pat wears the broad and satisfied smile of someone thoroughly enjoying the thing for which he's waited long and hard. He's sailing, and the new engine is working "tickety-boo"! The sense of fresh adventure is as tangible as the cool breeze on our cheeks.

Soon we join the mainstream of traffic in the busy naval port of Norfolk. The water becomes choppy, stirred by boats of all sizes and purposes crowding the waterway. We take the opportunity to practise the marine rules of the road: keep the green markers sticking out of the water to starboard as we go out to sea, and the red markers to starboard when we return from the sea. " Red right returning" is the alliterative mnemonic device summarizing those traffic rules.

Erin is below decks when a large speedboat roars past us, creating two huge furrows of water at its stern.

"Wake! Wake!" the boys shout down the companionway. They're not rousing her from sleep, but warning her to hang tight. A moment later, our boat wallows in the twin water troughs left by the speedboat.

That's when euphoria yields to dismay. A piece of debris leaps with the wake and strikes one of the davits. The cast iron arm breaks in a freak accident, leaving the dinghy to dangle in mid-air.

"What rotten luck, on our very first day out," Pat glowers. "And not a half-day after we finally left the repair facility."

I take the helm while Pat jury-rigs a temporary fix. He amazes me almost every day with his previously unrealized mechanical talents. I'm beginning to see how essential Pat's aptitude and resourcefulness are to this new cruising lifestyle.

When we drop anchor in the late afternoon, just outside Willoughby Bay, Virginia, frustration gives way to serenity. We are utterly alone in this wide, still anchorage off the vast Chesapeake. The sky is awash with streaks of purple. Erin cooks a fine meal. We light a candle, read the Bible, and utter a prayer of thanks before turning in to our berths. Safely anchored and rocked by wind and waves, our boat is an ideal cradle.

Lying here at anchor in the gently swaying water of the harbour is very pleasant indeed, I write in my diary. *What a range of emotions we've felt today: exhilaration, wistfulness, elation, dismay, and now, peace.*

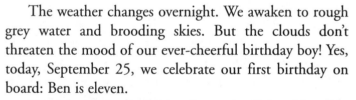

The weather changes overnight. We awaken to rough grey water and brooding skies. But the clouds don't threaten the mood of our ever-cheerful birthday boy! Yes, today, September 25, we celebrate our first birthday on board: Ben is eleven.

To kick off the festivities, I surprise Ben with a rare treat, his favourite sugarcoated cereal. This package even comes with computer game software. Through the rest of the day, I continue to produce Ben's idea of culinary heaven: cookies during boat school, Ramen noodles for lunch, potato chips and pop as we play cards during the afternoon party, and baked ham and angel food cake smothered in whipped cream for supper. There are no balloons, treat bags, or rowdy friends this year, but Ben's eyes beam. He's completely satisfied to be presented with eleven blue candles, our thin rendition of "Happy

Birthday," and modest gifts of a puzzle, Juicy Fruit chewing gum, and American cash. His favourite gift is a thick volume entitled *Visual Basic 6 Unleashed,* whatever that means!

Later that night, as he prepares for bed, Ben sighs.

"Mom," he says, setting his glasses on the stateroom windowsill, "that was my best birthday ever!"

The stormy weather continues today, the 26th. We're still on the hook. The unrelenting and unmuffled motoring sound coming from our stern annoys me. I assume the noise is made by the constant traffic passing over the nearby bridge.

"Motorcycles sure are popular in this area," I remark. My kids give me a puzzled look, then break into laughter.

"That noise isn't motorbikes, Mom. It's the sound of our own wind generator!"

The wind generator looks like a huge propeller blade, mounted on a tall pole at our stern. On blustery days like these at Willoughby Bay, the generator's roar gets rowdy. Although it doesn't generate enough energy to power all the boat's systems, it and our solar panel deliver substantial juice to the boat's batteries.

Another familiar sound these days is the clipped and gravely digital monotone of the local weather service announced over the ship's radio, the VHF. That inhuman voice is nicknamed "Perfect Paul." The routine is well established. Pat turns on the VHF and tunes in to the weather channel. The kids' ears perk up. They know that because their dad has a deaf ear, he can't tolerate background noise. As if on signal, they hiss in unison, "Shhh! Dad's listening to Perfect Paul!"

Today's the 27th, our third day at anchor. We're especially eager for good weather news. We've been bucking so energetically at anchor that Liam and I are wearing acupressure sea bands, tight fabric bracelets that counteract motion sickness. Erin and I, unaccustomed to three consecutive days without showers, are anxious to get to land. We're not as desperate as Jasper, though. The water's been so rough that we haven't been able to dinghy our poor pet to shore for more than thirty-six hours. Despite Pat's encouragement to relieve herself on the Astroturf mat we placed on deck, Jasper refuses to "go."

"I wonder if we'll have to buy her a patch of real grass like the sailors we heard about," I remark to Pat. The crew I recalled purchased a square yard of sod and taught their dog to use it. Each day they'd toss another edge of the unsightly grass overboard, until one day they found their seadog literally guarding his turf.

After breakfast, the rain abates. Are the skies relenting? We crowd around the VHF to hear Perfect Paul's pronouncement.

"Sounds like the skies will clear off enough for a short trip this morning," Pat concludes. "About as far as the Hampton Roads area."

Erin pores over the cruising guide, looking for a marina.

"Here's one with showers!"

As we approach the marina at Salt Ponds Resort, we see it offers much more than just showers. It has a freshwater swimming pool, an upscale ship's store, and – quite obviously, since you're receiving this – Internet access. Even the docks are classy, made of narrow strips of smooth fine-grained wood. Compared to the planks at the repair facility, these seem like hardwood floors.

"The cruising guide has a rating system," Erin observes. "Salt Ponds rates 'four bells,' as compared to the last marina which is 'two bells'."

After three stormy nights cooped up in our thirty-seven by seventeen-foot home, we're delighted to enjoy the simple pleasures of walking in sunshine, taking a long hot shower, swimming in the deserted pool, and licking an ice cream treat. Imagine how happy Jasper feels!

Tomorrow we'll head out again for a more ambitious day, bound for Washington.

God bless and fair winds,

Love PJ+crew

Chapter 5
Weather

*The wonder is always new that any sane man can
be a sailor.*

— *Edward Emerson,* English Tracts

To be delayed by weather at Willoughby Bay, hard on the heels of nearly a month docked at the repair facility, was a challenge for our young crew. To lie at anchor in a storm for three nights, after only one day of sailing and just as we felt the first flush of liberty, was trying. That's why we felt so eager to loosen our docklines from Salt Ponds Resort the morning of September 28.

"Perfect Paul's prediction isn't the most promising, but let's head out anyways," said our captain. "We can always duck back in if it's too rough."

Pat pointed the bows toward the Chesapeake. I rang the school bell and assembled my students. As the morning progressed, the grey water grew rough. The sun shone, but the wind rose and whipped up the water. Because Chesapeake Bay is shallower than the ocean, the waves there tend to be higher and choppier than the sea's long swells.

"Mom, I'm too seasick to write," Erin complained.

"I'm sick just reading," Liam added. "Can I sit in the cockpit?"

*October 2000,
Wind Mill Point
on Chesapeake Bay.
Meara with her
stick family, and
the boys with their
moat.*

Pat watched as my green-faced students migrated one by one to the cockpit.

"I don't want to turn the kids off sailing right at the start of our trip. We'll duck in near Back River."

Once tucked into the harbour of Back River, conditions were ideal for a few hours of sailing drills.

"All hands on deck!" Pat yelled. "Let's practice tacking!"

First we'd take our posts. I'd stand at the helm. The three older kids would kneel on the cockpit benches where they could handle the jib sheets – the lines controlling the jib sail. One of them would take position on the lee side, ready to snap the jib sheet out of its cleat. The other two on the opposite side of the cockpit were poised to haul it in. Pat would sit at the stern, his hands on the mainsheet, ready to release the mainsail. Meara would keep Jasper in the salon so she wouldn't get underfoot.

As soon as everyone was ready, and when the arrow of the wind vane pointed straight into the wind, I'd yell, "Ready to tack!"

"Ready! Ready! Ready!" the three deckhands would respond.

"Tacking!" I'd yell, turning the helm hard to windward.

The lee side deckhand would release the jib sheet. The jib would move across the wind, ruffle a bit, then fill with air on the other side of the boat. The windward deckhands would lean back, haul in the jib sheet as quickly as they could, and wrap it around a winch. Using a winch handle, they'd take turns grinding the sheet more tightly, inch by inch, so the sail would catch as much air as possible. The stronger the breeze, the harder they worked.

Meanwhile, Pat would first ease, then pull in the mainsheet as the bows passed through the wind so that the

mainsail caught the wind. Then he'd cleat off the mainsheet, and gaze upward at the sails. If the edge of either sail
luffed, or rippled, then it must be trimmed. Pat would tell
the kids to let out or grind in the jib sheet, while he
adjusted the mainsail. Only when the sails were taut
would the crew cleat the mainsheet and jib sheet.

After a short rest, we'd repeat the drill. By moving the
bows through the wind, letting out our sails, and guiding
the boom back and forth from port to starboard, we led
our vessel on a zigzag path to take advantage of the wind.
It was great fun. The kids loved it.

"Now this is what I call *real* boat school!" Ben grinned.

Perfect Paul issued a "small craft advisory" for
Chesapeake Bay every day from September 28 through
October 3. Most of that time, *Cool Breezes* was anchored
offshore in Back River, so our crew continued to practise
not only sailing drills but also our live-aboard coping
skills. St. Christopher's Boat School was a Godsend during
that time, since it usefully occupied the children's time.
Once we finished book reports on our first novel study, I
assigned another Language Arts project to the older three.

"Make a list of items or ideas relevant to our new sailing lifestyle," I said.

Erin's list was the most ambitious: a chronological record
of everything our family had done to prepare for this boat
trip, beginning ten years before. Ben made a checklist of
chores to accomplish before leaving dock. His list was so useful that we posted it at the navigation station, and consulted
it regularly. But Liam's list, entitled "Overboard," was the
funniest. "When your yard is composed entirely of H_2O,
your possessions are in just as much danger as you are," he
wrote. "The following is a list of all the things that have
fallen or been mistakenly tossed overboard!" The list thus far
already included a flame starter that fell off the barbeque, an

unidentified book that flew out of a blanket being shaken, several beach towels and a welcome mat pegged too loosely on the lifelines to dry, a roll of electrical tape, and of course, the ill-fated davit.

While St. Christopher's was in session, Pat spent his hours happily scrubbing and waxing the decks and hulls of his beloved *Cool Breezes*. During afternoons at anchor, we'd each do our own thing. Meara would retreat to her little nook and play with her toys; Pat would recline on our berth, reading a novel and drifting into a nap; I'd sit in the salon and write. The laptop, where I composed emails, could be used for the two hours of its own battery's lifespan; plugging it into the boat's batteries while on the hook was taboo. If the laptop were off-limits, I'd write in my diary or sketch the outline of my long-planned novel.

Erin became an expert weaver of embroidery floss friendship bracelets, revelling in the nimbleness of her fingers and the rainbow of colours and patterns in her mind's eye. She made at least one bracelet for each of her friends back home and for everyone on board. She even persuaded Pat to wear one on his ankle.

"You must never take it off," she instructed her father solemnly. "You have to wait till it falls off, or else it's bad luck. But when it falls off, you get to make a wish."

When else but on a trip like this would a courtroom lawyer wear an anklet? I wrote in my diary.

Meanwhile, Ben and Liam would often play a board game or practise knot-tying in their stateroom. More often they'd read. They soon consumed everything we'd brought aboard, and devoured the most popular books several times. In those days, the boys' favourite book was *Planiverse*, named after its imaginary setting, a two-dimensional world. The premise of this slim volume caught their fancy and provided a springboard inspiring them to invent all kinds of machines that could operate in a two-dimensional world. They'd eagerly exchange ideas about how to accomplish certain activities without depth, and refer back to the original book to confirm physical laws. Then they'd fill their drawing books with images of invented motors, boats, submarines and rockets. Ironically, it was a lack of fresh reading material that fuelled the boys' ingenuity.

The brisk dry winds those days made it possible for us to air our bedding by pinning it, very securely this time, to the lifelines. The effect of our colourful duvet covers flapping in the breeze entertained the occasional fishermen passing by, but we didn't care. We prairie dwellers were just learning to cope with dampness. We were beginning to feel self-sufficient, like an island unto ourselves. We were gaining our sea legs.

Midway through this six-day stretch, we ventured out on the Chesapeake to see whether Perfect Paul was right about the small craft advisory. He was. But since we were out and about anyway, and at least two of us were desperate for a shower, we decided to check out the marina closest to our anchorage in Back River.

As we approached the marina, we could see it was geared to fishermen. Weathered, mastless and net-strewn fishing trawlers snugged up to the ramshackle docks, all bearing sweetly incongruent names like "Jenny-Lynn" and "Betty-Lou." Our low and beamy vessel looked sleek, like a spaceship from the future, docked beside its more rustic neighbours.

"You're the first cruising vessel to dock here in years," said the dockmaster, a short blond man with deeply furrowed cheeks. "I don't even know what to charge you."

Like the marina at Salt Ponds Resort, this one had showers. But the similarities ended there. Unlike the gleaming tiled bathhouses at the resort, the shower facilities in Back River were basic. The girls and I huddled together in the long, narrow and windowless wooden shack, wearing water shoes as a precaution against anything "icky" underfoot.

"I hope that bare light bulb doesn't electrocute us," Erin said, glancing warily overhead as she quickly shampooed her long hair. "Now I know why our cruising guide rates this as a one-bell marina!"

"I think I felt cleaner before my shower," Meara piped up, shivering in her towel.

Nevertheless, Back River had its charms. Set in an idyllic rural area, which Jasper and I explored on our runs, it yielded a big bouquet of variegated wildflowers. Pat was mildly annoyed whenever a wake tipped over my vase of flowers, but I didn't mind setting it right. Flowers on the table reminded me of home.

The local fishermen were friendly. Each day at 5:00 a.m., their boats rumbled out into the bay, and at 4:00 p.m., they returned with their haul. One day Pat bought a mess of freshly caught spotfish for a song from the fellow next to us, who also helped debone them. While Pat grilled the fillets, I boiled baby potatoes, slathered them with butter, and sliced fresh coleslaw with chopped apples. It was a delicious meal, savoured in the cockpit at sunset. The skies were saturated with shades of pink.

"As they say, red at night, sailor's delight," Liam observed, quoting the first half of the well-known weather prediction maxim. The other half, recited at daybreak all too often, was "Red in the morning, sailor's warning."

The harbour lay still and hushed. Then, as if to break the spell, a flight of Air Force fighter jets came screaming overhead.

"We're really close to Langley Air Force Base," Pat said. Nationals of a more pacifist country, we were constantly surprised by the obvious military presence along the American eastern seaboard. "Let's try to get out of here tomorrow," he added. "I'll go listen to Perfect Paul."

The dawn of October 3 revealed a wide and sunny weather window, a break in the weather enabling us to motor-sail north all the way to Windmill Point, Virginia. There we docked at a fairytale marina resort, set in a breathtaking and secluded wildlife and waterfowl refuge. The facilities included two pools, tennis courts, a golf course, plenty of bicycles, a sandy beach, a modern laundry room, clean and pleasant shower facilities, a restaurant, and Internet access. Our crew took full advantage of every amenity. *Who'd have thought I'd find it a treat to do ten days' worth of laundry?* I wrote in my diary.

"After six days of roughing it, I think we deserve a restaurant meal, don't you?" Captain Pat asked the crew. As the galley slave, I was all in favour. To be served a meal in the company of my well-scrubbed and freshly dressed fellow crewmembers was a delight. After tucking the kids into bed, Pat and I slipped away on a barefoot moonlit walk along the beach. The waves caressed the shore. Infinite stars glimmered softly in a navy velvet sky, and the dark water reflected a million points of white star shine. The romance was intoxicating.

The original plan was to head north the next morning toward Washington, D.C. Yet the weather gods conspired on October 4 to keep us at Windmill Point. This time it wasn't rain or wind that held us back, but a glorious summery day with clear blue skies, a light breeze, and balmy air that warmed to eighty degrees Fahrenheit.

"Boat school holiday!" I called out. The older three cheered, but Meara whined.

Jasper and I set out on a long run. While I was gone, Pat and the kids played tennis. Afterward Pat and Erin read by the pool, and I walked the younger three to the beach. There Meara and I played in the sand with her new stick family. Ben and Liam built a magnificent castle facing the ocean, flanked by a boy-made lake and mountain range. Only when an angry wasp hovered too near anaphylactic Liam did we reluctantly leave the shore.

That evening, after a family bike ride, Pat tuned in to the VHF weather channel. The next day's forecast was for gorgeous weather. How we longed to linger!

"We can't stay," Pat said. "We've got to keep moving. The weather is due to change soon. We want to be off the Chesapeake and well up the Potomac when it does."

I was just as happy to leave; I was eager to get to Washington, D.C. where my medical appointment was scheduled later that month. The burden of the lump in my breast had shrunk since I'd acknowledged its existence, but its size and my preoccupation with it remained the same. I thought of it every morning when I awoke, and worried about it every night in my berth.

On the brilliant morning of October 5, the beautiful beach at Windmill Point called to the crew of *Cool Breezes* like a siren. We prairie-born sailors had imagined our boat trip having more alluring days like those at Windmill Point than the many dreary weeks it had taken to get there.

Like Ulysses, our captain stuffed his ears against the temptation and the children's pleading to stay. We replenished our water and diesel tanks, and pumped the sewage from our boat's holding tank into the marina's government-approved storage facility. We took a last shower and sent one last bunch of emails. Then we loosened our dock lines and began motoring toward the broad Potomac River.

Though the winds were too light to raise the sails, our day on the water was lovely. Our young crew needed that pleasant kind of underway day. When fog rolled in at 4:00 p.m., after almost seven hours of travel, we coasted slowly into a small inlet up Smith Creek. The anchorage was delightfully mellow, and the atmosphere so still and clear that every sound was magnified. The air all but twinkled. We couldn't resist a late afternoon dip in the clean cold creek, swimming around our island, the anchored catamaran. Yet Jasper, who'd plunge with abandon into crashing waves on the beach, couldn't be coaxed into jumping off the deck into the calm waters of the pond. After a funny and furry struggle, Pat pushed her overboard. The kids were hysterical.

"Look, she's doggy-paddling to shore!" Liam laughed, pleased with his own pun. When Pat and the boys dinghied to the beach to retrieve her, they found some oysters, which we enjoyed raw on the half-shell as an *hors d'oeuvre* that evening.

The next few days were cold and blustery. No more dips in the pond, oysters on the half-shell, or tranquil evenings rocking gently at anchor for us! Erin and Liam began to show cranky signs of cabin fever and the wind was in a dither as we pulled into Sweden Point Marina, part of a Maryland state park, on October 7. Most of the docks were green with fresh seagull droppings, so we manoeuvred with considerable difficulty against countervailing winds to a relatively clean stretch of the dock. No sooner had we tied up after an ungainly docking, than the dockmaster arrived to say we'd have to move.

"We're having a bass-fishing derby today," he said. "All the competitors will be docking here."

We re-docked twice to accommodate the arriving contestants, ending up on one of the dirtier docks. Guano is not only unsightly, but also slimy. I learned this the hard way when the seat of my pants came into unexpected contact with the pier after a rather unceremonious leap off the bow of our boat. By then Pat was impatient, Meara was whiny, and I was irritable. Erin and Liam were already at odds, so that left poor Ben as the only cheerful soul of our cantankerous crew. Togetherness can be too much of a good thing sometimes, a sentiment exaggerated by the close quarters of a sailboat. The entire crew cleared off the boat, spending the afternoon in solitude or in pairs. Each of us took a long walk in the state park and an even longer hot shower before supper and bedtime. The high winds produced a sense of isolation that befitted our moods.

Through the night, Pat and I woke often. The halyard rattled inside the mast, the wind whistled, and the boat's rubber fenders squeaked and scraped against the docks. The waves rose and the temperature dipped. Even so, by dawn I felt rested. I listened for the children stirring. Nothing. I glanced over at my snoring husband and realized this was a golden opportunity to enjoy the rare gift of time to myself. I crawled over Pat, tiptoed to the salon, and immersed myself in writing for a precious half-hour.

Schedules, commitments and social pressures govern life at home, I wrote, *but weather rules life on board.*

October 2000, Washington, D.C. Left, the mast of Cool Breezes *passes under the Woodrow Wilson Memorial Bridge.*

Below, the children pose beside the White House gates.

Chapter 6
Sundowners in the Cockpit

I have learned to live each day as it comes, and not to borrow trouble by dreading tomorrow. It is the dark menace of the future that makes cowards of us all.
— Dorothy Dix

The morning of October 8, I brewed myself a cup of coffee, huddled into a blanket, and moved outside to the cockpit. There I gazed at the misty coolness hovering over the Potomac River. I let my mind drift like the water spreading outward from *Cool Breezes*. Back home, as I ferried children to myriad activities or dozed through yet another committee meeting, I'd imagined myself relaxing in what was then our imaginary cockpit. Pat had the same daydream, he told me. It was one of the visions that propelled us during those crazy frantic last few weeks at home. My specific mental image was of a tranquil evening, watching the orange glory of sunset spill onto a million blue facets of water. I'd be sipping a sundowner, the generic word sailors use to describe any beverage enjoyed at sunset. "Sundowners in the cockpit" became a shorthand phrase conjuring up the carefree interludes Pat and I both craved: niches of time when there was nothing but the sunset, the sea and ourselves, nothing else but the moment.

"Boo!" Meara called, breaking the spell. She and I tiptoed to the galley to mix and measure and bake. Soon breakfast aromas began to mingle and waft into the staterooms
and rouse the rest of the crew. Ben's head poked through
the window between his bed and the salon, where he
could see the galley goings-on.

"Hot chocolate and biscuits!" he exclaimed.

"And real coffee!" Pat added with *gusto*. To sip properly
brewed coffee, possible only when we were able to plug
into shore power at a marina, was a rare treat.

"Eat up!" I said. "Today we're on a schedule."

Cool Breezes was due to arrive in the Washington,
D.C. harbour that day. Enroute we must pass beneath a
bridge with a fifty-foot vertical clearance. Our mast measured forty-nine feet from the waterline. If we arrived at the
bridge at low tide, we'd gain a precious few inches, and
invaluable peace of mind. Since the journey would consume three hours, and low tide would fall at 11:30 a.m.,
we must leave the marina no later than 8:30 a.m.

The morning was chilly, on the brink of thirty degrees
Fahrenheit. Bundled in wool cap and gloves, Pat inched the
boat away from the guano docks at Sweden Point against
the northerly wind. It was just after 8:00 a.m.

"Jasper's dog bowls!" Liam hollered. There sat the
water and food bowls, lined up neatly on the docks. We
motored back to get them, and headed out again.

"My watch!" Ben yelled. "I left it in the bathhouse!"

"Sorry, buddy, we can't go back again to get it," Pat said.
"We're already pushing it to get to that bridge by low tide."

"Let's do boat school," I suggested, partly to distract
my sad young son. Attending St. Christopher's was a
much more appealing alternative to shivering in the cockpit. The kids and I took refuge in the salon, heated by our
own bodies, working out math problems.

The tide was ebbing as we approached the Woodrow Wilson Memorial Bridge. It was 11:35 a.m. "We're running late," Pat said.

Our rowdy crew fell silent. All necks craned, all eyes strained upwards, as our towering mast approached the bridge deck. From our perspective the feat of passing beneath it appeared impossible, even though the sign posted at the bridge trestle said fifty-one feet. What if our mast was really higher than forty-nine feet? We braced ourselves against hearing the crack of the metal mast on concrete. Even Jasper stood still, her tail pointing.

Six heads trained skyward began to turn backward. We had reached the other side.

"Hurray, Daddy, we made it!" Meara squealed.

Pat clearly enjoyed the hero's adulation. Yet, as he confided to me later, there was plenty of clearance – "a couple of feet anyway." No matter; from our vantage point it seemed like mere centimetres, and that we'd passed a formidable challenge.

From the bridge we glided effortlessly into the marina in Washington Harbour, and cruised serenely into our next few weeks in the nation's capital. The weather warmed to the mid-seventies. The skies were mostly clear and blue. Fresh food was both plentiful and readily available; laundry, shower facilities and email were all just steps away. The most memorable attraction of the marina, though, was the people. We'd docked in the midst of a thriving community, the village of live-aboards at Gangplank Marina.

The arrival of *Cool Breezes* created a significant ripple in this watery neighbourhood. Our crew included a beautiful Labrador retriever, a welcome addition to this marina full of dog-lovers. Within a day of our arrival, everyone seemed to know Jasper by name. Most were well versed in our kids' patient explanation that her red coat, though special, was simply at the extreme end of the normal range of colour for yellow Labs. Jasper quickly learned to take advantage of her popularity at the marina. She'd lie in the middle of the docks and roll over as each pedestrian approached, thereby snagging many extra tummy rubs in the sunshine.

Nearly as exciting as the presence of a new dog on the docks was the arrival of four children. The live-aboards were eager to talk to them, and to find out everything about us. Often, below decks in the galley while the children hung out in the cockpit, I'd overhear the kids answering all kinds of questions. "Where in Canada do you come from?" "How long is your sailboat trip gonna be?" "Did you sell your house back home?" "Have you ever sailed before?" "Do your parents teach you school?" "Where does your dog do her business?" – and even – "Where do all of you sleep?" When Pat discovered how willingly the children replied to these and other personal inquiries, he delivered a lecture on family privacy. It irked him that grownups would ask questions of a child that they'd not likely ask an adult.

The live-aboard community was not snoopy so much as genuinely interested in the details of a cruising family's life. The marina had accommodated plenty of "transients" who were couples. Some even had pets or one or two kids. A few were Canadian; a minority sailed catamarans; but we had it all. We were the most extraordinary, in their view; the most audacious, to recall Tevi's label; and the craziest, in our own estimation, at least part of the time. We began to appreciate, with typically Canadian quiet pride, how uncommon our common middle-class urban family had become.

Our first friend at Gangplank was Karen, the woman in

the houseboat next door. Friendly and pretty, thirty-some-thing and single, Karen would often putter with the profusion of plants on her huge veranda. We'd invite her aboard at the end of her workday. She'd sip a rum-and-cola and read a book to Meara. The two of them had a favourite, the pony story *Misty of Chincoteague*. Soon enough, Karen told us her own story. She described her choice to live the *Sleepless in Seattle* lifestyle as the outcome of a series of deci-sions, beginning with her dissatisfaction as an overworked, under-appreciated suburban schoolteacher in the American Midwest.

"I was heading toward burn-out real fast, and yet I was still young," she said. Then she noticed a newspaper ad for a horticultural position with the Smithsonian Institution. An avid gardener and student of botany, she applied for the job. To her surprise, she got it.

"This was my dream job," Karen told us, "but how could I afford to live in D.C. on a reduced salary? I knew housing prices were much higher here. Yet I also knew that job was for me. So I decided I'd take it and figure every-thing else out later."

After renting an apartment for a few months, Karen found out about Gangplank Marina.

"Although I'd never lived on a boat before or ever really sailed, I bought a houseboat. I've never looked back!"

Her contentment was obvious. It was clearly a charmed life. I looked at Pat.

"We could be live-aboards when we retire!" I exclaimed.

A few nights later, at a neighbourhood cocktail party, we met an older couple that had made that very choice.

"We'd been cruising for years, and loved being near the water, but we wanted a permanent community, too," they said.

We met and shared stories with a diverse array of people at that party, held aboard a lavishly appointed houseboat a few docks away. The hosts were a realtor, ironically enough, and his partner. We found there were as many different reasons for living aboard as there were varieties of people and houseboats at Gangplank.

Our days fell into a new and very pleasant routine. Pat and I would rise early those bright, cool and still mornings and take our dog for a walk. It was more important than ever for Jasper to exercise in the morning, because she usually spent her day left behind, tied up in the cockpit, while the rest of her "pack" went sightseeing. The first few days of our stay in Washington, we returned to the boat to find her gone, the leash or boat line completely chewed through. The friendly dockmaster found Jasper running around the marina looking for us, or standing stymied by the locked gate, and kept her until we returned.

At dusk each day, Jasper and I had another favourite routine. Feeling light as a breeze in a tank top and shorts, I'd take her on a run to Hain's Point, a lush and shady park across the channel. Running over the arched bridge, I could see *Cool Breezes* and her happy crew. Sometimes I'd see them walking to the fish market down the boardwalk to buy our supper. I felt very lucky indeed, and part of that good fortune was having an adoring and affectionate bodyguard to escort me on my runs. She was my passport. The beauty of it was Jasper loved me, and running, not necessarily in that order. We made a great team.

In between our morning and evening routines, we spent our days touring the sights of the nation's capital. We became expert navigators of the Metro subway system, but also gained a real appreciation for the capital's nickname: Walkington. First we visited the museums and galleries collectively known as the Smithsonian Museums. We approached these excursions as school field trips, with lessons in natural history, aerodynamics and space science. I was especially pleased when Erin noted that Ben had learned "about three months worth of Grade Six science" at the Air and Space Museum. The kids even absorbed art history. At the National Galleries of Art, we wound our way drop-jawed through the maze of masterpieces by Picasso, Mondrian, Degas, Monet and Rubens. All of us fell under the spell of the mobiles in the Alexander Calder gallery.

"Look, " I whispered to Pat, "we have our very own private security guards."

Two uniformed men followed us, none too discretely, keeping a watchful eye on Ben and Liam. The boys had a hard time keeping their fingers off the art.

"No doubt they've noticed our boys are tactile learners," Pat remarked.

The Hirschhorn Museum was a family favourite. Ben and Meara were especially inspired by the contemporary art. Meara began producing abstract images on paper, labelling them "modern art," and Ben, who was particularly drawn to sculpture, made a special request for an "art class" at St. Christopher's.

"We could do *papier mâché* in the cockpit," he suggested, and we did.

Other days we visited the Capitol building and the Washington Monument; toured the FBI building and explored the Washington Zoo; attended a concert at Kennedy Centre and clambered around the sleeping giant sculpture at Hain's Point; went to Mass at St. Matthew's Cathedral and the Basilica at Catholic University; dined on dim sum in Chinatown, and saw the White House. We couldn't help but become immersed in American politics during our stay because it was October of an election year.

In fact, it was the chits-and-chads election. We loved to tease our marina friends by pointing out that in our country, that very year, Canadians had not only held a federal election but also announced the outcome in a single day.

The American election campaign even entered our marina. Hilary Rodham Clinton had rented the *Sequoia* for an evening fundraiser (at a reputed price of US$10,000 per night) and President Clinton would be making an appearance there. The *Sequoia* was a former presidential yacht, magnificently refurbished, and over one hundred feet long. Since she was docked not more than seventy metres from *Cool Breezes,* we had a front row seat to all the preparations.

The President's expected appearance had galvanized the police, the secret service, the harbour patrol boats and marina security. Meara enjoyed the excitement, waving friendly greetings from our cockpit to the harbour police circling the docks. Untrained in the protocol of responding to disarming little girls, they'd wave back with obvious hesitation.

Pat decided that this was an ideal time to hoist the Canadian flag on our stay and eavesdrop on the VHF radio.

"He's here!" we heard a security guard announce. Moments later he said, "He's gone!" After all the hubbub and elaborate security measures, the President attended the party for a scant three minutes.

We also celebrated Canadian Thanksgiving in Washington. Since Americans celebrate the feast a month later than Canadians, we couldn't find cranberry sauce and pumpkin pie in the grocery stores. We settled for ice cream treats. Our galley oven was shallow, so we contented ourselves with roasting turkey breasts and thighs, and making a stovetop stuffing. Nobody cared. The object was thanking God for our blessings, and that was easy.

The half-dreaded, half-hoped-for day of my clinic appointment approached. The night before, I lay still in my berth, yet churned within. Both the breast lump and my worst fears loomed larger than ever. I could do nothing now but pray, and that I did with fervour.

The next morning dawned crisp and sunny, hopeful yet surreal. Despite the crowd of commuters on my subway ride to the university clinic, I felt alone, isolated, poignantly aware of nothing but how momentous the day's diagnosis would be.

The women's clinic waiting room was inundated with brochures on breast cancer. When I read about the increased risk of breast cancer among users of aluminum antiperspirants, I felt sure my brand contained that evil carcinogen. Just thinking about it got me in a sweat. I took refuge in watching fellow patients in the waiting room. That's when I witnessed an amazing five-second slice of life.

A middle-aged woman swept into the room and fell into the arms of her mate.

"It's okay, I'm okay, it's not cancer," she sobbed. Joyful tears overflowed the cups of her dark eyes.

The man took her wet cheeks into his two hands and kissed her lips.

"Thank God," he said softly, a crack in his voice.

Then it was my turn. Stripped to the waist and wrapped in paper, I waited for the physician in the examination room. I felt apprehensive, yet loathed my fear. At forty-two, my body was much too young to betray me.

A sparrow-like woman stepped briskly into the room.

"Good morning," she smiled pertly. "Let's see then what this lump might be." She moved her thin deft fingers beneath my rustling gown. "Ah yes, there it is. Well, the good news is that it's round and smooth, not typical of a

tumour. Likely a cyst. But it's a good size, so you'd better get a mammogram. How about next week?"
I explained my transient situation. Who knew where I'd be in a week?
"Well then, we'll have to schedule you in today," she said. "No small feat, since mammography is booked solid during breast cancer awareness month. But they owe me a favour, so I'll see what I can do." A moment later she returned. "You're all set," she chirped, as if she'd just pencilled me in for a cut and colour. "Come back at 2:00 p.m. They'll squeeze you in then."
The intervening three hours passed with glacier weight and pace. A mild autumnal ambience graced the tree-lined streets, sun-dappled and strewn with golden leaves. Yet I felt anxious. I went for a long yet aimless walk. I bought a muffin, yet tasted nothing. I looked at a newspaper, but found I couldn't read. My gut felt encouraged with the preliminary diagnosis, but my head cautioned against premature hope.
And then there was the mammogram to face, my first. I winced to recall those mammogram jokes women send each other on the Internet, the ones that describe the best ways to "practice" for a first mammogram. "Visit your garage at night when the cement floor is just the right temperature," the typical parody reads. "Remove your shirt and bra. Lie comfortably on the floor with one breast wedged under the rear tire of the car. Ask a friend to slowly back up the car until your breast is sufficiently flattened and chilled. Turn over and repeat for the other side."
At the appointed hour I returned, braced for the onslaught. My credit card took the first assault. Lacking a domestic health plan, I had to pay up front. Various charges added up to more than nine hundred American dollars. That gave me another source of negative energy:

guilt. Then came the personal hit. The mammogram was just as predicted – excruciating, even alarming. Feeling sufficiently flattened and chilled, I went for a sonogram. Last I visited an oncologist.

"Nothing tumourous shows up," she said. "Let me check you out myself."

Again I stripped to the waist. The doctor examined me. "I can't find any lump," she said. "Show me where it is."

My fingers moved instantly to that memorized place, but I couldn't feel a thing. My breast was totally numb.

"I wonder where it went!" I exclaimed.

But I did know. That lump got squished until it popped during the mammogram.

"Then it's just a harmless cyst," the oncologist smiled. "Visit your doctor once you return to Canada. "Until then, you can just relax."

I'm free, my spirit sang, as I burst out of the clinic into the resplendent sunshine. I was grateful to the physician for fitting me into a tight schedule. I felt greater appreciation than ever for the Canadian public health system after paying that staggering bill. But gratitude and appreciation do not begin to articulate the sensation of sweet relief that flooded every cell of my body upon receiving the news of its good health. Every possibility in the world, every adventure and dream, suddenly and wonderfully opened up to my family and me.

The marina was a few miles away, a distance I relished. Walking down Pennsylvania Avenue past the black iron rails fencing the White House, I discovered tears flowing down my cheeks. My eyes were wet not only with relief, but also regret. For two months, I'd worried for nothing, allowing an imagined dark future to undermine the joy of dwelling in the moment, within this long-awaited trip. With a sigh I dried my eyes and smiled. I felt freshly washed. Raising my face and folded hands heavenward, I breathed thanks.

Back at the marina, I ran down the docks to tell Pat.

"I told you it was nothing to worry about," he said, yet his hug was especially long and tight.

Late that night, I hunkered down in the salon of our boat with my diary. *Today I learned the meaning of 'a new lease on life',* " I reflected. *And I know where that joy comes from. It comes from suddenly arriving at a point where you can live in the present.* Until then, I'd simply replaced the cares and stresses of my land-locked life with a new hard little worry. Learning to be in the moment – every moment, whether it be worrisome or joyful – was harder than packing up and moving onto a boat, leaving a home and setting out on a journey, turning off one switch and turning on another. The lesson of living in the present – of being truly present, of presence – may be more easily acquired while travelling, but it wasn't automatic. *Will I always live by today's lesson?* I wrote. *I doubt it, but for the moment, I'll enjoy it.*

The next day, souvenir shopping at the Natural History museum, Pat asked me to choose a ring, something to replace the diamonds tucked away in a safety deposit box back home. Later, back on board, he popped in a CD. The soulful words of "When a Man Loves a Woman" wafted out to the cockpit. Pat settled me there on the cushions with my children, and gave me a glass of red wine. Then, one knee bent before me, he propped open a grey velvet box. There it was: the chosen silver amethyst ring.

"Will you marry me, Jake?" he asked.

The kids giggled. I laughed out loud. I remembered the tension breaking on that dear man's face in the waiting room, and wondered whether release from fear had any bearing upon the timing of Pat's gift.

"Yes, I will," I replied.

Then I noticed it was sunset. A million facets of blue water were tinged with orange. Aha, I thought, as I sipped my wine. At last, a sundowners-in-the-cockpit kind of moment.

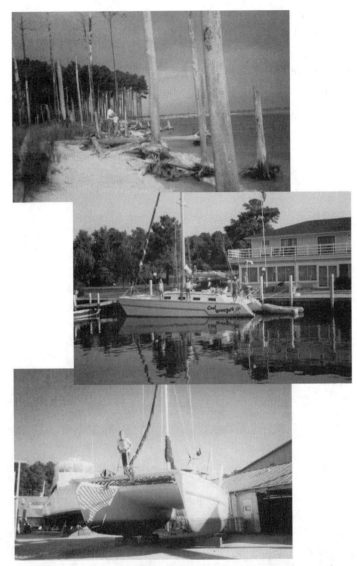

October to November 2000, Windmill Point on Chesapeake Bay. Top, the remains of a cypress forest at the point. Middle, our boat is docked in the marina basin. November 2000, Great Bridge, Virginia. Bottom, when Cool Breezes *spends a night on the hard, Erin re-creates the "bow scene" from* The Titanic.

Chapter 7
South to Warmer Climes

*Do not struggle. Go with the flow of things, and
you will find yourself at one with the mysterious
unity of the Universe.*
  – Chuang Tzu

By late October, our main focus was to get south. The
weather was noticeably nippy, even frosty some
mornings. Without a heating system or insulation
aboard, we longed for warmer climes. Besides, we'd promised Pat's mom Mary and her husband George that we'd
join them for Christmas in Largo, near St. Petersburg and
Tampa Bay, Florida. Pat calculated a two-month journey,
considering that a sailboat's top speed is only seven knots,
and factoring in variables like weather and boat repairs.

Yes, boat repairs. Pat felt strongly that we should get
the second diesel engine replaced. The new port engine
had performed perfectly thus far. Although the original
starboard engine was also operating well, Pat worried that
it might give out at an inconvenient time and place. Our
intermediate destination on the waterway from Washington, D.C. to Tampa Bay, therefore, was the same Virginia
repair facility at which we'd docked for four weeks in
September.

On October 23, we turned our twin bows southward
down the broad Potomac River to Chesapeake Bay.

Weather conditions were excellent the first three or four days of our travels, and we made good use of them. We'd get underway by 8:30 or 9:00 each morning, Pat standing at the helm and the kids and I seated at boat school in the salon. By noon St. Christopher's would be dismissed. We'd eat lunch in the cockpit, and continue our passage south-ward through mostly clear skies and still waters. At sundown we'd putter into yet another lovely, silent anchorage. Once anchored, we'd dinghy Jasper to shore for her day's respite, and eat supper. Afterwards Pat and the kids would squish together on one of the forward stateroom beds to read. They'd chosen the difficult but rewarding classic *Kidnapped*, inspiring Ben to adopt the protagonist's exclamatory "Voot, voot!" in his daily lingo.

Meanwhile, I'd sit at the salon table. With Pat's singsong reading voice as background music, I'd tap out one of my chapter-length emails at the laptop, or work on my novel. By October, I'd fleshed out my characters and plotted my plotline. Now I could weave the story. A few hours would slip by before our vigilant captain worried about waning energy supply. Between 9:00 and 10:00 p.m., he'd send one of the kids to check the meters on the control panel show-ing our supply of "juice," or battery charge.

"The needle's getting pretty close to red," Liam would report.

"Lights out!" Pat would holler.

During that time we celebrated Pat's birthday. October 26 dawned still and misty. We were docked at a marina at Point Lookout, Maryland, where the Potomac meets the Chesapeake. Since *Cool Breezes* was immobilized until the fog lifted, we enjoyed a languid morning.

"The weather's cool and grey, like me," quipped the silver-haired birthday boy. "I declare this to be a St. Christopher's Boat School holiday!"

All but Meara were jubilant. Pat celebrated his temporary reprieve from the helm by savouring freshly brewed coffee, toasted bagels and a newspaper. These basic ingredients of a typical urban morning were available to him that day only because we'd docked overnight and accessed such amenities as shore power and grocery stores. An additional benefit of docking was our proximity to a nearby playground.

"Why don't you kids play in the mist?" Pat suggested to the kids. Pulling me closer, he added, "And Jake, why don't you stay here with me...."

By noon the fog lifted and the wind picked up. We loosened the docklines and listened to Perfect Paul.

"I do believe we'll actually be able to sail today," Pat said.

He was right. After days of travelling under engine power, to sail was exhilarating. The wind blew at our stern. The boat responded with a surge of effortless drive. For the first time on this boat trip, conditions were ideal for Pat's favourite sail-set, "wing-on-wing." With the mainsail set to starboard and the jib to port, our boat looked like a soaring bird.

"Now I get why they call it wing-on-wing," Erin said. "It feels like we're flying!"

That evening we anchored at another idyllic inlet called Anti-Poison Creek, named for the mud the natives took from its bottom to make a poultice for stingray wounds. We arrived just in time to enjoy a brilliant sunset. The sky shimmered from shade to shade and moment to moment in a glorious moving light show, reminding us of the aurora borealis, that iridescent drapery that so often unfurls in Edmonton. After dinner, I presented Pat with another glorious moving light show: a cake laden with forty-four candles. The kids gave him gifts such as hand-written coupons for a shoulder rub or breakfast in bed, and poetry composed and dedicated to him. Pat responded by reading aloud another chapter of *Kidnapped*.

"Now that was a perfect birthday," Pat sighed, shutting the book with a satisfied clap.

This jewel of a day shone all the more brilliantly because it was rare. The very next morning, Perfect Paul issued a small craft advisory for the waters near Hampton, Virginia, our day's destination.

"Let's head out anyway and see how the water really is," I suggested. I had two motivations: our quest for warmer climes, and our hope to be close to a major centre like Hampton by Halloween.

Perfect Paul was annoyingly accurate. Less than an hour into Chesapeake Bay, the water began to climb. At first the kids were thrilled – running up and down the narrow hallways of our bucking bronco pontoons – but then they were ill. As usual, Liam and I were the first to feel queasy, then Erin, then Meara. Last, but clearly not least, came Ben. Taking stock of his green-faced and ineffectual crew staring numbly at the horizon from the cockpit, our iron-gut captain decided to change course.

"We're headed to Windmill Point," he announced.

"Voot, voot!" Ben shouted.

Though nausea dampened our show of enthusiasm, we felt elated to return to Windmill Point. When we passed the point, the waters suddenly calmed, the skies cleared, and the sun emerged. The difference from the conditions we'd just left was dramatic.

Bob the dockmaster appeared at the docks, astride his bicycle.

"Welcome back!" he shouted with a wave. A nimble and gregarious fellow in his seventies, his purpose on earth seemed obvious: to spread gladness. Bob made each guest feel that she personally brightened his day. I daresay he had a true soft spot, though, for Meara. "Sweetie-poops," he'd call her, much to her chagrin.

In no time we were hooked up to water and power, and to the kids' glee, cable TV. Our miniature television and VCR unit had gone neglected for weeks. That evening, Pat suggested we leave the children on board watching "Who Wants to be a Millionaire," while we ambled to the resort lounge.

"Are you sure it's safe to leave the kids alone on board?" I worried aloud.

"They're just fine," Pat assured me. "The lounge has a VHF radio, so the kids can call us anytime. It's almost like having a cell phone. The marina has a security guard, and Jasper's there as back up. Erin has babysat the others dozens of times. And besides, we can see the boat from the lounge."

To be off-duty, even for just a few hours, was intoxicating. We drank Irish coffees and flirted as if we'd just met.

A foursome stopped by our table on their way out. We recognized them as the two middle-aged and noticeably affluent couples in the berth next to us. They'd arrived late that day in a well-appointed trawler flying the Canadian ensign and bearing the distinctive markings of the Royal Canadian Yacht Club. When Ben and Liam saw her approach, they leapt to action and ran to the dock, ready to catch the docking lines of a fellow countryman. The captain's obvious apprehension melted to surprise when the boys efficiently snagged the lines and wrapped them around the dock cleats.

"Aren't you the couple with four kids on a cat?" the captain asked. "I just wanted to say we think what you're doing is impressive."

"Really?" I blurted in surprise. They'd appeared to me to be more aloof than impressed.

"You're doing exactly what we wanted to do while our kids were still young," he went on. "Only we didn't have the guts to do it."

Guts. That earthy term stuck in my mind for two reasons. For one thing, it was an unexpected word choice coming from a fellow exuding such refinement. But mostly it didn't ring true. We didn't have guts so much as perseverance, or perhaps audacity. I said as much.

"No, what you've got is guts," the man said firmly, with a deferential nod. "I mean it, I really mean it," he added as the group moved toward the door. I wondered if the regret of an unfulfilled dream lay beneath that cultured exterior.

Buoyed by the sincerity of the compliment, Pat and I toasted each other's guts, drank to our audacity, and finished our cups. We felt infatuated with each other and the dream we were living. The kids were still watching TV when we returned to the boat, so we cranked up the volume, stuffed a pillow in the window between our stateroom and the salon, and shut our door tight.

Our days at Windmill Point began to run into each other, each sunny and breezy but increasingly cold. Each day Perfect Paul predicted high seas on the mighty Chesapeake Bay, and warned small craft to stay away. After boat school, we'd while away the afternoons playing tennis, running the dog, and riding bikes. It was too cool to play in the water, but we still enjoyed the beach. We found a secluded stretch of sandy shoreline right at the point, where the ebb and flow of the tides had eroded a cypress forest. A stand of tall tree trunks, weathered white and bare, their roots exposed, bore witness to the destructive forces of nature. Pat and the boys gathered driftwood and built a sturdy chair. It's likely still there, a sentinel facing the grey-green water and the grey-blue sky.

As Halloween approached, we began to feel stranded. At secluded Windmill Point, truly a land's end, we had no access to a neighbourhood, much less costumes, and the weather prevented any move by boat to a more populous area.

"Are we gonna get to go trick-or-treating?" wailed Erin, the most theatrical of the bunch. "And what kind of costumes will we wear?"

"Let's ask Bob what kids around here do," Pat suggested.

We had no trouble finding the friendly dockmaster, riding about the property on his bike. "If I were you, I'd rent a vehicle and head to Williamsburg," he recommended.

We arrived in colonial Williamsburg on a brilliant autumn afternoon, just in time to watch a parade of costumed children marching down the main street. After exploring the historical site, our kids bustled into some washrooms with bagsful of gear they'd gleaned from our boat lockers. Moments later they emerged, laughing. Erin had dressed as a spelunker, wearing a harness, ropes, and a headlamp. Ben was costumed as a scuba diver, sporting snorkelling equipment. Liam wore a yellow sou'wester and rain gear, like any worthy sea salt. Meara, wearing a cape made from a Canadian flag and a homemade red mask, brandished a Canadian flag on a stick.

"I'm Canada Girl!" she proclaimed.

I shook my head to recall our family's perennial Halloween charade. Each October we'd agonize over what to choose, buy and create for the four children's costumes. This year, costuming had been not just easy but also fun: less was truly more. The other bonus this year was that for the first time, Pat and I could accompany the kids on their quest for treats; neither of us need remain home to answer the door.

Once we'd done Halloween, we were more than ready to move on, but each day, Perfect Paul would enunciate a fresh small craft warning.

"It sure is getting very cold, isn't it?" Meara asked one morning, as we cajoled her out of her little sea berth.

"Fall weather isn't any different here than it is at home," Pat replied.

"Except that our house has heat and insulation, not just a Fiberglas hull," I said.

"Yeah, it's more like camping here on the boat," Liam added.

"And we're ready for something other than 'cool breezes'!" Ben joked.

At dawn on November 2, Pat tuned in to the weather radio on the VHF. Perfect Paul predicted three-foot waves, but no small craft warning, so Pat and I loosened the docklines and stole away before 7:00 a.m. The children slumbered.

"It's a pyjama day!" Meara pronounced upon waking. She and her siblings spent the day in their berths, reading books and eating Halloween candy. The wind and waves remained at our stern, affording us a marvellous sail all the way to the repair facility.

"As they say, been there, done that," Liam observed. The modern adage summed up our second stay at the Virginia marina while the second engine was installed. In November, the marina was almost empty. Our first boat friends, the crews of *Clover* and *Jasper J*, were well on their way to points south. Our days grew tedious. When the mechanics arrived at 7:30 each morning, my St. Chris students and I were already fed, dressed and out the companionway, headed to the marina salon on frost-coated docks. After lunch, we'd browse at the public library, do errands, or provision. When the mechanics quit at 6:00 p.m., we'd dine late and go to bed. Pat would often stay up entertaining himself with news coverage of the botched American election. Despite the passage of eight successive colourless days, I didn't chafe to leave. I accepted the time and place for what it was, and became one with it.

The only bright spot of excitement during that dull second visit to that humdrum marina happened the day before we left. The new starboard engine had been installed. Our bilge pantries bulged. Our umpteen loads of laundry were done. Our bedding was freshly aired and our photos were developed. The kids were tickled with their new soccer ball and books. Erin had a fresh supply of embroidery floss for friendship bracelets and Ben a brand new watch. I'd bought Christmas cards and photo albums, and Pat had stockpiled batteries and those elusive, essential engine filters.

"While we're still here, we should adjust the pitch of the propellers," Pat said.

"Do what to the what?" I knew what propellers were, but not much about pitch.

"The new engines will be a lot more efficient if the propellers are properly angled," Pat explained. "Only thing is we'd have to get a haul-out."

"A haul-out!" the kids shouted with excitement.

"Voot, voot!" Ben exclaimed.

By then we'd seen many boats literally hauled out of the water by the hull on a lift with two slings, then left to rest on piles in the boatyard like ungainly ostriches with gangling legs. Some crews, unwilling to climb ladders into their boats, took a hotel room while hauled out. Not our kids. They'd visited *Jasper J* during its haul-out and thought it delightful to be on the hard, perched high as if in a treehouse. Pat and I were game to spend a single night that way, but Jasper was less than thrilled. Unable to negotiate the steep ladder, and unwilling to be far from the crew, she slept cold and alone upon her beanbag on the chilly asphalt.

"Poor baby," I said as we bid her goodnight from on high.

"She must think we humans are crazy," Liam mused.

"What the heck are they doing with their boat way up there?" Ben added, projecting the dog's thoughts.

That night was strange. Our berths were not only elevated, but also still. By then we'd become fondly accustomed to the gentle sashay of the boat as we drifted off to sleep.

The next frosty morning, the mechanics re-pitched our propellers. Then they lifted *Cool Breezes* back into the water, and accompanied Pat on a sea trial. All seemed well. But when Pat finished paying the repair bill, his first comment was, "Let's get out of here quick, before we spend any more money!"

The kids and I were happy to oblige. We cast off the docklines in the early afternoon. Since it was still hurricane season, our captain charted an inland passage along the Intracoastal Waterway or ICW, a winding ribbon of canals and locks, rivers, creeks, lakes and inland channels running parallel to the Atlantic Ocean, all the way to Florida. Although an ocean passage would be quicker and more exciting, the ICW would be safer if a hurricane struck.

That evening we anchored in the languid waters of Deep Creek, Virginia.

"Hey, let's dinghy to the park over there," Liam suggested.

Pat stayed behind for a respite from the crew, while the rest of us puttered over to a small island. There pungent campfire smoke filled the air, and mounds of crackling potato chip leaves blanketed the ground. The kids knew exactly what to do. They heaped up a huge pile of leaves and took turns launching their bodies into it. For the first time in forever, there was no need to rake and bag those leaves; it didn't matter a whit whether all the work of amassing them was undone. *Carpe diem,* I thought, feeling inhibition flee my limbs as I lunged toward the heap. As soon as I landed, gleeful, in the middle of the amazingly spongy mound, the kids began to bury me in leaves. It had been years, I ruefully realized, since I'd done this.

Back in the dinghy, put-putting to the anchored boat, Meara sighed fondly.

"It was my dream come true to jump into leaf piles on this boat trip," she smiled, pulling a stray brown leaf from her yellow hair.

"I'm glad," I replied. "I expected we'd be among palm trees by mid-November."

"Let's cross our fingers her other dream doesn't come true on this trip," Liam grinned. "Her wish to build a snowman!"

After almost a week at Windmill Point, and a week and a day at the repair facility, it felt right to be underway again. The next morning we'd embark southward on our next adventure, a cruise of the Great Dismal Swamp Canal.

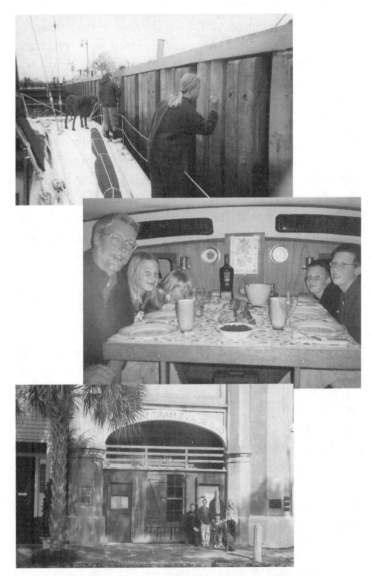

November 2000. Dismal Swamp Canal, Virginia,
where we inscribed our boat name and the date.
Charleston, South Carolina, where we celebrated American
Thanksgiving and visited the Old Slave Market.

Chapter **8**
Waterlogged

To travel hopefully is a better thing than to arrive,
and the true success is to labour.
  – *Robert Louis Stevenson,* Virginibus Puerisque

By November, weather had already dictated frequent changes to the travel plans and course of *Cool Breezes* and her crew. The soggy conditions that lay ahead, though, revealed how weather affects not only decision-making, but also frame of mind.

We rose at dawn November 12 at our Deep Creek anchorage, keen to get underway. To reach Elizabeth City, North Carolina by nightfall, we must navigate three locks, and the first opened at 8:30 a.m. Besides, we were eager to experience the Great Dismal Swamp Canal.

Construction on this historic canal began in the 1700s. George Washington was one of its first surveyors. Its principal use for a few hundred years was as a commercial transport route between Norfolk and Albemarle Sound. Now it's a protected waterway, bound on each shore by the Great Dismal Swamp Wildlife Refuge. Lock openings and maximum speeds are minimized to prevent erosion and preserve water levels.

By 8:25 a.m., *Cool Breezes* was admitted to the concrete chamber of the Deep Creek lock. Recalling the amateurish way we handled the boat the first time we entered a lock, back in August, we were intent this time to snug up and secure ourselves smoothly to the lock wall. Our skipper beamed when we succeeded.

"Look, the lock walls are covered with graffiti!" Liam exclaimed.

On closer inspection, though, we observed that none of the writing was obscene. Ben pointed.

"Everyone using the lock autographs their boat name and the date!"

"Quick!" Erin ordered Meara. "Go get the felt pens!"

Four youthful hands scrawled our credentials in each of the three locks. *Cool Breezes'* passage through the Great Dismal Swamp Canal is well documented.

The canal was well named. Our route along it was straight and narrow, bordered on each side by overhanging cypress limbs and cedars draped with grapevines. Behind them, the oaks shivered, clad in the dry remains of their fall foliage. The sky was a fitting shade of cheerless grey, the air perfectly dank and still, the water stained brown like over-steeped tea. Far from gloomy, though, our crew was entranced.

It wasn't until we emerged from the Dismal Swamp that we grew dismal. On Albemarle Sound, winds from every quarter funnel onto the shallow water, creating rough and confused seas. There we felt the chill of the lonely wind and a miserable discomfort bordering on nausea.

We motored sixty-five nautical miles on the ICW that day, a considerable distance considering the waiting time involved at locks. The feeble sun was sinking when we arrived cold, damp and weary at the municipal docks of Elizabeth City. The unexpected greeting from an elderly couple on the dock was thus all the more welcome.

"We're from the Rose Buddies welcoming commit-tee," they said, stretching out eager hands to help us tie up at the docks. "Would you care to join us for refreshments?"

"Yes, let's," I said, smoothing the kids' hair and jackets. In a big warm tent on that blustery dock, just fifty metres from our boat, friendly Elizabeth City citizens served up wine and cheese, pop and chips, and the camaraderie of fellow sailors. We learned this was a daily event. As we left the tent, a gentleman presented me with a single rose bud. *It's amazing how a cheerful word and kind gesture can revive a literally damp spirit,* I wrote in my diary that night.

The next four days rolled into each other, indistinguishable in their consistency: cold, grey, and wet. Pat and I would rise with the sun at 6:00 a.m. and embark on a nine- or ten-hour motor trip down the ICW. When the kids woke, we'd do a morning of boat school, and then I'd set the pot to simmer on the stove. Meals like clam chowder, stew, corned beef and cabbage, spaghetti and homemade sauce, and chili con carne seemed made-to-order for weather like this.

"You've no idea how great it is to come inside from the wet and cold to smell a hot supper cooking," Pat said at the end of each travel day. We'd anchor at sundown, after another sixty-five to seventy-five-mile day, in yet another swampy creek. By 8:00 or 9:00 p.m., it was lights out.

After five days of this regimen, the crew grew restless.

"Instead of the ICW, they should call it the 'icy W'!" said Ben.

"My scalp feels totally gross," Erin complained. "I need a shower!"

"Tonight we arrive in Beaufort," Pat said. "We'll get a berth at the marina there."

The marina at Beaufort, North Carolina was a treat, and not just because of the showers. The town was hip, especially after a succession of dull days. Even more important, half-dozen families were docked there and, like us, they were eager to socialize. Freshened up, we shopped, toured a museum, got a dose of email, and dined on grits and shrimp. Although we were on a steady march south, we decided the next morning to stay an extra day in Beaufort. It would be good for morale. A few families had planned an outing to Carrot Island, North Carolina, a dinghy ride across the marina, where wild horses roamed. The weather had brightened and the beach beckoned. It was a day to play hooky.

Our day on Carrot Island was golden. The weather wasn't mild enough to swim, but it didn't matter. We exulted in a barefoot day at the shore, beach-combing and collecting shells, climbing and sliding down twenty-foot sand dunes, watching the horses through binoculars, and warming our bones. Just soaking up the company of fellow cruising families under a canopy of cirrus clouds and brilliant sun was enough.

"Have you been to the Beaufort bar yet?" asked Mick of *Goldeneye*. "It looks just like the one in the movie *The Perfect Storm*." We hadn't seen the bar, or indeed the movie, fearing the trepidation it might inspire in our supposedly audacious crew. Since the establishment seemed to be a landmark, and it was only steps away from our docked boat, Pat and I left Jasper on guard, and completed our perfect day at the perfect bar.

We sidled up to the long wooden counter, intricately carved with myriad initials, and took our seats along the bank of leatherette bar stools. The oblong room was festooned with fishnets and seashells and beer logo mirrors, and lined with shelves of sparkling glasses and liquor bottles. The air was dense with a thick fog of cigarette smoke and the din produced by a duelling jukebox and television. There at the bar, flanked by groups of rowdy fishermen predictably dressed in baseball caps and plaid shirts, we faced the archetypal buxom and gap-toothed barmaid, a horsey woman with tight jeans and an unfortunately bare midriff.

"You guys are cruisers, ain't cha?" she asked with a friendly smile. We were surprised at her accuracy until we looked down at ourselves. We realized that in our rumpled shirts, weathered jeans and Sperry topsiders, we too wore a stereotypical uniform.

Back on the boat, we faced two new problems. First, Erin had killed a humungous cockroach on board. The sight of it triggered both alarm and disgust. In Edmonton, cockroaches are rare, but I knew from living in Toronto how resilient the pests could be.

"Don't worry," a fellow cruiser reassured us. "A cockroach that big lives and breeds on the docks, not boats. It must have crawled over on your docklines. It doesn't mean you have a whole nest." This advice was encouraging, yet on my next morning jaunt with Jasper, I bought cockroach traps, tucked them into our cubbies, and checked them daily.

The second problem, not as quickly remedied, was that our salon cushions were thoroughly soaked. We'd washed the covers the day we went to Carrot Island, and left them and the interior cushions to dry on the decks. It rained the evening Pat and I were at *The Perfect Storm* bar, but the children hadn't thought to bring the cushions and covers inside. Now they were wetter than ever. For the next five days, our coolest yet, we sat on the cold hard wooden benches of the salon until the drenched cushions and covers dried out, propped up in various inconvenient places in the staterooms.

Our next passage was as sodden as the upholstery. On November 18, Pat rose at 6:00 a.m. with the first sign of tepid light, dressed quickly in multiple layers and hustled out the cockpit. I roused myself to wipe down the sweating windows. Condensation dripped from them. We could see our frosty breath, even in the cabin. As Pat steered *Cool Breezes* into the channel, I poured hot coffee into him. An hour later, after setting breakfast on the table for the kids and fixing a bowl of steaming oatmeal for Pat, I took over the helm while he enjoyed a reprieve from the fog and rain, sleet and wind.

This became the pattern of our next five days. The kids and I would work at boat school for three hours, breaking at noon. I'd layer up in one of our ugly heavy-weather jackets, and take the helm while Pat ate lunch with the kids. The children hung out in the afternoons. I'd put a pot of supper to simmer on the stove, and scrub away the spots of mildew dotting the fabric overhead. Sometimes I'd work on photo albums or Christmas cards or, on the rare day Meara napped, my novel. Mid-afternoon I'd spell Pat off for a while. At sundown, about 5:00 p.m., we'd set anchor after a numbing day's journey of fifty to seventy-five miles. Locals told us seasonal temperatures were ten to twenty degrees below normal. We believed it.

After the first two days of this, the kids and I felt mired in a misty drizzle, as dispirited as the weather. Meanwhile Pat, half-frozen from his hours at the helm, would burst through the companionway positively exhilarated. "I just saw some dolphins!" he'd report, or "There was an incredible flock of birds flying overhead!" He was in his element, even as he battled the elements. When I asked him how he occupied himself, passing marker after weary marker on the tedious route down the ICW, he said he spent a lot of time thinking: mulling over legal problems, envisioning the future, or simply watching the world around him.

On one of those boat school mornings, I read aloud the day's entry from the kids' book of reflections, a piece called "The Oyster and the Pearl." The question for the day asked, "Is there some irritation in your shell that might become the seed of a pearl for you?"

"Yes," Ben answered immediately. "The weather."

I realized that in weathering the irritating cold and damp, Pat was already reaping the pearl reward. He was mentally far better off braving the weather outdoors, living in the moment, than the rest of us hiding from it.

In those days we made excellent progress at boat school. One downcast day, sequestered in the salon, we hauled out all the shells we'd gathered at Carrot Island. We identified them using a guidebook, labelled them and organized them into related groups.

Once that was done, Ben piped up, "Let's have a beauty contest!"

Erin and Meara perked up, but Liam was skeptical. "Whaddya mean?"

"We each vote on the shell we think is the most perfect specimen from each group," Ben explained. Boat school stretched into the afternoon that day, with the kids immersed in their beauty contest. Like most pageants, it got political. By sundown, my scholars had assembled an impressive array of scientifically named shells. That gave me an idea.

"Let's do student-led conferences with your dad tonight," I suggested to my enthusiastic pupils, recalling the concept of a portfolio from the kids' regular school. "Choose examples of your best schoolwork to show him."

"And we could show him the display of our best seashells," Erin added.

Among my students' proudest school assignments were their comical essays entitled "My Strangest Year, by Jasper Kirwin." The inspiration for that project was our haul-out and night on the hard, as we gazed downward at

Jasper stranded at the bottom of the ladder. It had struck us then as perversely funny how unfathomable human behaviour must seem from a dog's point of view. The children ran with it, and the results were telling.

"One of the oddest things about my pack's new house is that it floats on water," Erin wrote. "My tummy feels floaty too. We keep on staying and moving. I hate the journeys, but I always love the destination. As long as my pack is together, I want it to last."

A new form of family entertainment emerged in those lacklustre days: the after-dinner dessert production. Every night, Erin would pull out a box of brownie or chocolate cookie mix, light the oven, and assemble the ingredients. We'd wait, salivating, for dessert to bake. We'd play cards at the salon table or read, basking in the radiant heat of the oven and the waft of warm chocolate permeating the boat. At long last, Erin would ascend beaming from the galley, bearing a plateful of cocoa decadence. The tradition became addictive.

Another night, anchored in the waterway, we experienced a more thrilling form of entertainment. Reading in my stateroom at the bows, I became aware of the approaching rumble of a large marine engine and the blare of powerful lights through the bow windows.

"Pat!" I shouted out into the salon. "Something big is heading right for us!"

We scrambled to the cockpit to witness a huge barge, barrelling down the waterway straight at *Cool Breezes*. We'd done everything right. We'd turned on our mast lights. We'd tucked the boat off the marked route. Pat flashed our thousand-candle flashlight, yet the barge didn't swerve from its course. The throb of the barge engine and the glare of the lights grew overwhelming. I huddled the kids close to me.

"Why can't they see us?" Liam cried.

Then the barge made a sharp and sudden L-turn. We watched, limp with relief, as it ran off in the distance. We realized it had been merely swinging wide to negotiate the creek's curve.

"Whew, that felt like a close one," Ben grinned.

The next day, we arrived at Barefoot Landing, a shopping complex with dockage along the ICW, a much-anticipated reprieve from our travels. We fastened the bow and stern lines to the dock cleats and locked up the cabin.

"Jasper, come!" Liam called, holding out her leash. Jasper leapt off the deck of the boat. Her back two paws missed the dock. She fell with an icy splash into the frigid water.

"Jasper! Jasper!" the kids cried out.

Pat helped our bedraggled pet struggle onto the dock. The kids and I rushed to her with dry towels from the cockpit lockers. Her tail wagged eagerly as we rubbed her red coat. Meanwhile Pat descended the swim ladder to pull the dinghy up closer to the stern. That's when we heard the second chilly splash of the day.

"Dad! Dad!" the kids shouted.

Pat pulled himself up from the swim ladder, unlocked the cabin and changed into dry clothes. If he had a tail, it wouldn't have been wagging.

"Two more things to add to Liam's list of stuff gone overboard!" Ben quipped.

When we finally left the dock and climbed a staircase to the mall, we found it was lined with boutiques and factory outlets, when what we sought were groceries, showers, a laundromat and post office. We cheered ourselves with coffee, hot chocolate and cinnamon buns at a warm café, and trundled back down to the boat for another few valuable but miserable hours of travel.

To be rocked to sleep by the boat each night was delightfully lulling, yet Pat and I rarely enjoyed unbroken sleep. We
were ever on guard, always attuned to the wind and the
waves and the dread that our anchor might have loosened
and our boat might be dragging. For several nights during
that passage, I was roused in the wee hours by a rustling
noise. Did we have mice, or heaven forbid, rats? Had that
one cockroach we found aboard while in Beaufort now mul-
tiplied? One night my curiosity overcame my lassitude. I rose
to investigate, determined to catch the culprits in action.
First I inspected the cockroach traps, hidden in the galley.
Nothing there. I could tell the crackling came from beneath
me, so I stealthily pulled the bilge covers off the floors and
aimed my flashlight inside. Nothing amiss in the bilges.
Mystified, I clambered over Pat to my place on our berth.

"Where were you?" he asked foggily.

"Checking the bilges for critters," I replied. "Don't
you hear that crackly sound at night?"

"Oh that," he chuckled. "It's nothing to worry about.
In fact it's good. It's krill, feeding off the gunk on the bottom of our hulls!"

A recognizable pattern was beginning to emerge not
only in our daily routine, but also in the succession of
days. Despite the fluidity of our travel plans and course,
there seemed to be a design. After a bout of wet, cold and
dreary days, we'd enjoy a short spell of golden sunshine.
The sequence had emerged when we landed at idyllic
Windmill Point, then repeated itself during our interlude
in Washington, D.C. and, most recently, on our holiday in
Beaufort, N.C. *As in life,* I wrote in my diary, *we struggle
and push for a long while, and then we enjoy a short but
golden reprieve.* I imagined these glimmering gems of time
to be like the occasional shimmering oasis to a weary
desert trekker.

By the sixth morning of cold and wet, we were over-
due for an oasis. By then, even our cheerful captain
seemed worn down by the cold wet conditions. The
weather gods must have sensed this, for as we travelled
that morning, the skies cleared. At midday November 22,
when we arrived at City Marina in Charleston, South
Carolina, our spirits lifted with the clouds.

The next day would be American Thanksgiving. All
stores, restaurants and amenities would be closed, we
heard, so we made hay while the sun shone. Showers, grocery shopping, deck swabbing, a thorough airing of the
cabin, a pump-out and fuel-up consumed the balance of
the day. That evening, I accomplished the usually tedious
task of laundry in a decidedly convivial manner. Since the
marina laundry room was conveniently located next door
to the restaurant, I could run loads of wash in between sips
of white wine and forkfuls of peppered salmon.

Thanksgiving Day was indeed a day to give thanks.
Everyone slept in. It was such a treat to see Pat snuggled
under the sailboat duvet, instead of bundled up in the cold
cockpit, that I served him breakfast in bed.

"Hey, I never got my birthday breakfast in bed," Ben
reminded me.

"Okay, you too then," I laughed. Ben's gangling legs
scrambled back into his berth.

Sunshine streamed in the portholes. After a cozy pyjama
morning reading in our berths, our family set out on an
excursion. Jasper and I led the crew to the historic quarter,
the destination of our previous day's run. The storied city of
Charleston, founded in 1670, retained much of its eighteenth-century architecture, mostly because the post-Civil
War depression there prevented the modernization of its
cityscape. The outcome of this historic, economic and
architectural accident was an intriguing tourist attraction.

As visitors from the Canadian prairie, where anything a hundred years old seems ancient, we were more impressed than most. We ambled along the winding cobblestone and brick streets, lined with palm trees and bougainvillea. We admired rows of fine old residences painted pastel colours, with white trim about the windows and doors, lacy black wrought iron balconies and railings, and tidy brick-walled yards. The Creole influence was enchantingly pervasive. We found the waterfront park, overlooking the convergence of the Ashley and Cooper rivers, and strolled to the point. Then we came upon the ancient pink whorehouse and the old city slave mart. Despite having seen the prettiest parts of town, it was these sites that provoked the greatest response from the kids.

"You mean they used to sell people?" Liam exclaimed.

When Pat explained the history of the American Civil War, the kids were appalled.

"I can't believe slavery was right here such a short time ago," Erin said, her blue eyes wide.

"Everywhere we look we see Confederate memorials," Ben added. "It's almost as if the people here are proud of the Confederates and slavery."

"This is turning out to be a social studies field trip," their schoolmarm murmured.

Soon our scholarly pursuit became a quest for food. Nothing, not even a hot dog stand, was open for business on Thanksgiving Day. By mid-afternoon, Pat was unbearably ravenous, so we returned to *Cool Breezes* for a snack while I cooked our second Thanksgiving feast. Meara sat perched on the countertop, helping me stir and chop. We made honey-glazed ham, cranberry sauce, baked herb potatoes, cabbage and apple salad with honey-mustard dressing, and served pumpkin pie and whipped cream for dessert. At sundown we dined by candlelight on our best seashell tablecloth and with real cloth napkins.

"Didn't we already have Thanksgiving in Washington?" Meara asked.

"You're right, we did," I replied, launching into an explanation of how the Canadian harvest arrives earlier than the American.

"You can never thank God too often," she said in her wise little way.

The next morning dawned cool but bright and windy, perfect for travel. After one last hot shower, we untied the docklines. Charming Charleston had provided a dry and satisfying respite from the soggiest stretch of our journey.

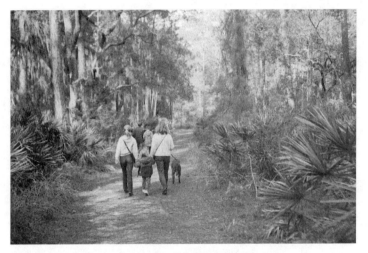

November 2000, Jekyll Island, Georgia.
Taking a stroll toward Millionaires' Village.

Chapter 9
To Florida

How a little thing can make us so happy when we feel we deserve it.
— *Mark Twain,* Tom Sawyer Abroad

As Charleston receded on the horizon, the weather became drier. Cool breezes blew *Cool Breezes* southward through South Carolina and Georgia. The ICW route became more intricate. Instead of droning along straight canals and dredged cuts, known as "the ditch," we wended our way along rivers and across sounds and coastal inlets. One night we docked at a marina at Port Royal, South Carolina, but otherwise we anchored in wide and lonely salt marshes, in the company of birds and the occasional dolphin. We were gunkholing, meandering from one secluded anchorage to another, our boat a mobile island.

While *Cool Breezes* put on the nautical miles those last few days of November, St. Christopher's covered a lot of ground.

"If you work hard in November, we can take off the whole month of December!" I cajoled my pupils. With this incentive, the children set ambitious but realistic goals for themselves, and worked diligently and cheerfully toward them. Most days, that is. One morning there was a crisis in my classroom.

"I've finished three-quarters of my math already,"
Liam announced with pride.

"Well I'm actually a grade and a half ahead," said Ben.

Erin was two-thirds of the way through her math, but
there was no satisfaction in that; her younger brothers had
surpassed her.

"Braggers!" she shrieked.

The rest of us watched, astonished, as Erin slid from
the salon bench seat onto the floor, crawled under the
table, and fled to her berth, raging at the injustices in her
life.

I waited a few minutes before approaching Erin, but it
wasn't long enough.

"Are you feeling better?" I asked, pushing aside the
sea-blue curtain hanging in the arched doorway to her
stateroom.

"No!" she screamed. Her face was puffed and pink
from sobbing. She sat up in bed, pushed the hatch over
her head and escaped into the cockpit, where Pat stood at
the helm.

"Aagh!" Erin yelled in frustration. "There's no place to
be alone on this boat!"

We watched through the portholes as she stomped
howling towards the trampoline.

"What happened?" Pat asked, poking his head into the
companionway.

The boys and Meara shrugged.

"A pubescent meltdown, I'd say," I replied. Her fury
was like a storm, I thought, to be waited out until spent.
An hour later, Erin returned to the salon, eyes cast down,
head held high. She slid into her spot as if nothing had
happened, and returned to her math.

Later that afternoon, I re-appeared at her stateroom
doorway.

"Oh, Mom," Erin sighed, as soon as she saw my questioning face. "Sometimes I can't believe how I act. I just can't control my feelings. What's wrong with me?"

"You're growing up, is all," I said, caressing her long gold hair. I well recalled my own sullen early teens. "Don't worry. It's normal. And don't feel you must compete with your brothers. Remember your marble analogy?"

"Yes, I remember," she smiled, propping herself up on an elbow. "It's like God gives all of us a hundred marbles when we're born. The boys have pretty much all their marbles in the brains department, but I've got mine spread around a bit more. I've got, say, eighty marbles in the brains department, ten in the art department, and ten in the music department. You told me if I could come up with that marble analogy, I must have plenty of marbles in the brains department. So now what do you think?"

"Well, after this morning's performance, I think you have lots of marbles in the drama department!" I joked.

"Really, Mom," she said, looking me straight in the eye. "What do you think?"

"You've got way more than a hundred marbles, sweetheart," I replied.

Despite that late November class commotion, St. Christopher's finished its first term on an upbeat. The older scholars were finished far more than half the year's schoolwork. Dear Meara, who could have been playing instead of sitting at the salon table, was working at her Grade Two math book and had taught herself to read. With a deep sigh of satisfaction, I dismissed St. Chris for a one-month vacation at noon on November 30, and retired to the cockpit. I sat, bundled up, my eyes at rest, my face turned to the sunshine and brisk wind.

"Don't you think your teacher deserves a beer?" Pat yelled down to the kids from the helm. It's not easy to be a teacher, I reflected, never mind the teacher of my own children. My class may have been small, but it came with unique challenges, like sibling rivalry, intellectual competitiveness, multiple grade levels, and adolescent angst. Liam hustled out to the cockpit with an uncapped bottle. It was lukewarm – like all beverages aboard *Cool Breezes* – but rewarding. Yes, I did deserve that beer.

As we continued our journey, it became increasingly obvious we'd joined the mass migration of boaters heading south. "You know it's time to head south when all you hear on the VHF are the voices of French Canadians," Jim of *Jasper J* had warned us. This year, since the weather had been unseasonably cool, there was a prematurely steady flow of southward traffic along the ICW, and plenty of Québécois accents on the radio.

On November 28, we docked at the marina of verdant Jekyll Island, Georgia. Once the summer retreat of the "robber barons" – the famous Morgan, Vanderbilt, Rockefeller, Pulitzer and other wealthy families – this secluded property was now a year-round refuge for wildlife, protected by conservation laws. Palm trees, palmettos and live oaks draped with Spanish moss all thrived in luxuriant forests. Flowers abounded. The weather grew mild our second day there, so we set out on an afternoon hike.

Our tour began with a stroll beneath an awning of branches. We soaked up the humidity, surrounded by exotic birdcalls. Soon we arrived at the grand and hushed Millionaires' Village, a cluster of multi-storey "cottages" once used by the original families, now a national historic site. Some of these mansions were converted to museums, and some were now shops, but all lacked the same amenity: a kitchen. During the first incarnation of these buildings, their occupants always dined at or ordered their meals from "the club." That clubhouse, now called Jekyll Island Club Hotel, was the village centrepiece. There we ordered a snack, served outdoors on a sunken patio with wrought iron tables and chairs and a garden of colourfully striped umbrellas. As I sipped my exorbitantly priced glass of iced tea and observed dapper patrons at other tables, I couldn't help but notice that we looked out of place. Wearing rumpled jackets, faded caps, salt-stained deck shoes and baggy shorts, our crew appeared to be on a camping trip, not a holiday from prep school.

"There are three standards of dress," I mused aloud. "There's the city standard, where you shower and wear something different every day. There's the camping standard, where you might shower every second day and wear the same clothes except if they're really dirty. Then there's the cruising standard. You don't shower for four or five days on end, and you wear the same thing most every day, dirty or not, because your cubbyholes don't hold more than a few clothes, and the next laundromat is days away."

"Yeah," the boys chimed in. "And guess what standard we like best?"

That evening Pat plugged in the television cable cord at the docks so the kids could watch, appropriately enough, "Who Wants to be a Millionaire?" Since the marina was guarded and its lounge overlooked the docks, he and I nipped up the hill for a nightcap.

"What'll y'all have?" drawled the Sea Jay's barkeep, a tanned young man in a polo shirt.

"I'll have Southern Comfort, and my wife will have Cointreau," Pat replied, as we seated ourselves on the bamboo barstools. White fans whirred lazily overhead. Leafy ferns graced the room. The textiles and artwork were muted and floral. A light wind chime of crystal and laughter, ice cubes and jazz notes filled the air. A thin curl of smoke from a solitary cigar drifted upwards. I was glad I'd taken the trouble to throw on a summer dress.

The bartender put a pair of tumblers in front of us and began to pour.

"This must be what they call 'southern hospitality'," Pat remarked, as liquid levels rose and our eyes popped out.

The bartender grinned.

"Well, as we always say down south, if you're gonna have a drink, have a drink!"

Good thing our drinks were generous, for Pat and I had much to discuss. We needed to find a canvasmaker to replace our salon cushions, make new cockpit cushions, and repair the gaps in the mosquito net that zipped up to our cockpit enclosure at night. This work would consume at least a week. Should we get it done in St. Augustine, Florida, our next destination, or in St. Petersburg, where we'd spend Christmas? We'd also planned to take the kids to Disneyworld for a few days. Should we drive to Orlando from Titusville, near Cape Canaveral, Florida, or should we wait until we arrived in St. Pete's? How did a Disneyworld side trip fit in with the concept of our boating adventure? And what could we afford?

"It's a good thing to talk it all over, but in the end," I said, "doesn't most of our decision making depend on the weather?"

A day and a half later, we crossed into Florida. Our first port of call was the magnificent city of St. Augustine. The inlet leading to this historical city was crowded with sailboats, shrimpers, and sportfishing boats, all milling about in tight circles awaiting the lift-bridge opening on the half-hour. From the water, we could see a tall white cross, a fort, and the twin spires of a cathedral: a fitting entrance to the oldest permanent European settlement in the continental United States. The grand and aptly named Bridge of Lions was raised to allow *Cool Breezes* a stately entry into the wide harbour. The city beckoned us to explore, but first we must find our marina and contact local canvasmakers.

Both these tasks proved frustrating. The marina entrance was difficult to find, and the dockmaster didn't answer our VHF call for directions for over an hour. When we finally docked, we found the marina to be less than ideal. Located in a rough neighbourhood, it was tumbledown, and lacked proximity to grocery stores.

"There's no Internet access," said Ben.

"Or courtesy cars," said Liam.

"But at least the showers are brand new!" Erin offered.

"And so are the laundry facilities," I added, and set the mechanical drums to shaking.

Inquiries with local canvasmakers proved fruitless. Most said they couldn't begin our project for at least three weeks. The one who was immediately available estimated he could complete the job in ten consecutive days, yet his arrival almost two hours later than promised undermined our confidence in his ability to deliver on time.

"Well that certainly helps point us in the right direction," Pat remarked. "We'll order the canvaswork and do Disneyworld once we get to St. Pete's."

In the meantime, the sun smiled between briskly passing clouds. Lured by the brilliant weather and the charm of the old city, we decided to linger another day in St. Augustine. This was an auspicious decision, since it happened to be a festival day in the historical quarters. We sat on a grassy hill to watch the re-enactment of a military drill just outside Castillo de San Marcos National Monument. Afterward, we toured the diamond-shaped bastions and the dungeons of the Spanish fortress, made of coquina, a natural shell limestone. From there we poked around the narrow cobbled streets of the old Spanish Quarter, dating back to 1565, now lined with boutiques and restaurants. No traffic was allowed, not even on bicycle. At sundown, when we peeked into the oldest Catholic church in North America, the Cathedral Basilica of St. Augustine, we saw the evening vigil Mass was about to unfold, so we stayed.

It was dark by the time we emerged from the Basilica, and we were hungry. After dinner at a hopping pizzeria on Old St. George Street, we set out for home, only to discover a crowd had gathered on the streets.

"What's going on tonight?" I asked a passerby.

"Tonight is our annual Grand Illumination," she replied. "There'll be a parade in the Old Spanish Quarter." Street performers and a marching band dressed in period costume led the way, followed by hundreds of spectators, each bearing a candle or lantern. Someone gave us candles, and so we too became caught up in the winding procession of this centuries-old tradition. The children's eyes danced. A thousand lights sparkled. It was spectacular.

After such an exhilarating day, the next was somewhat anticlimactic. We untied the docklines at 7:00 a.m. and pushed southward to Daytona Beach, Florida against blustery northerly winds. By sundown, the growing strength of the gusts discouraged us from anchoring. We were blown onto the fuelling dock of the Seven Seas Marina, then swept along to our berth.

Erin and I set out on a quest for food, beginning with a walk down the long palm-lined boulevard bordering the famous beach. The supermarket was more than a mile away, a distance intensified by heavy winds and spats of rain. The cab driver we hired to get back to the marina with our groceries claimed to have difficulty finding it. By then night had fallen. Erin and I exchanged frightened glances. I wished for my cell phone back home. An hour later we finally arrived at our marina. Erin and I felt overjoyed to see the glow of warm light from our salon chasing away the shadows, and to smell the alluring aroma of fresh *carbonara*.

Pat was as relieved as we were. He paid the driver, returning with a pronouncement: "That's the last time you'll be getting the groceries after dark."

The winds were as spirited as our freshly showered, well-fed crew when we set out for Titusville, Florida later that morning. Conditions were not as treacherous as the day before, but it was nonetheless challenging to buck both the breeze and the current to get away from shore. Erin took one parting glance backward at the docks.

"Jasper!" she yelled.

We all turned to look. There stood our beautiful red Lab on the edge of the dock, watching forlornly as our boat sailed out to sea.

"How the heck did that happen?" Pat growled, rotating the wheel about.

"She must have jumped off the foredecks while we were getting ready to leave," suggested Ben, eager to smooth things over.

Once again we were swept forward as we retrieved our retriever, and once again we struggled away. The effort required taught our crew a valuable lesson.

"From now on, Meara, your job is to keep Jasper in the salon with you whenever we leave port," our captain ordered. Meara nodded solemnly. But it appeared Jasper also learned a lesson: whenever she sensed the family was preparing to leave, she would lie right in our path, determined never to be left behind again.

Several hours later, we approached Titusville, where we expected to find two of our first boating friends, Jim and Edwina.

"*Jasper J, Jasper J,* this is *Cool Breezes,*" I called on the VHF radio.

"*Cool Breezes,* this is *Jasper J,*" came the reply.

"Hurray!" yelled the big kids. Meara was conspicuously silent, though. Her expressive face revealed the churning of her mind. The last time she'd seen Jim and Edwina, they'd invited her to come live aboard *Jasper J,* with the promise of brownies and ice cream for breakfast and candies for lunch. She worried they'd ask again.

"I'll just tell them sorry, but I'll miss my family too much," she rehearsed. "Or else I'll just say no, all that candy isn't good for me. I know – I'll tell them I might get cavities!" An hour later, though, when we showed up on the dock beside *Jasper J*'s cockpit, Meara was tongue-tied and simply gave Jim and Edwina big hugs.

"You're just in time," Edwina told the kids. "There's gonna be a satellite launch tonight from Cape Canaveral and we'll be able to see it from here!"

The whole marina came out to watch in the chilly night air, creating a festival atmosphere. Equipment aboard one of the sailboats picked up NASA radio transmissions, so we knew the launch would take place between 8:00 and 10:00 p.m. Jim and Edwina joined us on the broad bow deck of our catamaran, huddled under blankets with our hot drinks. Finally the big moment came. A round orange glow appeared at the southern horizon, followed by the burst of a yellow ball of fire, shooting high into the sky. After the ball began to arc, we heard the thunderclap of an explosion. Then the ball disappeared. Although the spectacle lasted less than two minutes, it was well worth awaiting.

"It's all about creating memories, isn't it," Edwina murmured, patting my arm.

The next morning, we departed Titusville, heading southward once again. *It was one of those perfect days,* I wrote in my diary. So was the next. The weather was grand. Clouds blew fleetingly across the bright sun, and the air warmed enough to allow Pat to bare his chest. The kids, now free of boat school and with the warm sun beckoning, kept him good company in the cockpit, setting up the sails whenever possible, and taking the helm under his watchful eye, sometimes for hours at a time.

At sundown on December 7, we anchored just off Jensen Beach, Florida. A light blanket of breeze caressed us. We were alone in a languid bay. Pat was the first to recognize the ripeness of the moment: "Let's have a sundowner!"

Long waiting sweetens the reward, I mused, as I sipped my gin-and-tonic, our first cockpit sundowner in months.

Our passage from Charleston to Jensen Beach was a breakthrough in several ways. Grey November had given way to more festive December. St. Christopher's Boat School had finished its first term and taken a month-long break. We'd shed the topmost layer of our clothing and felt the sun most days. And we'd crossed the imaginary but symbolic state line into Florida, the last of our mainland milestones.

The kids joined us in the cockpit.

"So where are we going next?" Liam asked.

"We'll start our trip westward on the Okeechobee Waterway tomorrow," Pat replied. "Should take us four days or so to reach the Gulf of Mexico. From there we head north to St. Petersburg, to meet your grandparents for Christmas!"

"I meant after Christmas," Liam said.

"Hurricane season will be over, so we'll cross to Cuba," said Pat. "After that, who knows?"

"Do you think we'll cross the ocean?" Ben asked.

"Not likely," Pat said. "The passage would be too long, with four kids and a dog."

"Yeah, just think of Jasper," Erin exclaimed. "She needs her daily trip to shore."

"Besides," Pat went on, "the point of this trip isn't to travel a certain number of miles, or to see as many countries as possible."

"I know, I know," said Liam. "As Gandhi said, the reward is the journey."

By then I recognized this axiom as simply another way of expressing the idea to live in the moment.

"The way our lives are set up back home, we focus on what lies ahead instead of what's happening right now," I added. "Planning ambitious destinations would put us in exactly the same situation. We want to start living more in the present."

"The neat thing is, the trip is actually teaching us to live that way," Ben added.

"Yeah, things like the weather teach you to live that way," Liam nodded.

"And meeting new people and finding great places," Erin chimed in.

"And deciding to stay an extra day if you like a place," said Pat.

Meara sighed.

"I want this trip to never end!"

Chapter 10
Outlandish

You are meant to be what you dream of becoming.
It is never too late to be what you might have been.
— George Eliot (Mary Ann Evans)

Over the next six days, the good ship *Cool Breezes* cruised the Okeechobee Waterway. The heart of this system, located in the centre of the lower Florida peninsula, was Lake Okeechobee, accessed both from east and west by a series of rivers and manmade canals. Since the water level of Lake Okeechobee was higher than in the channels leading to it, there were five locks to navigate. If we cut across the Florida peninsula on this waterway, we'd save several days' travel, avoiding the numerous bridge openings and traffic jams around Fort Lauderdale and Miami to the south.

The morning of our first day on the Okeechobee Waterway, we awoke to a purple sunrise in a peaceful anchorage. A pod of leaping dolphins greeted our gleeful children. After a few hours of motoring under a temperate sun, we arrived at St. Lucie, where we found the first lock. There, along with a dozen other boats, we waited two hours for the lock opening. Pat trolled restlessly in circles, alert to avoiding other vessels.

"It's a lot harder to manoeuvre the boat in circles than it is to go straight ahead," he complained. "From now on

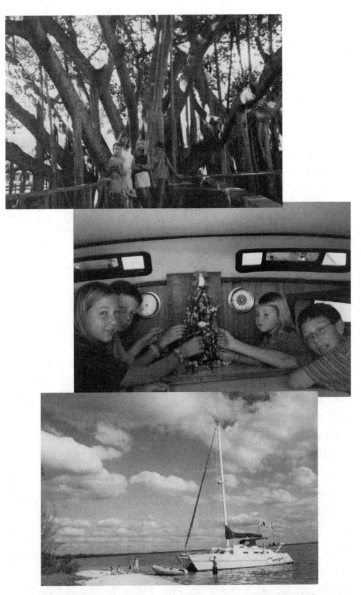

*December 2000. Above left, Fort Myers, Florida, under
the banyan tree at the Edison estate. Above right, the children
decorate their Christmas tree. Bottom, Boca Grande Pass, Florida,
where we beach the boat on a small island.*

I'm going to find out exactly when the locks open, and make sure we arrive just before."

Meanwhile, I cleaned boat. I'd anticipated it would take less time to clean the tiny spaces of a boat than the large rooms of a house, but I was wrong. Seven of us, living intensively in close quarters, created a lot of dust and crumbs. Coarse red hairs from Jasper's coat accumulated in every nook and cranny, even in the staterooms, despite the fact our dog couldn't descend the steps into the hulls. Our broom handle was less than a yard long, so I spent many an hour bent over at the waist, sweeping up the salt, the sand, the debris of our life. And then there was the head. Sometimes the chore of cleaning it would make me gag. On this day, though, I was in a cleaning frenzy. The two-hour wait flew by.

Once past the first lock, we arrived at our first ever boat-in campground, complete with docks, water hook-ups, showers, laundry facilities, campfire pits and a playground. We made use of every amenity. The children played and Pat tinkered. I dragged all the bedding, even the mattresses, out on the decks to air. Then, while the sun shone and the breezes blew, Jasper and I took a long and happy run. That evening we roasted wieners over a fire, and Liam pulled out his guitar for a singsong. We lingered by the campfire as long as possible, driven to bed by a light drizzle and the first mosquitoes in weeks.

On our second day, the scenery took a few dramatic turns. We rose before dawn for an early getaway. Pat was determined to arrive at the next lock before its scheduled opening at 10:00 a.m. Our passages through that lock and the next were uneventful, bringing us to Lake Okeechobee. The breeze freshened just as we approached the lake, so for the first time in days, we cut the engines and sailed on a wide expanse of placid water under a

nearly cloudless sky. We turned our faces upwards, straining, yearning for that sunshine.

"A perfect day to suntan!" Erin exclaimed. "I'm putting on my swimsuit!"

"Me too!" Meara chorused. I slathered her with sunscreen.

We lounged about the cockpit and foredecks for most
of the afternoon as the boat majestically crossed the lower
corner of the lake. The sheer breadth of wind, sky and
water that day swept through us like a yogic cleansing
breath, as refreshing to the spirit as my bout of cleaning
had been to the boat. It was invigorating. It was grand!

Three hours later we finished our crossing. The exit off
the lake seemed abrupt. Just as sudden was the slump in
atmosphere. The sparkle of brilliant clarity on the lake
grew swiftly sombre, as brooding as the swampy canal we
found ourselves cruising. Trunks of leafless trees bordered
the waterway. Behind them, the landscape was flat.
Hordes of black turkey vultures, their wrinkled red necks
craning, huddled on the barren tree branches. Pieces of
black cinder from nearby burning sugar cane fields drifted
onto our decks. The air was thick, heavy with the sweetly
acrid scent of torched carbon. Alligators waddled along
the shores, their heads swaying slowly, scanning for food.

"This would be a poor time to fall overboard,"
observed Liam. I pulled my smallest child close.

Soon the surreal eeriness passed, and we arrived at
Clewiston, Florida.

"It's not quite dark," Pat said. "Let's do one more
lock."

I agreed, but it was a poor decision. By then we'd been
on the water for over twelve hours, and were sagging. We
almost bumped another vessel as we tied up in the lock.
When we emerged from the lock at Moore Haven,

Florida, the sky was black. To find a place to tie up at the city docks was frustrating. And our sloppy docking rankled the skipper.

"I'm going for a walk," Pat announced brusquely. He leashed up the dog and disappeared in the night.

Familiarity breeds contempt, goes the old saw, and it began to feel apt for us. Too much togetherness in too little space began to rub the wrong way. The next day in particular, it seemed none of us could do anything to please anyone. Liam darted in my way just as I was trying to push the boat off the Moore Haven docks. I lost my grip, with the result that the starboard stern got scraped.

"Liam, look what you've done!" I yelled. It was not my finest moment. Liam scowled. His every inconsiderate word and gesture leapt immediately to my memory. I was "sick and tired" of his rudeness, and said so.

"Leave him alone!" Pat retorted.

I was astounded he would speak to me that way. Not just angry, I felt wounded. That familiar knob of hot emotion clogged my throat and as much as I resisted them, tears seared my cheekbones. I retreated to my stateroom and indulged myself in weepy wreckage. I felt like a failure in every way that mattered, as a sailor, a mother, and a wife. Not even my writing was going well: another failure. After some time, a new conviction emerged: to give myself more space. Instead of returning to the cockpit I remained on my berth, taking refuge in the creation of my novel. Almost a month had passed since I'd touched the piece, I realized. No wonder I was cranky: my creative spirit had been stifled.

Later that day we tied up stern-to at the small city docks of Labelle, Florida, a pretty little town on the Caloosahatchee River. We stuffed the big blue sailbag full of laundry and headed downtown. Twenty minutes later we found the laundromat, a huge room that held not only rows of churning machines but also a bar serving beer, soft drinks and snacks.

"Did you see that?" Pat whispered to me. More than a few male heads had turned as our tall blond daughter crossed the threshold, and her vigilant father's antennae were up. We six were the only gringos in a room occupied by more than eighty Mexican itinerant workers. All the signage was in Spanish. Even at the supermarket next door, Spanish was clearly the predominant language.

"It's time we got on with our Spanish lessons!" I remarked to the kids, as we puzzled over a product label.

The next morning, December 11, we carried on westward down the complacent Caloosahatchee River, bordered on each side by extravagant homes, boat launches and gardens. Sunshine flooded the salon. It was an ideal time to make the Christmas tree ornaments we'd planned. The girls and I painted a rainbow of cockleshells with watercolours, and attached gold ribbons to them. Next we pulled out an origami instruction book and papers. That's when the boys – even Liam, who is not exactly "crafty" – became interested. We made dozens of origami balls, fish, and good-luck cranes, and threaded them with strands of silver.

While the kids were engrossed in folding, I dug out the notes from my Spanish conversation classes in Edmonton, and made some cue cards of elementary Spanish greetings, responses, and variables. Soon the children were engaged in a scintillating exchange of pleasantries.

"¿*Buenas tardes*, Erin, *como esta?*" Ben asked with exaggerated politeness. Good afternoon and how are you?

"Terrible, just terrible," came the hilarious reply, *en español.*

"How wonderful," Liam added in Spanish, delighted more with his own sense of humour than his grasp of the language.

"*Hasta la vista,* baby!" said Erin. "Guess what, that just means 'until I see you later'. I used to think it was really rude."

I disappeared for a moment to rummage through the depths of my cavernous hanging locker, and reappeared with my great find.

"Hey kids, look what I had tucked away!"

"A baby Christmas tree!" Meara shouted with delight.

"That's the one from the book swap back in Virginia," said sharp-eyed Erin.

The kids festooned the miniature branches with our new shell and origami decorations. Although we pushed the laden tree against the bulkhead, it consumed a sizeable portion of the salon table. We didn't mind; or at least five of us didn't.

"A Christmas tree on the salon table?" Pat exclaimed. Noting our collective swell of pride as we gazed at our creation, however, he prudently let it be. He'd face mutiny if he put up a fuss.

That evening we docked at Fort Myers, Florida, where *Cool Breezes* was built.

"Aw, we're bringing our baby home," Erin said.

A sultry wind rippled the fronds of the palm trees along the docks of the city marina. It was eighty-two degrees Fahrenheit. Pat and I sat on a bench facing the water, sipping a glass of wine, lost in private thought. I recalled the recent tension aboard, and my realization that we needed more space.

"I'd like to do more writing when we return to Edmonton," I began.

"Do what makes you happy, Jake, not what you think

you should do," Pat replied. "You may decide not to practice law at all."

"Not practice law at all!" The concept astounded me. All those years of law school and the bar admission course, completing articles of clerkship and navigating the political waters of a large firm, building a client base in my specialized field, re-establishing myself at Pat's small office, juggling career and home life – all for nothing?

"No effort is totally wasted," Pat replied. "It's your life, not anyone else's."

To leave my certain and lucrative profession altogether was scary. To become a writer, a calling much more speculative and notoriously poorly paid, was daunting. Yet looking out on the water this mild and languorous December evening, far, far away from my cold urban Canadian existence, anything seemed possible.

If any place symbolizes limitless possibility, creative industry and innovation, it would be Fort Myers, the summer home of Thomas Edison and Henry Ford. At dawn the next morning, Jasper and I left our slumbering family on board and ran toward the magnificent Edison and Ford estates. It was easy to find, at the end of a long avenue flanked with palms of every variety. Edison was not only a remarkable inventor, but also a notable horticulturist. He collected and planted every specimen of plant life possible in his beloved city. Visiting foreign dignitaries would present him with a young sapling or unique seed as a gift.

When Jasper and I reached the Edison estate, the gates were wide open. In we ran, unaware then that the property is an attraction, with an admission price, regular hours of operation, and a rule forbidding dogs. Yet no one troubled us in the morning hush. The occasional gardener simply nodded at me and smiled at my dog as we jogged along the paved paths. An enveloping lushness, an embrace of profuse oxygen greeted us. Dewdrops glistened in the bright Florida sun, the fragrance and colour of exotic blossoms graced the air, and a flock of songbirds greeted the day. But it was the majestic vigour of the Indian Banyan tree that impressed me most. This single tree, the third largest of its species in the world, covered almost an acre. Its unique biological adaptation was the ability of its branches to reach down and take root, to join the ranks of a thousand fellow tree trunks, more trunks than in a herd of elephants. The life force of this Banyan tree was palpable.

Our family spent a very happy and balmy half-day absorbing the science of Edison's hundreds of inventions, learning the history of the inventor's friendships with Henry Ford and Harvey Firestone, and taking in the glory of the botanical garden.

The boys led the way as we headed back to the marina. As usual, they walked like pals, Ben's arm resting on Liam's shoulder. Their footsteps fell into rhythm. Their heads were bent, absorbed in conversation. I nudged Pat's arm.

"Don't you just love it?" I said, gesturing to our sons.

Suddenly the boys stopped in their tracks and turned to face us.

"Guess what, we just decided we're going to share a bedroom when we get back home," Ben announced. "We'll put our two beds in my room. Then in Liam's room, we'll put our desks and books and computer, and set up a real science lab!"

"Yeah, and we're talking about *real* science experiments, you know," Liam added. "Not just one of those little kids' chemistry sets!"

With reluctance the next morning, we threw off the bowlines and pulled away from the docks at Fort Myers. After a few hours of motoring along the Caloosahatchee River, we turned north into the Boca Grande Pass and raised the sails. The famous islands of Captiva and Sanibel shone on the horizon of the blue-green sea, their palms waving greetings on the balmy breeze. The sun peeked through a checkerboard of white clouds.

"We're making really good time today," Pat said. "Let's stop for a few hours at one of these little islands." He checked the cruising guide. "I bet we could even beach the boat!"

Sailing magazines are full of photos of catamarans tied up to coastline trees, but in reality the conditions for beaching a cat rarely converge. The sea bottom must be sandy, with a fairly steep underwater approach, and the winds, currents and tides must cooperate. Pat was delightfully right. For the first and last time on this year-long cruise, perfect weather, availability of time, and coastline prerequisites happily conspired allowing us to beach *Cool Breezes* on the soft shores of an uninhabited green island.

The children were tickled with the novelty. Instead of stepping out of the cockpit onto a dock, or clambering into the dinghy off the stern, they leapt off the bows onto the sand a few feet below. Pat beamed. Jasper too was joyful, racing up and down the beach, pawing at bubbles in the sand and sniffing out the cranky horseshoe crabs.

I paused to watch my family from the deck. Their pleasure was my pleasure. Moments like this went a long way to balancing out the cramped quarters and cloying closeness of life aboard.

"Look, I found a gastropod shell!" Ben exclaimed.

"Come over here, I see a hermit crab!" Liam shouted.

Erin found the rarest treasure: the pale and fragile, exquisite round shell of a sea urchin.

Time flowed like the shimmer of a falling silk scarf. But the tide was ebbing, and soon our boat would be stranded, not beached.

"All hands on deck!" Captain Pat yelled, and thus the reverie ended.

An hour later we lay the anchor in a sunlit inlet in the Gulf of Mexico. Dolphins leapt and played only a few feet away from our cockpit. I found myself marvelling at how a family like ours had found itself in a place like this. My mind's eye recalled the myriad vistas we'd seen just in the last few weeks.

"Doesn't it strike you sometimes just how exotic all this is for our prairie eyes?" I murmured.

It's outlandish, I thought, simply outlandish.

December 2000.

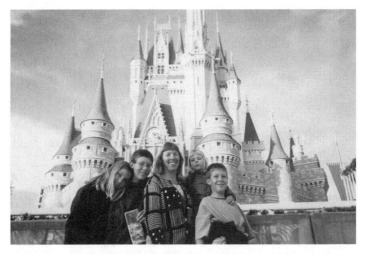

Orlando, Florida. Holiday in Disneyworld.

Largo, Florida. The children with Mary and George.

From: The Kirwin crew
To: Kith and Kin
Subject: **Greetings from *Cool Breezes*: Back to the Land**

It's 7:00 a.m. on December 15. *Cool Breezes* is anchored off Longboat Key, Florida in the Gulf of Mexico. Although we're eager to weigh anchor, the fog is too dense. Since Pat wants to sleep and the laptop battery still has a half-hour's worth of juice, I find myself with a golden opportunity to start this group email.

We've made many decisions in the last few days. We'll dock at the Harborage Marina in St. Petersburg, Florida for a month. During that time we'll get our canvaswork done, rent a minivan, and visit Disneyworld. We'll celebrate Christmas and New Year's with Pat's mother Mary and her husband George. After that we'll re-provision *Cool Breezes* and head south to Key West, Florida, our jumping off point to Cuba.

Pop goes the kettle on the propane burner, a signal it's about to reach a boil.

"Boo!" goes Meara. The golden moment dissolves. I'll close now and reconnect later.

We arrive at Harborage Marina mid-afternoon. As soon as we're tied up, Erin and I run to the marina captains' lounge to use the phone.

"Hello Gramy, this is Erin."

"Who?"

"Erin."

"Erin?"

"Yes, it's me, Erin," she laughs. "We're here!"

Mary and George are surprised. They'd expected us to arrive three or four days from now. We're docked about an hour's drive from their winter home in Largo, and they're uncomfortable driving in the dark of evening, so they promise to come for lunch tomorrow.

It's Saturday the 16th. Mary and George are coming, so we clean boat like crazy! Pat's mired in a holding tank repair. I open the portholes and hatches to air out the boat, and hurry to the marina laundry room with a sailbag of dirty clothes. The kids sweep the cabin and swab the decks. Liam bakes fudge brownies. When Ben downloads our email from the captains' lounge, we retrieve more than a dozen emails from you good people! I buy a platter of sandwiches and cold Corona beer from the marina canteen, while Pat dashes off to pick up a rental minivan.

"I see them!" Meara squeals, pointing. We run down the cement docks to greet our guests. It's fun to show our boat to those who knew us long before the trip began, and therefore appreciate the difference in our new lifestyle. *Cool Breezes* shows off well today in the sparkling sunshine. The buttons on Pat's chest are busting.

Now it's the morning of December 20. The weather has become unseasonably cold again, hovering just above the freezing point. In the last few days, plans have fallen into place. We found a canvasmaker and placed our order. We shopped for Christmas gifts. We booked a condo and a dog kennel near Orlando, did twelve loads of laundry, bought four days worth of groceries, and filled six duffel bags. We're up early to pack the minivan for what Liam calls "our holiday within a holiday": our trip to Disneyworld.

Pat and I are enjoying this resting place from our boat travels, this reprieve from Perfect Paul, anchoring and charting, guarding water supplies and battery power. We're delighted to take showers and wear clean clothes every day, and to have ready access to telephones and the Internet. But there's a downside. When I record here what we've accomplished in the last four days, my head spins. We seem to be living in fast forward.

Here are some vignettes from our Disneyworld days:

Effervescent excitement in the minivan that sunny morning, headed for Orlando.

Pat and the big kids pumped for the thrill rides, and even more pumped getting off.

Seeing the Magic Kingdom through the eyes of Meara, who truly believes in magic.

Taking Pat's favourite ride, Splash Mountain, at nightfall. It's just us six crazy Canucks out there in the cold and dark!

Watching Ben perform on the set of "Home Improvement" as the volunteer audience participant. He wins a nail-pounding contest against a virtual Tim Allen.

Experiencing the Fantasmic light show from front row seats, the Osborne Family Spectacle of Lights, and the Illuminations light show. Tears often spring to my eyes at the sound of music, but rarely do they come prompted by the sight of beauty.

The lush, green, worldly and "eco" feel of Animal Kingdom.

Enjoying the condo. It includes three bedrooms and two clean, bright and modern bathrooms – both equipped with the luxury of knowing no stranger will intrude – and a long hallway Meara loves to use as a sprinting track.

"You know why she does that, don't you?" says Erin. "It's because she can't do it on the boat!"

Visiting Canada at the Epcot pavilion, and yearning for the prairies and mountains.

Shopping at Millennium Place, where artisans from the world over demonstrate their crafts. Ben buys a turtle and Liam an elephant, adding to their growing collections.

Leaving an email message at the "Wailing Wall" in the Jerusalem pavilion, investigating mechanical dolls in Japan, and dining in Morocco, entertained by belly dancing!

Returning to our boat close to midnight today, December 23. After months of no colds or flu on board, Pat and Meara have come down with sore throats and coughs. Catching flu bugs: now that's another price to be paid for re-entry to civilization!

It's Christmas Eve 2000. The marina is filled with decorated boats. White lights are twined along our boat's lifelines. Colourful strings of lights are mounted on the masts or stays of the surrounding boats. The effect at night, with the circus of reflected colours upon rippled water, is unfamiliar and not especially seasonal to our prairie eyes. Yet it's dazzling. Time to close up the boat and drive to Largo. We'll attend Christmas Eve Mass there and stay with Mary and George "for three sleeps," as Meara says.

It's December 27, and we're happily snugged back on board, after three easy days with Mary and George. Mary is a tall and gracious woman with a kind and gentle manner. George is affable and articulate, and loves to play chess. He's a retired country doctor, and she a former schoolteacher. Their Maritime roots are evident in their unhurried approach to each day. They are perfect hosts to our ailing, coughing crew.

This Christmas seems unscripted, for once. There's nothing to do Christmas Day but open gifts (which we interrupt for brunch and stretch out for almost six hours), cook a turkey, and walk the dog. Americans don't observe Boxing Day on December 26, but we do, by playing shuffleboard, eating, and connecting with many of you kith and kin by telephone. One of the callers was my mom, Eldean, who tells us she's booked a flight to Varadero, Cuba, to meet us on January 31!

Driving back to the boat this morning, I worry that our crew, having burst open like a Christmas cracker at our Disneyworld condo and then at Mary and George's house, might have trouble squeezing back on board. It turns out we humans are just fine re-acclimatizing; the problem is our gear. Before we can unload the van of our luggage, Disneyworld purchases and Christmas gifts, we must purge our lockers and cubbies. We fill a few bags of things to give away in Cuba, a box of stuff to mail home, and a few pails of garbage. Pat stows the Cuban treasures in a deep locker at the bow. I mail the parcel, and the kids haul away the garbage. Only then can we move back in.

Now it's December 30. The weather continues wet and cold. The water in Jasper's bowl has a thin layer of ice most mornings. Pat and the kids are in Largo for the evening. The idea is to clear the boat of extraneous small bodies and Pat's innumerable projects so that I can do a thorough cleaning. As soon as the sun sets and the good light disappears, I forsake my chores and take Jasper for a long run. I return to solitude. I bundle up in layers, light three candles, make a light supper, brew a pot of green tea, and flip on the laptop switch. Heaven!

Time to turn in to my c-c-cold berth. God bless, fair winds, and Happy New Year!

Love PJ+crew

Chapter **11**
Watercolour Days

I recommend to you to take care of the minutes: the hours will take care of themselves.
  – Lord Chesterfield, Letters to His Son

The few weeks after Christmas ran together like a blur of watercolour paints, mostly grey and blue. The weather, too, was watery. The same system that walloped the northeast coast of the continent with record snowfalls also touched Florida.

A few spots of high colour appeared those blurry grey days. New Year's Eve was one of them. Pat and I left Erin in charge at George and Mary's so we two couples could attend a dance at the seniors' lodge and the house party to follow. Most of our fellow partiers were Canadian, Maritimers in particular. And what do Maritimers do at a party, but make music! The host pulled out a guitar, the hostess played the piano, a guest played "the spoons," and the rest of us sang along to all the old folk songs. The undoubted star was George on harmonica. He was transported. Eyes pressed tight and chin raised high, he played with such intensity that the tiny instrument resonated. *I wish I could write like he plays,* I wrote in my diary the next day. That was New Year's Day morning, a day to make resolutions. *This is the year to seize and savour,* I wrote.

143

January 2001.

Largo, Florida at New Year's.

A day sail on Tampa Bay, Florida.

Taking our cue from local schools, St. Christopher's resumed in the New Year. Our days began to take shape again: studies in the morning, while the custodian ran errands or tinkered on board; provisioning in the afternoons; visits with Mary and George in the evening. The silver lining to those cold and cloudy days was that they were ideal for schoolwork.

Another bright spot in that watercolour mural was the serendipitous single day the sun shone, the same day we'd promised Mary and George a day sail on Tampa Bay. At noon our preparations were complete. We'd installed the newly upholstered salon and cockpit cushions, laced on the repaired trampoline net, polished the portholes, and swabbed the decks. Our boat was shipshape. Down in the galley, the porthole crystals sparkled in the light. Steaks marinated; homemade potato salad and a plate of veggies and dip lay stowed in the fridge; a platter of fruit waited on the counter. Tinned beverages cooled on ice, and the aroma of Erin's brownies filled the air. To top it off, the wind was freshening.

"Look here, it's actually getting warm!" Mary laughed from her seat in the cockpit.

The twin diesels readily sputtered to life. The docking crews let go the lines with synchronous grace. Once underway, Mary and George inched their way along the lifelines to sit on the foredecks, and were rewarded with the exhilaration of oneness with the wind at the bows.

"Let's see if I can get Otto to cooperate," said Pat. Our autohelm had been unreliable lately. That day, however, our most fickle crewmember agreed to collaborate with the boat's compass. "Otto's working perfectly," Pat marvelled, as he reclined his long frame on the deck.

An hour later we reached the middle of the big blue bay. The glistening office towers of Tampa Bay surrounded

our island, the boat. Pat cut the engines and fired up the barbeque. I set plates and food buffet-style on the salon table. We dined in the cockpit.

"You know, there's enough wind now to actually sail," Pat said. The kids leapt to their feet. It wasn't every day we could ply the waters under sail alone. Liam was especially eager to strut his sailor-boy stuff. He described to Mary and George how sailboats manage to sail against the wind.

"You take the boat on a zigzag path in the water, by bringing the bow back and forth across the wind. That's called tacking. The opposite is when you bring the stern through the wind, if you want to change direction while you're going downwind," he explained. "That's called jibing."

George, familiar with the concepts, smiled.

"That's the best explanation I've ever heard."

Cool Breezes felt frisky that day. In fact, she showed off. A pod of dolphins came out to play with her, dozens of them, leaping and splashing in her twin wakes. Mary and Meara screamed in delight. Those squeals must have reached just the right pitch, for the dolphins took them as encouragement, and returned for several encores. When sun descended at 5:00 p.m., we returned to the marina. Even our docking, despite weeks without practice, was perfect.

"Wasn't our day incredible?" I said to Erin later that evening, as we washed up in the galley. "One of those amazing days when everything goes better than a dream."

"I'll etch it in my memory, like you always tell me, Mom," she laughed.

That was January 7. A few days later, Pat asked his mother a favour.

"Would you take the kids overnight so Jake and I can take the night off? I'd like to take her out for dinner."

Mary agreed. I felt grateful, not only toward her, but also to Pat. He knew what I knew, that what our marriage desperately needed then was some time to ourselves, an injection of romance: a date night.

A bitter wind blew that evening, but at the *tapas* restaurant, the hearth was lit and the Shiraz glowed. We talked about everything, beginning with the mundane. Pat was engrossed in the frustrating task of prodding assorted bureaucrats to produce various papers for us. Obtaining extended coverage for travel in Cuba from our American boat insurer was harder than getting a sailboat fridge to produce ice.

"The agent just can't seem to grasp that we're Canadians, that we have no embargo, that we're actually allowed to go to Cuba," Pat complained.

The Canadian government had its hang-ups, too. We'd requested our Canadian boat registration papers be sent to Largo, knowing the Cuban coast guard would demand to see the originals. Yet, months later, no certificate had arrived. When Pat first called to complain, the office staff was mystified. They claimed they'd mailed the envelope weeks ago.

"When I called again today, the woman said she'd just found out the mail was returned. They had the wrong address," Pat said.

"Should we wait for them to send the certificate again?"

"No, we can't wait for it," Pat said. "I told them to fax it to us at the marina. If we want to get to Cuba before your mother arrives there at the end of the month, we've gotta leave St. Pete's the next time there's a break in the cold fronts."

Sailing to deadline – the deadline imposed by my mother's flight to Varadero – was a sore point I knew better than to explore on our date night. Timing is everything.

From the mundane we delved deeper. We indulged in all parents' favourite subject: their kids. Pat and I marvelled at each child in turn. The distance between them, in Largo with their grandparents, and us, in a cozy restaurant overlooking the water, only magnified their virtues.

"They're so smart," I effused. "You should listen to them learn Spanish."

We'd picked up some Spanish language software on one of our recent reprovisioning trips, and had begun using it at school. The program even had a pronunciation function, measuring the user's speaking skills by means of a gauge linked to the computer microphone. The user would repeat the instructor prompt, and a little needle on the screen would rate the user's accent on a scale from "native," the most sophisticated, to "tourist," the least competent. I regaled Pat with tales of his children's brilliance at grasping *español*.

"Jake, you're doing an amazing job teaching," he replied. "It's gotta be the hardest job on board, and you're doing great."

"Thanks," I murmured at the unexpected compliment. Flattery will get you everywhere, I thought. "You're not doing so badly yourself, prairie boy."

"What do you mean?" he asked, refilling our wineglasses.

"You ought to be proud of yourself, as captain of our boat," I said. "Let's face it, we are somewhat audacious, as Tevi said. We're landlubbers, the reverse of fish out of water. We couldn't do this without you." I made a mental note: must practice our man-overboard drill soon.

"I couldn't do it without you, either," he replied. "Not every woman would agree to take a trip like this."

Perhaps I was more adventurous than many women back home, more willing to forego creature comforts and colour outside the lines. That possibility made me more inclined to make the most of our journey. Yet sometimes, new experiences revealed personal characteristics that I didn't always like, such as my tendency to deny worrisome situations, to dwell in the future, and to avert my eyes from the painful present. My breast lump scare had certainly shown me that, and taught me not just to live in, but also to face up to the present.

"So what do you think of the boat trip so far?" Pat asked.

"The weather has been much colder than I expected," I replied. "I had no idea how common boat repairs are, or that I'd crave solitude as much as I do. You should see my diary. Every single moment I get to myself is written down, it's all there. But in many ways this trip is way better than I ever imagined."

"How's that?"

"I had no idea living on a boat could be so satisfying, and yet so confining, at the same time. I thought I knew my children well, yet I'm still learning about them every day. Little did I know you're such a capable mechanic and sailor, or how refreshing living mostly outdoors could be. And water everywhere – I love it, and yet sometimes I can't stand it."

"What do you mean, you can't stand water?" Pat laughed.

"When it's rain or sleet, or it splashes into the hatches or condenses on the windows or drips on the beds, or makes mildew, that's when I can't stand it," I said. "And what about you, Pat? What do you think, now that four months have passed?"

"Well, I gotta agree about the weather," he answered.

"What bad luck, that the year we happen to be sailing the eastern seaboard is the coldest in ten years. Another thing I expected was more interaction with other sailors."

"Like we had in Virginia, at the very beginning," I nodded.

"Yeah," he agreed. "But maybe that's more of a fair weather thing, getting to know your neighbours. And maybe it depends on how long we stay in one place.

"But what I really enjoy is my kids. I just love every minute with them," he continued. "What a gift, this rare bit of time with them. And what I also really love is the sense of perspective this boat trip gives me."

"How do you envision the next eight months?" I asked.

"Who knows?" Pat smiled. "Part of the joy of this year is spontaneity, just going somewhere on a whim – if the weather allows, of course," he laughed.

He was right. As much as we wanted to see the entire Caribbean, cross the ocean, even complete a circumnavigation, that's not what this year was about. It was about dropping off the edge of the earth, challenging our comfort zones, trying something completely different. It was about getting closer to our children, showing them first-hand there's more than one way to live a life, that despite Disneyworld and packaged food and computers and everything else we hold so dear, our North American lifestyle isn't necessarily the best. And it was becoming increasingly clear that for me, this year was about letting go that North American mindset of multi-tasking, maximizing efficiency, and projecting into the future. Amazing, those moments of clarity induced by a good bottle of wine.

Back at the marina, Jasper was shivering, overjoyed to see us, and eager to get on board. Not that it was any warmer inside than outside. We couldn't believe how frigid it felt, without the children's four extra bodies to generate warmth.

"Let's heat things up a bit," I said. I lit the oven, the oil lamps and every candle I could find.

"Yeah, let's," said Pat. He produced a bottle of port and a deck of cards. "I know a kind of poker we could play, now that the kids aren't on board."

We played one of those card games in which even the loser wins. Amid the *mélange* of those blue and grey watercolour days, that evening evoked a splash of red.

January 2001.

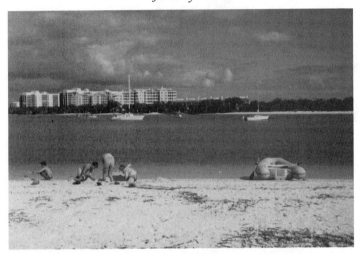

Marco, Florida. The children build a sandcastle on Coconut Island, with our catamaran and the city in the background.

The finished product.

Chapter 12
Cruising the Gulf of Mexico

*I must go down to the seas again, for the call of the
running tide is a wild call and a clear call that may
not be denied.*
— *John Masefield,* Sea Fever

By mid-January, we had docked in the St. Pete's
marina for almost a month, and had journeyed in
the United States for almost five months. We'd over-
stayed, yet technically we were unready to leave.
Confirmation of our Cuban insurance coverage hadn't yet
arrived. While we awaited it, Pat worked on an improved
davit repair so we could hoist the dinghy on board when we
crossed the Florida Straits. And there was the reprovisioning. Not knowing what resources lay in Key West or in
Cuba, we filled our bilge food stores to bulging. Pat fulfilled
his quest for three other necessities: a doggie life-vest, a
stockpile of oil and water filters, and the perfect SSB, a single sideband radio. We'd need an alternate source of weather
information as soon as we ventured beyond the range of
Perfect Paul, that gravel-voiced weather predictor on the
VHF. The rest of us searched for books. Who
knew when we'd find English-language reading material
again?

The day we finally received our insurance confirmation was the day we found a bountiful used bookstore. We

filled two big brown grocery bags for only US$80, and with that, our provisioning was complete.

It was time to leave, something we looked forward to; time to leave Mary and George, something we didn't.

"I'm so sad because Gramy and Grampy are going to miss me so much!" Meara sighed sadly. Then, when it occurred to her there was a flip side to this coin, she burst into tears. "And I'm going to miss them, too!"

Once the fog lifted the morning of January 14, the boys threw off the docklines and we turned our bows south. It was a Sunday, an auspicious day to begin the next leg of our journey. The kids and I sat on the foredecks with our faces turned to the emerging sun and the freshening breeze. My, but it was grand to get away!

After a whole month tethered to land, we were glad to sail all day and anchor out at night. With full water and fuel tanks and replenished food stocks, we lived self-sufficiently for days aboard *Cool Breezes*. Only Jasper had difficulty with the concept of boat as island; she could find no scrap of grass on board, no piece of earth upon which to relieve herself, and so our daily trips to shore resumed. But Jasper did take a few steps on the path to becoming an old seadog. Once petrified at the leap of faith between the boat stern and the dinghy, Jasper now jumped freely. Sometimes upon emerging into the cockpit those foggy mornings, we'd find her already in the dinghy, ready to be ferried to shore.

Our southward cruise in the Gulf of Mexico to Key West was easy. The weather was sunny, the winds favourable, and the time fluid. Now that hurricane season had passed, we ventured confidently to open seas. No longer confined to the narrow borders of the winding inland waterways, we could use our autohelm. Pat would put Otto to work after boat school each morning, when the whole crew could bask in the afternoon sun on the foredecks and trampoline. We revelled in it.

Not just the weather, but also the length of our cruising days was comfortable. Foggy mornings made for late starts, and early sunsets made for long and leisurely evenings at anchor. Pat and I revived the tradition of sundowners in the cockpit before supper. Then, after a barbequed meal, Pat would pick up Sir Walter Scott's *Ivanhoe*, one of the classics he found at the used bookstore, and read aloud to the kids. As with *Kidnapped*, the plotline was enthralling, but the text tortuous. I'd often listen in. Every few minutes, one of the kids would ask, "What does that mean?" I chuckled at Pat's predicament, well aware one of his personal goals this trip was to enlarge his patience.

Every night at 10:00, Pat and I would pull out the SSB and practice tuning in to the weather report. Obtaining weather information on the often-feeble airwaves was more difficult than we expected. We'd take turns huddled close to the radio speaker, straining our ears to catch the tinny voice over the sea of static. Our fingers made tentative, minuscule adjustments to the tuning dial, then scribbled frantically upon the notepad close at hand. Most nights we'd give up and turn to Perfect Paul on the VHF for hard information.

One afternoon, we entered the bay across from the white towers of the city of Marco, Florida, and anchored in the lee of Coconut Island.

"I wonder how the island got its name," I said. The spit of sand that lay before us seemed to support nothing but grey-green tufts of grass. "I don't see a single palm tree."

"Let's check it out," Pat replied.

The islet lured all of us. The whole family accompanied Jasper on her trip to shore in the dinghy. We were rewarded with a treasure of seashells, heaps of them often two feet deep, surrounded by sandy hillocks. Meara caressed the soft mounds with slender fingers.

"This is the softest sand I ever felt!" she exclaimed.

"And this is the biggest number of seashells I've ever seen at once!" Erin added.

"Let's do beauty contests!" the boys shouted.

The next day was momentous. Pat and I rose at 7:00 the morning of January 17 to listen to the weather report. The forecast was for light winds and calm seas.

"Let's do an overnighter," Pat suggested.

"An overnighter!" I said eagerly. In my student days, the term referred to a sleepless night of studying or writing a paper. In this context, though, it meant sailing through the night. We'd never done that before. Our preference was to travel by day, and thus far all of our excursions had been twelve hours or less. Longer voyages required more careful timing. The top priority was to avoid arriving in a strange port in the dark. The far safer alternative was to spend the night hours in deep water, away from shoals, rocks and docks.

"It would be great to do a practice run before we sail from Key West to Cuba," Pat said. Our passage to Cuba would require sailing through the night across the Gulf Stream. "From here to Key West is a perfect overnight distance if we leave in the afternoon."

We planned our day with the expectation that we'd spend a nearly sleepless night. To prepare for that, Pat napped while I taught boat school, and I rested in the afternoon while he and the kids returned to Coconut Island.

After a delicious hour of sleep, I awoke and waved to my family on shore. They were beachcombing. Feeling recharged, I prepared a cold supper and snacks to eat while underway. Soon I found myself wiping down and sweeping up, seizing the opportunity presented by a crewless boat to get it shipshape. So much for my New Year's resolution to 'seize and savour', I thought ruefully, mopping the sweat from my brow. I intended to seize and savour moments of solitude for reflection and writing, not cooking and cleaning.

Then I remembered I hadn't showered for three days, and decided to take a dip in the Gulf of Mexico. I shed my shirt, shorts and eyeglasses, and sauntered out to the foredecks in my little black bikini. From there I plunged headfirst into the beckoning blue.

The dull pound of air hitting water filled my ears. A blizzard of bubbles dazzled my eyes. I felt freshly cleansed, stripped clean as a dolphin, when I pulled my slippery self to the surface. After a languorous float in that salty bath, I climbed the swim ladder to recline in the sun on the foredecks.

Better do some callisthenics, I told myself, glancing beyond my chin at the bumps along my torso. No time like the present, especially if I'm alone.

Rolling over, I did a series of push-ups, followed by tummy crunches. I had a little routine going, counting aloud in a different foreign language with each set of ten. English to start, then *français*. Next the more challenging German and Cree numbers I'd learned as a teen. Finally, my newly learned *español*. By the end of this regimen, my numbers came out as grunts and heaves. I stood up. That's when I heard a loud chorus: "Way to go!"

Only then, squinting through nearsighted and unaided eyes, did I perceive a charter boat full of tourists pass directly in front of our twin bows.

"Here's to the lady on the catamaran!" male voices shouted. I made out a blurry image of them raising glasses toward me.

I fled, mortified, to the sanctuary of my stateroom. Neither my athletic prowess nor my little black bikini was intended for public consumption.

A short while later, the crew returned from the beach. "That was quite the show you put on!" Pat remarked.

"Oh no, did you see it too?" I cringed.

"I sure did," he chuckled. "But the guy with the best view was that lucky fisherman anchored off our bows. He even pulled out his binoculars!"

By late afternoon, we were ready to head into the vast blue sea, stretching away to the limitless horizon right off our bows. I stood at the helm, watching the breakers roll toward us against the moody sky. I waited while Pat pulled up anchor, and felt the awe and trepidation of embarking on adventure. Although ours would be but a toe-dip in the shallows compared with much greater voyages made by far braver sailors, I couldn't help but ponder the many metaphors of the main. The ocean: a blank canvas, a representation of the vast unknowable; a symbol of yearning or escape from worldly chaos; the restless water a sign for human alienation or unresolved emotion. The Protean sea personified: a harsh and unmerciful taskmaster, unrelenting and uncaring as the pounding surf; a seductress, sparkling and flirtatious; a roaring avenger with a tempestuous temperament, a monster to be feared. What did the water hold in store for us tonight?

Pat heaved the anchor into its slot and signalled to me at the helm. I steered the twin bows southward. Yes, this journey was but an overnight passage on calm seas in a shipshape vessel. Yet this was no story. This was real. This was my family, our boat, right now, sailing upon the deep and into the dark. I caught a glimpse of what I imagined all intrepid voyagers must feel at the poignant point of departure: that anything might happen, anything is possible.

"All hands on deck!" Captain Pat shouted down the companionway.

The kids were in the galley, cleaning and sorting their newest shells. They hurried up to the cockpit.

"This is the drill for overnight passages," their father announced. "The moment you step into the cockpit, you put on your life vest."

The kids scurried down to the wet locker and returned with their gear.

"Here's Jasper's vest," Liam said. It was a garish thing, brilliant yellow with purple paw prints. No sooner had Pat snapped it on, than Jasper began to chew it off, much to the children's amusement.

"Your mother and I will be taking turns on watch," Pat continued. "Most of the time there'll be only one of us parents in the cockpit. If you want to keep us company while the other parent is below decks, you must clip on a harness." He showed the kids how to wear the straps around their torsos, and to clip the line to the helm.

"Don't worry, we'll all be awake all night!" the kids assured us.

And so at sunset that day, instead of setting anchor, we sallied forth. I gathered the crew to say grace before our cockpit picnic.

"Wait, wait," Meara interrupted, just as we began to breathe Amen. "I just want to say, St. Christopher, keep us safe!"

January 2001, approaching Key West, Florida.
The boys sight land after our glorious first overnight sail.

From: The Kirwin crew
To: Kith and Kin
Subject: **Greetings from** *Cool Breezes*: **Now This**
                 is Sailing

Now *this* is sailing.

As I tap away here at the laptop, it's just past 5:00 a.m. on January 18. We're sailing on the Gulf of Mexico, only a few short hours away from Key West. This passage of sixteen hours and about ninety nautical miles, beginning near Marco, Florida, constitutes our first overnighter.

Pat and I take turns at the helm on two-hour watches, but in fact neither of us spends much time sleeping. The air is cool and still. The sky is partly cloudy, almost moody. The ocean is tranquil as a mountain lake. It seems strange, even surreal, to be so placid ourselves, so accepting of what lies ahead as we hurtle forward in the blackness, unable to see a thing beyond the twin bows of our catamaran. On a rational level, our mental comfort rests on the fact that we're wearing not just life vests but also harnesses, and that we're receiving a wealth of information from our radar, depth sounder, autohelm, GPS units and charts. Nevertheless, a visceral level of spiritual acquiescence is at work here on board. What delivers this inexplicable trust and nearly ecstatic peace is a hyper presence, our willingness to be one with the sky and water, with the great unknown. It's an exquisite awareness that God is with us.

Imagery from the evening's journey will be forever etched in my mind's eye. Visions of the sky and water: the Orion constellation, appearing in the eastern sky, and disappearing in the west; the white bow lights of an interminable line of freighters, visible both on our radar screen and to the naked eye, twinkling like a string of sparkling diamonds in the shipping lanes about four miles to the west; the quarter moon rising at midnight, casting a surprisingly helpful glow on the water; the phosphorescence in the water, flashing a million points of light in our wake. Images of our young crew: Jasper, sleeping away the entire experience on her bean bag under the salon table; Meara slumbering in Erin's narrow berth, having finally collapsed there at 1:30 a.m.; Erin sprawled on the bed of the master stateroom, and the boys, crashed, fully-dressed on their own berth, despite earlier vows to stay up all night with us.

The latest image, as I return to this missive now at 6:50 a.m., is of the pink edge of light growing brighter to the east. The whole crew is now awake, ready to witness its first and much anticipated daybreak on water. All of us feel it: this is a life moment. We're sailing not into the proverbial sunset, but toward the hopeful sunrise.

Once the sun is up, Liam notices something amiss.

"Dad, look! We're dragging something behind us!"

We turn to see a crab pot bouncing along at the stern. The line usually affixing the crab pot to a fisherman's buoy has somehow wrapped around our rudder.

"Thank God the line didn't wind itself around our propellers!" Pat remarks, releasing it. "That would have been a huge headache."

"Just think," says Ben, "None of our 'high tech' equipment detected that piece of 'low tech' equipment!"

Ben's feeling especially chipper this morning. Reprising his role as the trusty navigator upon whom Pat so heavily relied during their early days bringing the boat to Portsmouth, he expertly guides the helmsman through the maze of markers and buoys into Key West Harbour.

As we approach landfall I call various Key West marinas on the VHF, seeking a berth for *Cool Breezes*. None can be found. Everything is booked because it's Race Week on the island, and boats from all over the world are competing in the regatta.

"When will you have space for us?" I ask each marina dockmaster.

"Check back on February thirtieth," one of them replies sarcastically.

Resigned to anchoring out, we drop the hook, find something – anything – to eat, and collapse on our berths.

A few hours later, the uncomfortably rough water in the anchorage rouses me. Queasiness motivates me to call the marinas again to see if a spot has opened up.

"You're in luck!" exclaims the dockmaster at the marina hosting the regatta. "One of the boats just got wrecked in a race and went home. Hurry in if you want a slip."

My mother hen instincts kick in. Excited at the prospect of getting to a marina so we can do laundry and take showers after four days of deprivation, I wake Pat. I know he'll be equally eager for the marina's other amenities: fresh water and diesel. We weigh anchor and motor in. As we approach the stone breakwater, we hear the peal of a starting horn. A string of sleek racing yachts follows us in the main channel. Just when our beamy catamaran idles slowly to the fuel pumps at the marina, hundreds of other boats stream in behind her after their day at the races.

Liam is thrilled.

"Hey, it looks like we won the race!"

What a zoo! We've never docked in such a busy, crowded and exciting situation, surrounded by such expert sailors and magnificent boats. Our vessel looks like a sturdy Clydesdale stabled among lean thoroughbreds. The Canadian flag flying off our stern and the prairie port of call labelled there make us even more conspicuous.

"Slow is pro," Tevi taught us. *Cool Breezes* makes its stately way down the lane toward our assigned slip. As we get closer, though, we can see that the racing sailboat in the slip beside ours is floating sideways, occupying our berth as well as its own. Its crew of large and beefy men, wearing identical sets of spanking new Izod shirts, struggles to align the wayward vessel alongside the finger pier. We wait. Captain Pat at the helm sighs with frustration. It's no small feat to control the direction of an almost idle boat in a narrow lane amid the wind, the underlying current, and the wakes created by other boats.

When the race crew finally snugs its last line to the dock cleats, the crew of *Cool Breezes* springs into action. To prevent Jasper from leaping prematurely onto the dock, Meara leads her to the salon and locks the companionway door. Pat orients our bows to the slip and guides our vessel slowly in. Ben, at the bow, secures one end of a line to the bow cleat and neatly tosses the other end to Liam. Surefooted Liam has jumped onto the dock, where he snags the line and wraps it tightly around the dock cleat. Erin and I repeat the same procedure at the stern. In mere minutes, our relatively youthful crew executes an expert – dare I say perfect – docking.

Our seemingly effortless effort isn't wasted on the men aboard the neighbouring American race boat. They pause mid-swig to watch us. One of the crew points at us.

"Hey, you reprobates," he shouts to his mates. "That's how we dock back in Canada. Even the kids can tie up better than you!"

Pat's exasperation with the neighbouring crew

instantly melts. Saluting a fellow Canadian is always a treat, but to be recognized as a skilful crew in company such as this makes all of us feel like strutting.

"No need to admit that we haven't always docked so well!" I whisper to Pat.

Although we feel foggy – overtired from the previous nearly sleepless night – it's easy to catch the bright and breezy post-race buzz. A festival spirit prevails. Mostly male crews dominate the docks and crowd into cockpits, drinking to success or drowning sorrows. Our own crew fills the water tanks, smooths the sail cover over the boom, arranges the docking lines into Flemish coils, and connects the electrical cord. Meanwhile Pat and I put up our feet on the cockpit cushions. We feel like we're in a beer commercial.

"It's one of those 'it don't get much better than this' moments," Pat says.

"And the beauty of it is, we know it," I reply.

Now *this* is the cruising life.

God bless and fair winds,

Love PJ+crew

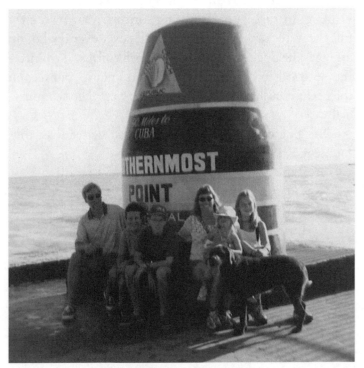

January 2001, Key West, Florida.
Only ninety miles to Cuba, the message reads.

Chapter 13
Awaiting a Weather Window

There is a poetry of sailing as old as the world.
  – Antoine de Saint-Exupery

The morning after we arrived at the Key West marina dawned bright and breezy: perfect regatta weather. I crawled out of bed and set the kettle to boil on the stove. The crystals in the galley portholes danced, casting rainbow reflections everywhere.

I smiled to recall the delight of our first overnight sail. "How many of your friends back home have sailed a boat into the blackness?" Pat had asked. I'd been standing watch, harnessed to the helm. The children had all collapsed. Pat pulled me close and nibbled my neck. At that deep blue velvet hour, he and I were delectably alone in the cockpit. So close were our quarters, and so numerous our children, that opportunities for luscious and lingering romance aboard were rare. The ancient adage urges *carpe diem,* seize the day, but we had seized the night.

An excited buzz on the crowded docks snapped my reverie and woke the rest of the crew. As I poured hot water from the kettle into the teapot, I peeked out the portholes to see Jasper, lying underside up on the dock, her eyes shut tight, lapping up a steady succession of tummy rubs.

"She sure knows how to handle a crowd," Liam observed.

167

We dressed quickly and hurried to the cockpit to watch the goings-on. Dozens of brawny sailors milled about the docks, pumped with the adrenaline of anticipation. Then, as if on signal, they dispersed. As the finger piers emptied, the channels filled. We watched a steady stream of haughty yachts head out to the races. A moment later, a plaintive horn blew. The races had begun.

After a short morning at boat school, we packed the laptop, leashed the dog, and headed out to see the town. First up: a big and greasy brunch at Harpoon Harry's. There we raised a juice glass toast to the success of our overnighter, our first big test as sailors. Next order of business: downloading our email at the cyber-café. A few dozen messages awaited us. We opened these precious gifts with all the excitement of a six-year-old at a birthday party. The longer and further we travelled, the more we welcomed contact from home.

Sated with food and news, we set out to feast our eyes. We walked the narrow and colourful streets toward Duval, the town's main drag. The air was warm and humid, the atmosphere breezy and hip. The sidewalks on Duval were crowded with people of all configurations. Bronzed beach babes in bikini tops brushed shoulders with pasty-faced couples in matching jackets; Rastafarian males strode past little old blue-haired ladies; male lovers, strolling hand in hand, crossed paths with pierced and tattooed teens; ragged beggars slumped at street corners. We six and our dog were but another float in the parade. We walked downhill to the water, past chic boutiques, trendy cafés, appealing watering holes and tasteless T-shirt shops, to an immense concrete buoy marking the southernmost point of the USA. There we posed for a photo beside the brightly painted message, "Ninety miles to Cuba."

By then it was sundown, time for the nightly street

performer celebration at nearby Mallory Square. We made our way there via a side street. Though it ran parallel to Duval, it seemed a world away, a neighbourhood marked by run-down dwellings, rickety picket fences, and dozens of free-range chickens. We could barely restrain Jasper from the instinctive chase.

Mallory Square was more an event than a place, a sunset street festival set in a cobblestone park looking west over the water. There we found not just booths offering food, jewellery, art and psychic services, but also a steady flow of street performances. As each busker finished his act, another one called out to the crowds. We swarmed round each like bees to a pot of honey. Liam was chosen as an audience volunteer in a balancing-act routine, magnifying the entertainment value for our crew. Pat and I beamed as our nine-year-old capably threw plastic bowling pins to the high-heeled and top-hatted woman propped on a platform. Then Jasper became an unexpected participant.

"Hey Mo, get back here!" shouted a clown. Mo, his sidekick dog, had just abandoned the ring on his nose and the ramp he was navigating to check out our pretty Labrador retriever. The crowd roared with laughter.

A cold front rolled in that night, bringing unsettled conditions. The months of January through March brought a steady succession of cold and wet weather systems on the American eastern seaboard. We resigned ourselves to awaiting a weather window – a space of time between cold fronts – to cross the Gulf Stream.

Every morning and evening, Pat listened to Perfect Paul on the VHF for local weather predictions, and to the SSB for offshore reports.

"Shhh!" the children hissed to each other, as soon as they heard metallic voices broadcast in our salon. Pat, with

his one deaf ear, groused if he missed a word or two due
to background noise. Those lost few words might be key
to our safety.

In addition to getting radio reports, we also picked up
daily printouts of the online weather forecast from the
marina office. We had an abundance of weather information, all of it consistent, and none of it promising. The
days marched inexorably forth – January 20, 21, 22 –
without a foreseeable break in the cold front.

That prickly old subject arose again. Pat worried we
might not arrive in Varadero, Cuba by the time Eldean
flew there on January 31. Meanwhile, I was anxious that
he was anxious. Because it was my mother who was visiting, I felt responsible for the pressure created by her
imminent arrival.

"You know how dangerous it is to sail to deadline," Pat
complained. "Committing to arriving at a certain place by
a certain date makes for poor decisions. People take more
risks than they should because they want to arrive on
time."

"I've explained our situation to my mom," I replied.
"If we're still here on January thirtieth, I'll phone her and
she'll cancel her flight. She bought cancellation insurance,
so it's no problem. Or else she might fly to Varadero and
spend a few days there by herself. She wants to see us so
badly, she's willing to take the risk we might not get there
in time."

Every time we played out this exchange, or a variation
of it, I felt torn between the wishes of my husband and my
mother. Mostly though, we loved our time in Key West.
What a fine place to await a weather window, no matter
how anxious that wait may be! After mornings at boat
school, we spent the afternoons running errands or sightseeing. Our favourite museum was the Shipwreck

Historeum. There, aided by animatronics and live actors, we were transported to the morally dubious world of wreckers, the men hired to salvage the cargo of ships wrecked on the off-lying rocks. All too often, they were the very men who set up false lighthouses that lured those same ships to their ruin.

Another day we took a tour of the Turtle Kraal Museum at the end of our dock. This qualified as a science field trip, the kids told me, since we learned about the now banned practise of capturing and serving sea turtles, Ben's favourite animal. Yet another afternoon I took Erin shopping along Duval. The excuse was necessity: our adolescent had outgrown her clothes. The truth was, Erin loved to shop, and I loved spending time alone with her.

One of my favourite pastimes while we waited was writing. Each morning I rose at dawn to a quiet boat, lit my candle, and opened the coiled notebook where the private realm of my novel was stowed. I became immersed in my plotline, charmed by my characters, consumed by my private world of words and imagination.

My cast had five protagonists, most of whom had children. There was a savvy teenaged girl who loosely resembled Erin, a lanky big-hearted boy like Ben, and a wisp of an angel child who reminded me of Meara. It took two boys, a pair of rambunctious twins, to capture the essence of Liam. My husband's generosity and wry sense of humour, and the traits of other real life characters, could be traced in my fiction. The seed of my novel had been planted years ago, but time and circumstance had never been conducive to nurturing it. At the outset of our travels, the magic bean of my story had sprouted. I originally expected my novel would be written within our year aboard, but now, in January, with only five chapters written, I was less ambitious. No matter, the gift lay in the process. Merely the exercise of writing had stirred latent fonts of creative urging, and I threw myself into them.

One late afternoon, as Pat and I walked the dog, I gazed longingly into the windows of the various eateries.

"Let's go out tonight," I suggested. "The marina is guarded, so the kids would be safe."

"We could use some adult time before we get to Cuba," Pat agreed.

Legendary establishments on Duval Street, like Sloppy Joe's of Hemingway fame and Jimmy Buffet's Margaritaville, were out of reach; we were unwilling to venture that far down Duval. Two other restaurants were just a few steps away from our boat, however, so we turned on the VHF, left Jasper on guard, and stole away for a few hours.

"Hurray, Mom's gone, we can play our favourite CD!" the boys cheered.

Yes, even aboard *Cool Breezes,* that age-old tension was playing out: the kids clamoured to play their loud and obnoxious top-forty music, and I could hardly bear to hear it.

"Mom," Erin wailed, "how can you complain? We've got only one 'kids' music' CD on this whole boat!"

"Yeah, and only one video!" Ben snorted. That would be *Maverick*, a Mel Gibson/Jody Foster comedy the kids had already watched a half-dozen times.

"Yeah, and most of our measly software games came out of cereal boxes!" Liam whined. They were right, and I said so. I knew that although our pre-teens occasionally complained about being unplugged, they were remarkably tolerant.

Our first stop that evening was the "raw bar" down the dock, where the specialty was raw oysters on the half-shell. There we downed margaritas, sampled the delicate flavour of stone crab, dined on conch chowder, and learned to pronounce *conch* like *conk*.

"Let's check out the place next door," I suggested. Pat ran back to the boat to tell the kids where to reach us on the VHF, while I ordered two more margaritas. Now we were actually barhopping. In no time our conversation moved from the humdrum to the philosophical. Once we'd covered the wet and ruffled weather, I effused about my love of writing, and how my book had begun to fill my waking thoughts.

"What book?" Pat asked.

"My book! You know, the novel I started back in Virginia," I replied, feeling a touch tetchy. Of course he must know what I meant by "my book."

"Well, Jake, you know you're actually writing two books," Pat smiled.

My brows knit in puzzlement.

"There's your novel, yes, but there's also the book about this boat trip," he explained. "All those emails you've been sending every few weeks are like chapters in a book. You're already writing the first draft."

What a revelation that was! My perception of those fortnightly reports was transformed. We'd received requests from far-flung people across North America to be included in our group email list; perhaps there was a readership after all for my tale of a boatful of displaced prairie folk.

The next morning I awoke with a start. A jump-start, actually. I craved the blank page, especially after the previous evening's revelation. More than ever I was eager to write, to play with words. Like my children with their seashells, I had a wondrous and luminous, ever-expanding collection of words. Pages and pages of them; single words, neat turns of phrase, snippets of wisdom, and even whole passages from the great books I'd read along the nautical miles, books like Robertson Davies' *Fifth Business*, Pearl Buck's *Mandala*, Marilyn French's *The Women's Room*, Marianne Frederickson's *Hanna's Daughters*, Barbara Kingsolver's *The Poisonwood Bible*, and the Bible itself. I always kept a yellow legal notepad nearby, eager to capture an especially golden word, fitting name, or telling insight.

Sometimes, when I sat down to write and found the muse had fled, I'd survey my trove of treasured words, and locate them in that ultimate collection, my dictionary. *Effulgent:* diffusing a flood of light, radiant. *Pellucid:* perfectly clear, translucent. *Sublime:* exalted, eminent, inspiring awe and adoration. *Kith:* one's friends. *Halcyon:* calm, peaceful, tranquil and happy. *Serendipity:* the faculty of finding valuable or agreeable things not sought for. *Limn:* to paint or draw, to portray, depict. *Aerie, augury, miasma, dun; fawn, acerbic, glib, visceral; feckless, reckless, gloze, glaze; evocative, execrable, winsome.* Words: tumbling out of the air, flowing like the water, polished with use, worn with abuse. Words: gems not to conceal but to reveal, morsels not to swallow but to savour. Words: tools, symbols, mysteries. The more I read, the more I came to appreciate the well chosen, the well written, the subtly alluring array of words, and the more I rejoiced in each new discovery, just as an artist delights in a fresh tint or shade of colour. The more I read, the more I wanted to write, to use my overflowing jewellery box of nuances. The more I wrote, the more I wondered whether I could ever really write.

I scribbled, enraptured, for over an hour before Pat stirred.

"Time to listen for the offshore weather report," he said, joining me in the salon.

The fractured voice over the SSB was barely discernible.

"Sounds as if there'll be a narrow weather window tomorrow, between the end of this cold front and the start of the next," Pat announced. "Looks like we'll be sailing to Cuba tomorrow!"

The news prompted me to hustle away to buy yet another load of groceries. I returned to find Pat had taken over boat school. The kids were engulfed in charts and weather diagrams, irrepressible in their eagerness to tell me all they learned.

"The wind is coming from the northwest tomorrow," Ben explained. "That's good, because the Gulf Stream comes from the west and so the wind and the Stream won't oppose each other."

"The Gulf Stream will push us east," Liam continued. "That's good, too, because Varadero is east of Key West."

"At seven or eight knots, our passage will take about eighteen hours," Erin chipped in. "Since we want to arrive in the morning, we'll leave tomorrow afternoon."

Later that evening, Pat hooked our television cable to the marina outlet so the kids could watch TV. Then he and I took the dog for a short walk to mail postcards and send email from the cyber-café. Little did we know that it would be months before we indulged again in television and the Internet. Nor did we then appreciate that the continuity of North American culture had been a lifesaver, enabling us landlubbers to tread water in our new environs, this cruising lifestyle, without drowning. The next day we'd quit treading water and begin to really swim. We'd undergo a sea change.

Part Three: Cruising the Cuban Cayos

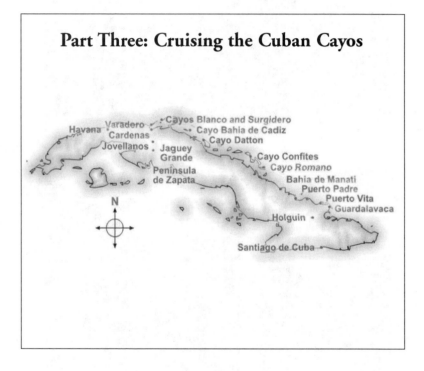

January 2001.

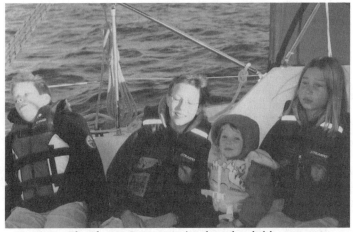

Key West, Florida, on January 24, when the children experience different stages of seasickness.

Right, Varadero, Cuba, at dawn on January 25.

From: The Kirwin crew
To: Kith and Kin
Subject: **Greetings from *Cool Breezes*: Cuba,
               Ahoy!**

Gathered in the cockpit at sundown, watching the Key West harbour fade away at our stern, we pray not only for a safe and uneventful journey across the Gulf Stream to Cuba, but also to keep our suppers down.

The latter prayer turns out to be the most necessary. The wind at our stern pushes us forward, and creates lumpy following waves. The motion of the sea, compounded by the fact we've been lying in still waters tied up to a dock for over a week, produces a distinctly queasy sensation in our pits. Despite taking motion sickness tabs, wearing sea bands, and drinking ginger tea, we feel green. All of us, that is, but our skipper. Pat stands stalwart at the helm and stares at the horizon, the best antidote to seasickness.

Pat and I intend to be much stricter with our two-hour watches tonight than we were on our first overnight passage. That way we might get some real rest through the night. At 8:00 p.m., Pat retires to our berth, and I take my first watch. Soon the rest of my faithful crew begins to drop off. At first I'm surprised that none of them try to stay up all night. But conditions are different this time. Motion sickness meds have subdued the kids' high spirits. This night crossing doesn't hold the same novelty as our first. And tonight's rough and cold waves and wind make for a much less hospitable cockpit than we enjoyed during our first overnighter.

My second watch is much harder. I'm glad Pat's actually sleeping, and proud to be managing single-handed. But mostly I feel sorry I took those seasickness pills: they did nothing but induce a somnolent haze. Alone in the night, I pray the entire rosary, then play games in my mind. One challenge is to recall as many Spanish words as possible. Another is to sing my entire repertoire of lullabies, in sequence, just as I did to my nursing infants years ago. Another is to watch the blinking blips on our radar screen, and imagine stories about the boats they represent, the ships we pass in the night. Once in a while, I stretch out my legs and hips. On a night watch, I remind myself, to live in the present is not optional but mandatory.

Precisely two minutes past the end of my watch, I heave a sigh of relief. I conduct a final check of our panoply of equipment, the trim of our sails, and the wind vane at the top of our mast. All must be shipshape when I turn over the helm. Then, the rope from my harness trailing behind me, I descend to our stateroom and rouse Pat. Then I unleash myself from the wheel, nestle into the warm spot left by my mate, and drift away for a few hours.

I awake for my third watch at 4:00 a.m. feeling much more alert. The winds are constant, and we're still travelling under sail alone. Pat decides to stay up with me.

"Soon we'll enter the mighty Gulf Stream," he says. "I wanna be here."

He ignites the twin engines. We wait for the jolt when our boat hits the Stream, but our confluence with it is gradual. Our charts and GPS tell us we're in it, but we can't feel it.

"It seems to me the Stream has been a bit over-glori-fied," Pat remarks.

Then we notice we're straying off course. We alter the autohelm twenty degrees off our compass direction, just to compensate for the pull of the Stream.

"Never mind what I said," Pat says. "The Stream's more powerful than I thought."

The sun crests as *Cool Breezes* approaches landfall on January 25.

"There she is!" Pat exclaims, pointing to the headland on the horizon. "There's Cuba."

The coastline is rugged and mysterious, yet beckoning. Heavy orange-tipped clouds scud across blue-grey skies. I hurry below decks to rouse the children.

"We're here, kids, we're in Cuba!" Drowsy and bleary-eyed, they straggle to the cockpit for their first view of this new land.

"Look, a flying fish!" Liam yells, suddenly alert. He snatches up a poor specimen that has landed on our stern deck sometime during the night.

"And look, dolphins!" Erin calls out, pointing ahead. As if to temper the drama of the seascape, an escort of playful dolphins appears, leaping in the wake of our twin bows. To be greeted by dolphins is a lucky omen.

The sun peeks through rifts in the streaked skies. A half hour later, we hear a staccato bark over our VHF.

"*Coo-Bree-zes, Coo-Bree-zes!*"

It's the Guarda Frontera: the infamous, ever-vigilant, overzealous Cuban border guard. We've read all about Guarda soldiers in our cruising guide, and now we hope to pass muster with them. We're especially anxious to find out how they'll handle Jasper, knowing that Cuba imposes a two-week quarantine period on canines. As the crew of a newly arrived vessel, we humans are effectively quarantined as well. We raise our solid yellow Q-flag, the international signal that we have yet to be cleared in.

It's almost 8:00 a.m. as we pass between the rock sentries guarding the entrance to Varadero. From there we make a sharp dogleg turn left onto the Canal Kawama, leading toward our destination, Marina Darsena. The canal is flanked on the peninsula side by high-rise hotels, and on the mainland side by a modest village. Cruising the canal on a catamaran, two boys perched at the forestay and a red dog lounging on the foredecks, we draw more than our fair share of attention from the villagers. Pat chuckles.

A squad of officials awaits us on the dock in the Varadero marina, watching as we approach the slip assigned to us over the VHF radio. We expect the group to include the Guarda Frontera and marina dockhands. Yet when Liam tosses a bowline to the cluster of Cubans, the young man who unwittingly catches it stands there awkwardly. He seems unaware that he should fasten the line to a dock cleat, and that due to his inaction, our boat is drifting away.

"Our boys could have done much better without him," Pat mutters. A moment later, annoyance dissolves into sheepishness when we learn that the fellow who caught the line is the port medical doctor.

Clearing in is a complicated process, involving so many officers and quadruplicate forms that not everyone can sit at our salon table at once. The kids retreat to their staterooms and peek out at the goings-on, while Pat and I take turns sitting down, then jumping up to fetch yet something else the officers request. The first four Cuban government officials to board are the doctor/health officer, the customs officer, the immigration officer and the agriculture officer/veterinarian. The pretty dark-haired vet confiscates our three dozen eggs, but redeems herself a few minutes later by allowing Jasper to enter the country without enduring the quarantine.

Thanks to the advice in our cruising guides, our papers are in order. We pass out photocopied sheets detailing the specifications of our boat, the birth dates and passport numbers of all the crew, and Jasper's most recent vaccinations. These information sheets, together with gift bags of lollipops and lukewarm cans of Coke, help grease the wheels of this painstaking process.

After the first four officials disembark, we must lower our Q-flag and fly the Cuban courtesy flag, an ensign with brilliant blue and white stripes. But we aren't yet done with officialdom. The humans and dog are cleared in, but the boat isn't. Enter the Guarda Frontera. Two Guarda soldiers come aboard as soon as the first officers leave. Compact, moustached men in khaki uniforms, they demand to see our Canadian boat registration certificate. I shrug nervously as I pass them a fax of it; the original had not arrived before we left St. Petersburg. Pat and I exchange worried glances.

A sigh of relief. Neither officer insists on seeing the original. They do question us closely on the direction we intend to travel. A half hour later, they issue a *despacho*, a navigational license permitting us to travel to the next port of entry. Once we reach that port, they carefully explain, we must obtain a new *despacho* from the next Guarda outpost.

"You mean we have to go through all of this again every time we arrive somewhere new?" Ben asks, once the Guarda soldiers are gone.

"We don't have to go through new inspections from the immigration officer, the customs officer, the medical doctor or the vet," Pat replies. "But we do need to surrender our old *despacho* and get a new one every time we reach a Guarda Frontera station."

"Wow, that's incredible," says Erin. "We're just a family on a cruise. What kind of threat do they think we are?"

At that point, we think we're done; admitted, if not welcomed, into the country. Then two more Guarda soldiers approach our boat. They insist upon inspecting the boat itself to judge its "seaworthiness." Once again we produce our sheaf of papers, tins of cola and gifts of candy. We're beginning to understand that these offerings are expected not as bribes, but as gestures of courtesy.

Then one of the Guarda officers crosses the line. It's one thing to accept a gift, quite another to request one. A tall, husky man with the fair skin and eyes of his Soviet Russian father, he gladly takes our proffered bag of sweets for his children, then asks, "Do you have any pantyhose for my wife?"

Unfortunately for him, I'm unable to oblige; fortunately for me, sailors don't wear pantyhose.

Despite its lack of hosiery, *Cool Breezes* is issued a seaworthiness certificate. With this last document, we are now officially processed. We begin to settle into the marina. Pat is particularly impressed with the electrical hook-ups. Our cruising guides forewarned us that the marina electrician, armed with a jumble of wires and electrical tape, would connect us to shore power. As likely as not, we read, our electrical system might get fried. But these hook-ups are effortless. Pat examines them more closely.

"They're made in Norfolk, Virginia," he smirks. "So much for not trading with the enemy." He's referring of course to the United States embargo forbidding Americans to buy from or sell to Cubans. That means

Americans are permitted to be in Cuba, but forbidden to buy anything while here.

The girls and I walk down the docks to check out the marina facilities.

"Wow, look at the showers!" Erin effuses. The bath-house is gorgeous, replete with ceramic tiles, marble countertops, and sparkling chrome fixtures. Yet it lacks both toilet paper and a reliable supply of hot water.

We're hungry and tired after our overnight sail and the protracted process of clearing in. As if on cue, a clean-cut young man wearing black slacks, a crisp white shirt and black bowtie appears dockside with an invitation.

"Good day, I'm Emil from the marina restaurant," he says pleasantly, in very good English. "You are new here. We have a *speciale* price just for you today, only eight dollars, all-inclusive, five dollars for the children. Please join us."

How could we – especially I, the galley wench – resist this delightful invitation to our first Cuban meal?

Sitting with my family in the restaurant, sipping red wine after a dinner of shrimp and rice with beans, I can't help but marvel. Only twenty-four hours ago we loosened the docklines from our slip in Key West. Only ninety miles across the water from there lays an entirely different world, and we are in it.

God bless, fair winds, and *adiós*,
Love PJ+crew

January 2001, Cuba.

The palm-lined avenue leading from the Varadero marina to Santa Marta.

Our first Cuban friends, the three artisans, posing with the children.

The kids dig for clams and search for sea treasures ashore Cayo Blanco.

Chapter 14
Sea Change

Sea change (n.) 1. A major transformation, often for the better. 2. A change or alteration brought about by the sea (Gage Canadian Dictionary). A notable or unexpected transformation; a radical change (Canadian Oxford Dictionary). A marked transformation (Nelson Canadian Dictionary of the English Language).

Many destinations of our year-long cruise were deliberately undefined, but the *cayos* and *ciudads* of Cuba had always been among our planned ports of call. Pat and I wanted to show our children – and see for ourselves – life in a country truly foreign to Canada. Cuba was alluring in many respects; its language, history, geography, and political system were completely new to us. Cuba's people, however, would impress us most.

The morning after our arrival dawned clear and, especially after a good night's sleep, promising. I took Jasper for an exploratory run. We ran down the docks to the gate of Marina Darsena, where three uniformed young guards politely nodded. Outside the marina gate the main highway led west to Havana, one hundred and forty kilometres away, and east to Varadero. On the south side of the highway stood two rows of palm trees, a majestic entrance to

the village of Santa Marta. Having so much to see, and
such a gloriously wide-open agenda, produced a tingling
sense of anticipation.

The only way to reach Varadero on foot was to cross a
bridge from the mainland, where we were docked, to
Peninsula de Hicacos, the skinny finger of land lined by
high-rise hotels facing a long stretch of beach. I could easily see the narrow bridge from the marina gate. Jasper and
I turned east and ran through the grassy field along the
highway toward it.

Clusters of men and boys fished from the shore of
Canal Kawama. The highway shoulder was dotted with
pedestrians, their thumbs stuck out. Cars stopped regularly. Hitchhiking appeared to be a common mode of
travel. While I took in these sights, I noticed Jasper and I
were creating one. The sight of a woman running with a
leashed dog must have been rare, for we drew a lot of
stares.

Traffic on the curved bridge was choked. Our gait
slowed to a walk. The narrow walkway was made of metal
grating, which Jasper found difficult to navigate. Passersby
gave us a wide berth, wary of my beautiful red *perra*. I
stopped midway across the bridge beside a small glassed
room, manned by a guard. From there the charms of
Avenida Primera, the bustling palm-lined main street of
Varadero, lay arrayed below me. I turned back at that
point, but only so I could soon return with my family.

Once the kids were showered, schooled and fed, the
six of us took the half-hour walk to town. By then Avenida
Primera was packed with tourists. Yet to our eyes, scanning for everything foreign, they were all but invisible. We
saw schoolchildren in uniform, chickens and stray dogs
running freely, and artisans selling colourful wares at craft
tables. We saw rundown homes and laundry hanging on

clotheslines in front courtyards, right next door to modern towering hotels. We saw smiling people everywhere, greeting each other warmly, grasping arms and pressing kisses on both cheeks.

Dogs barked, horse hoofs clopped, horns blared, laughter rang, music from sidewalk cafés sang out. An underlying stream of rapidly spoken *español* tempered the cacophony of the street. Immersed in a wordy stew I couldn't comprehend, I wondered if this was the experience of infancy, straining to make sense of language. How I wished we could express ourselves better! Nonetheless, we found that the greeting *"¡Hola!"* goes a long way.

Our children provided us with an instant connection to the Cuban people. A Cubana attending a craft table asked, *"¿Cuatro niños?"* Her gesture, pointing in a circular motion to my children and then to me, expressed her question whether all four were mine.

"Sí, sí," I replied. The Cubana nodded appreciatively, eyeing my full length as if to size me up, clearly impressed with my productivity. This happened more than once. A family of six was by Cuban standards large, rare and admirable. Cubans, we learned, love children.

We waded eastward through the crowds towards the tourist telephone office. The hotels along the peninsula became more glamorous, and the local influence less noticeable. Halfway to the end of the Avenida, we found the telephone office. There Ben and I waited in line to call Eldean while the rest of the crew strolled onward. Laden with pastries and bread from the sweet-smelling *panadería* on Calle Forty-three, they found us a half-hour later.

"What did she say, what did she say?" Erin asked breathlessly.

"Well, Nanny sounds pretty excited to get here," Ben replied. "Before we got cut off she told us the name of her hotel and the time her flight arrives on Wednesday."

"Only five more sleeps till she gets here," I told Meara.

We hired a horse and buggy for the return trip to the marina. Our seven-kilometre journey began with a gentle trot westward along Avenida Primera. From there we crossed the bridge. Once across, the road bore right onto the buzzing *autopista*, where the horse broke into a canter. There we joined peak rush hour traffic. Cars whizzed by, honking as they passed us in the carriage. The horse and driver took no notice. Soon we turned onto a road leading to the dusty village of Santa Marta. We could barely glimpse it as we bounced along its outskirts on an abandoned airstrip. Beside us, a string of bobbling pumpjacks drilled for oil. Then we veered onto a lane flanked by swaying palms, the same majestic entrance I'd seen from the marina gate that morning. Our ride ended there. We crossed the highway to the marina, where the guards greeted us at the gate. It was past sundown.

We woke the next morning to find that the sulphurous fumes from the local oil refineries had blown northward over the marina, producing a stench in the air and a fine, greasy film over the whole boat. Perhaps that was a good thing: it motivated us to venture further afield. Pat visited the local detachment of the Guarda Frontera to get a *despacho*, while I checked out laundry options at the marina.

I'd read in our cruising guides that the marina had no laundry room; indeed we would find no such facility during our whole time in Cuba. Instead, Marina Darsena offered a laundry service. What luxury, I thought, but at what price?

"*¿Cuánto cuestas?*" I inquired.

"*Nada de nada,*" smiled the well-groomed Cubana; it's nothing.

My impression was not that the service would be free, but that it would be economical.

"*Bueno*," I said, dropping off a sailbag full of laundry. Later that afternoon, Erin and I retrieved our clean clothing. It smelled lovely, and was folded so carefully that it looked pressed. I was delighted until the friendly worker presented me with the bill. The laundry service charged not per load but per item of clothing. Our order of thirty-eight socks, twenty pairs of underwear, ten shirts, and six pairs of shorts added up to US$18, more than dinner for two at the marina restaurant.

"*¿Es muy caro!*" I whispered to Erin, very expensive. "From now on we'll wash out our own socks and underwear!"

That evening Pat and I sauntered down the concrete docks to the bar at the marina. Pat ordered a *cubalibre*, but rum and cola didn't appeal to me.

"What's another Cuban drink?" I asked Emil, who was tending bar that evening.

"You could try a *mojito*," he replied. "That was Hemingway's favourite."

With a few deft squeezes and shakes, he produced a delicious light rum concoction with lime juice and soda, garnished with a sprig of crushed *yerbabuena* – fresh mint. Like the infamous crusty writer, I was hooked.

"So you're a bartender as well as a waiter," Pat said to Emil.

"Oh yes," Emil replied. He detailed the extensive training he had received after high school to equip him to work in the tourist industry. "The government realizes how important tourism is," Emil went on. "If we do well in school at English, we're invited to take the hospitality course. It's great for us because we get tips in American dollars." In Cuba, we learned, the best and the brightest take on serving roles. "We make more money than doctors and lawyers."

A few moments later, we were joined at the bar by fellow cruisers Danny and Debbie from Ontario, aboard *La Vida Dulce*. Our foursome connected instantly. Since we were so fresh from our overnight passage across the Florida Straits, Gulf Stream stories were the immediate conversational gambit. That's when Jacques, a lean and weathered Québécois, joined our group. As a single-hander, he had the best Gulf Stream crossing story of all.

"I am in de middle of de Gulf Stream," he told us. "De wedder is gettin' worse. De wind, she come' up and de wave' is getting really 'igh. Dat's when ma boat she jes' stop. I don' know wha' 'appen a' firs'. I check everyt'ing; dere's nut'ing wrong. Den I t'ink, *tabernac*, I bet somet'ing is catch 'round ma propeller. So, I tie one en' of a line 'round ma wais', an' de odder en' I tie to ma 'elm. I stick a knife in ma teet', an' dive overboard.

"*Sacre bleu*, I am scare'! I swim under de wadder to ma stern, *et oui*, I see it; some ol' piece of fisherman' line is all tangle' in ma prop. I am runnin' oudda air, so I come up to de surface. I 'ope dere is no shark in de wadder tonight, I tell myself. I dive back dow' an' start cuttin' de tangle' line. Up an' dow', up an' dow' I go. It take more den an 'our to cut t'rough. Where in de 'ell am I now, I wunner, 'cause de Gulf Stream, she is sweeping ma boat away. Finally I finish. I check my bearin', *et oui*, I am many many mile' off course. It take me 'ours to get to Varadero, an' I am exhaust'."

Jacques had clearly rehearsed this story before numerous previous audiences, but it was still a treat to hear.

"What brings you to Cuba?" I asked.

"I kem to fin' a wife," he replied with an assured shrug. I couldn't help but start, not only at that antiquated idea, but also at the man's seemingly bleak prospects. Jacques was tall and stringy, rumpled and poorly groomed, with a grey beard and ponytail and yellow teeth. Yet, I thought, he can speak *español*, he's resourceful and brave, and he has that certain *je ne sais quoi*, that appealing rogue ingredient, confidence. His best attribute by far was his sense of humour. A guy who can make a woman laugh is more than halfway there.

"*Bonne chance*," I smiled.

The next morning, the Guarda Frontera met us dockside, as planned, to issue our *despacho*. We were permitted to cruise the Bahía de Cardenas for the next few days, with Marina Darsena listed as both our point of departure and our ultimate destination. Our course was eastward, but the only way out into the bay would be to retrace our route westward down the Canal Kawama.

As soon as we passed between the two rock sentries guarding the Canal and turned our bows east, we felt the salt breeze on our faces. At first the wind felt brisk and invigorating, but our young crew soon grew tired of beating against it and the choppy waves. Our boat too felt the strain. The topping lift, a cable supporting the boom, snapped under the pressure. Pat groaned. We hoped to avoid boat repairs altogether in Cuba, where parts were notoriously difficult to order and local expertise was patchy.

Just as we approached the twin islands Cayos Blanco and Surgidero, we met with mishap again.

"Look, Daddy, our dinghy is floating away!" Meara shouted.

We turned back to see our grey inflatable growing smaller by the instant. We'd been towing it behind us, attached to our stern by a painter. Pat examined the short line. The ring to which it was tied had broken off the dinghy, and was dangling in the water. Pat groaned again, then brightened.

"At least we can still see it. Let's go rescue our dinghy!"

The exercise of retrieving the dinghy proved to be a good man-overboard drill. The first step in the drill is to appoint someone to fasten his eyes on the overboard person or object, while the helmsman turns the boat about.

"I'll spot it!" Liam shouted, without being asked. As our unofficial "dinghy captain," he was the perfect candidate. Ten minutes later we ran alongside the dinghy and pulled it toward the boat with a long pole, then secured it to the stern by passing a line through one of its bow handles.

We arrived in the early afternoon in the lee of Cayo Blanco. As we approached what the cruising guide billed as a white and unspoiled beach, we saw to our dismay that it had changed. Thatched roof cabanas, a volleyball net, and dozens of chaise lounges now dotted the shoreline. A twenty-foot high ferroconcrete sculpture of Atlas bearing the world was under construction, and three boatfuls of tourists were swarming the beach.

"That's okay, we'll just anchor out for now while I fix the topping lift," Pat announced. "You'll have to hoist me up on the bosun's chair to the top of the mast."

The older three were eager to help. The prospect of using the little canvas seat, rigged up to a rope and pulley mechanism, seemed exciting. The charm quickly wore off, though, when it became evident that the three of them couldn't pull hard enough to raise Pat's one hundred and ninety pounds a mere inch. Even with my additional labour it was an arduous task to hoist Pat only two-thirds of the way up.

By the time Pat had jury-rigged a repair, the day catamarans began to load up their passengers. Boozy sunburned North Americans – people like we might have been on a holiday from our former life – sprawled across the boat decks. None of them wore life vests, and some of them were perched precariously close to the lifelines, but the tour boat operators seemed indifferent. As soon as the convoy left, we hopped in the dinghy and rowed to shore. By then, the late afternoon, the tide was out, so we dug for clams.

"Look at that spout hole!" shouted Ben.

"Wow, the mother lode of clam holes!" said Liam.

The boys dug feverishly, only to unearth an angry six-inch sand crab that snapped its claws and scuttled sideways to safety. Jasper couldn't help herself. Within seconds the crab was in shreds.

"No, Jasper, no!" the kids wailed, but to no avail. We'd soon become accustomed to Jasper's canine instinct to chase and kill everything that moved. This particular incident taught our dog to dig in the sand for prey, one of her favourite pastimes, and the rest of us to avert our eyes.

The children's voices on the beach must have carried, for just then three Cuban men emerged from the forest behind the beach.

"¡Buen' tarde!" they called out. They dropped the final "s" in their greeting in what we came to distinguish as the Cuban inflection.

"Come see our little *perro!*"

Pat and I recognized the men as the sculptors on the beach, but the kids were more interested in the drowsy blond puppy in their arms.

This trio of artisans proved to be exceedingly congenial. They seemed delighted to share their paradise with us. Pietro's English was very competent, and so assisted by my rudimentary *español*, we could communicate easily. We learned they'd been hired through their union to produce the sculpture, and lived in a small hut on the island until their commission was complete.

One tremendous aspect of our cruising lifestyle – indeed one of its main attractions – was that if we liked a place, we simply stayed. That's what happened at Cayo Blanco. The anchorage was so tranquil, the water so sublimely crystal blue, the white beach at daybreak so alluring, that we decided to linger an extra day. Right after breakfast the next morning, we dinghied to shore, where our three new friends met us. The kids snorkelled and built sandcastles while Pat and I conversed with the artisans. The men divided their little pot of *espresso* into two extra portions, and we sipped the intensely sweet thick brew together.

Not only the coffee was stimulating. Pietro, a gangling man with tattered clothes, a broad grin and thick black ponytail, proved eager to answer our questions. We wondered how the Cuban economic system worked; we had expected socialism but by then had noticed that individual entrepreneurial endeavours were not only well rewarded, but in some cases encouraged. Private taxis, home restaurants, street musicians, all seemed to thrive among the state's run-down schools, farms, factories and hospitals. The government regulated most of these enterprises, Pietro told us, but not all entrepreneurs followed the regulations, and the authorities did not vigorously enforce them.

The artisans had questions for us, too, mostly about Canadian weather. Pietro had been invited to work on a sculpture in the Muskoka Lakes region of Ontario, and wondered how cold the winters were.

"Could be minus twenty degrees Celsius," I warned him.

The three Cubans laughed, certain I was exaggerating. How could I tell them the truth, that it might well be minus thirty or colder? And how could I describe the blue beauty of etched frost and the ice blossoms on water, the muffled magic of fresh fallen snow and the tingle of ice crystals in sunshine, that we Canadians know so well? The sights, sounds and sensations of true winter were so far removed from their balmy, palmy world that even were our *español* fluent, no language could conjure them up.

As soon as the day catamarans arrived, loaded with tourists, we returned to *Cool Breezes* for boat school and chores. As soon as the tourists left, we returned to the beach, where the artisans waited. Andreas, with his black beret and flamboyant shirt, greeted us on the beach with a portfolio brimming with drawings and an album of snapshots of their sculptures. We were impressed by the artwork, but mostly we admired the three men, their faces glowing in the sunset light, so passionate about their work.

The next morning, we couldn't wait to get to shore. We'd gathered a bag of treats, North American things like candy, soap and Coke, to give our new friends. To our surprise, the artisans had also prepared some gifts for us: opalescent pink conch shells they'd found and cleaned themselves. It didn't escape us that their gifts were far more meaningful.

Soon the fleet of day catamarans appeared on the horizon, loaded with their day's catch. It was January 30, the day before my mother arrived in Varadero, and time for us to return there. A shadow of wistfulness tinged the brilliant day as we waved goodbye to our first Cuban *amigos*.

The wind blew at our stern on the sail westward from Cayo Blanco. We had time to stop at Cayo Piedras del Norte, an islet with a small sandy beach, coral reef snorkelling, and a striking white lighthouse. Goats, fowl and dogs roamed freely among the rocks. Two open-faced men, officers of the Guarda Frontera, met our dinghy on shore. They led us on a tour all the winding way to the top of the rustic lighthouse, where a steel guardrail surrounded a spectacular vista. From there we could see *Cool Breezes*, bobbing white and wide in the sparkling sapphire sea.

Liam was so taken with the view that he lingered a few extra moments while the rest of us wound our way down the steps. That's when one of the young Guarda cornered him, and pointing to his own bare feet, asked Liam to give him his water sandals. Liam began to remove them, then paused and ran to Pat and me.

"I didn't know what to do," said our nine-year-old, "so I just said no."

This encounter provoked a lively moral debate in the cockpit as we returned to Varadero. Liam was young and confused; he shouldn't feel guilty, and we told him so. Yet the philosophical issues were intriguing. On one hand, it was inappropriate for an adult to ask a child for a gift, wrong for an authority figure to take advantage of a youth's isolation. On the other hand, the culture of sharing seemed different in Cuba. Our crew had plenty of footgear, and therefore we should share. It was a vignette showing a typical North American reaction to the more friendly and open, yet less affluent Cuban character. We had much to learn.

Chapter **15**
Becoming Acquainted with Cuba

He that will learn to pray, let him go to sea.
  – *George Herbert,* Jacula Prudentum

"There she is!" Meara squealed.

For over an hour, she and I had waited outside the Varadero airport terminal, denied entry because we lacked airline tickets. Meara had churned with worry that we'd missed my mother's arrival. When the automatic doors finally parted, grandmother and grandchild flew at each other, all arms and grins.

We taxied to my mother's hotel, the Cuatro Palmas on the Varadero peninsula. Pat and the older three had walked there, and were waiting when our taxi arrived.

"Your hotel looks pretty fancy schmantzy, Nanny," Erin said, surveying the lobby.

"Yes, I hadn't expected such luxury in Cuba," Eldean replied.

After Eldean checked in, she treated us to a restaurant meal. The food was savoury but the ambience more flavourful. The children tripped verbally over each other trying to tell their grandmother everything about our trip in one sitting. Meanwhile, she was eager to share all the gifts and letters she'd brought from home. I sat back, content to watch the interaction between my children and my mother, a lean woman with short dark hair. I'd often

February 2001. Clockwise from top left: Meara greets Eldean at the Varadero airport; the alluring little girl in Jaguey Grande; the baths of St. Miguel; vintage cars in Matanzas city; the street vendors in Varadero.

chafed at my mother's solicitude, but now I was beginning to appreciate the depth of her devotion. By travelling to Cuba, she'd found a new way to show her love for my family and me. And to see someone from home, my mother above all, warmed my heart.

As we bid goodnight that evening, I promised to meet Eldean in the lobby of her hotel at 11:00 a.m. the next day. I'd run into town with Jasper, and then the three of us would walk back. The next morning, realizing I couldn't teach and run the dog at the same time, I asked Pat to be the substitute teacher. He looked startled, and not necessarily pleased.

"Let's set up work stations," suggested Erin, our organizational wizard. "Each of us works at one subject for an hour and then rotates to the next station."

Pat grinned to hear Erin's scheme.

"Meanwhile, I'll supervise from the cockpit with my coffee and newspaper!"

Eldean had brought a fresh copy of the *Globe & Mail*, a coveted treasure in any marina that would be carefully folded and passed from boat to boat with a gravity disproportionate to its weight. Whoever first received it would owe us a favour.

When Eldean and I returned to the boat, St. Christopher's was dismissed.

"Now we can do 'show and tell' for Nanny!" Erin announced. The kids were eager to show their grandmother how the boat was laid out, how to hand pump the flushing mechanism of the toilet, and how to use the floor pump to send water to the sink faucets. They demonstrated how to manage the steep stairways into the hulls by descending them backwards like a ladder, and how to turn sideways to pass each other in the narrow hallways. They explained how we conserved water and battery power, managed sewage, and wore the same clothes as long as possible.

Observing my children's explanations and my mother's astonishment, I witnessed a landlubber's reaction to life aboard. I realized how much our living quarters differed from our suburban home, and began to appreciate how well we had adapted to our new lifestyle. It had been seven months since we'd left Edmonton, six months since we'd left the prairies, and five months since we'd begun life on the water. No longer fish out of water, flopping about the docks, yet not quite seasoned sailors, we'd become amphibious.

The next day, we sunbathed on the Varadero tourist beach. It was a hot and hazy, breezy day. The kids played in the water and sand, while Pat devoured a novel and Eldean and I read up on Havana in our travel guides. Then Erin, Eldean and I took a leisurely walk along the leggy blond beach. We covered a third of its twenty-two-kilometre length.

Back at our family's staked-out patch of sand, Erin asked the question of the day.

"Did anyone else notice all the topless ladies?"

"I did!" Meara piped up. "Why did they forget to put on their tops?"

"Okay, I admit I noticed," Ben drawled, his voice heavy with disapproval.

"Me too," Liam added quickly, "but I only looked at their backs, not their fronts!"

"That will soon change," Pat observed dryly, and in an aside to me, added, "Too bad I forgot my sunglasses!"

On each of the next two nights, Eldean retired to her hotel room with a pair of grandchildren. One night she took the girls, and the next she took the boys. Each time we sent the laptop along, hoping in vain that the hotel would have Internet capacity. We later learned that Cuba had no internal Internet access. We wouldn't be able to send our saved-up messages and receive news from home for months.

Back on board, our quarters seemed suddenly more spacious with two fewer bodies, and quieter with only two children.

"The odds of squabbling are reduced by five-sixths when there are only two children instead of four!" Ben calculated.

My mother had booked her Varadero hotel room for only three nights, at our suggestion, since we hoped to take her on a short cruise to an island destination. But the weather proved improvident for sailing. Although the sun shone, the wind was too brisk to safely venture out to sea. When Eldean tried to extend her stay at the Cuatro Palmas, though, she found the hotel was fully booked.

"That's okay, you can stay on board with us," Pat offered.

Since Eldean felt uncomfortable on water and our boat was small, accommodations aboard required adjustments for everyone. Our guest and her hard-sided luggage occupied the master stateroom berth, closest to the head. Pat and I moved to the boys' stateroom, and the boys slept on the salon floor. These cramped arrangements made for a good story.

"Guess what just happened at the bathhouse," Eldean giggled. "A lady came up to me while I was standing by the mirrors. She started telling me about this boat full of Canadians – 'four kids, would you believe, and a dog on a catamaran. The parents must be crazy. Not only that, now the grandmother is visiting and she's sleeping on board too'."

"What did you say?" I asked.

"Nothing," she replied. "Because just then Meara and Erin came in and called out, 'Hi Nanny!' The lady just stared, stuffed her things into a bag and ran out the door!"

By then the crew of *Cool Breezes* was accustomed to being the talk of the marina. One evening, sharing a *cuba libre* and a cigar with Danny of *La Vida Dulce*, Pat met Gary, an affable American sailor aboard *Randy G*. He seemed keenly interested in seeing for himself how we coped, so Pat invited him for a tour of our boat the next day.

The next morning, Gary knocked politely on our hull.

"I brought my notebook and camera, because there's a story here," Gary explained. "I'm a freelance writer and hoped to write a piece about your family. Okay with you?"

Pat and I exchanged glances.

"Sure," we said.

Gary's interview gave us the opportunity to reflect on how we were doing, and what it took for us to get to where we were.

"A year out of our life doesn't make a lot of difference in terms of money, but it can make a huge difference to us, to our kids, to the family," Pat said.

"We had to overcome the fear of losing what we had – our so-called security – in order to realize the even more important goal of spending time with our children in their early years," I said. "It's so great to really get to know your kids, and I get to do that at St. Christopher's Boat School. We can take all day to explore one little subject or thought if we want to."

"That's the best part for me too," Pat added, "watching my kids twenty-four hours a day, discovering new sides to them. We get to teach our kids our own values. Plus for me personally, I'm getting time for reflection."

"What's the hardest part about sailing?" Gary asked.

Pat's answer was quick.

"Docking! Well at least at the beginning it was, but now we all know what to do and we do it well. We're really hot stuff!"

"What about you, Jake?" Gary asked. "Is it laundry, meals, or cleaning? Teaching the kids?"

The frankness of my reply surprised us both.

"I miss the intensity of close relationships with other women," I said. "I miss my best friends at home. Pat can just pick up and enjoy the casual company of fellow cruisers at marinas, but it's harder for me. I know any friendship I make at a marina will be fleeting, and that's not enough."

Five months later, Gary's piece appeared in *Living Aboard* magazine. At the end of his article, Gary wrote: "I suppose some people would say the Kirwins are living a dream, maybe even say they are living in a dream world, far from reality. But are they?"

After he finished interviewing us, we asked Gary about his own life. This weathered and bearded sixty-year-old revealed he was once a business executive.

"I ran the rat race till I collapsed," he said. "I moved to the coast and bought a little boat. Now I do carpentry work and freelance writing to pay the bills, and whenever I can, I set aside money to go sailing. Right now I'm running low on cash so pretty soon I'll go back to Florida and build a few cabinets. Then I can get out on the water again." Gary's kind smile and serenity showed how much at peace he was with his new life.

The next day Liam turned ten. The birthday boy abandoned his makeshift bed on the salon floor, and climbed back into his own stateroom berth, where I served him breakfast. The fare was simple – Honeycomb cereal purchased in Key West and set aside for this special day – but Liam was thrilled. Aware no breakfast cereal could be found in Varadero, he hadn't expected the treat.

After opening St. Christopher's Boat School for the day, I turned my students over to the professional: Eldean, a retired teacher who still loved the classroom. The children each took a turn at "demonstration of learning" with her. Meanwhile, I made Liam's favourite dish, peach pancake, along with pineapple ham. In the afternoon, we had a party complete with microwave popcorn, the Harry Potter board game, and a real novelty, birthday balloons. The kids scampered in and out of the breezy cockpit and along the docks, whooping and chasing balloons. Then the inevitable happened; Ben, in an overzealous attempt to rescue a balloon from the water, fell into it himself.

"Something else to add to the list of things fallen overboard!" Liam cheered.

Only a few days remained in Eldean's week with us. A day trip to Havana, escorted by our own driver and car, was already scheduled. The day after Liam's birthday we planned a beach day, but the wind that rose that morning was far too brisk for comfort.

"Let's rent a car instead and go for a drive in the country," Pat suggested. Within an hour, the shiny red Daewoo ordered by the marina staff appeared at the marina gates.

"It's a little small for all of us," said Liam, peering inside. "I see only five seatbelts."

"It's the only size available," Pat replied. "Besides, Cuba has no seatbelt laws."

We seven crawled into the subcompact. Danny, the first recipient of the fresh *Globe & Mail*, agreed to keep Jasper for the day in the company of his own dog Lobita.

The glee of new adventure was palpable as we turned the car southward toward the interior of Matanzas province. Once through the dusty brown industrial town of Cardenas, we reached the country roads and passed through the quieter centres of Jovellanos, Pedro Betancourt and Jaguey Grande. We saw a variety of crops – citrus groves, coconut palm stands, banana orchards, and sugar cane fields – and variable geography – flatlands, marshlands and distant blue-green hills. Even the vehicles on the road came in assorted shapes. Dozens of 1950s automobiles overtook slower traffic: trucks piled high with harvested cane, horses pulling carts loaded with farm workers, bicycles, crowded buses, and even teams of oxen. The dwellings of the intermittent settlements were consistent only in their tumbledown modesty. We saw houses made of cinder block, some with thatched roofs and marble floors, and rows of pastel apartment buildings, laundry flapping on the balconies. The greatest homogeny was among the Cuban people: elementary school children in red-and-white uniforms, matrons in faded print dresses, wrinkled and gap-toothed older men, all appeared lean and laughing.

Just outside Jaguey Grande, where sugar cane ruffled in a light breeze, a pretty child with dark curly hair and a cheery brown face appeared on her doorstep and waved.

"She's the one!" I said.

We'd been waiting for just the right situation to give away our trunkful of saved-up clothing and household items. Pat stopped the car. When the girl's mother emerged from her house, Meara and I hopped out of the car. The beaming child walked right up to Meara, kissed both her cheeks, and took her small white hand.

When Pat popped the trunk lid, I began giving its contents to the girl's mother. Eldean and the older three entered into the festivity, and a second Cubana joined us. The two ladies, clearly accustomed to sharing, quickly divided up the items. Those unsuitable for their families would be given to the *escuela*, the school, they said. Soon the trunk was empty.

"Looks as if we're about to be swarmed," Pat said, nodding toward an approaching group of ten or fifteen people. "And there's nothing left to give. Time to go."

"*Adiós!*" we called out, about to hop back into the tiny car. Before we left, though, the two ladies and child bestowed us with startlingly affectionate embraces. As we pulled away, I waved back at the villagers standing on the roadside.

"What a rush," I said. "That's the most fun I've had in a long time."

From Jaguey Grande we drove south to the shoe-shaped Peninsula de Zapata, all the way to the infamous Bay of Pigs, and stood on the deserted beach. That was our turnaround point. On the return trip north, we took a detour through San Miguel de los Baños – St. Michael of the Baths – set in the cool blue hills we'd seen earlier from a distance. The most prominent building in this sleepy little town was the once grand but now disintegrating bathhouse, made of white marble. Despite its fallen condition, it appeared proud and alluring, especially in the golden twilight. It was surrounded by overgrown gardens, dotted with stone seats, and etched with an intricate system of wells and canals, now dry, that once brimmed with mineral waters. It would have been idyllic in its prime five decades ago.

"It's beautiful," Eldean breathed, aiming her camera lens at the sight.

"*Gracias,*" female voices replied. Two young women stopped, smiled, and posed for my mother's photo. They'd assumed Eldean's exclamation was a personal compliment.

By then the sky was ochre. We squeezed ourselves back into the car for the last leg of our day trip. We got lost, briefly – entangled in the black labyrinthine streets of Cardenas – but emerged at last on the road to Varadero.

As we stepped out of the car and through the marina gates, the warm and vibrant images of the day began to twinkle away, to dissolve at the edges until they disappeared. Back in the fluid and breezy blue setting of water and sails, the province of Matanzas seemed nearly as remote as our prairie home.

The children's choir in the Catedral de San Cristobal.

Eldean with a jinitera.

Sitting on the Malecón, el Morro in the background.

From:	The Kirwin crew
To:	Kith and Kin
Subject:	**Greetings from *Cool Breezes*: Ah, Havana!**

Today's the day our family – including Eldean – takes a day trip to Havana. Pat found a driver, who for a fee of US$100, will drive us there and back in a vintage car!

We rise just after 6:00 a.m. to shower, but the taps in the bathhouse run dry.

"Oh well, at least that saved us a little time!" Meara chirps. She dreads her showers here in Varadero. The hot water has turned suddenly cold once or twice too often.

An hour later, we seven are fed. The knapsack is packed, and the boat padlocked. We drop Jasper off at *La Vida Dulce* to spend the day with her doggie friend Lobita. We've arranged to meet our driver outside the guarded marina gates; Cubans are forbidden to enter marinas for fear they'll defect, stowaways aboard an American boat. Our driver, a dark, powerfully built man in his early forties, awaits us. Beside him, leaning on the back fender of a glossy green '51 Oldsmobile, stands a small and wiry youth with a ready smile.

"Good morning," says the younger man. "I'm Ramon, and this is my stepfather Leo. He doesn't speak English, so I'll be your tour guide." Ramon's English is lilting but perfect.

With Leo and Ramon, our party numbers nine. Recalling our road trip to Matanzas, when seven of us squeezed into the little red Daewoo, I feel apprehensive.

"How will we all fit in?" I quietly ask Pat.

Ramon overhears me.

"Hey, this is Cuba! *No problema!*"

He's right. The interior of the Olds is much more spacious than I envisioned. It's actually comfortable, with cream-coloured bench seats and plenty of legroom for everyone.

"It's like a living room in here!" Liam exclaims.

We head west. Along the way Ramon answers questions about the car – it now boasts a 1999 Fiat engine – and his education. A recent high school graduate, he's now taking mandatory military training. Next year he'll attend university tuition-free.

Our first stop is upon a one-hundred-and-twelve-metre high bridge, a viewpoint overlooking the Río Yurumi. At this early hour, the verdant river valley seems bottomless, steeped in rising mist.

At 9:45 a.m. we arrive at *la ciudad* of Havana, home to three million Cubans. Leo parks close to La Plaza de la Catedral, in *la Habana viega*, or old Havana. As we step onto the sidewalk, a street musician approaches and bows. The tiny man, his face creased with care, coaxes the plaintive melody "Guantanamera" from his violin. Pat drops some American money into his open fiddle case as we walk away.

"That must be a *jinitero*," Erin remarks. The kids and I have just learned that word, Spanish for street hustler.

Ramon leads us to Plaza de la Catedral, an eighteenth-century cobbled square, where we join the throng of fifties cars, horses and buggies, and colourful characters.

"Look at that lady!" blurts Meara, pointing. An elderly and extremely thin Cubana sits on a door stoop, dressed in bright pink slacks and a loud floral blouse, smoking a big fat stogie. For a dollar, she permits her photo to be taken, her hand on Eldean's shoulder.

As we pass the baroque Catedral de San Cristobal, we discover Mass is about to begin. We slip into a pew. Since the bishop presides, it's a high Mass lasting an hour and three-quarters. Our Spanish is too rudimentary to comprehend the words, yet because Mass rituals are so universal we know what's happening. Besides, we have much to occupy our eyes and ears. The church architecture, described by Cuban novelist Alejo Carpentier as "music set to stone," is magnificent. The altar, made of Carrera marble and inlaid with precious metals and ebony, is a marvel. The exuberant children's choir, however, is most enthralling. Dressed in white blouses with bright turquoise collars, the children clap and sway to the drumbeat and the piano descant, and raise clear and joyful voices up to the ornate dome. Their spirit resounds.

Pat gestures toward a clutch of tourists strolling the side aisles in skimpy beach attire.

"I can't believe they're talking out loud and taking photos in the middle of a church service," he whispers.

"I can't believe there's a Mass at all," I reply. "Isn't Cuba communist?"

Satisfying the spiritual yearning can whet one's physical appetite.

"I know a great *paladero* for lunch," says Ramon. "It's not a touristy place, not too expensive," he claims.

He leads us down dark, narrow and winding streets. A *paladero*, we've learned, is a restaurant operated from the dining room of a private home. In the entrance to this *paladero*, we see the walls are inscribed with the signatures of patrons from all over the world.

"For a non-touristy place, there seem to be quite a few foreign signatures," Ben remarks. Nevertheless, we add our names and nationality to the collection.

Our pork meal is light, delicious and well presented, but not inexpensive. When it becomes clear that we're expected to pick up the tab not only for ourselves but also for Ramon and Leo, Pat is peeved.

"We've been stiffed," he scowls, forking over an American hundred.

After lunch Leo drives to the Capitolio. The third largest indoor statue in the world, a gleaming bronze Indian maiden representing liberty, dominates the marble hall. The oak doors, several storeys high, are decorated with bas-reliefs depicting historical events.

"Why are some of the names and faces scratched out?" I ask Ramon.

His dark eyes dart furtively. His voice drops.

"Because they showed Batista!"

Our driver and tour guide whisk us off to the next famous monument, La Plaza de la Revolución. Since it's Sunday, all the buildings are closed, but we're content to sit on a row of cement benches facing an imposing marble podium. Re-enacting a black-and-white photo from the 1960s, Pat and Liam take turns taking the head honcho seat, stroking their imaginary long beards, pretending to be Fidel Castro addressing the multitudes. The rest of the family finds the imitation amusing, but Leo and Ramon look nervous.

We hop back into the car for a roadside view of several other landmarks. Adjacent to opulent architecture we see tenement buildings festooned with lines of laundry. Ah, Havana – so ancient and crumbling, yet so magnificent and vibrant! The city has been likened to a beautiful mature woman who has let herself go, but still has great bones. Pat sees her decline more clearly than her origins.

"If you like the distressed look in furniture or architecture," he says, "then Havana is the place for you!"

I am entranced by Havana's romance, especially when we come upon the Malecón. Lined with once grand but now decrepit buildings, this seawall promenade winds its egalitarian way through both affluent and poor neighbourhoods. On this balmy Sunday, all walks of life stroll the Malecón with us: pairs of affectionate lovers, loud and persistent *jiniteros*, and dozens of small brown mutts. The backdrop for this surge of humanity is the steady crash and foam of the pounding grey sea. We pause at the east end of the Malecón to gaze across the *bahía* at El Morro, the fabled lighthouse flanked by fortresses and adorned with seaspray spilling over the ramparts. The sight is stunning. It's also rewarding; we've seen so many photos of it that to behold it firsthand gives a distinct sense of satisfaction.

Around the corner from the Malecón is Avenida del Puerto, another pedestrian walkway. It doesn't border the water, but it boasts a kid-friendly modern sculpture gallery.

Pat turns to Ramon and Leo.

"We'll head out by ourselves from here," he says. "Could you meet us here at six-thirty?" Aside to Eldean and me he adds, "I'd rather find our own restaurant this time, wouldn't you?"

From Avenida del Puerto, we walk to La Plaza de Armas, home to a centuries-old solid-rock castle, Castillo de la Real Fuerza. Its ceramic display intrigues my mother, its collection of weapons and armour, my sons. We climb to the tower on a staircase so steep and broken down that in North America, it would have been cordoned off as a hazard.

From La Plaza de Armas we step onto the bustling Calle Obispo. On Sundays the cigar factories are closed, but we poke around many fine galleries and cafés, including a few claiming to have been patronized by Ernest Hemingway. Later on we relish a filling array of *tapas*, complemented with red wine, for less than US$50.

We amble the Plaza de San Francisco toward Avenida del Puerto at twilight. Passing by a flowing fountain, Fuente de los Leones, Erin sighs.

"Don't you just love the thought we're walking the same streets as other people did five hundred years ago?"

Leo and Ramon are already waiting when we reconvene at our meeting spot, so we clamber back into the Olds. We're bone-weary, happy to be returning to our dog and boat. But when Leo turns the engine, he sputters a foreign profanity. No Spanish phrase book is required to discern there's car trouble; the headlights won't work. Driving without them on Cuban roadways at night would be suicidal. When we realize this will be no quick fix, we exit the car. The kids distract themselves exploring the modern sculptures on the sidewalk. Ninety minutes later, though, they're bored. Pat's face is stern, and Eldean looks anxious. I wonder whether finding a hotel for the night will be next on the day's agenda.

"Look," Pat finally says to Ramon. "We've waited long enough. Get us another car, and I'll split the hundred-dollar fare between Leo and the other driver however you decide."

Ramon hustles off to find another driver and returns with Enrico, a young fellow with a red '57 Chevrolet.

The mood pervading our return excursion is less buoyant than on the trip out. The Chevy bench seats are shorter than those of the Olds, so we're more crowded. Also, since it's now dark, we can see nothing outside our windows, nothing but the lights of every single gas station enroute. Loathe to waste his portion of the fare on fuel, Enrico parks on the curb beside each gas station, pulls a jerry can out of the trunk, and fills it with cheap coloured marine gas. Then he pours the contents of the jerry can into his gas tank and drives away.

After five or six such stops, Pat pipes up.

"That's the last time we stop, Enrico." The driver's English is poor, but he seems to get the message. Perhaps he thinks we object to his illegal use of marine gas; in fact, we're just weary. It's almost 11:00 p.m. by the time we board our beloved *Cool Breezes*.

Eldean and the children are sleeping. Pat's gone to retrieve Jasper. Judging from the amount of time he's been away, I predict he's enjoying a *cubalibre* with the dog-sitters. I'm sitting on my bed, tapping away at the keyboard. I strive to capture the day for you, to portray the sense of displacement, as we roam the magnificent but disintegrating streets of *la ciudad*, and of warping time, as we ride in a '57 Chevy in the big dark night.

God bless, fair winds, and *hasta la vista!*

Love PJ+crew

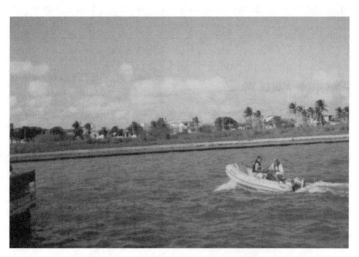

February 2001, Varadero, Cuba.
Pat and Liam are off to rescue a fellow cruiser!

Chapter **16**
The Rescue

*A guardian angel o'er his life presiding, Doubling his
pleasures, and his cares dividing.*
  – Samuel Rogers

February 7 was yet another bright but windy day. My
mother and I worked below decks, dismantling the
beds and packing her suitcases. She was flying home
that day and had agreed to take our duvets back to Canada.

"A boat's just arriving," Pat called down to us from the
cockpit. "They must've just crossed the Gulf Stream. I'll
go help them tie up."

A few moments later Pat returned, shaking his head.
"You remember how dog-tired we felt the morning after we
crossed to Cuba, even though we had good weather? Well,
this new boat, *Pegasus*, crossed on a miserable night, so I'm
thinking the crew must be pretty young and capable." He
chuckled. "Imagine my surprise, standing on the dock waiting for someone to toss the bowline, when an elderly fellow
– he's gotta be eighty – shuffles out of the cockpit to the
bow with the dockline. Where's the rest of the crew, I'm
thinking. Then out comes his wife, almost as old, with the
stern line. Can you believe it? They're almost twice our age,
and they crossed the Gulf Stream on a night like last night."

Pat was right: Alex was eighty, and Elaine seventy-
eight, when we met them that blustery February morning.

The weather had been wretched, with wicked winds and gut-wrenching waves, yet the crossing itself was relatively uneventful. A gash on Elaine's forehead from a bump on the companionway presented the only injury. Pat and I were impressed, and humbled.

Pat and Eldean walked to town to buy government certified cigars. The kids sat down to boat school. They wrote letters for their grandmother to mail back in Canada – a Language Arts assignment – while I slipped away to do some boatkeeping.

Since the wind was brisk and dry, and the beds were already dismantled, I hauled the mattresses up on the decks to get some sun. I pinned the duvet covers and sheets to air on the lifelines and strung some freshly washed socks and undies to dry on a line strung across the bows, out of sight of passersby. The vision of so much fabric flapping in the breeze reminded me of that very first marina back in Portsmouth, Virginia, the one with the sign forbidding the hanging of beach towels on lifelines. I smirked to think what the dockmaster would say if he saw my display today!

Pat and Eldean returned eager to show off their heavily ornamented, stamped and sealed cigar boxes.

"You're not really going to smoke those things, are you?" the kids asked their father.

"Yes, I probably will. Cuban cigars are famous the world over," Pat replied.

"That's just gross," Erin said, her face screwed up in disgust.

Soon it was time for Eldean to take a taxi to the airport.

"We'll all squeeze in with you," I said. "We're used to squishing ourselves into cars!"

On our way to the marina gates, we ran into our friend Gary, the magazine writer.

"I'm leaving today," he said. Pat and I were surprised.

"You're crossing to Florida in this wind?"

"Well, I've been waiting for a weather window for over a week. I've depleted my sailing kitty, so I gotta go," Gary explained. "The winds are supposed to be five knots lighter today than any other day so far, so I figure I'll make it even if I have a rough time."

The prevailing easterlies had been averaging thirty to thirty-five knots, with gusts to forty-five, for ten days. That wind speed, rated as a strong breeze or light gale on the Beaufort scale, was too brisk for a trip across the Gulf Stream. Winds of only twenty-five to thirty knots blowing against the current could kick up dangerously high waves.

"I expect your crossing will be a bit lively," said Pat.

Gary chuckled at the understatement, but his laughter sounded nervous.

"Well, goodbye then," I said, hugging Gary. "We'll turn on the VHF as soon as we get back from the airport. Keep in touch with us as long as you can."

I glanced at my mother's face.

"Don't worry, we'd never do that," I assured her.

Our airport farewell was emotional. My girls and I always keep tears at the ready, but my mother's were particularly copious.

"Take care," she said, with emphasis. "I love you," she added as she pressed each of us close. What a parting image she must have, I thought: her dearly beloved, cramped in a small boat cluttered with fluttering laundry, surrounded by a community of risk-takers. And six months remained of our year away.

Taxiing back to the marina on the shoreline highway, I looked out to sea. When I thought of Gary aboard *Randy G.,* my gut felt uneasy.

"I have a sinking feeling," I confided to Pat, then

clapped my hand to my mouth at the unfortunate choice of words.

"Just look at the water," he said, gesturing. "It's choppier than I've ever seen it."

Back at the marina, we found Debbie of *La Vida Dulce* pacing the docks.

"Another boat headed out with *Randy G.*," she reported. "The crew of *Companion* was waiting to get to Florida, too. It's good the two boats are travelling in tandem."

The six of us ran down the docks to our boat. We gathered round the VHF, just like those families in the black-and-white photos huddled to listen to an old-time radio show. We couldn't reach *Randy G.,* so we tried *Companion.*

"*Companion, Companion,* this is *Cool Breezes,*" Pat radioed. "Where are you and what's it like out there?"

"*Cool Breezes, Cool Breezes,* this is *Companion,*" replied her captain Sterling. "It's way too rough for us out here. We're turning back."

"Great to hear! What about *Randy G.?*" Pat asked.

"She's going on ahead without us," Sterling replied, his voice crackling.

Pat and I stared bleakly at each other. I had a soft spot for Gary that developed during his interview of us, widened when I heard he was a Canadian wannabe, and deepened when I learned he'd turned a sharp corner to make permanent changes in his life.

Five minutes later we heard from *Companion.*

"We just talked to Gary," Sterling reported. "The good news is he's turning back. The bad news is his engine's raw-water cooling pump gave out, so he has to make it back under sail alone."

We waited again, ears keened for the next radioed

word. The next transmission came from *Randy G.*, barely within VHF range. Gary's voice quavered on the airwaves.

"So far I'm okay, but I'm worried about the canal entrance. I can't make that dogleg turn under sail alone, right into the easterly wind. Could any of you dinghy out and give me a tow?"

Debbie and Danny were the first to radio back.

"We'll be right there!"

"Dad, we gotta get out there and help!" said Liam, our dinghy captain. "Debbie and Danny's dinghy outboard has only five horsepower, but we've got fifteen!"

"You're right," said Pat. "They'd have a hard time towing *Randy G.* against the wind."

The Guarda Frontera had prohibited cruisers from using dinghies in Varadero, but we didn't care. This was an emergency. We sprang to action.

Since *Cool Breezes* was backed stern-to into her marina slip, the dinghy was now lodged beneath the docks. We'd have to pull the boat forward to free the dinghy. That's when I remembered the bows were draped in clotheslines. Pat groaned.

"Help me!" I called to the kids. The older three and I scrambled over the boat decks, feverishly gathering pins and bedding and socks and underwear. We hurled everything into the salon and shoved the mattresses down the stairs. Meanwhile Pat started up the boat's engines. I took the helm, inching the boat forward, as Pat dislodged the dinghy.

"Okay, it's free!" Pat shouted.

"Oh no, it's full of water!" Liam wailed. He jumped down and began bailing while Pat lowered the outboard engine and secured it to the dinghy.

"Get me two life vests!" Pat yelled. Ben threw them to him.

"Find me a tow line!" Ben tossed him one.

Against the urgency of the moment, it seemed as if we'd never get our dinghy ready in time to actually be of help. At last, Pat and Liam set off, off to the rescue!

I dashed into the salon and radioed a message to *Randy G.* that Pat and Liam were on their way. Then I grabbed the binoculars and headed out to the docks, where the rest of our crew had joined a crowd of anxious fellow cruisers. *Companion* returned first. We helped tie her up and welcomed her wild-eyed crew with hugs and backslaps. Then all of us craned our necks toward the canal, eager to see *Randy G.* arrive. Twenty minutes later, the boat landed, pulled along by Debbie and Danny's dinghy and pushed by ours. Our roar of cheers was drowned by the wind, but there was no mistaking our elation.

"Thank-you, everyone," Gary smiled, as soon as *Randy G.* was safely docked in her old slip. "Thanks, Debbie and Danny. Seeing you head toward me was an indescribable relief. Thanks, Pat and Liam. Without your push from behind, I'd be struggling against the wind till nightfall!"

Then his voice softened.

"I tell you, what happened out there was the doing of my guardian angel. I shouldn't have been out there in the Gulf Stream in those conditions. I knew it, but I went out there anyways like a stubborn fool. I should've turned back when *Companion* did, but still I was too stubborn. Then the cooling pump broke. It shouldn't have broken. It was brand new. But it broke anyway, and that's what forced me to turn back. You know what made that pump break? My guardian angel. Who knows what would've happened if we didn't turn back when we did? My guardian angel has been looking after me my whole life long, and I know she was out there today, making me do the right thing."

An uncomfortable silence followed. Spiritual openness is something to which we North Americans are unaccustomed. I caught Gary's gaze and smiled. "I believe you," I said quietly. "And we're so glad you're back."

Later that evening, Sterling invited Pat and me aboard *Companion* to rehash the day's events. Sterling was a Canadian ex-patriot, a beer company executive hired by a Cuban brewery. Gary joined us.

"I still say it was a blessing that pump broke when it did, instead of halfway into the Gulf Stream," he said. "It would've been a lot more dangerous to turn back then."

His account stirred others to spin yarns of other mysteriously provident turns of event at sea. This was just the kind of scene in which Pat delighted, swapping sea stories as he sipped his whiskey and pulled at his Cuban cigar. Then we heard a giggle, and looked up to see the flash of a camera and four childish faces pressed against *Companion*'s portholes.

"The kids have never seen their father smoke cigars," I explained. "They seemed shocked at the prospect, but I'd say they've adjusted quite well to their harsh new reality."

"The rescue," as we called it, worked like a catalyst turning a marina full of transients into a community. We'd run errands for each other at the Varadero *panadería* or the Santa Marta vegetable market. Our crew became regulars at that outdoor market, pointing to the vegetables we wanted and paying for them by holding out a handful of American coins for the bemused vendors to pick out. Once when we walked there, the market was closed.

"That was not only a fruitless effort, but also a vegetable-less one," Ben quipped.

In the evenings, the adults would meet for drinks at the marina lounge or, weather permitting, for sundowners in each other's cockpits. More often than not, it was Pat who initiated or promoted this socializing, a major role reversal from our social pattern back home. Sometimes, craving an "alcohol-free day," I'd stay back on board with the kids.

One day, as Pat sat reading in the cockpit, Pierre from *Prudencia* stopped to chat. Pat invited him and his crewmate Jorge for dinner aboard *Cool Breezes.*

Pierre and Jorge were pleased to join us. They brought a bottle of red wine, a perfect accompaniment to our meal of barbequed roast beef, market vegetables, pasta with pesto, fresh bread with garlic mayo, cookies and fruit. Pierre told us he was born in France, and became a NATO pilot. When he retired he met a beautiful Argentinean woman, and became a citizen himself. He learned to speak Spanish, in addition to English and his native French. Jorge, however, spoke only Spanish. We explained that we were trying to learn *español* using a software program.

"Really?" Pierre replied. "Could we try it?"

Ben and Liam hustled to their stateroom and set up the "How to Speak Spanish" software on the laptop. They showed our two guests how to repeat the narrated phrase into the computer's tiny microphone so the software could evaluate their accents.

"It says I'm a 'tourist'," Ben said. "Now it's your turn. I bet you'll be 'natives'."

Our guests laughed. Clearly this was way too elementary for them, but they couldn't resist the technology. They listened to the narration, then rattled off a repetition.

"Ha, ha!" Liam shouted. "It rated them 'tourists'!"

Pierre and Jorge looked flustered.

"No, no, no, no!" they retorted rapidly.

They repeated the prompts with clearer enunciation,

and watched intently for the needle on the display screen to rate the outcome.

"'Natives!'" Pierre exclaimed, raising a triumphant fist in the air. For the rest of the evening, our two guests entertained themselves (and us) "learning" to speak Spanish. Everyone's pronunciation improved that night.

One Saturday evening, Gary came by to tell us he was definitely leaving the next day. His pump was fixed, and the weather would be cold but calmer.

"Elaine planned some send-off festivities this evening," he went on. "First, Mass at Our Lady of Fatima in Varadero, and then to a *paladero* in town for dinner."

"I didn't know you're Catholic," Pat said.

"No, but I wannabe!" Gary laughed.

Our party comprised eleven – the six of us from *Cool Breezes,* Alex and Elaine from *Pegasus,* Gary from *Randy G.,* and Sharon and Lou of *Question.* The latter two were recent arrivals, originally from Fort Myers, the owners of an adorable terrier puppy. Keeler had been fished out of the water with a large net after so many spills off the dock that she now sported a bright yellow doggie life vest as she trotted about the marina.

It didn't matter that some of us weren't Catholic and that Mass was in Spanish; we were all pleased just to pray together. From church we walked to the modest home of our *paladero* hosts and crowded into their dining room. The small table was crammed with dishes, including tender lobster tails, crispy fried plantains, a starchy vegetable called *yucca* sautéed with garlic, the ubiquitous *arroz con gris* or rice with beans, a salad of tomatoes and cucumbers thinly sliced and laced with oil and vinegar, and *espresso.* Our waiter, the very large and hairy husband of the chef, found it unnecessary to wear a shirt in the privacy of his own home.

"I guess we didn't really need to get dressed up after all, eh Mom?" Ben remarked, an eyebrow cocked.

As the blustery days wore on, a few more boats arrived at the marina. Fellow Canadians Heather and Al aboard *Keegunoo* tied up beside us, after a short sail from Havana. The same day, Dale pulled in from Florida aboard his mammoth motor cruiser *Outsized*. These arrivals prompted Emil, the friendly marina waiter, to organize a "family *paella*" dinner at the restaurant.

"The price is right, so everyone can welcome our new friends," he urged, thus managing to lure twenty-five cruisers to dinner. Since the restaurant entrance was outside the marina gates, Debbie and Danny invited their Varadero friends, a family of four.

"After all these years, Carlos and Luisa still haven't seen our boat," Debbie lamented. "The guards know them, but they won't let them beyond the gates because they're Cuban."

"What about their two boys?" I asked. "Are they allowed in?"

"Oh sure," Carlos replied. "*No problema.*"

Our kids perked up. They dashed off, eager to show off our boat, with the two young Cuban brothers following close on their heels.

"How did you two couples meet?" I asked.

"Danny and I met Carlos fourteen years ago when we honeymooned in Varadero," Debbie explained. "Carlos was the concierge at our hotel. His English was excellent, and we hit it off right away. The next year we cruised from the Great Lakes to Varadero and tied up here for a month or so. We saw Carlos nearly every day, and had such a great time we decided to visit every year."

"One year when we showed up, Carlos was married to Luisa," Danny went on. "The next year, they had a baby boy named Dany. Three years later, they had another baby boy named Daniel." He chuckled. "We explained that in Canada, Dany, Danny and Daniel are really the same name, but they don't care."

"Yeah, we name both our sons after you, and then you laugh at us," Carlos accused with mock indignation.

Over the next few days, we became well acquainted with the crews of *Keegunoo* and *Outsized*. Heather and Al were from Nova Scotia. Al, a banker, had enjoyed puttering around in his little sloop, but it was only when he retired that he and Heather took up the cruising life. Now they spent summers playing with their grandkids at their cottage on the South Shore of Nova Scotia, and their winters cruising in the Caribbean.

"Now that's the way to retire," Pat said. I agreed.

Dale, meanwhile, was not on a cruise. He was on a mission.

"I'm here to find a Cuban wife," he explained. Compared to Jacques, the scruffy French-Canadian in the dilapidated sailboat, we thought Dale had a better chance of success. He was almost fifty, but had boyish good looks, a toned physique, and money. Within a day or two he reported he'd fallen in love with a beautiful Cubana lawyer.

"I'm meeting her family and taking her out to dinner tomorrow night," he said excitedly one morning. That would be Valentine's Day.

Cubans celebrate Valentine's Day with *gusto,* as we learned on February 14. They call it *El Dia de Amor* – the day of love – or *El Dia de los Enamerados* – the day of the lovers. I surprised my crew by arising early and tucking some "sweet nothings" under their pillows: a little love note for each of them, slipped into the curling folds of a small seashell. Then, when I emerged into the cockpit, I found my own surprise. Sharon of *Question* had left a small bowl of Hershey's kisses and pink paper hearts for every boat. That gift inspired Erin to bake some of her famous brownies for our favourite fellow cruisers. She decorated them with some of the cinnamon hearts from Eldean.

"Come with me when I deliver them, Mom," Erin begged, "in case I feel shy."

"*Bueno Dia de los Enamerados,* Jorge *y* Pierre," I said, as Erin and I made our delivery.

"Ah, *gracias,*" Pierre replied. "I need a hug today. Today I am sad, because I especially miss my lover, my beautiful Jacquelina," he sighed. "She left me years ago, but I still love her."

"Oh my goodness," I said, my heart melting. How could we not hug this poor heartbroken man? Our hugs became farewells, because Pierre and Jorge sailed north to the Yucatan peninsula that very afternoon.

Our next delivery was to *La Vida Dulce,* where we found Debbie and Danny shelling and deveining *camarónes,* baby prawns Carlos had given them.

"Take some!" said Danny. "There's way too much for us. And here's an extra crawfish tail, too."

"Wow, sure!" Erin exclaimed. This was a huge "black market" treat. The Cuban government exerted a monopoly on seafood, and we had been unable to buy it anywhere except restaurants.

Our last delivery was to *Pegasus.*

"You two newlyweds are invited to Valentine's Day dinner aboard *Cool Breezes,*" I said.

Liam and I spent the afternoon sitting on the dock, our legs dangling down, shelling and deveining shrimp for the first time. Then we threaded them on skewers and laid them in a marinade. When Alex and Elaine arrived a few hours later, Pat barbequed the skewers and the crawfish tail. We served it with spicy rice, a tomato salad, fresh bread from the *panadería*, and of course, some of Erin's brownies. Our guests brought along a fine bottle of wine.

"What a memorable Valentine's Day," Elaine smiled. A diminutive but feisty woman, she'd raised six children. Alex, a chief engineer for the American merchant marine, had spent much of his career years travelling. That's when he first heard the call of the sea.

"We bought our first boat when I retired at sixty-five," Alex said. "So you see, you needn't be young to fulfil your dream."

"Speaking of fulfilling dreams, where are you off to next?" Elaine asked us.

"We're not sure," Pat said. "What do you veterans recommend?"

"Your kids would really enjoy the Cruising Regatta Week in George Town, the Bahamas," said Elaine. "It takes place mid-March each year. Three or four hundred boats show up, many with kids aboard."

"Wow, we gotta go!" Erin effused. "I haven't talked to a girl my age for months."

We cleared the salon table and spread out some charts.

"Sail east along the north coast of Cuba all the way to Puerto Vita," Alex said, tracing his knarled finger along the route. "There's a modern marina and a little village there, a perfect jumping off point to Ragged Island in the Jumentos, one of the southernmost archipelagos of the Bahamas. From Ragged Island, make your way north towards George Town in the Exumas chain of islands. It'll take a few weeks to make your way there from Ragged Island."

"Sounds perfect!" I said. Pat's eyes gleamed. The children were ecstatic.

That night, I sat up late at the laptop with my tea and my candle, composing another chapter-length email home. Although we couldn't send instalments, I kept writing them.

"The wind has just changed," I reported. "The southerly wind brings the stench of the sulphurous burn-off at the Santa Marta oilfields and the throb of the nearby night-club. But that's okay. It means the prevailing easterlies are finally on the wane, making it possible for *Cool Breezes* to embark on further ventures eastward."

As I shut down the computer and slipped into bed, I sighed with satisfaction. This marina community had been wonderful. We'd met some remarkable people, the likes of whom we'd never have encountered at home. But it was time to move on. The Cuban *cayos* and the Bahamian cays beckoned.

Chapter 17
A Need for Change

God, grant me the serenity to accept the people I can-
not change, the courage to change the one I can, and
the wisdom to know it's me.
– *Anonymous*

I was wrong about the wind. The shift in direction was
temporary. The morning after I'd composed the email
announcing a break in the easterlies, they returned. Every
morning we'd listen to the weather, but each day brought
more of the same: a strong and constant wind, coming from
exactly the direction we intended to face in our travels. I
wish we'd known then that we'd be holed up for at least two
more weeks. With that knowledge, we might've had a different mindset. Without a crystal ball, though, we expected to
leave, and because it never happened, we became frustrated.

More accurately, it was the kids and I who were frustrated. Cruising Regatta Week in George Town had
become a shimmering oasis in the desert for us, but Pat
was just as happy to stay in Varadero. Instead of charting
and sailing all day, he could swap weather reports and
reading material with the neighbours by day, and enjoy
nightcaps with Danny and Debbie by evening. I found
myself more reclusive aboard than at home, where my
established friendships lie, but Pat liked the more casual
and transient marina social life.

Not just crew mates, but life mates.

"I don't mind if the weather forces us to stay docked," he remarked. "For the first time on this trip I can actually sit down with a book during the day."

At first I was pleased to see him relax. As the days wore on, I became resentful. My daily chores of cooking, cleaning and teaching boat school remained the same whether we were at sea or tied to a dock. Yet, perversely, I was too proud to ask for help. I wanted it offered to me. I expected Pat to read my mind, even as my demeanour grew steadily cooler. This was deeply ingrained behaviour on my part, nothing new to Pat.

Even when Pat accomplished a major repair, like a permanent fix of the topping lift or, with Alex's help, a rock solid replacement for the dinghy davit, I stewed. I hated the fact I'd allowed myself to become trapped in this traditional division of labour. I hated the fact that because Pat was the superior sailor, I'd become a disappointing role model not only for my daughters but also my sons, who would one day be husbands. I hated the feeling of resentment, that tight and narrow fist of selfish triteness. I especially hated feeling that way in the midst of our long-awaited journey.

The whistling of the wind did nothing to lift our moods. Oftentimes I'd have to hold Meara's hand so she could make forward progress against the hot gusts, or avoid being blown off the docks. The kids and I sat dutifully at the salon table doing boat school, but we felt restive, and the wind fed our restlessness. The kids expressed their agitation with sullenness and I responded with a short temper.

"I'm getting kind of worn out by the wind," Liam said to me one day, when I asked him to justify his cranky behaviour. To imply that every moment was snarly or that we didn't laugh in those days would be wrong. Yet to paint a picture of placid family life without a ripple to its surface, a setting in which children never squabbled and spouses never disagreed, would be dishonest.

The other burden that weighed me down was the daily cooking. We had by mid-February depleted our stores of traditional North American breakfast foods, things like cold cereal, hot oatmeal mixes, and yogurt. We could find no stock of such things in Cuba. That meant that preparing breakfast became just as labour intensive as the other two daily meals. One day, when I finally blurted out my feelings over the work imbalance, Pat announced brusquely that he'd be making breakfasts from then on. Still I was sour. *Why didn't he offer gently instead of making me feel guilty?* I ruminated in my diary.

Another contributing factor to my malaise was that I missed running with my dog. Jasper was injured. She'd cut her back paw on a piece of glass. Pat and Erin disinfected and bandaged the big gash. To prevent Jasper from chewing off her bandage, Pat secured Meara's navy blue sock to her foot using that versatile invention, duct tape. When Erin tied a navy blue polka-dotted bandana tied round her neck, Jasper looked jaunty. When her paw healed a week later, everyone felt pleased. My gladness was more selfish, however; now I could resume my daily escapes.

It was truly a joy to embark on a run with Jasper, to stretch not just my legs but also my vista. She and I usually ran to the beach just west of the marina, the one sporadically used by Cubans and never by tourists. The waves swept as relentlessly as the wind, but I found the steady rolls of water reassuring in their resurgence. I'd sit and watch the rhythm of the sea while Jasper sniffed around. Sometimes I'd bring my diary along and write for a few minutes. My questions began to change. Instead of venting, I began to examine my own flaws. *Why can't I just happily do things for others even if they don't appreciate it?* I wrote one day. *Why can't I simply give of my time without expecting my generosity to be reciprocated? I suppose it's because I am so human, and have so much growing to do.* After a while I'd re-engage with reality, call my dog, and return to life aboard.

One blustery morning, just like the one before it (and the day after it), Liam sank into his place at the salon table with a sigh.

"As they say, this too shall pass," he said.

"That reminds me of another bit of wisdom," I replied. I reached for the book in which I'd first read it. "Here it is. It's a centring prayer by Dame Julian of Norwich, a thirteenth-century English mystic:

All shall be well, and all shall be well,
And all manner of things shall be well."

Liam repeated it. Meara poked her head up.

"I like that," she said.

I did too. The parallel structure of that piece of wisdom appealed to my ear, not only as writer but also as sailor. The phrases had a mysterious, repetitive, yet pleasing rhythm, like those breakers on the beach.

With a pang in my chest, I remembered the first time I'd read that passage: in the weeks leading up to my visit to the clinic in Washington, before I learned the lump in my breast was only a cyst. That recollection was sobering. How could I become so emotionally mired in petty problems, when that lump had already taught me to move beyond, to find the beauty in this very moment? Although one of my worst faults had been to live in the future, lately I'd been dwelling in the past, letting old issues discolour my perception. More than ever, I must revisit the life lesson taught by that lump, to live in the present.

But the true turning point for me came one day at boat school. The day's morning reflection was an excerpt from Chapter 13 of St. Paul's first letter to the Corinthians, the one so often read at weddings, including Pat's and mine.

"Love is patient, love is kind," I read aloud. "It is not jealous . . . or selfish or irritable; love does not keep a record of wrongs."

The words gave me pause.

"Love is not selfish or irritable," I repeated.

Even the children were still and pensive.

"Love does not keep a record of wrongs."

The timing of that passage was providential. It couldn't have come at a better moment. I'd heard and reflected upon St. Paul's words countless times, yet on that particular day, it was a gift. *Why does it take me so long to learn the same lesson?* I wrote in my diary. Then I recalled the last words from Corinthians 13: "For we but see through a glass, darkly."

Several months later, when I heard one of Eileen Quinn's nautical ditties, I recalled this period of our journey with a wry smile. In that particular song, with her tongue in her cheek, she aptly asks, "if I killed the captain/really, who would know?" A little later on, she sings, "perhaps I'd better kill the captain/before he kills me."

Chapter **18**
Varadero Vistas

We can't direct the wind, but we can adjust the sails.
– Anonymous

My attitude may have changed, but the weather did not. Since we couldn't sail onward, we sought out diversions. The first one fell into our lap.

Debbie and I ran into each other one morning in the bathhouse.

"Remember our Varadero friends Carlos and Luisa?" she asked, towelling dry her cropped blond hair. "They've invited us and your whole family to dinner tomorrow night."

"We'd love to come," I replied. "What should we bring?"

"Not a thing," Debbie said. "They want to cook a big traditional Cuban meal. Carlos does all the cooking. I've asked him to teach us how to make *arroz con gris.*"

Next afternoon the crew of *Cool Breezes* walked across the bridge to Varadero, bearing a fresh package of play-dough and a new deck of cards as icebreakers for the kids, and for the adults, a case of *cerveza,* beer. We'd never visited the residential part of the tourist town, but our hosts' address was easy to find. Inside the gate of a large fenced property, we saw a main house surrounded by smaller

February 2001, Cuba.
Santa Marta, approaching Martin Klein junior high school.

Matanzas city, awaiting a guagua.

dwellings. The yard was alive with a flourishing garden, rabbits in hutches, free-range chickens, and stray dogs.

"Come in, come in!" Carlos stood, arms outstretched, in the doorway of the big house.

He led us on a tour of his home. Compared to the house in which we'd eaten a *paladero* meal, this was a mansion, a concrete illustration of the rewards reaped in this socialist country from the income of Carlos's after-hours industry. In the spacious foyer with its large screened windows, we saw a large TV and VCR, along with an aquarium and a caged parakeet named Rosita. Dany and Daniel each had his own bedroom. In the kitchen, recently upgraded with new appliances and glossy ceramic tile, sat Debbie, Danny and Luisa, drinking *cervezas* and *cubalibres*. Carlos, Pat and I joined them. Armed with English/*español* dictionaries, aided with gestures and nods, assisted by Danny and Carlos' teamwork translation, and fortified by our beverages, we conversed with relative ease. All the while, Carlos taught Debbie and me how to make *arroz con gris* and tended the fat suckling pig in the oven.

A few hours later, Luisa ushered us to a long table set in the breezy foyer. Her mother, grandmother, and siblings arrived bearing heaping platters. Along with roast pork and *arroz con gris,* we sampled *yucca* served with garlic sauce, raw tomatoes and cucumbers laced with oil and vinegar, and fried plantain.

"*Delicioso!*" exclaimed Erin, pleased to practise her newly acquired vocabulary, as she dished out a third helping.

To our hosts' delight, all of us ate heartily, especially the kids. They'd been outside working up their appetites, playing tag and hide-and-seek with Dany and Daniel, climbing trees and chasing lizards. My icebreaker strategies for surmounting the language barrier had proven unnecessary. Becoming acquainted with Carlos and Luisa's older son Dany made us curious about the junior high school he attended in nearby Santa Marta.

"Would the school allow our kids to visit?" I asked Carlos.

"Oh yes, you just have to ask," Carlos replied.

When the meal ended, I turned to our hosts.

"To thank you for your generous hospitality," I said, "our children will sing some Canadian songs for you." Our children groaned. Yet when Carlos translated my message for the other guests, the family clapped in anticipation. The kids delivered passable renditions of some old choir songs, culminating with a spirited version of *O Canada*. After each song, Rosita squawked, and Luisa's old grandmother clapped with *gusto*. When our kids sat down, the matriarch jumped up and led her family in belting out a fiercely patriotic song that could only have been the Cuban national anthem. Rosita was delirious.

"Cubans sure are proud of their country," said Liam. Our dinner with Carlos and Luisa's family turned out to be not only a culinary, but also a cultural experience.

A few days later, I laboured over an hour, composing a seven-sentence message *en español* requesting permission of the local school to pay a visit. Jasper and I ran to the school to deliver the note. When I presented it to the teacher at the entrance, she nodded.

"*Sí, sí,*" she said, passing back the note. "*Mañana, por las ocho horas*" – tomorrow at 8:00 a.m. I was glad not only that my faltering note could be deciphered, but also to receive permission so readily. My students were delighted with the prospect of a "field trip."

Next morning, the teacher and students of St. Christopher's Boat School arose early to attend Escuela Martin Klein. We walked to the school in a light drizzle, along the boulevard of majestic palms, past the pumpjacks and abandoned airstrip, across a field and through narrow streets of tiny houses to the *escuela*. We appeared conspicuous in our salty denims, surrounded by hundreds of students uniformed in mustard slacks or skirts and crisp collared shirts, as we awaited the morning bell.

Promptly at 8:00 a.m., the friendly teacher of English opened the door and whisked us off on a tour. The two-storey school had fallen into disrepair. The hallways had no operating light fixtures. The science lab had no running water, and the library a dearth of books. A single computer served the entire student body and – as in the rest of Cuba – the Internet was unavailable. We climbed the dingy staircase to a crowded classroom, where the teacher introduced us to rows of assembled students. The average class size was just over forty pupils, she said, and eight hundred and eighty students attended the school. Classes ran from 8:00 a.m. to 5:30 p.m., five days a week, eleven months a year. From there our guide led us past a wall entirely covered with posters.

"What's that all about?" Ben asked.

"This mural tells how badly the United States has treated Cuba," the teacher explained, pointing. "This part is about the Bay of Pigs and that part is about the many communicable diseases and illegal drugs Americans have brought to Cuba." I was surprised that the propaganda flowed in both directions, since we'd found Cubans to be fascinated by everything American, and American currency was at that time a big part of their economy.

At the end of our tour we sought out young Dany, and gave him a bag containing hundreds of pieces of packaged chewing gum. He might have hoarded them, but when we left we saw him swarmed by schoolmates, enjoying the role of magnanimous hero.

That Sunday we took a day trip on the Hershey train. In the pre-*Revolución* heyday of capitalism, this train route was used to transport village workers to and from the Hershey chocolate factory. To us, it provided a charming ride through the verdant valley of the Río Yurumi, and a chance to savour a slice of everyday Cuban life.

We took a US$20 taxi ride from the marina to the bright blue train station in nearby Matanzas city, at the east end of the line. There we boarded the nearly empty five-car train. A few moments later the engine cranked up and the train lurched forward.

The train rattled so loudly that we couldn't hear each other speak. Each *estación* was a mere shack, and each village brown and dusty. Not only the usual goats and chickens, but also pigs and oxen roamed the dirt roads of these small settlements. Not a car was in sight. Between stops, however, the countryside was a visual cornucopia. Misshapen green hills called *mogotes* erupted from the plains, royal palms stretched regally to blue skies, and the slender river winked as it slithered its silver way to sea.

"It looks like the Garden of Eden," Erin breathed.

At the hamlet of Canasi, a horde of teenagers boarded. The train became suddenly crowded and boisterous. Young girls sat in each other's laps, and boys perched on up-ended pails in the aisles. To them, everything appeared hilarious, especially our family, the only foreigners aboard. Having by then stopped at twenty-four *estaciónes*, we disembarked at the town of Hershey, eager to view the factory.

"Maybe we could buy some chocolate here!" chirped Meara, a chocoholic like me. At three, she'd captured the essence of chocolate rapture in a phrase: "When you take a bite of chocolate, it's a whole new world."

Hershey was no tourist attraction, we soon discovered;

no cocoa delight suffused the atmosphere there. The buildings, with their barbed wire fences and boarded-up windows, were eyesores. The now defunct chocolate factory, with its twisting tunnels and rusted funnels, might have been the transplanted set of a *Mad Max* movie.

Back at the Hershey train station, the children wished to use the *baños*. I located a key for each bathroom and handed them out. The boys and girls emerged from their respective washrooms only a few moments later, their noses wrinkled.

"We think we'll wait," Erin explained.

"You gotta wonder why they bother locking up rooms like that," Ben said.

When we disembarked from the train at the Matanzas station, we discovered no taxis were available for hire. A tall slender man named Javier noticed our predicament and offered to help. His English was impeccable. With his greying Afro and aquiline nose, he had the noble bearing of a Biblical wise man.

"Cross the road to that sign," he said. "Take the *guagua* to the main station where you can catch another *guagua* to Varadero."

"The 'wa-wa'?" we asked.

"Our local slang for 'bus'," he laughed. "Perhaps in imitation of the bus's horn."

When we thanked him for his kindness, Javier bowed his head graciously. "It's a pleasure for me," he said, "and a chance to practice my English." Despite his university education, he said, he worked as a labourer.

When the ancient *guagua* arrived, we paid our twenty cents fare, and stuffed ourselves into the aisle, where we were supported by the crush of human bodies. Our ride was hot and sticky, yet mercifully short and therefore fun. The bus wobbled and the locals laughed.

"Well, now we know the feeling of that expression, 'squished in like a can of sardines'!" Liam said brightly as we disembarked at the main bus station.

By then the children were desperate to find a bite to eat, and a decent washroom. Pat hunted down these necessities while I inquired about buses to Varadero.

"No buses go there on Sunday," the ticket clerk told me.

Dusk was falling and yet again, we found ourselves in a strange city without transportation for our large brood. Once again, Cuban entrepreneurial spirit came to the rescue.

"You like to hire my car?" asked a cheerful young fellow. He gestured toward a gleaming red 1955 Chevrolet BelAir. "Only twenty-five dollars."

"A bargain," Pat agreed. We gratefully slid into the cream tufted leather seats.

This driver didn't use illegal coloured gas to get us home; nevertheless, his business was not quite legitimate. Instead of taking the highway, he drove the scenic route, avoiding every settlement possible. Whenever we emerged from a back road to a little village, he'd motion for us to duck our heads. And when we finally approached Varadero, he dropped us off far from the marina gates, out of sight of the guards. The kids were puzzled at the driver's incongruous behaviour.

"He doesn't have a taxi license," Pat explained.

Meanwhile, life at the marina was unfolding like a soap opera. Two new boats had arrived. One of them was crewed by a couple that wore nothing but thong swimsuits as they strolled down the docks. The crew of the other, an Irish fellow and his American buddy, drank beer and argued at top volume. As well, Alex and Elaine's daughter Claire had just arrived on a flight from Montreal. A vivacious woman with long wavy hair, Claire was a radio journalist. She'd spread the word that she was eager to interview everyone on Gulf Stream stories, to be broadcast on American public radio. And the latest scuttlebutt was also out: both of the marina Romeos had found their Cubana Juliets.

Jacques, the impecunious French-Canadian, had moved in with a woman and her family in a town near Havana. Unable to pay dockage, he was forced to surrender his weary boat to the Cuban authorities. Now he was trying to raise cash by selling off his other possessions. It was illegal for foreigners to trade goods without paying duty, but most of Jacques' fellow cruisers felt sympathy for him and agreed to buy something.

"I 'ave a Wes' Marine sea kayak. Perhap' ze children would like dat?" he asked Pat. Pat could hardly refuse; Jacques had offered within the children's earshot. That's how we acquired a bright yellow kayak in excellent condition for a quarter of its retail price, and that's the last we saw of Jacques.

Meanwhile Dale, the romantic entrepreneur from Florida, conferred daily with Pat – over beer – on the situation with his beautiful Cubana.

"Carmel is a lawyer. She lives with her family in Matanzas. I rented a car so I can drive out to see her every day. I'm in love with her, and she says she is with me," he sighed, "but I don't know if she'll ever leave Cuba."

"Have you asked her to marry you?" Pat asked.

"Yes, just yesterday I proposed," Dale answered. "But she said she has to think about it. She loves her grandmother very much, and she loves Cuba too. She isn't sure she would like to live in America. And I know I couldn't live here."

The pathos of the situation fascinated me. The fact that a professional Cuban woman wouldn't yearn to live in North America was intriguing.

As the days marched on, the weather began to improve. Our family often visited the west beach, as we called it, instead of the high-rise hotel beach to the east. One day Pat took the older three horseback riding there. Most days the children took turns paddling around the marina in the sea kayak. Along with improved weather came the sailors' itch to loosen the docklines. Sharon and Lou and their doggie-vested terrier were set to sail north to Mexico, and Claire was due to fly home.

"Let's have a dock party to send them off," I suggested to Pat. He spread the word around the marina, and took the kids to the west beach for the afternoon so I could prepare. We knew our neighbours would expect a tour of our catamaran – in effect, a glimpse into our personal lives – and so we may as well show our "sunny side up."

Not a minute past the designated happy hour, our guests began to arrive. Soon they spilled out of the cockpit and onto the dock. The older three kids gave tours of our boat. It was then that Claire became acquainted with our children and asked to squeeze in one last radio interview with them before her departure. When we agreed, she hurried off to get her fancy headpiece, microphone and recorder.

"What's the worst part about living aboard?" she asked the kids.

"Sharing a bed with my brother," Ben answered.

"What have you learned about your family on this trip that you didn't know before?"

"How many times a night they make a trip to the head," Erin replied.

The older three sniggered. I muttered something about bathroom humour always finding an audience.

"Not bathroom humour," Meara giggled. "You mean head humour!"

The next morning dawned sunny and calm. Weather predictions were for increasing winds that day, but light winds the next.

"I do believe we'll be able to set sail eastwards tomorrow," Pat announced.

"That'll be a month to the day since we landed in Cuba," I said.

The last day of any marina stay was always busy. A long list of errands and chores had to be accomplished in a time frame that somehow seemed short and sudden, despite weeks of anticipation. Laundry must be done, children showered, and fuel and water tanks refilled. Here in Cuba, the Guarda Frontera must be notified and a new *despacho* issued. One of the most important items on my personal agenda that day was to buy the small oil painting I'd seen in an art gallery on Avenida Primera. It depicted the verdant Río Yurumi valley, a perfect memento of our Hershey train ride. I told Pat about it.

"Okay, let's take Jasper for a walk into town," he said with a trace of resignation in his voice. He hated shopping. "The painting can be an early anniversary gift to each other."

Once inside the gallery, though, Pat's enthusiasm was unleashed. We found Cuban art wildly creative and diverse. In addition to the small landscape, we bought a watercolour portrait of a young Cubana smoking a cigar by the roadside, a rooster at her feet. Then we found four large and colourful acrylics, each depicting a child's fanciful face, one image to correlate with each of our children. Since the gallery didn't accept credit cards, we paid in American cash, necessitating another errand: a trip to the bank. That was an ordeal in itself, involving the production of profuse identification and completion of copious forms under the eye of watchful armed guards.

Back at the marina, Dale was pacing the docks.

"Word's out you're leaving tomorrow," he said. "I've got enough canned and dry goods to sink a ship, so why don't you come aboard and do some provisioning?"

Pat and I were more than pleased with the convenient location and prices offered at the *Outsized* grocery store. The storekeeper was only too happy to lighten his load, and our kids were delighted to have a fresh supply of North American food. We stocked up on Erin's favourite dessert mixes, rice and canned beans for making *arroz con gris*, and dried soup packets. We were especially pleased to buy a store of flour; Heather had given us yeast and taught us to make bread. There would be no *panadería* where we were going.

"How about you, Dale? How much longer are you staying?" Pat asked him.

"I gotta be back by the end of the month," Dale replied, a furrow crossing his suntanned forehead. "I just hope Carmel makes up her mind by then."

"She still hasn't given you an answer?" Pat asked. "You poor fellow."

"You're such a romantic," I sighed. "I love it."

We never did hear the outcome of Dale's wistful romance, but as a would-be writer, I had a plotline all worked out from this point of indecision. I envisioned torrid scenes involving sweet surrender, a concealed nighttime passage to Florida, a beach wedding, and a child. A visit to Cuba to see a dying grandmother, and a failed return trip to Florida. Dale's broken heart. A bit over the top, that story, but what fun it would be to write.

While we shopped aboard *Outsized*, we received three invitations. The first was from Emil, delivering his daily promotion of the marina restaurant's nightly *speciale*.

"Yes, Jake and I will come at nine o'clock," Pat replied.

"But without the children, so we can celebrate our anniversary." I was surprised – our anniversary was days away – but tickled.

Then Alex and Elaine stopped by to invite us to a farewell sundowner party at 6:00 p.m. Danny came by with the third invitation, to bring Jasper to say goodbye to Lobita and have one last nightcap with him and Debbie.

Before we enjoyed any of these social outings, though, we attended evening Mass.

"Who knows when we'll get to church again," I told the kids. "I need you to pray for our safety!" I believe God is more receptive to the simple and sincere prayers of children.

After Mass, the crew of *Cool Breezes* enjoyed one last walk across the bridge, through the fields, and back to the marina. We joined Alex and Elaine and the convivial crowd enjoying sundowners aboard *Pegasus*. When Pat and I left the party for our dinner reservation, the kids returned to our boat, where Erin cooked supper for her siblings. Emil welcomed us to the restaurant. He served a delicious meal of grilled red snapper and *arroz con gris*. Then, with a gleeful smile, he surprised us with a dense, heart-shaped cake.

We brought most of the cake back to our voracious children, then strolled down the dock with Jasper to the cockpit of *La Vida Dulce*, where Debbie and Danny waited with Lobita. Tears lay close to the brink as we bid them goodbye. Walking back to *Cool Breezes*, I conjured an image of each of our marina friends, so that by the time I crawled into bed, my tears overflowed.

Leave-taking was never my specialty.

February 2001,
Cuban cayos.

Top to bottom:

The lighthouse at Cayo
Bahía de Cadiz;
Learning to fillet the fish
we traded for fresh
water;
Beachcombing at Cayo
Datton.

Chapter 19
Golden Days in the Cuban Cayos

It is a more fortunate destiny to have a taste for collecting shells than to be born a millionaire.
– Robert Louis Stevenson

The morning of February 25, Pat and I planned to sleep late. The Guarda Frontera weren't due to deliver our *despacho* until 10:00 a.m., and we were tired after our late night of goodbyes. At 7:00 a.m., however, Erin roused us.

"Mom, Dad, the Guarda Frontera officers are waiting for you!" she called. From the hatch opening in her stateroom, she could see the squad standing at our stern.

Pat bounded out of bed, pulled on a pair of shorts and greeted the officials. We wouldn't be ready to leave for a few hours, he explained. In fact, the marina had not yet delivered our diesel. Unlike American marinas with fuel docks, Marina Darsena ordered jerry cans of diesel from a supplier and delivered them dockside.

The Guarda didn't much care about convenience.

"Tell us where you got the sea kayak," they demanded. "You did not have it when you arrived."

Pat decided not to name Jacques as the vendor, since the Guarda would then report the sale back to the government, which would then find Jacques and force him to pay the proceeds. So Pat told the story vaguely, referring to

253

a transaction with a boat that was already gone. Still, the Guarda insisted we pay duty as purchasers before they'd issue our *despacho*.

Shortly after the Guarda left, marina staff delivered wheelbarrows full of diesel jerry cans. Pat decided to filter the diesel before pouring it into our tanks.

"If the diesel is old, it will contain clumps that can really clog our fuel lines," he explained to the boys, who stood watching. "Then we'll have fuel delivery problems and our engines will stall. And that will be sure to happen at the worst possible moment!"

The filtering process was laborious and time-consuming. Al gave Pat a hand. In the meantime, Heather came aboard and, for the last time, supervised my dough kneading. The dough rose well in this warm and humid salt air.

"Your cat cruises so flat, I bet you could bake the bread while you sail," she said.

By 10:00 a.m. we were ready to leave. We heard Elaine calling fellow cruisers on the VHF to bid us goodbye. A small crowd gathered on the docks to help untie the docklines and wave farewell. Having already bid my private goodbyes the night before, I felt confident my eyes would remain dry. But when I hugged Elaine's tiny frame and saw Debbie's tear-stained cheeks, I succumbed again, along with my girls.

"As they say, all good things must come to an end," Liam pronounced wisely.

We motored slowly down the canal, made the dogleg turn, and headed into open water. When Pat pushed the levers to accelerate, however, the response was lethargic.

"I can't believe how sluggish the boat feels," he said. A moment later, the light bulb went on in his head. "I bet the propellers are encrusted with barnacles, after a month in one place," he said. "I should've dived down and scraped them off."

"What an ugly job that would've been, swimming below the hulls in the dirty marina water," Ben said.

"Yeah, you're right," Pat nodded. "I'll do it once we're anchored at Cayo Blanco."

"I'll help!" Liam piped up. If any of our kids grows up to buy a boat, it will be he.

Besides the accumulation of barnacles on her hulls, the lapse of a month without sailing had other adverse effects: the rustiness and queasiness of her crew. We floundered when we set about raising the sails, and our captain grew frustrated. And when we turned eastward and faced twenty-knot winds and five-foot waves, we discovered some of us had lost our sailing stomach. Meara and Liam were seasick, I felt nauseous and tired, and Pat was weary and irritated, when at last we approached Cayo Blanco. We held a slim hope that our artisan friends would still be there, but when we lay the anchor we saw their magnificent sculpture was finished and the beach deserted. Pat stretched out for a nap, while I made an early supper to eat with our fresh bread. By 8:30 p.m., everyone was fed and in bed.

After a night of deep sleep swaying gently on the hook, we awoke to an exquisitely golden anchorage morning. The air glistened and the sea twinkled. Wavelets lapped our hulls, and a soft breeze wafted our hair as we enjoyed breakfast in the cockpit. Pat and Liam dove under the hulls to scrape off the propellers, while the rest of us dinghied to shore for Jasper's morning respite.

"Time to go!" Pat called. He pointed to the horizon where the day cats, loaded with tourists, their salsa music blaring, bore down on our little paradise. We pulled up anchor and pointed our bows eastward.

The next five days were much the same: gleaming weather, achingly picturesque island anchorages, and gentle easterly headwinds. We ate breakfast, dinghied Jasper to shore and back, and pulled up anchor. The kids and I studied three hours at boat school, while Pat took the helm. If one of my students finished the day's regular schoolwork, he or she joined Pat in the cockpit, writing a journal entry and helping out as deckhand. After an underway lunch, I took the helm while the kids lounged about their staterooms or on the trampoline. We wore swimsuits and bare feet all day, and bathed in crystal clear waters. We rose with the sun at 6:00 a.m. and twelve hours later, retired shortly after sunset. We were gunkholing, exactly the kind of subtropical cruising we'd envisioned in our ten years of planning this boat trip.

One day we stopped at Cayo Bahía de Cadiz, known for its striking lighthouse made of steel sheets painted a checkerboard black and white. The only approach to the lighthouse was via dinghy along the winding rivulet maze among the mangroves. The lonely lighthouse keeper and his drove of goats ran forward to greet us as we beached the dinghy. Though he spoke no English, the keeper insisted upon giving us a guided tour of the lighthouse display in *español*. We nodded politely, but learned little.

"*Gracias, señor,*" I said. Walking toward our dinghy at the end of our tour, my nostrils flared to absorb the island's delectable scent. As if on cue, the lighthouse keeper plucked some limes from the trees beside us, and presented Erin and me with generous handfuls.

"A welcome addition to your gin-and-tonic sundowners, eh, Jake?" Pat grinned.

On another of those idyllic days, Pat and I celebrated our fourteenth anniversary. The day began auspiciously. We rose early, as usual, with that delicious sense of well-being and fresh promise brought by a good night's sleep.

The anchorage lay perfectly still. I assembled a breakfast frittata while Pat and the boys dinghied Jasper to and from the nearby island. On their return trip, they met two fishermen eager to trade fresh fish for fresh *agua.* "*No problema!*" Pat replied. In exchange for three red snapper and two large silver fish we couldn't identify, he filled the fishermen's bucket from our fresh water tank, and pressed some American bills into their hands. Then each of us took a turn cleaning and filleting the fish under Pat's supervision. We lay the fresh fillets in the fridge, and took our sea baths.

By that time in our cruise, we'd developed a sea bath regimen. We brought the shampoo and conditioner to the stern, close to the swim ladder, then plunged head-first into the clear salt water. After a shampoo and rinse, we applied conditioner and rinsed again. Next we pulled ourselves into the cockpit and rinsed off with fresh water on deck. The fresh water came from a black rubber bag that hung from the mast in the sun, absorbing warmth. It looked like a giant hot water bottle with a sprinkler attachment. We unhooked the sprinkler and sprayed the tepid stream on our heads. Then we wrapped ourselves in beach towels, and dried off in the sun. By the end of this routine, our skin felt aglow.

"Let's make it a short travel day today," Pat said. "Cayo Datton is only four hours from here. And in honour of the teacher's wedding anniversary, I declare it to be a boat school holiday!" The cheers of my older three students drowned out Meara's protests.

We pulled up anchor and turned eastward, ever eastward. The day shone. I went below and tried a new bread recipe, pita pockets, the basis for our lunch that day. The kids hung, as they would say, doing nothing but day-dream. Meara watched Erin embroider beads on their jeans. At times they burst into song. Ben sat in the cockpit whittling, and Liam lay on his berth, twirling his pencil and letting his imagination fly.

Later that afternoon, we approached Cayo Datton. Liam was overwhelmed by the sheer splendour of the display before him. He lifted the hatch opening to Erin's stateroom and hollered, "You gotta get out here! We've just arrived at heaven on earth!"

He was right. Cayo Datton was a low-lying island, separated at that moment of low tide into two islets. Mostly rock and coral, with a sprinkling of shrubs and a white crescent beach, the *cayo* was not lush. Yet once ashore, we discovered that it teemed with life, and yielded a treasury of shells for our collection. We collected conch shells, starfish, sea fans, helmet shells, tiger shells, and many yet unnamed offerings from the sea.

"We decided to call that half 'Tresoria,' like treasure," Ben and Liam announced, pointing to the separate islets, "and this half 'Emporia,' as in a store full of treasures."

The evening brought another gift from the sea. Pat and I sipped sundowners in the cockpit, as the fish fillets grilled and the smells of rice, asparagus and brownies drifted up the companionway. Our children were cooking an anniversary dinner. Just then another boat of fishermen puttered to starboard and offered us a bucket full of fresh fat crawfish tails. Crawfish, unlike their lobster cousins, have no claws, but their tails are well developed, making for a plump and tasty meal.

"*Gracias, gracias!*" Pat exclaimed. "*Momento, momento!*" he added, signalling with his index finger to wait a moment. He ran below and found fish hooks and cash, while I rummaged in a cubby for candy and soap, to give in exchange. The three men accepted the gifts, but refused the cash. With a nod and a smile, they motored away.

"I wonder how they knew it's our anniversary?" I marvelled, as we watched them disappear in the deepening dusk. The kids looked puzzled at my apparent lapse in logic. "Of course they couldn't know, but God does," I explained.

Liam's bit of heaven on earth lay glistening and alluring the next golden morning, so we dinghied back for a few more hours. The kids held seashell beauty contests on the beach. By noon, the sparkling morning spell had dissolved like a sigh, and we set sail eastward again. We couldn't help but glance back as we pulled away from Cayo Datton. This place and time was the golden pinnacle of our cruise in the Cuban cayos.

The next few nights we anchored near islands with Guarda Frontera detachments. At Cayos Barracho and Diablito, the Guarda radioed us as we approached.

"How many on board?" they demanded.

"Six," Pat replied. "Two adults and four children."

"¿Cuatro niños?" they asked in disbelief.

"¡Sí, sí, cuatro niños!" Pat confirmed.

"No, no, not possible," they replied.

"Come on out, kids, let's show them how many of you there are!" One by one they joined Pat and me on the foredecks and waved in the direction of the Guarda.

"Okay, okay, okay!" came the tinny voice over the VHF. "You can stay."

The Guarda allowed our boat to remain in the anchorage, but wouldn't let us bring Jasper to shore, even for a moment. At dawn the next morning, however, Pat quickly dinghied her back and forth before we pulled up anchor and motored off.

The next night we anchored near Cayo Paredon Grande, where an imposing yellow and black lighthouse dominated the seascape. Once again we endured the

Guarda's radio inquisition, and once again, for no discernible reason, we were forbidden ashore.

In counterpoint to the stricture of the Guarda, a boat full of fishermen arrived to port at dusk to borrow a screwdriver. When Pat passed them the tool, they handed back a plastic bag full of crawfish.

"They're alive!" Meara squealed, when Pat dumped the bag's contents in the cockpit. She jumped onto the bench seat and clutched her fists to her chest. The six fish scurried around the Fiberglas cockpit in a frenzy. Jasper lunged and the children shrieked. When Pat pulled out an axe, the girls and I disappeared into the salon while the boys held Jasper back.

"Ew, gross!" Liam shouted with audible delight. "Did you see the way their heads and feelers scrambled around even after Dad chopped them off?"

"No I didn't, but somehow I think I can live without that experience," Erin snapped.

The next night we landed at Cayo Confites, yet another idyllic subtropical island that had it all: palm trees, coral reefs, a white sand beach, and its own Guarda Frontera detachment. This detachment permitted Pat to dinghy Jasper to shore, but just to the edge and then promptly back.

"The Guarda have definitely become a dampener on this cruise," Pat complained.

Other problems cropped up. One was a fuel delivery problem in the port engine. The engine often kicked out while underway, due to impurities in the diesel that clogged the fuel line.

"Couldn't be the diesel we just bought in Varadero," Pat said. "We filtered that. It must be the fuel we got way back in Key West."

He lifted the cover of the port engine compartment, and showed me how to pump the fuel line bulb so fuel could flow past the clump. It was a nasty, reeking job, guaranteed to produce nausea, especially since we pounded into the waves as we beat against the easterlies. "At least only one engine kicks out," offered Ben, ever the optimist. "Imagine the trouble we'd be in if the starboard engine didn't function either."

Another difficulty was obtaining weather reports. Since we were now well out of Perfect Paul's range, we had to rely upon the regularly transmitted, though irregularly received, reports picked up on the single sideband radio. Weather for our area of the Caribbean was read aloud at 5:00 a.m., 5:00 p.m., and 11:00 p.m. We missed the 5:00 p.m. report two consecutive days, once because the hour slipped by unnoticed, and the second time because the reception was too poor to be comprehensible. That meant that for two days in a row, we had to remain awake past the 11:00 p.m. report and rise before the 5:00 a.m. report to get our indispensable weather fix. At first, since I was such a novice at the delicate art of tuning in, Pat and I would both get up to listen to the report. Then, as the days went by, the job of getting weather fell mostly to me. *How ironic to be keeping my usual sleep-deprived schedule on a year away from it all,* I wrote in my diary.

The morning of March 4, I heard a cold front was coming, with westerly winds. When I reported this to Pat, he looked at the charts and decided we'd better tuck in behind Cayo Romano, just a short distance away from Cayo Confites.

Cayo Romano would hold many misadventures for us. The initial golden glow of our idyllic early cruising days had already begun to fade. As Liam had observed, all good things must come to an end.

March 2001, Cayo Romano, Cuba.

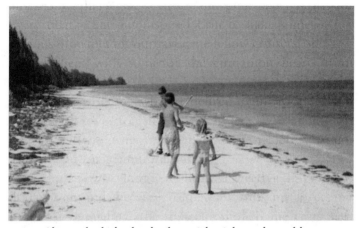

*Above, the kids play hockey with sticks and an old coconut
among flotsam and jetsam.
Below, Ben wears the turtle skull he and Liam found.*

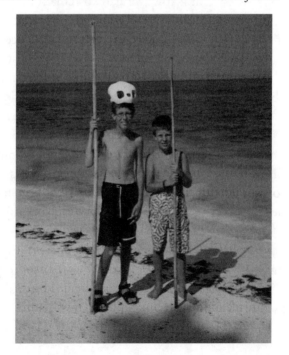

Chapter 20
Adventures and Misadventures

He that would go to sea for pleasure would go to hell for a pastime.
— *A sailor's proverb*

The distance from Cayo Confites to Cayo Romano was short, and the journey pleasant. A cold front was on its way, yet the sun shone and the wind and water lay down. To our surprise, no Guarda Frontera detachment radioed us the moment we anchored.

"Perhaps there's no detachment on this island," Pat said, so he and the kids dinghied Jasper to shore.

I stayed back, intending to snatch a moment to write. First, though, I washed two bucketfuls of hand laundry and set some bread dough to rise. That was a mistake. I had only just retrieved my coiled scribbler from its cubby when the crew returned.

"We had two adventures!" Meara reported, her eyes bright. "The dinghy engine quit on us, and then we almost scraped the bottom on some coral!"

Pat's face confirmed that the expedition had indeed been stressful.

"Don't worry, I got the dinghy engine going again," he said.

We sat down for lunch, ready to say grace, when Pat looked out the porthole and groaned.

"Oh no," he said. "The anchor is dragging, really dragging."

Our boat was headed toward the dreaded coral reef that could seriously damage our Fiberglas hulls. We sprang to action. Liam grabbed the ignition keys, Pat hurried to the foredecks, and I took the helm. We motored further offshore, and Pat re-set the anchor.

"I think I'll set a second anchor too," he murmured, just as we gathered round the salon table a second time. When Pat returned to the table, we assembled a third time and bowed our heads for grace. Just then, Erin glanced out the companionway toward the stern.

"Oh no!" she shouted. "Our dinghy is floating away!"

Pat swam out to retrieve it, tied it more securely to the stern, and returned to the table with a lecture to the one whose knot had been too lax.

"Wow, we've already had four adventures today!" Meara exclaimed. She'd be less excited, though, about the misadventures to come.

After lunch, we dinghied to the beach. We wanted to explore Cayo Romano, and check out what our cruising guide said was good snorkelling just off shore. When we arrived, however, we found the coral reef dead and black, and the beach strewn with fragments of objects lost to sea and washed ashore. Bottles, pails, cups, shoes, basins, even dolls, littered the white sand of this island paradise.

"Hey Mom, this is what they call flotsam and jetsam!" Ben quipped. I too had longed to use that pair of words.

Despite the debris, the children amused themselves. The girls drew pictures in the sand with short sticks. Ben and Liam found a pair of longer sticks and played hockey, using an old coconut for a puck. Pat laughed.

"You can take our boys out of Canada, but you can't take the Canada out of our boys!"

Just then we noticed two dark figures in the distance. As they strode closer, we discerned two tall young men, barefoot, wearing tan-coloured Guarda Frontera shirts.

"Here we go again," Pat grumbled.

The Guarda were assertive.

"Not possible to come ashore, not possible to play on beach."

"Why not?" Pat asked.

"Not permitted," one replied. "We protect Cuba from drug-runners."

"Drug-runners!" Pat exclaimed. "Do we look like drug-runners? We're just a Canadian family on a boat trip."

"*Sí, sí,* you have a beautiful family," the fellow replied. "Still, you must leave. And also you must show us your *despacho.*"

"The *despacho* is aboard our boat," Pat said, pointing to our anchored cat. "I'll go get it and bring it back." Deflated, morose, we walked to the dinghy in silence.

"We'll go back with you when you bring the *despacho,* Dad," said Liam and Ben, as the dinghy approached our stern.

"Okay, wait here," Pat said. He headed to the nav station where we kept a plastic file folder full of important documents like our birth certificates and passports, Jasper's veterinarian report, our vaccination records, the boat registration certificate and, of late, our *despacho.* The girls and I decided to stay aboard *Cool Breezes.* Just as we climbed out and Pat back into the dinghy, the elastic wrap on the file folder gave way and its contents spilled into the sea.

"Oh no!" Pat yelled. "Quick, help!"

Pat, Ben and Liam scooped most of the papers before they sank, while I used the net to nab the few others that had drifted away. The *despacho* was soggy but legible.

While Pat and the boys roared away with it, the girls and I spread the other papers out to dry.

"I can't believe this day!" Meara said, her eyes wide.

"Oh well, nothing has happened that can't be fixed," I replied.

"Hey, Mom, it's just us girls aboard. Let's do our nails!" said Erin.

"I have a better idea," I said. I'd noticed the fellows were mere dots on the sand when they pulled their dinghy ashore. "If it's just us girls aboard, let's go skinny-dipping."

"Mom!" Erin exclaimed in shock. "Skinny-dipping?"

"What's that?" Meara asked, suddenly interested.

"Swimming naked," I replied.

"No way!" my daughters chimed in unison.

"Well, you gotta try it at least once in your life," I advised. "And without the guys around, it's a perfect opportunity."

I'd last gone skinny-dipping as a teen in the dark at a lake in the Canadian Shield. Then it was the cool thing to do, both literally and figuratively. This time – in the sunshine and the warm Caribbean waters – felt much different. Delicious, even, as I reported to my girls, who bathed in their swimsuits beside me.

A moment later Erin threw her wet swimsuit in the cockpit.

"You're right, Mom," she said, immersing herself and floating to the surface. Her long blond hair spread around her head like a peacock's tail. "It kinda feels free!"

Meara declined to participate. She finished her sea bath, and climbed the swim ladder into the cockpit. She suddenly squealed.

"Quick, quick! They're coming back!"

"Quick, Meara! Pass us a towel!" Erin shrieked. She and I scrambled aboard, slippery and laughing, and tugged our wet suits over our wet legs. By the time the dinghy arrived at the stern, we were sitting on the bench seats wrapped in towels.

"Hey, Jake," Pat shouted out, "Could you pass me a couple of Cokes? We're gonna go back and give those guys some pop and our extra goggles."

"You are?"

"Yeah, they're actually really nice young guys, just following orders," Pat said.

As they dinghied off, I wiped my brow in mock relief. The girls giggled.

"Oh great, they're gone again," said Erin. "This time let's just do our nails."

That evening, Pat and I listened to the SSB weather report. The cold front would arrive the next day, we heard.

"Hard to believe," Pat remarked. Even at twilight, the water lay so still and clear that we could see through eight or ten feet of it to the ocean floor. "If the forecast is correct, then we're in the right place, sheltered behind Cayo Romano," he went on. "But if the cold front is delayed, we'll make tracks tomorrow."

Conditions remained so calm the next morning that we decided to motor southeastward for a few hours, then tuck in when the cold front hit in the afternoon. Pat turned on the ignition to the port engine. It sputtered and died, still clogged with bad diesel. Then he turned the ignition to the starboard engine. The harsh clatter of shattering metal assaulted our ears. We could feel the shards shuddering through the boat. The kids, seated at boat school, looked up from their books startled and wide-eyed.

"Dad, what was that?" Liam yelled.

"I don't know, but whatever it is, it isn't good," Pat muttered, squeezing past us enroute to the starboard engine compartment. I could tell from his expression that this was not a moment to be asking questions, so I shushed the kids and redirected them to their schoolwork. Meanwhile, I baked bread, tossed a bean salad, and set chili soup to simmering.

A few hours later, Pat emerged from the stinky engine compartment.

"The coupling between the engine and the transmission is completely stripped," he reported. My vacant expression prompted him to explain. "The new starboard engine was installed improperly, at a slight angle instead of vertically. So over the last few months, the gear to the transmission has been gradually wearing away. Today when I turned the engine, the last remains of metal gave out. Now, even though the engine works fine, it has nothing to turn. The coupling is shot, and it's beyond me to fix."

The kids and I sat mutely, absorbing the news, while Pat wiped his greasy hands on a rag. His lips were pressed thin, his eyes cast down.

"So what are our options?" I asked.

"I don't really know. It's gotta be fixed, but where and how I've no idea."

I heaved a deep sigh. More trouble in paradise. I looked outside. The sky was brewing. Dark clouds were clustering, and the wind was whistling. I gathered the laundry from the lifelines. The kids packed their books, battened down the hatches, and replaced the porthole screens with Plexiglas. We sat down to lunch.

"Looks like the weather forecast is right after all," I said, looking out the companionway. At high noon, the sky was nearly black.

Pat swabbed the last of his bean salad with a morsel of fresh bread. On a full stomach, he felt more optimistic.

"God is looking out for us today," he mused. "With that transmission breakdown, He made sure we didn't try going anywhere in the storm. He might have been subtle about it, though. He could've given us some problem I can fix."

By then the boat rocked uncomfortably. The kids retreated to their staterooms. Weary from nights of broken sleep trying to catch weather reports, and queasy from the erratic motion of the water, I reclined on my berth. Pat joined me.

"If only both the fuel delivery and the transmission problems happened to the same engine," he sighed, stretching out. "Now, even though we have two engines, we have no backup." A moment later he added, "I find it so frustrating. We spent thousands of dollars and weeks of delay doing the right thing – getting our engines replaced back in Virginia – yet this has to happen."

An hour after falling asleep, I awoke. The boat was bucking. Through our stateroom portholes I saw Pat standing at the bows, examining the anchor lines. He returned for the anemometer.

"Thank God we were dragging yesterday," he said. "Otherwise I might not have laid the second anchor. We should be okay through this gale."

"Gale?" I asked. "Is this a gale?"

"Oh yeah." He held aloft the wind gauge. "She's a strong gale, blowing well over forty knots."

That the weather was serious was perversely reassuring; it meant we weren't wimps. It was also perversely exciting. The drama of a strong gale appealed to my pioneer spirit, in the same way a blizzard would back home. Yes, it was something to dread, and something to hate. It was also something to love to hate.

Drama and excitement often come with discomfort. The boat was rearing on its anchors in a predictably violent pattern. First the bows would rise and fall in two humungous rollercoaster humps, and then the boat would gyrate from port to starboard. All but irongut Ben and Pat felt nauseous. The rest of us sat miserably huddled in the cockpit, oblivious to the rolling sea and dense streaks of foam and spray. We were content just to be out of the cabin, staring at the horizon. Jasper hid under the salon table and slept away her misery.

When suppertime approached, Ben and Pat went below to heat the chili soup. I was glad I'd started cooking early; I could never have managed to descend to the galley.

"Try some, it's good!" Ben laughed, holding a bowl beneath our noses. The four of us almost retched in response.

"Really, you should try to eat. It'll do you some good," Pat urged. He passed tentative portions to each of us in the cockpit. We nibbled to make him happy, found it sat well and tasted good, and ate some more.

Although days seemed to have passed, it was only 7:00 p.m. All we wanted to do was go to bed. I was approaching that catatonic state of seasickness, past nausea and into a mute stupor. Pat and Ben wanted to play poker, however, and Liam, sick as he was, couldn't resist. Sheets of rain began pelting down, so we abandoned the cockpit and dealt cards at the salon table. Every so often, Liam would rise, green as a goblin, and run gagging to the cockpit.

"I haven't lost it yet!" he'd announce cheerfully upon his return.

At 8:00 p.m., we wrapped up the game. It was impossible to play on our careening table. Pat set the anchor alarm so we'd be alerted to any dragging, and we lurched to our sea berths. Despite the early hour, no one cared to read, and no one whined when Pat announced lights out.

"This was the worst day of my life," Meara confided tearfully after nighttime prayers. The day's adventures and misadventures, once exciting, were now overwhelming.

"Don't worry, Meara deara," I said, tucking her duvet cover under her chin. "The important thing is we're all still safe."

Liam overheard the exchange.

"As they say, this too shall pass," he offered.

The night was long and uncomfortable. The TV broke free of its strappings. Dishes and glassware rattled in their cupboards. Companionway doors griped on their hinges. The halyards jangled inside the mast. The wind screamed, the waves smashed our hulls, and the hulls heaved and slapped back at the sea. It was the fiercest weather we'd encountered.

When I awoke the next morning, after eleven hours in bed but half as many hours of sleep, my stomach hurt. I couldn't be sure whether the soreness came from internal bruising, having been tossed around for hours on end, or from tension, having braced itself against losing its contents all night long. None of us lost our suppers, however, and both anchors held tight, all that long night.

By sunrise the weather had calmed enough to permit moving the boat. A more protected anchorage lay off Cayo Verde, further east. Pat tried turning the port engine over, but it kicked out after each try, clogged with diesel clumps. When he changed the fuel filter, however, the port engine agreed to perform. *Cool Breezes* battled the wind and waves, and its crew braved nausea once again, but by mid-afternoon the reward was tangible: a much calmer anchorage. We could study, cook, eat and play cards. The worst was over.

The next day was blessedly peaceful. For a change of pace at boat school, we played cards in *español,* and identified our Cayo Datton seashell treasures. In the afternoon, after sea baths, Pat hooked the bosun's chair to the mast and gave the kids rides. I sat in the cockpit, mending tears in our sailboat duvet covers. After a while, Ben joined me with his whittling, and Erin with her friendship bracelets, softly singing. Meara sat in the salon, creating a picture. Pat read a book. Liam reclined on the wrapped up mainsail, twirling his pencil. So tranquil and domestic was the scene that it conjured a vignette from *Little House on the Prairie*. Instead of a landscape, though, we beheld a seascape. Instead of rippling yellow wheat fields, we saw swelling blue water and whitecaps. How intriguing, I thought, that though the boundless prairie is usually compared to the ocean, we landlubbers find the reverse: the sea's expanse and undulation remind us of furrowing, folding fields of grain.

The similarity of seas of grain to seas of water went further.

"Big skies and vast horizons, that's another thing they have in common," I mused aloud. Ben and Erin looked up from their introspective work and thoughts. "Coming from Alberta, we're used to big skies. The flatness of our land gives us almost a full circle of horizon. Being surrounded on all sides with water is similar. You see great big sky and limitless horizon both at sea and on the prairie. It's good for the soul."

At the end of another day at anchor at Cayo Verde, the SSB weather report predicted a window of light winds for the next twelve hours. Since the next good anchorage was over sixty nautical miles away, Pat and I arose very early – at 3:00 a.m. – to get a head start before the winds built. We weighed anchor in the dark and quiet, and puttered away. The children nestled more deeply into their berths. I felt my mind lift to that surreal place of acute and suspended awareness. Just as I contemplated this might be one of those sails I'd never forget, something went bump in the night.

That something was our boat. And the bump was caused when our daggerboards – surfboard-shaped panels inserted vertically into deck slots to control sideways motion – hit an uncharted shoal of sand and coral. There is nothing like the sound of one's boat scraping on coral to set a sailor's teeth to grinding.

One by one, the children appeared in the cockpit.

"Mom, Dad, we're stuck!" each announced in turn.

By the fourth announcement, Pat snapped.

"Yes, we know! Now get back to bed!"

Pat raised the daggerboards and pushed the boat off the shoal while I stood at the helm, the engine engaged in reverse. The power of a second engine would have been very useful. Twenty minutes later, we pulled away from the shoal and continued eastward.

"Good to see you got yourself out of that scrape!" Ben called out from his berth.

"Yes," Pat bantered back, "we got off to a rocky start today, but it'll be smooth sailing from here on out."

He was mostly right. We sailed onward into a spectacular sunrise, and enjoyed light and pleasant winds all day. Another tense moment arose when the fuel delivery problem cropped up again in the port engine, and we were caught without power. After Pat changed the filter, and I pumped that rancid fuel line bulb one hundred and sixty times (I was counting), we got out of that tight spot, too. By sundown we'd covered sixty nautical miles. We anchored in Bahía de Manati, one of the deep pocket bays enroute to Puerto Vita. That's when, despite Pat's prediction, things got rocky again.

March 2001, sunrise on the Cuban cayos.

From: The Kirwin crew
To: Kith and Kin
Subject: **Greetings from *Cool Breezes*: Adversity**

Adversity strengthens character; hardship leads to self-discovery. These proverbial words of wisdom seem banal but ring true these last few days. In fact, as this latest chapter of our family's adventure unfolds, I find that old adage sings a constant refrain.

The last few days have been trying, for several reasons.

First, there's the weather, pivotal in every sailor's daily life. Lately ours is miserably wet and windy, the worst we've experienced in our seven months at sea.

Then there's the food, the centrepiece of every day on the water.

"I'm absolutely starved for 'normal' food!" Liam gripes when I send him to retrieve dried beans and rice from the bilge pantries. Our cupboard is far from barren, but our stores of brownie mixes and packaged pasta are depleted.

Next there are the mechanical breakdowns, inevitable for every sailor. Right now, *Cool Breezes* has problems in both engines. On the port side, bad diesel clogs the fuel line, especially in rough water. On the starboard side, the coupling between the engine and its transmission is worn away.

Social deprivation, stormy weather, near starvation, and engine troubles are not the worst of our tribulations. For Pat and me, the most disagreeable aspect of our recent travels is the Guarda Frontera. Cuba's over-zealous coast guard has prohibited us from visiting the last several alluring *cayos* we've approached.

It's sundown now on March 8. We anchor in a pond-like bay called Bahía de Manati. What a blessed relief it is – after twelve long hours beating against the wind and struggling with engine troubles – to strike the sails, lay the anchor and cut the whiny diesel engine! Even the kids appreciate stillness and solitude. There's no Guarda detachment here, judging from the long silence when Pat hails them by VHF. He and the boys dinghy Jasper to shore. The girls retreat to their pockets of space while dinner simmers.

The sun sets as I pass hot plates up to the salon from the galley. Pat pours two glasses of red wine. That's when we hear the deep bellyache of a large vessel approaching. Ben peers out the companionway into the dark.

"It's a Guarda Frontera gunboat!" he exclaims.

The crew crowds into the cockpit to watch the ancient yet imposing boat rumble toward us. Fifteen or twenty soldiers stand on deck, most of them shoeless, all in tattered clothing. Several yell. Some shake their fists. They don't like our spot in the anchorage.

"We no move!" Pat shouts above the engine's thrum. "Too dark! Not safe!" He motions to the expanse of dark and unfamiliar water.

In response, two of the officers hop into a wooden skiff and paddle to our stern. One of them clambers aboard. His hand-held radio goes off. After a lengthy radio conversation with a gruff-sounding commander, he inspects our staterooms and the jumbled collection of clothes, books, games and gear in our lockers. Little Meara clings to my side. The older three watch, their faces wary. We've heard of cruisers being boarded by the Guard Frontera, but never endured the experience.

Prompted by the brusque radio voice, the Guarda officer makes a triggering motion with his finger, and asks Pat if we have any *armas*. Pat thinks the fellow is referring to the VHF. Mimicking the thumb gesture used to operate the radio, he points to it.

"S*í, sí, armas!*" he nods agreeably.

The Guarda frowns, puzzled. I suddenly remember that *armas* means weapons.

"No *armas*, no *armas!*" I pipe up, pointing to the four children. "We have *cuatro niños!*"

The Guarda laughs out loud.

"Okay, okay, okay," he says in staccato.

Thanks to the presence aboard of our *cuatro niños*, he allows us to remain where we're anchored, provided we surrender our *despacho*. Without it we'll be immobilized. Somehow we communicate that we'll need our *despacho* by 6:00 a.m., when we plan to pull up anchor, bound for Puerto Vita on the northeast coast of Cuba. Somehow we come to understand the Guarda's promise to return it before dawn.

At 5:45 a.m., we make out the hazy outlines of a Guarda rowboat. The children are still asleep, but Pat is on deck, preparing the lines for departure, and I'm in the galley. A peach cobbler is baking, the yeast for our daily loaf of bread is soaking on the counter, and a pot of freshly brewed Cuban coffee is ready on the stove. When the young officer arrives at our stern, *despacho* in hand, we invite him aboard for a cup of *café americain*. A typical Cuban, he graciously accepts our hospitality. Despite our language barrier, we part with a shared sense of mutual goodwill.

Pat manoeuvres *Cool Breezes* out of the anchorage at Bahía de Manati and into the mainstream of Old Bahamas Channel.

"Oh no," he groans. "The swells are coming from the southeast, straight at our bows."

When the boat begins rearing like a bucking bronco, the rest of the crew stampede from their berths to the cockpit, the best place to avoid motion sickness. The heady and fruity aroma of baking peach cobbler and the earthy scent of blossoming yeast summon me down to the galley. The cobbler is ready to come out of the oven. Normally sweet, today it smells cloying. Our daily bread needs kneading. Usually redolent, the dough reeks of fermentation. My stomach lurches as I work. I nearly toss the iota of coffee I consumed at dawn. Measuring flour into a sliding bowl on a rollercoaster countertop and rescuing a pan of cobbler from sudden impalement may sound comical, but I'm not laughing.

"Peach cobbler, anyone?" I ask the crew weathering it out in the cockpit.

The kids nearly gag. No one can stomach a biteful of anything.

Soon the winds and waves build and, like the swells, rush headlong at our twin bows.

"We won't be able to reach Puerto Vita by nightfall in these conditions," Pat predicts. No more lovely little *cayos* lie in this part of the northern Cuban coastline behind which to anchor; we must seek shelter in the closest pocket bay, Puerto Padre. Against the wind and water, relying upon only one temperamental engine, we'll have to tack on a zigzag path the whole way there, steering clear of the coral reef bordering the shoreline.

Erin shows not just musical proclivity but also emotional maturity when she strikes up a singsong, beginning with Pat's favourite ballad, "Four Strong Winds." Meara sings along for a while, then collapses on the salon cushions. Jasper slinks off to her retreat, a refuge of dreaming

in the den-like space under the salon table. I take the helm
while Pat trims the sails.

Taking the wheel of a boat in rough seas works wonders to restore equilibrium. Feeling physically stronger, I
take stock of my present circumstances. What a transformation! I marvel that someone like me finds herself in a
place like this. Prairie-born, a landlubber prone to motion
sickness, a lawyer trained to be risk adverse, and an over-
protective mother, I'm not the average sailor. As a child,
the product of a secure but homogenous small town
upbringing, I'd write adventures rather than live them.
Now here I am, steering a small vessel containing my nearest and dearest, in high winds and on high seas, off the
coast of a foreign country. But my smug self-appraisal is
premature.

"Things are getting a little more 'adventurous' than I'd
like!" observes Liam, when the port engine kicks out. The
fuel line is plugged again. The only way to get the engine
going is to pump that rancid fuel line bulb. Captain Pat
dispatches me to the engine compartment to squeeze the
bulb.

"At least a hundred pumps!" he yells down to me. I
emerge from the engine locker ready to retch. Luckily, my
stomach is still empty.

The engine chokes a half-dozen times. Each time I
pump the bulb, Pat holds the helm under sail alone.
Whenever the engine re-engages, we quickly tack. Pat turns
the wheel sharply as the kids and I loosen one line to the jib
and rein in the other, pulling the sail across the bows of the
boat. If we don't work quickly enough, the jib flaps wildly,
leaving a morass of cloth and rope for Pat to disentangle.

This happens more than once. I take over the helm –
holding my course as steadily as any old sea salt – and
watch my man, the father of my four children, manoeuvre

his way along the deck to the trampoline of our catamaran. Poised against the heavy winds, amidst swells and waves that by then have grown over eight feet tall, Pat unsnarls the jib and lines. Each time it happens, time and I hold our taut breath.

"Please God," I beg. "Anything, anything, just please keep him safe."

Meara wakens and crawls into my lap. Whenever the port engine dies, she trots off, unbidden and uncomplaining, to the salon, while I descend yet again to pump the fuel line. Tromping down the steps to that stinky dungeon, I feel close to tears, yet lack the luxury to indulge in them. A weepy mother would be worse than engine trouble. Get a grip, I tell myself. After all, this isn't a hurricane, a shipwreck, or a shark attack, the calamities Mary and Eldean fear will befall us. Nonetheless, I feel much less the capable, venturesome woman I so recently imagined myself, and much more the original small child within: humble and seasick.

By mid-afternoon, *Cool Breezes* reaches the long channel leading to Puerto Padre. Our zigzag path measures forty nautical miles, yet in over seven arduous hours, we've reached a distance only eighteen miles away. Conditions are much calmer in the protected waterway.

For the first time since the morning, I remember my unbaked bread dough, and descend to the galley. A culinary disaster awaits me. The dough overflows the bowl. The rest of the galley is in a state of upheaval, having heaved for hours upon the waves.

Almost an hour later, I emerge into the cockpit. The scenery is dramatically changed. At the end of the channel stands an immense commercial pier, about six feet higher than the deck of our boat. A huge freighter is docked there, and a gigantic crane loads bags of sugar onto it. As soon as

we tie up – our docklines like strings beside the tree-trunk
lines of the freighter – four officials leap down to our deck.
They include a veterinarian, an immigration officer, a doctor, and of course, a Guarda Frontera soldier. They inspect
our papers, which are in good order, and our boat, which
certainly isn't. We tell the Guarda we'll rest overnight, and
leave at sunrise tomorrow.

The Guarda soldier points to where we must anchor.

"Could we please anchor there instead?" Pat asks, indi-
cating an area upwind from the spewing smokestack of the
nearby sugar factory.

"Not possible," comes the brusque reply.

"Could we get some fresh water?"

"Not possible."

"Could we please bring our dog ashore for a
moment?"

"Not possible."

Incredulous, exhausted, immensely sympathetic to
Jasper's plight, we limp off to the appointed spot and drop
anchor.

"It's too bad our travels in Cuba have to end on such
a sour note," Pat remarks, surveying the dreary environs.
"If the Cuban government is so keen to promote tourism,
it should call off the Guarda Frontera."

We gather in the cockpit. Pat pours sundowners. We're
finally off duty. Sitting beside the husband I felt I could
have lost today, I finally let go my bravado. A single hot
tear escapes the corner of my eye.

"Why are you crying, Mommy?" Meara asks, brushing
the wet from my cheek.

"Just a tear of joy," I explain, snuggling her closer.

"You know, some adventures are better left in story
books," says Liam, shaking his head. His observation
about books triggers my recollection that the children and

I haven't yet begun boat school. We deserve an easy day, I rationalize, perfect for a novel study. We discuss Johanna Spyri's *Heidi*.

Meanwhile, Pat conceives and executes the brilliant idea of exchanging the two engines' fuel delivery systems. That way, the starboard engine with its transmission breakdown also has the fickle fuel delivery problem. In theory at least, the port engine can operate problem-free.

Erin and Ben make supper by throwing together a few things: things like a can of chili, a can opener, and a pot! Not one child complains when Pat and I announce a very early bedtime.

That was yesterday. Today, Pat and I rise before first light. 'Tis no idyllic golden morning in the Cuban *cayos*! Acrid fumes hang in the air. A greasy film of sulphur coats the decks and glass of our boat. Yet bolstered by sleep, our spirits are high. The gloom does nothing but motivate us to reach Puerto Vita by sundown.

I listen to the early morning weather report on the SSB.

"The weather gods are with us today!" I shout to Pat. He's on the foredecks, pulling up the anchor. The sun rises.

Our journey is a breeze. Fresh winds face our bows, but the seas follow at our stern. We eat lunch in the sunshine, watching the topography change before our eyes. *Mogotes* rise where scrubby lowlands once lay. Stands of palms spring up to replace the interminable miles of mangroves. The shoreline no longer threatens, but beckons.

Best of all, to me at least, the port engine fuel line remains clog-free all day.

"Oh, joy!" the older three exclaim in ironic voices, as I expound on this blessing. I'm thrilled that Pat's brilliant idea works.

The lighthouse at the Puerto Vita entrance appears mid-afternoon, luring us like a siren's call. From there we follow a winding channel. Lush vegetation springs from craggy rocks fringing the shore. The waterway is laced with blond beaches and framed by knobby blue hills.

A voice hails us by VHF.

"Welcome to our beautiful little paradise," we hear. "May you have a beautiful time!"

We stare at each other, startled. The contrast between this day's reception and those of the last several days is astonishing.

Round the bend we find a brand new marina, its white stucco walls and red roof tiles dappling the green hillside. Our boat glides into port on glassy water. We are awed.

Sitting at my laptop late at night with my candle and my wine, I realize adversity not only strengthens and reveals the fibre of character, it also bolsters the thread of a story.

Till next time then, God bless, fair winds, and *adiós!*

Love PJ+crew

March 2001, Puerto Vita, Cuba.
"Welcome to our little paradise!"

Chapter 21
Plenty

*If we had no winter, the spring would not be so
pleasant; if we did not sometimes taste of adversity,
prosperity would not be so welcome.*
 – Anne Bradstreet

E verything we needed – companionship, better
weather, fresh food and mechanical expertise – we
found in the lovely village and marina of Puerto
Vita.

Shortly after sending its warm (if startling) VHF greeting, the marina staff dispatched a small guide boat to escort
us into the marina. The pilot then helped tie our bow to
two mooring balls. Two dockhands waited on the pier to
wrap our stern lines to the dock cleats. Even Captain Pat,
who loved to show off his young crew's excellent docking
skills, was grateful that day for the expert assistance.

The moment we were snugged up, the usual team of
officials came aboard to inspect our papers and boat. The
doctor, veterinarian and immigration officer seemed satisfied, and soon left. The two Guarda soldiers were not
pleased, however, when we indicated we'd anchored
overnight in the harbour at Puerto Padre. Although our
current *despacho* listed Puerto Vita as our ultimate destination, and we hadn't set foot on land at Puerto Padre, they
said we should have received a new *despacho* when we were

285

there. That we hadn't properly cleared out was a huge problem for them, causing no end of headaches and paperwork. As if to retaliate, they subjected our boat to an exhaustive search, turning our cubbyholes and lockers inside out.

"I feel mortified," I confided to Pat as the two officers pawed their way through bags of dirty laundry. "We're not exactly showing our sunny side up."

The boat was a disaster. Jasper's coarse red hairs lay everywhere. Seawater had leaked through the hatches during our adventures in the high seas the day before, and our duvet covers were wet. Salt spray encrusted our greasy portholes. Metal trim had begun to rust. The teak floors were sprinkled with sand and salt, the nav station and countertops strewn with clutter. After more than two weeks of anchoring out with seven bodies aboard, our small boat was not shipshape. We lacked not only access to hoses and plentiful fresh water, but also sheer manoeuvring room in order to do a proper clean-up.

Despite the disarray, our top priority once we were finally cleared in was a freshwater shower. What a morale booster that proved to be! The water felt warm and soft on my weather-beaten hide. The bathhouses were clean and bright. The marina also boasted hook-ups for one hundred and ten volt electricity and water, a ship's chandlery and food store, an open-air restaurant at the top of the hill, a thatched roof lounge with a cool tile floor, blossoming flower beds, a diesel fuel dock, and even a mechanic on duty. The welcoming voice on the VHF was right: we had indeed arrived in a little paradise.

By the time we finished our showers and tour of the marina, our stomachs touched our backbones.

"Let's try out the food in the marina restaurant," Erin suggested. I smiled to myself; Erin had noted that the crew of a nearby boat included children, one of them a young girl about her own age, and she hoped to encounter them. We did see that family, but only in passing. The crew of *L'Alouette* was leaving just as we arrived. Both families were racing toward their respective destinations to avoid a sudden deluge, and crossed paths on the stairway from the docks to the hilltop restaurant.

"Hello there!" I called out.

"*Bonsoir!*" they replied.

"*Des Québécois!*" I remarked to Erin. I was pleased; our boat school lessons *en français* had become instantly practical.

The next morning, the sun shone with golden brilliance. Yet to me, the light seemed harsh, revealing the flotsam and jetsam of our life aboard. Instead of revelling in the verdant hills, glistening with dewdrops, and the flight of a shockingly white flock of birds across pavonine water, I couldn't see past the mountain of chores to be done. In addition to yesterday's boat-keeping challenges, we must also contend with damp towels from our showers, wet clothes from the previous evening's downpour, and dew-covered salon cushions from forgetting to close the hatch at night. So what did I do first? I grabbed the dog's leash and fled!

Jasper leaped when she saw the leash; because we'd anchored out each night, we hadn't gone running for more than two weeks. We jogged past the bemused guards at the marina security gate and into the lanes of the humble hamlet of Vita. A whole other world was butted up to our little marina paradise. The streets were brown and dusty, but Vita was teeming with life. The villagers were awake, visiting their neighbours.

"*¡Hola!*" they called out, waving as we ran by. Animals abounded: pigs, roosters and chickens, turkeys, oxen, and horses lined the road on which we ran.

Mainly, though, Jasper and I took note of the dogs. The road was over-run with them. That children's classic, *Go Dogs Go*, sprang to mind. Unlike the storyline of my girlhood favourite, however, this was no dog party. There were no big dogs, just little dogs; there were no blue, yellow or black dogs, only brown mongrel dogs. Each barked incessantly, following us to its own territorial limit, where the next dog took over. I was determined to remain undaunted by these small strays, but when a German shepherd loped toward us, I succumbed to intimidation. Jasper and I turned back to the marina. Running in Varadero, a tourist town, created a scene. Running in Vita caused a village uproar!

When Jasper and I returned, the rest of the crew was awake. Pat was hanging wet bedding and towels on long lines strung across the deck. Wet cushions and mattresses were propped up to dry. The children swept and swabbed.

"Here's some coffee for you, Mom!" Ben said, producing a steaming cup.

"And Daddy says if we finish all our work we can eat breakfast at the restaurant!" Meara piped up.

But Pat had the best news of all.

"I was just talking to Bernadine, the marina's public relations person," Pat said. "She says there's a lady in the village who takes in laundry!"

Back to the village I went, accompanied by Erin, both of us burdened with sailbags full of wet and soiled garments, towels and sheets. Just a few steps from the marina gates, we found Alba's modest home. A short, brown woman with wavy black hair, she greeted us with a gap-toothed smile and a kiss on each cheek. Pablo, her impish-looking white-haired husband, hobbled to the door on his cane and clasped us warmly.

"*Buen' dia'!*" said Alba.

"Come in, come in," added Pablo in English.

The laundry business was clearly not only a commercial venture but also a fine social opportunity for this middle-aged couple. They insisted we take a seat in their living room and become acquainted. When we said we were Canadian, they were delighted. Pablo announced proudly that as a former seaman with the Cuban merchant marine, he had visited Toronto, Montreal and Halifax, where he learned to speak English. Erin's news that her relatives lived near Halifax prompted Pablo to limp away to fetch a black-and-white photo of his younger self in a sailor's uniform, standing on a Halifax dock before a huge freighter.

When she saw how enthusiastically Erin and I admired Pablo's photo, Alba ran off to get some of her own. She returned with an array of framed photos of their daughters and grandchildren, who lived in Holguin, an inland city near Vita. While Alba proudly passed the photos around, Pablo described each family member in turn.

"Well, my husband and kids are waiting for us to eat breakfast," I said at last, intimating we should deal with the business at hand. I was especially glad I'd refrained from adding we would be dining at a restaurant when Pablo explained why Alba took in laundry.

"Without the extra money from laundry we'd have to live off our ration booklet plus my retired seaman's pension," he said, "And that's only five dollars a month."

"Oh my," I said. "What do you charge for laundry?"

"Anything you like to pay is fine with us," Pablo told us.

"Come, come," Alba gestured, and led us to their fenced backyard where, in addition to a goat and some chickens, there were several long clotheslines. Pablo pointed to a large wooden barrel standing close to the house. Attached to its exterior was a small motor.

"There is our washing machine," he said, and added with obvious pride, "I made it myself."

I glanced at Erin. Her face mirrored what I felt: utter amazement at the cheerful resourcefulness and pride of this modest couple.

"The sun is shining today, so your laundry will be ready this afternoon," said Pablo.

"*Gracias,*" I said. By then I'd have the chance to ask Bernadine what to pay Alba.

When Erin and I returned to the boat, we found Pat standing waist-deep in the starboard engine locker, showing the marina mechanic the stripped transmission.

"The kids are hungry, so go on ahead without me, " he said. A half-hour later, he joined us at the thatch-covered restaurant and delivered the verdict.

"The bad news is Manuel can't fix the gear shaft," Pat reported. "The good news is he knows someone in town who can manufacture a new part. And Manuel can install it at a rate of only nine dollars an hour!"

By then it was mid-morning and the sun was sweltering.

"Let's do boat school in the marina lounge," I suggested to the kids. We trooped up the couple dozen steps with our backpacks, and settled into two comfortable couches under the thatched roof. Jasper lay on the tiled floor beside us. The fresh breeze admitted by its open plan made the lounge far cooler than the boat. Its only drawback, at least from the teacher's viewpoint, was that it was so public. As usual, our arrival at the marina complete with four children and a red dog caused a stir. Everyone wanted to meet us, and there we sat, apparently just waiting to be met.

As we packed our backpacks to leave at 1:00 p.m., the French-Canadian family stopped by our makeshift classroom. Jeanne, a sprightly woman with short dark curls and excellent English, introduced her tall blond husband Laurent, thirteen-year-old Louise and ten-year-old Christophe.

"Would you kids like to get together for games after lunch?" she asked.

Lunch aboard *Cool Breezes* that day was the most quickly assembled and consumed meal ever. While the assigned crewmembers did dishes, the remaining two gathered board games. Everyone was ready when Louise and Christophe knocked on the hull. The six kids raced up the steps to the open-air restaurant, armloads of boxed games jostling all the way.

I can't be sure how Jeanne and Laurent passed the afternoon without children on board, but Pat and I couldn't have been less romantic. Pat pulled apart the engine compartments and puttered about on deck, surrounded by grease and rags. I could procrastinate no longer; no excuse remained; the interior would have to be cleaned. Determined to accomplish as much boat keeping as possible while the cabins were empty, I shooed Jasper outside, changed into my grubbiest gear and set to work. The protected bay in which our boat was docked was extremely still and as the afternoon progressed, the air below decks became increasingly hot. The sweat on my brow slid into my eyes.

"I'm heading up to the bathhouse," I shouted to Pat. Freshly showered and dressed, I checked on the crew at the restaurant. Juan, the waiter, had allowed the youngsters to sit at a table and play games all afternoon. He'd even served them bowls of creamy vanilla *helado*. The six kids were into to their fourth game by then, and everyone was still laughing. Meara, too young to play most of the games, had teamed up with Erin. Our children's *français* was not sophisticated, and Christophe's English nearly non-existent, but Louise spoke English fluently and acted as interpreter. A slim and lovely girl with curly brown hair and large blue eyes, Louise was an English immersion student in her native Montréal. It was easy to see she and Erin liked each other.

When I asked for Bernadine at the marina office, I met a tall shapely woman with boundless black legs and a knock-out smile. Bernadine could have been a fashion model, but she was far more than just a pretty face. Her laughter and charm were infectious, her wit obvious. The eyes of every male passerby devoured her every movement. Even shorter and less well-endowed females like me were charmed.

I asked Bernadine what to pay Alba.

"Ask how many loads she washed," she advised. "The going rate is ten dollars a load."

I tried to visualize the size of the wooden barrel washer, and to estimate the number of loads our sailbag contents would consume. There must be two or three, I calculated, walking toward Alba's house. When I arrived, Alba gestured to our fresh laundry, displayed in careful piles on the kitchen table, and invited me to inspect her work. After I expressed my admiration, Alba carefully placed each stack of garments into our big blue sailbag. Pablo held the bag open for her, then closed the drawstring and passed it to me as if it were a work of art. A month ago in Varadero, I'd balked at paying US$18 for laundry service, yet found it was a pleasure to give this resourceful and smiling couple three American ten-dollar bills.

Meanwhile, the duvet covers had dried and the mattresses aired. I reassembled the beds, tucked clean and neatly folded clothes into our cubbyholes, and made salads for supper. The cabin of *Cool Breezes* looked and smelled fresh and liveable at last. So rare and fleeting was this moment, I couldn't help but savour it.

After breakfast the next morning, the kids and I packed our school bags. It was sunny and hot already, well over thirty degrees Celsius. Once the morning mosquito infestation passed, we ascended the steep steps from the docks to the lounge to study. As we pulled out our papers and pencils, Juan the waiter beckoned us from the restaurant.

"Come sit at our tables!" he called.

"Really? May we?" I asked.

"*Sí, sí, señora,*" Juan smiled, his arms spread wide. "There is no one here till lunch. And perhaps the *maestra* would like an *espresso?*"

The *maestra*, I thought, I like that. And the *espresso*, how civilized. "*Gracias,*" I replied.

The kids pulled two square tables together at the edge of the covered room. There we could look over the lush hillside to the blue water, feel the cool breeze, and spread out not only our books but also our minds. It was such a delight to teach and learn there that we adopted it as our new classroom.

After lunch Bernadine came by wearing a mini-skirt and high-heeled shoes.

"You've got your crew hard at work, I see," she smiled. Captain Pat had coerced the entire crew into a thorough scrubbing and polishing of the decks. The spinnaker was raised to air out in the hot sun. Its rainbow colours barely fluttered in the sultry air. The sky was drenched in blue, the water mirror-like. "Manuel tells me his machinist friend isn't equipped to manufacture a new engine part for you," Bernadine went on. "But I know someone in Holguin who can certainly do it. I already phoned him for you. You need to rent a car and drive the part to him, though."

"*No problema,*" Pat grinned. He happily trotted up the steps behind Bernadine to make car rental arrangements.

In the meantime, the kids and I walked to the village

to visit Alba and Pablo. They wanted to meet all four children. We brought a bundle of small toys, outgrown clothing and new soap and toiletries for them and their grandchildren. Alba was clearly touched.

"*Gracias*," she said simply.

"The *niños* will love everything," Pablo added.

Alba ran to the kitchen and returned with a steaming little pot.

"For you," she said.

I opened the lid to smell a delicious concoction of seasoned beans and vegetables.

"*Gracias*," I said. This was becoming an indispensable word.

At sunset that evening, our freshly groomed family strolled to Vita to dine at a *paladero* recommended by Bernadine. Dora and her husband Aldo greeted us at the door.

"*Entre*," Aldo gestured. We followed him through the house's labyrinth of rooms, past the kitchen where Dora's sister stirred pots at the stove, to the backyard. There, overlooking a small inlet, a long table was set, complete with a floral tablecloth and candles in wine bottles. The thatched palm roof that sheltered the table was hung with colourful beer cans cut in zigzag shapes. The evening air was still and warm.

The moment we were seated, the food began to arrive. Dora and her sister served grilled red snapper, *camarónes* in a savoury sauce, *arroz con gris,* cucumber and tomato salads, and fried plantain. Their faces beamed with pride, and for good reason. Our hosts waited inside while we ate, but as soon as the *espresso* was served, the whole family pulled up chairs to join us, even the wizened old grandma, for a chat translated by Dora's cousin.

Back at the boat, we heard a knock on the hull. We

peered out the companionway to see Louise and Laurent standing on the dock.

"Hello there," Pat called out. "Come aboard!"

"*Merci*," Laurent replied. "Louise has been waiting all day to see Erin. Perhaps the girls could have a little visit now?"

"*Bien sûr que oui!*" I replied. The girls disappeared into Erin's miniature stateroom, now festooned with origami mobiles and watercolour paintings of seashells, dolphins, mermaids and rainbows. Erin lay on the bed while Louise sat on the fridge unit. Chatter and giggles wafted up to the salon, where Laurent joined Pat and me for *cubalibres*.

"Tell us," I said. "How long have you been cruising, and where have you been?"

Laurent was pleased to share his story. Like our family, his was taking a one-year sabbatical. Like us, they'd pulled up roots the summer of 2000 to spend a year cruising with their school-age children. They too had packed their belongings, rented their home, and lived with relatives for a few months before leaving. I felt amazed that thousands of miles away from us, another Canadian family had been living the same experience at the same time.

"I wish we'd known each other back then!" I said.

After Laurent and Louise left, Pat and I sat outside in the cockpit. Pat hankered for a cigar, and I for the open sky. Even the stars are abundant here, I thought.

"It was only two days ago that we arrived here in Vita," I mused aloud. "Isn't it incredible how much our life has improved since we got here?"

It was a moment of contentment, of feeling that life brims over with good things. How fitting then, that *vita* is the Latinate root for life.

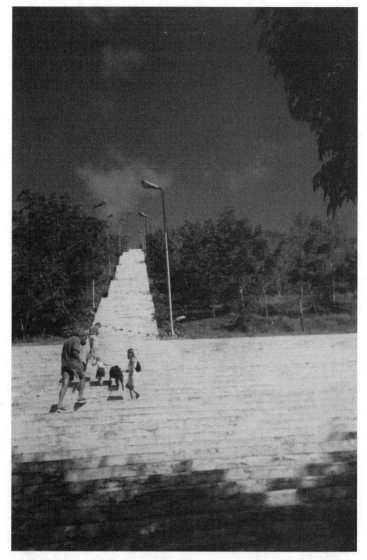

March 2001, Holguin, Cuba. Climbing the three hundred and ninety nine steps of La Loma de la Cruz.

From: The Kirwin crew
To: Kith and Kin
Subject: **Greetings from** *Cool Breezes*: **A Road
                Trip**

It's still and warm in Vita, Cuba, this brilliant early morning of March 13. The humid wind lies down. Except for
the drone of mosquitoes, the breathless air is hushed. The
teal blue water is an undulating mirror. The scent of fuchsia and bougainvillea is light and bright.

The new day is fresh, yet laden with expectation.
The blossoms will soon drip with cloying sweetness. Heat
and moisture will saturate the air. The flirtatious wink of
reflected light on water suggests ripples soon to come, and
the thin paper rustle of stirring palm fronds hints of brisk
winds to follow. The sharp cry of a distant bird punctuates
the stillness, heralding the day's cacophony. The day will
unfold, inevitably, into sweltering fullness.

Pat and the kids sprawl on their berths, their bed-
clothes kicked aside, resting up for today's road trip. When
they waken, time will likewise ripen for us.

Our rented Peugeot 206 subcompact is delivered to
the marina at noon. We pack a beach bag and head out on
a day trip to Guardalavaca, a small resort town down the
road.

The black five-seater is too small for six people and a
dog, yet renting anything bigger, let alone the minivan we
need, is next to impossible outside Havana. The four children press themselves into the back seat, Meara on Erin's
lap. Pat takes the driver's seat. Jasper curls up at my feet on
the front passenger side. To shut the door, I tuck in her tail.

"The name Guardalavaca means 'watch the cow'," I read aloud from my guidebook.

The children squirm with excitement as our car turns off the dusty village lane onto the main highway. The countryside's beauty enchants us. We drive past lime-green cane fields, flanked by the periwinkle ranges of the Sierra del Cristal and the Sierra de Nipe. An occasional nickel or cobalt quarry blots the landscape, but then, as if to compensate, a roadside stand of vibrant hibiscus waves in the wind.

Soon we turn onto the lane leading to the beach town. Guardalavaca and Varadero are both tourist resorts, but Guardalavaca is quainter. The amenities are fewer, but so are the tourists. There are significantly fewer hotels and *tiendas,* and many more Cubans. It's the broad beach at Guardalavaca that we find so much more inviting than its Varadero counterpart. A cobbled stone walkway winds its picturesque way around the shade trees growing straight up from the sugar-white sand. Easy-going vendors offer grilled Cuban sandwiches and *cerveza* in the shade of *ranchitos,* or thatched huts. The turquoise water, sheltered in the small horseshoe inlet, beckons snorkelling children.

"Even though it's easier to fly to Varadero, I'd pick Guardalavaca any day," Pat says.

"Yeah, but there are no cows to watch," Meara complains.

That was yesterday. Today, March 14, we drive to Holguin, the fourth largest Cuban *ciudad.* We plan to meet Bernadine at a public park there, so she can direct us to the machine shop that can make new parts for our broken transmission. Since *Cool Breezes* will be out of commission for a few days, we'll drive onwards from Holguin to

Santiago de Cuba. I plan to pack the laptop so I can continue on location from Santiago de Cuba tonight.

The one-hour drive to Holguin is a social studies field trip. Hundreds of workers march along the palm-lined highway towards the city, sticking out their thumbs. Every hitchhiker finds a ride. Thanks to an excellent map, we readily find Parque Calixto Garcia and the beautiful Bernadine.

"Jump in the front," I say, hopping out and climbing into the back seat with the kids. "Liam can sit on my knee."

Until that moment I doubted the car could hold another passenger, but Bernadine doesn't pause for a second, even as she folds her long legs around Jasper. She leads us through a maze of streets to the machine shop we'd never have found on our own, and translates Pat's explanation of the necessary repairs to the machinist.

Pat emerges from the shop with a huge grin.

"We're in exactly the right place on this planet for machining transmission parts," he says.

Holguin is an industrial centre of ingenuity in a country known for resourcefulness. The need to invent began after the 1959 *Revolución*, when scores of engineers, scientists and other technical professionals fled the country, and the United States imposed its embargo. That's when Che Guevara exhorted Cubans, "Workers, build your own machinery." The broad Cuban concept *inventar* – to do something new or different to survive – became even more critical when the Soviet Union collapsed in the early 1990s. Cubans are accustomed to re-using many machine parts that would be considered disposable in other countries. They throw away very little. Cuba's economic isolation, the mother of its inventiveness, certainly works to our advantage today.

A short drive later, we arrive at the base of La Loma de la Cruz, a large hill in the middle of a residential neighbourhood. From the street, three hundred and ninety-nine steps lead to a large cross that has stood at the hilltop since 1790. Even Meara makes it to the top! As we rest mid-climb at one of the regularly spaced benches, a trio of friendly boys joins us.

"We like to practice our Ingleesh, *por favor*," they say. Pat and Ben enjoy their lively company, and reward each of them with a loonie once they reach the summit. From there we can see the streets of Holguin spread out like the spokes of a wheel. Lumpy green *mogotes* surround the city. They resemble the hoodoos of the Alberta badlands, except that Cuba's limestone hills are covered with vegetation.

Back in the car, the air-conditioning turned up full blast, we set out for the second largest Cuban city, Santiago de Cuba, named for St. James. Despite the absence of consistent or clear road signs, we drive steadily southeast towards it. Then we somehow turn onto a more treacherous secondary route, nothing more than a laneway of gravel and hunks of broken concrete. More than once I yelp, certain we've just taken out the underside of our little car on a concrete shard. Each time I squeal, Pat glares. The kids grow cranky. They want water and washrooms. Those few hours on that *paso malo* are tense.

Soon the road gradually dwindles to become the only dirt lane running through a small hamlet. Every villager turns in surprise to watch us barrel through. They point, shaking with laughter. Not until the road approaches a bridge do we realize the reason. Pat slams on the brakes. Half the bridge deck has fallen into the water.

"Now this is what they call a dead end," Ben quips.

We sheepishly turn back. A villager directs us to the new six-lane *autopista*. Two hours later, we breeze into Santiago. The city is set in a lush bowl of green valley, surrounded by the soaring Sierra Maestra. It's easy to find Avenida Manduley, where our hotel is located, in the middle of a leafy residential area called Vista Alegre. Before the *Revolución*, the nouveau riche lived there in their art nouveau mansions, many of which are now converted into schools, restaurants and other public buildings. Our hotel is actually a *protocolo*, a collection of bungalows each with its own patio and backyard. Though forty years old, the *protocolo* is well kept, features a swimming pool and restaurant, and allows dogs. Jasper bounds from the car and sniffs around the shady yard, her tail wagging.

We unload our luggage, tie our dog to a tree beside a bowl of water, and squeeze into the car for another drive. We weave our way along the stifling hot and serpentine streets of the ancient city to its outskirts, drive fourteen kilometres south, and arrive at Castillo Morro.

This centuries-old limestone castle towers majestically at the edge of cliffs overlooking Santiago Bay. Castle construction first began in 1640, but re-construction became necessary later that century after the infamous English pirate Henry Morgan reduced the structure to rubble. Liam is impressed.

"The castle we saw in Havana is nothing compared to this!"

We cross the long drawbridge, inlaid with multi-coloured tiles, spanning a deep but waterless moat. From there we explore a maze of passageways, myriad lookout towers, and rows of prisoners' cells. At the end of a hallway, lined with a predictable and extensive collection of cannons and cannonballs, we find a chapel. There we sit in the original pews, gazing at a large wooden statue of

Jesus standing beneath a peacock blue ceiling. The juxta-
position of war in the hallway and peace in the chapel is
striking. The most compelling vista at the Castillo is from
what is called the queen's balcony. There, from a vertigi-
nous height, the spectacle of crashing waves below is
thrilling. I imagine how the castle must look from
Santiago Bay, thrusting skyward from its precarious perch
atop the cliff.

To end our tour, we visit the piracy museum, a collection of maps, wall murals, scale models, and weaponry
housed in glass cases. It's no surprise, after our visit to the
Varadero junior high school, to note that American
affronts to Cuba are presented as examples of contemporary piracy. The kids particularly enjoy looking at the scale
model of the castle itself. How we love to see the depiction
of something – whether in the form of literature, music,
or art – once we've experienced it personally!

Now, as I tap away, we're resting in our air-conditioned rooms after dinner at the *protocolo* restaurant. It's
blessedly cool. But also late. Lights out for this faithful
scribe.

It's March 15. We miss the gentle bob of the boat as
we slumber, but waken well rested in our air-conditioned
rooms. Lying beneath blankets and breathing cool air
seems to have induced sound sleep for everyone.

Nestled in a circle of wind-breaking mountains, the city
of Santiago swelters by day. Recalling yesterday's withering
heat, we decide to spend the morning at the *protocolo* pool.
We hike up the shady path to the outdoor pool, an enchanting oasis surrounded by tables, chairs, and gently swaying
palms. We've got the place to ourselves.

"Cannonball!" Liam shouts. We all plunge in.

Pat and I emerge dripping from the pool, and reach for our towels. A bow-tied waiter approaches.

"Would you care for a *cappuccino?*" he asks.

"*Sí, gracias,*" we eagerly reply. Pat and I grin at each other. Reclining in lounge chairs reading novels, sipping *café* served poolside, and watching our children swim and laugh and play cards, is a rare pleasure. We'd stay all day, except that checkout time is noon, and we have a whole city to explore!

First on our list of sights to see is the city centre, Plaza Cespedes. We park our car about a block away, engage a young *jinitero* to guard it, and amble in the mid-day heat. The plaza is small but urbane, well maintained and picturesque. Gas lamps, ornate railings and tall shade trees line the sidewalks. The pale yellow cathedral Santa Ifigenia Basilica Metropolitana dominates the colonial square. Its interior is cool and elaborate. Across from the cathedral stands the splendid Hotel Casa Grande, the chic place to stay in Santiago. On the first-floor veranda, beneath red and white awnings, tourists rub elbows with the city's bourgeoisie, sipping rum, puffing at fat Bolivars, and watching the crowds. Another important edifice on this plaza is La Casa de Don Diego Velasquez, the home of Cuba's first colonizer. This sombre mansion, said to be the oldest house in Cuba, was built in 1516.

When we return to the car, we find a young man lathering and scrubbing it.

"I hadn't noticed our car was especially dirty," Pat laughs, handing another American dollar bill to this second *jinitero.*

"We paid one guy to watch our car, and another guy to wash it!" Ben quips.

Our young crew is famished. We search for a restaurant with an outdoor patio where we can tie up Jasper. Disappointed in that exact mission but undefeated in our quest for food, we buy *pan jamón* – ham sandwiches – and cold drinks at a deli, and sit down to eat on park benches at the shady Plaza Marti. There we watch a less cosmopolitan Cuban world go by. Besides the ubiquitous pairs of kissing lovers, we see a cluster of Cubans reading what appears to be a bus schedule, as well as a daily newspaper, hung from strings in the trees.

Enroute to the car, I find a bakery. Waiting in the queue to buy bread, I note that everyone presents ration tickets instead of cash. I wonder whether the bakery clerk will take my money. I've worried in vain; cash is always accepted. For dessert, we sample world-famous Coppellia *helado*. Since the fridge aboard *Cool Breezes* isn't cold enough to keep ice cream, we always yearn for it. This brand tastes especially smooth, sweet and rich.

Santiago offers much more to see, but we must leave by late afternoon if we hope to drive in daylight. On the outskirts of the city, we pass the Plaza de la Revolución, where a stunning monument to the brilliant general and strategist Antonio Maceo stands. An immense bronze statue of his likeness, astride a rearing horse, faces soaring crystalline spikes. Then the city vanishes like a mirage.

Beyond the bold and jagged Sierra Maestra, the flat Cuban countryside resumes. At one point, fields of green cane give way to waves of golden grain.

"We could be driving from Edmonton to Calgary!" says Pat.

At 7:00 p.m. we're back on board. The night is not yet over, though! Taped to the companionway door is a note from Louise: "Come to Dora's *paladero* to celebrate Christophe's tenth birthday!"

Pat digs up a bottle of red wine, I find an extra souvenir Che Guevara hat, and the kids scribble a hasty birthday card with greetings in three languages: English, *français,* and *español.* Ten minutes later we arrive at the party. The traditional birthday feast of roast pig is finished, but we're in time for cake. Erin and Louise gab all evening. Meara and the boys play cards with Christophe. The women trade stories of recent road trips, and the men visit Aldo's neighbour who claims to sell authentic Cohibas. Pat returns with an impressive glass and wood case, a nauseating supply of slim cigars, and a big grin.

In fact, as I wrap up this email late in the evening, Pat is sitting in the cockpit, grinning at the constellations through wafts of pungent smoke. The children have collapsed on their berths. The hot and humid wind reclines once again. The water slumbers. Life is, for the moment, still, and good.

God bless and fair winds, *amigos,*

Love PJ+crew

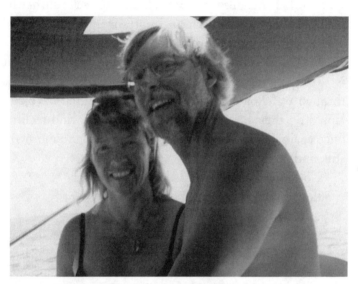

*March 2001. Feeling (and looking) like old salts
in our last days cruising the Cuban cayos.*

Chapter 22
Farewell to Cuba

Welcome ever smiles, and farewell goes out sighing.
  – William Shakespeare, Troilus and Cressida

Someone once asked Pat and me to name the place, of all those we'd experienced on our boat trip, to which we'd first return. In unison we answered, "Cuba."

Cuba was the first truly foreign country we'd travelled as a family, our first authentic ethnic journey. The country is physically beautiful, the nation culturally rich. Cubans are materially poor but spiritually generous. During our two short months there, we lived a lot of life and a breadth of emotions, ranging from excitement to boredom, fear to exhilaration, anger to joy. Cuba's geography and history may be captivating, but for us its most compelling national treasure was its people.

How ironic, then, to recall that by the end of March, we were eager to leave. As soon as the re-machined transmission parts were installed into our starboard engine, we'd jump off to the Bahamas, where new cultural experiences and social horizons lay.

The morning after our return from Santiago de Cuba, Bernadine stopped by our boat with a report from the Holguin machinist.

"Your transmission parts are ready. If you still have your rental car, I could drive with you to Holguin to get them," she offered.

"Our rental car isn't due back till five o'clock today, so this could work," Pat replied.

"You could drop me and the kids at Guardalavaca, pick up Bernadine at the marina, and drive to Holguin and back with her," I proposed, "then join us at the beach."

"Can Louise and Christophe come too?" Erin begged. She knew their company would bump up the number of passengers to eight, plus a dog, in a five-seater subcompact.

"Why not?" Pat replied. "When in Cuba, drive like the Cubans do."

Erin, Ben and Louise sat in the back seat. Liam and Christophe sat on their knees. Meara sat in my lap in the front seat. Jasper squeezed into the hatchback with all the towels, picnic food and beach toys. And Pat drove, very cautiously.

It was a glorious day at the Guardalavaca Beach. We laid our blanket under the shade trees. The kids snorkelled and swam and played in the sand. Pat and I joined them from time to time, in between chapters of our books. How therapeutic the combination of sun and water and rest can be! At the end of the afternoon, we joined in a beach volleyball game. It didn't matter that we spoke little *español* and our teammates little English. Everyone knew the rules and anyway, who cares about the rules?

"Let's stop at one of the upscale hotels in town and buy something for Bernadine," Pat said. "She's really gone out of her way to help solve our transmission problem. Did I mention the Holguin machinist charged only fifty-three dollars?"

It was fun to choose gifts for Bernadine, to buy luxury items in American dollars that her paycheque in Cuban currency could never justify. It was even more fun to deliver them. Bernadine beamed as she accepted our wicker basket brimming with perfume, chocolate, candles, and wine. Reading the children's homemade note of thanks, expressed in rudimentary *español,* brought a tear to her eye. I was glad the children witnessed first-hand how much happiness giving can bring.

Our last week in Cuba flew by. Pat often woke the boys at dawn and dinghied them out in the little *bahía* to fish. Though they didn't catch a thing, they always returned to the boat full of fresh energy. Meanwhile, I devised a new morning running route. I ran up and down the marina staircases, then out the security gate, as usual. Instead of turning right, where houses and dogs lined the road, I turned left along the shore of the bay, where the school and government store were located.

One such morning, I found the store open, so I ventured in to buy *harina,* flour for baking bread. My eyes took a moment to adjust to the darkness inside the long and narrow building. A few villagers leaned against the long counter that ran the length of the room. Behind the counter stood a clerk, ready to take my order, and behind her stood a long row of high shelves. It reminded me of the old-style general stores we see in sepia-tone photos, except that the shelves of this Cuban store were mostly bare. Among the few items I saw were children's black boots, plastic pails and jugs, tins of infant milk formula, bags of dry beans and sugar, and bottles of rum, but no *harina.*

After their short reprieve during our road trip to Santiago, the kids didn't mind returning to the boat school routine. Nor did I. When Manuel arrived each morning to install the new starboard transmission parts, we climbed the steps to the open-air restaurant. Juan the waiter smiled and waved as we spread out our books and papers and, a moment later, presented another *espresso* to the *maestra*. While the children studied, I sipped my java and gazed downhill at the Old Bahamas Channel.

The afternoons were stiflingly hot. After lunch on board, the kids hooked up with Louise and Christophe for a games afternoon and a bowl of *helado*, or a dinghy ride and kayak trip on the placid waters of Bahía de Vita. Pat and I attended to our sundry boat keeping tasks. After several such afternoons, the boat was truly shipshape, so that when Manuel left for the day, Pat and I could indulge in an afternoon *siesta*.

The sad day came when the crew of *L'Alouette* announced plans to set sail westward along the Cuban coast. The eve of their departure, our kids invited Louise and Christophe to a party aboard *Cool Breezes,* where they could watch our one and only video, *Maverick*. Meanwhile Pat and I hiked up to the lounge for drinks with Laurent and Jeanne and their boat buddies, other francophone Canadians planning to travel in a flotilla towards Havana.

A short while later, our group was joined by the crews of two recent marina arrivals. Gillian and Tony, silver-haired Australians who'd sailed *Seastage* for eleven years, pulled up chairs and made two announcements. First, it was Gillian's fiftieth birthday, and second, with their landing today, they'd just sailed to their fiftieth country. New arrivals Will and Nigel, aboard Will's stunning fifty-foot sloop *Easygoing*, were British. They were two of the tallest and in Will's case, widest, men we'd ever seen. Both men were extremely gregarious. Will had twelve years' worth of sailing yarns to spin, and young Nigel many adventures to retell from the races he'd crewed from Capetown, South Africa to Rio de Janeiro, Brazil. Candles flickered in the open air, glasses tinkled in toasts to "*¡Salud!*" and laughter rippled out to sea. Pat and I loved this international and bilingual nautical camaraderie.

Back at the boat, the movie was finished, and the two older girls had planned a sleepover in the cockpit of our cat. They spent the wee hours whispering and gazing at the stars.

"Louise and I plan to visit each other the summer of 2002," Erin informed me the next morning. To watch the two girls' emotional parting, after such a brief but intense friendship, brought tears to my own eyes.

Another evening that last week in Cuba, we patronized Alba's *paladero*. When we knocked at the door at the appointed hour, Pablo ushered us into the kitchen. The mint-green walls bore no decoration but a lone cross, and tea towel curtains framed the only window. A bare light bulb dangled from the ceiling. A festive cloth was spread on a large table, and a flickering candle offset the harsh overhead light. Alba stood by the stove and beamed.

"*Entre*, sit down," she gestured, as Pablo pulled out chairs for us. Dish by dish Alba served roast pork, two salads, fried plantain, *arroz con gris,* green beans with onions, and a cane-sugar pudding. Her subtle manner of seasoning the traditional Cuban foods was unsurpassed. After each course Alba smiled expectantly.

"*Bueno, bueno!*" we'd praise. Then she'd laugh and return to the stove.

"Come sit with us," I said. I felt we were *amigas*, not just customers.

"No, no," she replied with a laugh and wave of her brown hand. But Pablo sat down. He told us Alba had spent the previous day taking the *guagua* to and from

Holguin just to buy the meat and other ingredients. She also hand-stitched little *muñecas,* cloth dolls, for the girls, and polished some *conchas,* fiery gold seashells, for the boys. She presented her gifts so tenderly that the kids were touched. They sang their small repertoire of choir songs as a gesture of thanks, prompting Pablo to pull out his guitar and rejoin with Cuban songs for us.

It was almost 11:00 p.m. when we parted ways.

"Some new people arrived at the marina," I told Alba. "Should we tell them about your laundry service and your *paladero?*"

"*Sí, sí,*" Alba smiled. Then she held out a handmade seed necklace. "For you, *amiga,*" she said simply. My eyes filled with tears. I was beginning to see a pattern in the gift exchanges we'd made in Cuba: each time we gave something we'd purchased or no longer needed, we'd receive something in which the giver had invested time and effort.

We strolled back through the marina gates under starry skies.

"Look at that dark blue," Meara said. "It looks as if it might be soft, if only we could touch it."

"Look at Orion the Hunter!" Liam added.

"And look at the half-moon," Ben said. "I wonder why the bright side shines at the bottom here, instead of at the side like it does in Canada."

A few days later, Pat arrived breathless at our open-air boat school.

"Manuel says he's finished putting in the transmission, so we're going on a sea trial to test it out," he announced, his voice full of hope. "Up here from the top of the hill, you should be able to see us round the peninsula, heading to the fuel docks."

We watched from the restaurant tables with great anticipation.

"There's *Cool Breezes!*" Liam shouted. The children cheered. Their dream to reach the Bahamas by late March just might be fulfilled. We ran down the hill to the docks.

"Yes, the sea trial was a success," Pat reported. "Looks as if we'll be able to leave tomorrow, assuming good weather. Manuel, how long will the transmission parts hold out?"

"Maybe a hundred years, maybe only tomorrow!" Manuel laughed.

Our last day at the marina, as usual, was busy with chores and filled with errands. Most memorable of these was bidding farewell to our Cuban friends. First on the list was Dora, the chef of the first *paladero* we'd visited in Vita. Not one to miss an opportunity, she offered to sell us fresh *camarónes*. When she tucked the prawns in a plastic bag for us, she threw in some bonus plantains and cucumbers.

Then we trotted off to the marina office to pay our bill and say goodbye to our marina friends, Juan the waiter, and beautiful Bernadine. Meara and I gave big hugs, and Pat presented bottles of the best Cuban rum he could find to everyone remotely connected with the transmission repair.

We left the hardest leave-taking until last. As we walked along the fence toward Alba and Pablo's front door, we noticed their backyard clothesline was hung with huge pants and shirts. There too was Pablo, enjoying the evening air. As soon as he saw us he laughed, pointed at the clothes and gestured widely with his small hands.

"*¡Muchos grandes!*" he exclaimed.

"Ah, those must be Will's and Nigel's clothes!" Pat laughed.

We found Alba in the kitchen, scooping heaps of food onto platters.

"Are Will and Nigel coming for supper?" I asked her.

"*Sí, sí,*" Alba smiled, wiping her brow.

"*Muchos grandes,*" we replied, holding our hands up high and wide like Pablo.

"You're not going to make much money tonight, Alba," Pat joked.

Alba and I hugged tightly. I knew I'd never forget her. Erin stepped forward.

"This is for you, Alba," she said, presenting a small package.

Alba opened it to find a hand-beaded necklace. She held it like a treasure, then put it round her neck.

"*Gracias,*" she said simply, a single tear glistening. There in a gesture was the secret of Cuban generosity: to give freely, and receive freely.

On our way back to the boat that night, Ben found an unusually large carrier shell in an unexpected place, the pathway to the marina. Inside was a hermit crab.

"This is a sign," he said. "We're supposed to take this little guy to the Bahamas tomorrow!"

The next morning, March 24, Pat and I rose to listen to the 5:00 a.m. weather report. All would be well on our crossing to Ragged Island, the southernmost island of the Jumentos archipelago. We waited for the Guarda to check us out of the country at the appointed hour of 6:00 a.m., but the two soldiers didn't arrive until almost 8:00 a.m. After one last inspection to ensure there were no Cuban stowaways aboard (besides the hermit crab), the officers issued our last *despacho.* Exactly two months to the day after landing in Cuba, we departed her shores.

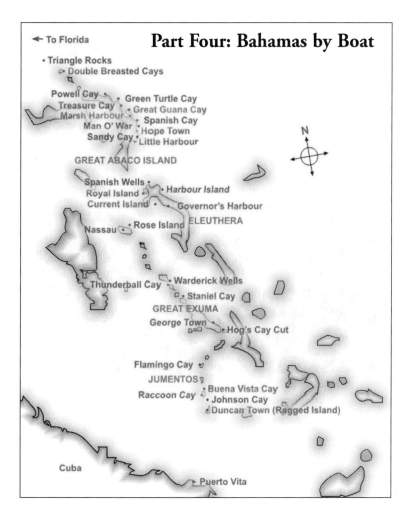

← To Florida   **Part Four: Bahamas by Boat**

· Triangle Rocks
  ∝ Double Breasted Cays

Powell Cay ·   · Green Turtle Cay
Treasure Cay · · Great Guana Cay
Marsh Harbour   · Spanish Cay
Man O' War · · Hope Town
Sandy Cay · · Little Harbour

GREAT ABACO ISLAND

                                              N

Spanish Wells ·
Royal Island   · *Harbour Island*
Current Island · · Governor's Harbour
                    ELEUTHERA
Nassau · Rose Island

Thunderball Cay · Warderick Wells
                  · Staniel Cay
GREAT EXUMA
George Town
              · Hog's Cay Cut

Flamingo Cay

JUMENTOS
              · Buena Vista Cay
Raccoon Cay · Johnson Cay
              · Duncan Town (Ragged Island)

Cuba

        · Puerto Vita

March 2001, Duncan Town Harbour,
Commonwealth of the Bahamas.

From: The Kirwin crew
To: Kith and Kin
Subject: **Greetings from *Cool Breezes*: Bahamas, Ahoy!**

It's 9:00 a.m. on March 24. *Cool Breezes* glides on placid waters past the candy cane lighthouse marking the channel to Puerto Vita. Our twin bows point northeast into the Old Bahama Channel toward Ragged Island, the southernmost outpost of the Jumentos island chain. It's a ten-hour passage, if all goes well. We're already behind schedule because the Guarda Frontera showed up to check us out of the country two hours later than promised. Still, we hope to lay anchor off Ragged Island by sunset.

The six of us sit in the cockpit, pensive. The rugged coastline disappears behind us. Wistfulness, an early nostalgia for Cuba, occupies our minds. Against the poignancy of longing weighs the buoyancy of anticipation; we're eager to experience the Bahamas.

Mostly though, our thoughts are consumed by a single problem: we're growing seasick. After two weeks tied to a mooring ball in the glassy waters of Bahía de Vita, the large swells pounding our bows seem to hit our gut. This time, the kids are beyond queasy.

"Pass the bucket!" Erin yells at Liam. Those two, predictably enough, are the first to succumb. Meara is next. Ben, as usual, is the last holdout, yet today even he can't stomach the onslaught of rolling water.

"Irongut bites the dust!" Erin and Liam gloat as Ben snatches the pail.

Ben laughs. He's never before been seasick, never mind lost his brekkie.

"Yeah, but you're the Green Queen, Erin," he retorts, "and Liam, you're the Duke of Puke."

Then comes the ultimate insult.

"You're no better than a bunch of landlubbers!" roars Pat. He secures one end of a line to the handle of a bucket, and the other to a cleat at the stern. The kids take turns using the bucket. They toss its contents out to sea, rinse the bucket in seawater, and pull it back into the cockpit.

As for me, I'm squeamish, but haven't yet relinquished my stomach's contents. This is an unexpected relief, since buckets and changes of clothing feature large in my childhood travels by boat and car. My insistence on taking the helm as Pat raises the sails is mostly selfish; holding the wheel and focussing on the horizon gives me equilibrium.

The water is lively, the sky bracingly blue, the wind burly. Our two white sails fill taut with big air, lying almost perpendicular to the hulls, what we sailors call a beam reach. No need for diesel. It's just us and the wind and the sea. We're having a brilliant sail.

"Hey, look!" Pat yells. "We're doing over eight knots! At this rate we might reach the Bahamas before nightfall."

The kids nod politely. They appreciate at a rational level today's co-operative sailing conditions, yet can't muster enthusiasm for anything. They lack energy even for their new pet, the hermit crab that dwells with a scrap of seaweed in a plastic basin in our cockpit. Jasper, normally enthusiastic about live food aboard, slinks to her refuge of sleep under the salon table. Meara is positively groggy, so Pat carries her to our berth, where she drops off instantly. Feeling green myself, I join her for an hour.

An hour later, I wake to brooding skies. At the halfway point of our passage, we alter course due north. The change in direction deflates the sails. Pat and the kids haul them closer to the mast, and fire up the diesel engines. Suddenly we hear the nerve-wracking clatter of disjointed metal.

"It's the starboard engine," Pat says tersely. He kills it. My heart sinks when I recall Manuel the mechanic's limited warranty: the re-machined transmission parts might last a hundred years, or they might last a day.

Now we're operating on the port engine alone, beating against the brisk wind. Our speed drops from eight knots to four.

"We're not gonna reach landfall by sundown," Pat says. "I'd better figure out where the heck we're going to anchor tonight."

Pat spreads the chart on the salon table. Just then another ugly sound rattles our nerves. I know what this is. It's the port engine, with its bad fuel problem, kicking out again. Wordlessly Pat and I exchange places. He takes the helm while I head below to the port engine locker to squeeze the stinky fuel line bulb. It's a scenario all too nauseatingly familiar.

Dozens of pumps later, I've got fuel flowing freely to the port engine. I return to the cockpit gagging yet relieved; we're making forward progress, and I haven't lost my lunch. The sun is setting more quickly than we're sailing. Sunsets don't linger in this part of the world. Night falls here like a dark and heavy curtain, not a dusky veil.

"Thank God for technology," Pat says. "We'll use the GPS to get ourselves as close to land as possible, until the depth sounder shows ten or fifteen feet. Then we'll anchor for the night and make it the rest of the way in the morning. Anyone hungry?"

The rest of us wrinkle our noses and shake our heads. The thought of eating disgusts us. Yet Pat's feeling hale and hollow.

"Would you fix me a sandwich, Jake?"

Down in the galley, the smell of sandwich meat overwhelms me. After a long day of self-containment, I lose it.

"The bucket, pass the bucket!" I yell, dashing up to the cockpit. The kids laugh, glad I've joined their ranks.

"Okay, I'll make my own sandwich," says Pat, leaving the wheel to me. I hold the compass direction, but the wind suddenly gusts and pushes us off course.

Pat feels the change and rushes back to the cockpit.

"What happened?"

"I can't tell. The GPS compass has gone wonky!"

Pat sighs with exasperation, wondering no doubt why his wife can't follow a simple compass direction, yet he too is unable to make sense of the GPS compass.

"Events are conspiring against us landing on Ragged Island tonight," I observe.

"Well, we can't risk going any further in the dark without the GPS," Pat says. "We'll just have to anchor here." The depth sounder shows over twenty-five feet, so Pat lets out every centimetre of our chain and line as he lays the anchor. It's 8:30 p.m., and time for bed.

What an anticlimactic day. We retire to our berths, sullen and seasick, well offshore from our destination.

I struggle to the murky surface of sleep, wakened by the beeping alarm on my wrist. It's 4:45 a.m. on March 25, time to listen to the weather report on the SSB. This isn't the first time I've been roused from my dreams this night. We're riding out a very bumpy night in a very rolly anchorage, so I've made several trips to the head. So have the kids.

I haul my leaden limbs out of my berth and check on our pets. Jasper hasn't moved, but Crabby, the hermit crab, has escaped his plastic basin. He's inching, shell and all, on the cockpit sole toward the stern. I wonder how he got out of the basin and drop him back in.

At 5:00 a.m., I tune in to the remote metallic voice of the SSB weather announcer.

"Sounds good," I mutter to Pat, clambering over him on our berth. "Seas two to three feet, wind from the east seven to ten knots."

At 7:00 a.m. the sun is up. I concoct coffee for Pat and return to bed, utterly incapacitated. Two hours later, I wake refreshed, the nausea gone. Liam and Erin are still confined to bed, but Ben and Meara have joined Pat relaxing in the cockpit.

"Good morning, Mom!" Meara cries, full of glee. "Guess what, Crabby was gripping the steering wheel when we woke up today. He wants to be the skipper!"

"That's his second adventure of the night," I say, and relate the story of his first.

"Speaking of adventure, let's see what happens when I try the engines this morning," Pat says. All of us wait in suspense. What does the day hold in store for us? Will the GPS and engines work today? Will we finally arrive in the Bahamas? And what lies ashore?

The GPS flickers to life instantly. The port engine turns over just as it should. Today its steady putter is not a whine but music to our ears.

Now for the starboard engine. Pat turns the ignition key.

"Wonder of wonders," Pat smiles. The starboard engine purrs like a well-fed cat. You'd never know it ever had trouble.

"Thank-you!" I exclaim, hands folded, eyes skyward. It's a miracle, inexplicable that the engine works today when yesterday it seemed on the brink of disintegration.

A few hours pass. Nautical mile by mile, we approach Ragged Island. Pat lowers the Cuban courtesy flag. He radios the main settlement where, according to our cruising guides, we can officially enter the Bahamas.

"Duncan Town Harbour, Duncan Town Harbour, this is Canadian vessel *Cool Breezes*. Just arriving from Cuba. We'd like to clear in," he calls.

"*Cool Breezes, Cool Breezes,* this is Duncan Town Harbour, Darlene speaking," comes the amiable reply. "This isn't a clearing-in point any more, but come ashore anyway."

"'Come ashore anyway'?" I laugh. "Can you imagine the Guarda Frontera saying that?"

"Thank-you, Darlene," Pat says.

"You're welcome," she replies. "Raise your yellow quarantine flag till you get to George Town, the closest clearing-in point. Then you can fly the Bahamian courtesy flag."

The water surrounding Ragged Island and in the channel leading to Duncan Town is notoriously shallow, accessible only to vessels with extremely low drafts. Most sailboats, with heavy keels extending five to seven feet beneath their waterline, must anchor out and dinghy to shore. But *Cool Breezes,* a catamaran, has no keel. Since our draft is only two feet, two inches and the tide is now high, we decide to slowly venture forth.

It's late morning. The air is still; even the blue sky blisters with heat. The kids sit in the cockpit, eager to witness landfall in a new country. Our fingertips brush the mangroves lining the narrow unmarked channel as we putter along. Pat tries to discern the water's depth. Landfall comes more quickly than we expect; with a soft whoosh our hulls dig into a sandbar. Pat groans. It's hard to say which is more trying, the embarrassment of running aground, or the struggle to get free.

A half-hour later, we're still stuck. Then we hear the efficient drone of a high-powered engine. Approaching our stern is a Jamaican canoe, a long and narrow boat equipped with a big outboard and piles of lobster traps.

"Kin I lend you a hand?" comes the singsong voice of the pilot. He's lean and lanky, a fisherman with black weathered skin, a faded plaid shirt, and cut-off jeans. Our rescuer throws us a line, and reverses his engine. A minute later, we're free.

"Folla' me in," he calls out. "I show you deh deeper parts o' deh channel."

Our new friend expertly guides us on a meandering route through the mangroves to a tiny bay. Around it the pastel dwellings of Duncan Town are perched. Once we reach the anchorage, Pat passes an American twenty to our guide. The man shakes his head.

"It's no trouble, no trouble a-tall," he laughs. He manoeuvres his red canoe tightly within the deep part of the bay, and speeds away.

"Well that's an auspicious Bahamian welcome," Pat says, heading to the bows to lay the anchor. "Boys, you'd better take your dog to shore."

Ben and Liam lower the dinghy from its davits and climb aboard. Jasper leaps in after them, eager for her respite on land. She's waited more than twenty-seven hours for relief.

"Gimme Crabby," Ben yells to Meara. "Time to let go of our little bit of Cuba."

Thus, at long last, we land in the Bahamas.

God bless and fair winds,

Love PJ+crew

March 2001, Jumentos islands, the Bahamas.

Ben at the bow of a Jamaican canoe.

Erin, the starfish slayer.

Chapter 23
Adapt or Run Aground

What is this life, if full of care,
We have no time to stand and stare?
– William Henry Davies, Leisure

B y the time we left Cuba, the notion that our voyage
was not merely physical had begun to penetrate.
Our journey wasn't just an experience of distance,
geography, culture and nautical challenges. It was also a
lesson in how to dwell in time, to put the past behind, to
push away the future. Life in the North American fast lane
rewards planning; the better we prepare for the future, the
more smoothly our schedules run. Yet cruising the Cuban
cayos and befriending the generous Cubans gave us shining insights into the rewards of being present, of giving
presents, of presence.

In the Bahamas, we met many people who, like
Cubans, were more attuned to the present than we. As our
early days in the Bahamas unfolded, we discovered other
lessons also lay in store.

No sooner had we laid anchor in the minuscule
Duncan Town harbour than our VHF radio began to
buzz. Fellow cruisers, all American, had eavesdropped on
our report to the Duncan Town harbourmaster and heard
that our last port was in Cuba. They were intrigued with
the concept of visiting Cuba. Before Pat and I could even

step ashore, a couple from Montana arrived at our stern, intent upon looking at our Cuban charts and borrowing our Cuban courtesy flag. Meanwhile, the children chafed to explore Duncan Town. Late in the afternoon, when at last our guests seemed satisfied with our information and suggested we go for a drink at the local watering hole, we practically leapt off the boat.

Duncan Town was small and still, hilly and charming. A smattering of modest and multicoloured homes and stores dotted the winding roads. The lanes were quiet, except for the pecking and squawking of chickens. Townsfolk sat in the shade cast by their houses and the intermittent palms, amusing themselves watching our vain efforts to restrain our dog from chasing the feathered bait. Compared to Cubans, we found the Bahamians' demeanour more guarded. In response to our greetings, they just nodded politely.

Our first stop was at Ponderosa Pub, a pale yellow two-storey building with an expansive wooden porch. The front door was open, and the proprietor waved us in.

"Yes, yes, deh children be welcome here," he laughed, noticing our pause at the threshold. He extended his hand towards Pat. "Hello mon, I'm Cyrus."

Our cold drinks, dripping with condensation, were as welcome and easy to savour as our host's comfortable company. Cyrus was a compact, wiry and sun-wizened fellow with grizzled grey hair and a ready smile. This little bar and the rooms upstairs were part of his bonefishing business. Judging from his smart apparel and after speaking with a few of his clientele, it appeared Cyrus ran a small but thriving enterprise catering to rich Americans.

We found it challenging at first to decipher his Caribbean accent. It wasn't the lingo so much as the unaccustomed rhythm and the lilting flow of words that our ears found difficult to discern. But it was easy to perceive the pride Cyrus felt in his little corner of the world. We must visit the abandoned salt pond businesses, he said. We should walk to the local station of the Bahamas telephone company, Batelco, to make long-distance phone calls and send email. And no visit to Duncan Town would be complete, he said, without a meal at Shelley's restaurant, or a pie from Flo's bakery.

Ben's eyes lit up.

"A pie?" he grinned. "Voot, voot! Let's go now!"

We bid goodbye to Cyrus and set out down the lane. By then, however, nothing was open for business but the mosquitoes. We fled to our dinghy, paddled like cartoon characters to our boat, and quickly zipped the mosquito nets onto the cockpit dodger. The sun then plunged behind the Duncan Town hills. Our boat, alone in the shallow harbour, lay at peace. Later that evening, the docile water rocked us to sleep. This was a delicious slumber, a welcome antidote to the previous seasick night in the rolly anchorage offshore. Had merely a single day passed since then?

Crowing roosters woke us at sunrise the next brilliant morning.

"It's not even six o'clock," Pat mumbled, rolling over on his good ear, but Liam bounced out of bed.

"Jasper, today you're six!" he said huskily, nuzzling his face in her neck.

"Happy birthday, Jasper!" Meara sang out. It was March 28.

"In honour of Jasper's birthday, we get breakfast out at Shelley's!" I announced.

Pat smiled at my newest excuse not to cook.

"Okay, but this time I'm not rowing ashore." He lowered the outboard engine to the rear of the inflatable. The boys screwed it on tight. Erin loosened the painter from the boat's stern. Then Pat yanked the outboard ignition rope. Nothing. He pulled again. Nothing.

"Guess I'll row to shore after all," Pat sighed. "The rest of you might as well head over to Shelley's while I find a mechanic."

The kids and I easily found Shelley's Fishermen's Lounge and its proprietor, a short and cheerful woman in her mid-forties. Shelley cooked eggs to order and a heap of fluffy pancakes.

"Wow, these pancakes are even better than yours, Mom!" Liam exclaimed.

"Humph!" I snorted, pretending to be miffed.

"Dat be my secret ingredient," Shelley winked at me. "A drop o' vanilla in deh batter." She sat down at the long table to chat while we devoured everything.

"Tell us about Duncan Town," I said.

"Back in deh fifties, it be a big town," Shelley sighed. "Dere be five hun'red people. Now deh population of deh whole islan' be down to ninety. Dat's because Cuba and Haiti done buyin' salt from our salt ponds."

"Could we buy some sea salt here in town?" I asked. Shelley shook her head.

"No one work deh salt ponds no mo'. Now all deh men gets dere living from deh sea. On a good day, a fisherman kin catch a couple dousand dollars wor' of lobster and grouper. Dey be workin' very hard right now because lobster season en' April first." We found out later that what Bahamians called lobster was the same as Cuban crawfish, a clawless cousin of the Maine lobster.

I recalled the fisherman who towed us off the sandbar, and described him to Shelley.

"Oh yes, dat be Leonard," she smiled. "He be my cousin."

"And Cyrus from Ponderosa's?" I asked.

"My cousin too," Shelley laughed. "Everybody lef' here on Ragged Island be related to each udder."

"We saw some kids on our way here wearing brown uniforms," Erin said. "Is there a school around here?"

"Yes, a primary school for mebbe twen'y children," Shelley replied. "My sister be deh teacher. Pas' Grade Eight, deh children go to Nassau for school. Once dey get to Nassau, not too many comes back to Ragged Island." Nassau, the capital city of the Bahamas on the tiny island of New Providence, was a few days away by boat. "But my son come back, and he bring Darlene wid him. So Darlene deh harbourmaster be new blood on dis islan'."

Just then Pat burst into the restaurant.

"The dinghy outboard is fixed!" he said with glee. "I found Sonny the mechanic, who figured it out in no time."

"Oh, Sonny," laughed Shelley. "He be my own boy."

"It sure would be easy to have a family reunion on this island," Liam observed.

From Shelley's we walked to the Batelco office to attempt email and long distance telephone calls home. Our phone calls to both grandmothers were cut off, and our emails were undelivered, because of the haphazard reception of the Batelco tower that day.

From Batelco we searched out Flo's bakery. Much to Ben's dismay, it was closed. We did find a small grocery, its shelves almost barren, and bought a bag of white flour. By then we'd explored the whole settlement, and walked to the deserted salt ponds. Shallow pools of the palest turquoise water lay desolate among drifts of off-white sand. By blurring my vision I could almost perceive sheets of ice bordered by heaps of snow. The mirage was marred, however; the air was more than twenty-five degrees too warm.

"Let's head back and do boat school," I suggested. We'd played hooky the last few days while underway. Back on board, however, the couple from Montana hailed us by VHF.

"We wanted to thank you for your help yesterday by showing you the best snorkelling grounds around here," they said. "And if you have spear-guns, we can show you how to spear lobster."

The older three cheered. They'd won another reprieve from boat school or, in Ben and Liam's estimation, they got "real" boat school. They gathered flippers and goggles, and Pat dug deep in the forward lockers to find the two spear guns left behind by the previous boat owners. Meanwhile, Meara pouted. She wanted regular boat school.

"I'll stay back and teach her math," I told Pat.

A few hours later, the four adventurers returned breathless with excitement. They'd learned how to use spear guns and discovered an enchanting underwater world, a vibrant coral reef.

That evening, ensconced within our mosquito net cocoon on the tiny Duncan Town harbour, we celebrated Jasper's birthday. We dined on the lobster Liam had speared and Erin's dessert of peanut butter and oatmeal sweets, shaped like dog bones and festooned with six candles. We sang happy birthday to our pet. Jasper seemed puzzled by the attention, but she did appreciate her own peanut butter treat.

Crowing roosters the next shiny morning gave us another early start. Before weighing anchor, we took one last trip ashore in pursuit of an email fix at the Batelco office and a fresh pie from Flo's bakery. Although neither quest proved fruitful, for the same reasons as before, we did receive an unexpected treat. When we bid goodbye to Darlene at the pink harbour office, she presented us with a half-bushel bag of sea salt.

"From Cyrus," she smiled, her perfect white teeth gleaming. "Shelley tol' him you wanted some salt from deh Ragged Island sea ponds, so he got it jes' for you."

We were touched by such thoughtfulness, and glad we also had a surprise in store for Darlene. We showed her a certain page in our Jumentos cruising guide where, in describing Duncan Town, the many virtues of the curvaceous young harbourmaster were celebrated.

"Dat's me!" she exclaimed, pointing to her name in print. She made a dozen photocopies of that particular page. "For my family back in Nassau," she said shyly.

By then the tide was in. Pat was eager to get underway, anxious to avoid sandbars in the shallow channel to the sea. We puttered out slowly and uneventfully. The thin waters and pervasive sandbars of the Bahamas force sailors to slow down and keep watch, said our cruising guide. Cruisers must accept and adjust to these realities, it admonished. In a phrase, we cruisers must adapt or run aground. Bearing in mind we'd run aground as soon as we entered the Bahamas, that lesson was real. By slowing down and keeping watch, I thought, we'd gain time to form impressions, absorb the glorious details, and replenish our hungry senses. Rather than resist the realities, we'd revel in them.

An hour later, we reached Pass Cay and set anchor in the impossibly clear blue water. Boat school was in session when a red Jamaican canoe pulled alongside. There was Leonard, the fisherman who'd towed us off the sandbar. Pat greeted him with a handshake. The rest of us crowded into the cockpit.

"Would deh children like t' go snorkellin' and fishin' dis afternoon?" Leonard asked.

"Sure!" came the chorused reply.

"I be back in a cuppla hours den," Leonard grinned. He whipped his canoe about and sped off. Pat made lunch while the kids and I finished our lessons in record time. When Leonard returned, we realized not all six of us could fit in his narrow fishing boat. Pat looked at me. It was unthinkable to send the kids without a parent, and awkward for Leonard to be accompanied by a woman.

"I'll stay back with Meara and Jasper," I said lightly. "I can get some cleaning done."

Meara didn't mind staying on board – she'd get her teacher to herself yet again – but Jasper did. She whined with longing as she watched the canoe head out. I knew how she felt. The bright note in my voice had been false. I hankered to see for myself the underwater paradise the children had described yesterday. With each menial task, I felt my resentment grow. Then I paused. Just like the Bahamian shoals and the shallows, boat keeping was part of my reality. I could resist it and grow sour, or accept it and be happy. Adapt or run aground: the choice was mine.

I ran the back of my hand across my sweating brow.

"Let's take a sea bath, Meara," I said. We plunged blissfully into our crystalline bath.

Later, as we towelled off in the cockpit, the Jamaican canoe appeared on the horizon. I remembered how modestly Bahamian women dress, and hurried below decks to cover up.

"Come aboard, Leonard," I called out a moment later. He spent the afternoon with us, showing Erin how to gut and preserve the twelve-inch magenta and tangerine sea stars she'd collected on their outing.

"So many cruisers tink all you need do wi' starfish is dry dem out in the sun," Leonard said. "But deh starfish jes' rot, and deh sailors jes' t'row dem back in deh sea, all stinky and wasted. Be okay to tek deh bigges' starfish if you clean dem out properly. But don't tek too many, and leave deh li'l ones alone."

The next morning we motored forty-five minutes north to Hog Cay, where we anchored in a pristine horseshoe bay under a smiling sun. We dinghied to shore to climb the cliffs, explore the caves, and play in the sand. "Let's go snorkelling!" I said. The kids said the Hog Cay reef wasn't as spectacular as those they'd seen the previous two days, but I thought it spectacular. To immerse myself in this secret and seemingly tranquil world, to not just see it but also to feel part of it, was an exquisitely joyful act. Bathed in filtered sunlight, a fantastic and fragile sunken garden lay arrayed beneath me. A dazzling variety of colours, from electric blue to shocking pink and saturated orange, swayed before my eyes. Brilliantly coloured fish darted about delicate white staghorn fern, sturdy brain coral, lacy sea fans, and brilliant purple sea anemones. Now this was revelry in reality!

By noon we were hungry, and headed back to the "mother ship" for lunch. As if on cue, and to our surprise, Leonard appeared in his red canoe, bearing gifts of crawfish. Pat fired up the grill, Erin sliced homemade bread, and I prepared a platter of cucumber and tomato slices, sprinkled with chopped onion and ground pepper, and drizzled with Italian dressing, an adaptation of the salads we'd enjoyed in Cuba. It was a meal fit for royalty, crowned with the ultimate treat, ice cream bars that Leonard produced from his cooler.

"You're so good to us, Leonard," Pat said. Leonard laughed.

"I like bein' wi' kids because I miss my own li'l girl," he confessed.

"You have a daughter?" I asked, immediately intrigued.

"Yes, Esmeralda, but she live in Cuba wi' she mudder," Leonard replied. "I met she mudder a few years ago when I go to Cuba to get some eyeglasses."

"You went to Cuba for glasses?" Pat asked. "You don't even wear glasses."

"Oh, but I do when I'm not on deh water," Leonard said. "I be far-sighted so I need eyeglasses t' read. And dey're much cheaper in Cuba."

"Then I bet you'd appreciate the prescription goggles left behind by the previous owner of this boat," Pat said. He rummaged around in a forward locker. "Here, try these."

Leonard pulled the goggles over his eyes. A wide grin spread across his face.

"Oh, mon, what a difference," he said.

Leonard stayed with us until mid-afternoon, then roared off in his big canoe. We pulled up the anchor and sailed off to Raccoon Cay, yet another uninhabited island, and tucked into yet another sparkling untouched anchorage.

The wind rose the next morning.

"We'd better stay here for the day," Pat said, snapping off the SSB. After boat school was finished, we dinghied to shore to go hiking.

The next morning the winds had not only strengthened but also shifted, so we moved to another anchorage, this time at Johnson's Cay. We anchored in a snug cove, sheltered by a white crescent beach and another incredible coral reef. We dinghied to the beach to hike, then waded into the water to snorkel. The moment we donned goggles, tubes and flippers, we were transported to the astonishing and silent sea world below. This time, instead of riding back in the dinghy with the others, I swam back to the boat and climbed up the swim ladder.

To be alone on the boat was a rare treat. Once I'd finished a few galley chores, I reclined on the foredecks and closed my eyes. I smelled and felt the refreshing breath of the breezes. I heard the flutter of flags on our stays, the cries of shorebirds, and the steady, soothing lap of waves against the hulls of our boat and the shore. A child's voice called me. I propped myself up on my elbows, and opened my eyes to an arc of blond sand, grey cliff faces with lush green brush cuts, and water dappled with turquoise, sapphire and emerald. I waved to my loved ones, poking happy faces from a cave entrance. Paradise!

Later that afternoon, Leonard found us yet again. This time he brought grouper fillets and a photo of Esmeralda, a three-year-old with cornrow braids and a beaming smile.

"Fishin' season en' deh day after t'morra'," Leonard said. "I be gone to Cuba preddy quick after dat."

Meara and I gave Leonard a bag full of picture books and clothing.

"Take these to Esmeralda," we said, with a hug. That was the last time we saw him.

When we left Duncan Town, we'd figured our passage of ninety nautical miles to George Town would take five days. Instead, due to weather, we were still gunkholing, puttering among quiet anchorages among the unspoiled and uninhabited Jumentos islands. No one in Bahamian officialdom seemed to mind our snail's pace; only we seemed concerned about meeting travel deadlines. Yet if we hadn't been delayed, we'd never have come to know Leonard.

We'd already run aground, and now we were learning to adapt.

April 2001, Flamingo Cay,
the Bahamas.

The Tyrene
Navigator.

Meara points to the sea cave
opening.

Ben and Meara relax
near one of the stone chairs
they built on the beach.

Chapter 24
Don't Worry, Be Happy

Incessant company is as bad as solitary confinement.
  – Virginia Woolf

The day after we parted with Leonard, the winds shifted again. Along with two other boats anchored nearby, we motored from Johnson's back to Raccoon Cay, where the horseshoe bay protected us from the wind. Other boats joined us, until there were seven of us waiting out the cold front. At the whim of the wind, we all shuttled back and forth between the two anchorages.

The days slipped like sand through our fingers. After our morning migration to the alternate anchorage, and two or three hours of boat school, we dinghied to shore for an afternoon hike. On Raccoon Cay we searched for a blue hole, an unusually deep and promising fishing spot, but instead found huge cube-shaped salt crystals in an abandoned salt pond. On Johnson's Cay, we found a herd of thirty white goats and a trash-strewn beach the kids dubbed "Death Valley." On both islands, Pat and the kids built cairns using flat shards of loose limestone. Many were fashioned after inukshuks, the human-shaped Inuit landmarks found in Canada's north. Months after we had left them behind, Pat would proudly remark, "I bet those markers still stand today."

We met a handful of other cruisers in our island explorations. Tim and Carolyn, a middle-aged couple who had managed to stretch their sailing sabbatical from one to fourteen years, took an interest in our children. One evening they buzzed by in their dinghy to bring three new pets: more hermit crabs in shells. Although the kids added sand and other shells to Crabby's basin so that David, Goliath and Titan would feel more at home, the new crabs attempted escape daily. Another night, Carolyn and Tim gave us sea beans, heavy chocolate brown legumes, about three inches across, brought ashore from Venezuela by the sea currents.

"They're all the rage among the cruising kids in George Town," Carolyn reported.

"Really?" said Erin, grateful for the tip. Even at sea, she liked to keep up with the trends.

Like most batteries, ours re-charged when the engines ran. Daily migrations between anchorages took a half-hour or less, not long enough to replenish our battery juice, so Pat would idle the engines intermittently each day. Still, many evenings the cabin lights grew alarmingly dim. When they began to flicker, Pat would fire up the engines, while the rest of us snapped off all lights. Sometimes we even turned off the fridge and freezer.

"At this rate our diesel tanks will run dry before we reach George Town," Pat worried.

One morning, so little battery power remained that Pat couldn't start the engines. I confessed to having used battery power the day before, tapping out an email on the laptop. My yearning to write had got the better of my judgement. Pat was angry.

"How could you?" he demanded. "It's something I'd expect from the kids, not you."

Feeling the wind knocked from my sails, sorry to have been so foolish, I set to work, cleaning out long-neglected cubbies and lockers. If only the energy derived from my guilt could be funnelled into the batteries! Pat turned on the wind generator and solar panels. Over time they'd build up enough battery power to start the engines, so the engines could in turn re-charge the batteries. When the wind direction changed later that morning and our neighbours migrated across to the adjacent anchorage, *Cool Breezes* stayed behind. We spent a miserable day in the rocky anchorage, waiting for battery power to build. *How I wish I could turn back the clock*, I wrote in my diary. When the engines finally sputtered to life at dusk, we limped off to join our fellow cruisers.

Late in the afternoon of the next day, April 2, the weather gods opened a slender window permitting a short sail northward. We anchored in the lee of Buena Vista Cay, seven miles away. Although this progress brought a change in scenery, crew morale did not rally. In fact, our three nights anchored at Buena Vista marked a new low.

Part of our slump was related to dwindling food stores. Forced delays affected our provisions and therefore our meals, those all-important morale boosters. We expected to have arrived in George Town by then, and to have replenished our supplies of flour, eggs, fresh vegetables, and meat, never mind snacks. All that remained in the bilge pantries were tins of Spam and beans, and bags of rice and pasta. What we had was plentiful, but none of it resembled a conventional breakfast. In a vain attempt to simulate the Cream of Wheat porridge of my childhood, I began to cook rice for breakfast, and serve it with a dollop of Cuban *marmalada*. The children just stared at it, their pampered North American sensibilities shocked at the low culinary standards to which their lives had sunk.

"Cereal and yogurt are things of the past, that I know,"

Liam sighed wistfully one morning. "Mostly, though, I miss eating bread."

Then we began to lose things overboard, important stuff like the multi-purpose screwdriver, Pat's snorkelling flippers, and one of the dinghy paddles. All of these, Pat analyzed, had been left on deck by an absent-minded child and snatched by the wind. Even the dinghy went missing, drifted away in the night because one of the kids had failed to tie its painter securely to the stern. Fortunately for that unnamed child, a fellow cruiser rescued the dinghy and towed it back to us. No longer were these overboard items amusing additions to Liam's list. Pat became increasingly discouraged. One day, sitting in the cockpit with bowls of five-bean salad, we watched one of the fuel tank caps roll off the deck and fall in the water. I knew that Pat had asked the boys to check the diesel level, and therefore one of them was at fault for leaving the unscrewed cap on deck. I watched Pat's expression register the same thought, and the boys' faces fall.

I can't bear to hear another complaint about another lost thing, I thought. To my family's surprise, I stripped off my shorts, dove into the tepid water, and retrieved the sinking cap. When I surfaced a moment later, the kids cheered.

While Pat grew frustrated with our ineptitude and anxious over fuel and water supplies, the kids became testy boat school students. The north winds not only stalled our northward passage, but also blunted our spirit. Because we were straining toward George Town, we felt anxious. There's a big difference between puttering at will, choosing to gunkhole, and compulsory waiting for weather. Despite my best intentions to adapt or risk running aground, I was tired of keeping up with the accumulated salt, sand and dog hair, head smells, rust, mildew and clutter that overtook our cramped quarters. We'd neither showered nor done laundry for days on end. We were grumpy, grown weary of each other's incessant company.

The bloom is off the rose, I wrote in my diary. To simply accept and adapt, as the Bahamas guidebook admonished, seemed ridiculous, even laughable. The advice seemed irrelevant aboard our thirty-seven-foot cat with its crew of six and a dog, yet that was exactly what we must do. The lilting melody of that Caribbean mantra – don't worry, be happy – ran a continuous refrain in my mind. I realized I'd slipped back from the steps forward taken in Washington and Varadero. Waiting for the future to arrive – whether it was the resolution to my medical problem, leaving a marina after a month's stay, or getting to George Town – had become my focus. The difficulty lay not in the situation itself, but in my approach to it. Although unskilled in overcoming the problem, at least I now recognized it.

A bracing day sail on April 4 broke the stagnation. The early morning weather report on the SSB forecast decreased wind velocity. Although we'd still beat against north winds, it was feasible to reach the next major island. Once we'd released David, Goliath and Titan on the shores of Buena Vista, we weighed anchor and headed for Flamingo Cay.

The pounding of the bows against the oncoming waves produced nausea in our young crew, especially after twelve days of lying at anchor. We gave up on boat school after the first hour. Yet no one complained, not even after the fifth hour. To move again, to feel the big wind and the big water, was liberating. In the early afternoon we dropped anchor in a small bay on the lee side of Flamingo Cay.

This island was well known in the Bahamas for two reasons apart from its pink inhabitants, which had long

since flown the coop. Its first claim to fame was as backdrop to an international drama. In 1994, when the crews
of three sailboats anchored exactly where we were and
dinghied to shore, they found one hundred and fifty hungry and thirsty Haitians. Their refugee boat had been
shipwrecked over a week earlier on the windward side of
the island. The cruisers radioed for help and sustained the
Haitians with food and fresh water from their own boats.
Two days later, a Bahamian rescue vessel arrived with provisions. By then two Haitians had died, and were buried
in the hills. In a cruel denouement, the survivors were
deported to Haiti.

Flamingo Cay's second claim to fame was its natural
wonder, a majestic sea cave. At low tide it was possible to
float right into the cavern, but we chose to dinghy to the
beach and hike to the entrance. It was a rugged excursion
over the coarse limestone rocks, especially for Meara, but
she cheerfully persevered. We descended into the cave from
a hillside opening, and waded into the gently lapping
water. The children's high spirits settled immediately into a
hushed awe. Above us rose a dramatically vaulted coral ceiling. Sunlight streamed through breaks in the lacy
limestone, bounced off the shallow ripples, and produced a
dappled green lightshow on the cavern walls. We basked in
the cathedral effect, uttering barely a word.

Back at the beach, the kids discussed what to build
with the large flat slabs of rock.

"Let's build stone seats right into the sand bank," Pat
suggested. He transformed our young crew into a team of
quarrymen, engineers and labourers, who in turn produced
a row of surprisingly comfortable chairs facing the sea.

The next day's early morning weather report predicted
strong winds from the northeast, the same direction in
which we were headed.

"Should we go anyway?" I asked.

"Let's give it a try," Pat said. "George Town is still two days' sail away."

Out in the mainstream, the swells were steeper and the winds mightier than expected. The new question was whether we should turn back.

"Look!" Ben shouted. "The wind blew a hole in our jib!"

"The decision has been made for us," Pat said. He lowered the jib and cranked the wheel one hundred and eighty degrees. In an instant, our experience of the weather was transformed. The wind was now at our stern, pushing us forward, filling the mainsail. We flew back to Flamingo.

We remained at anchor there for three more nights, waiting for the north winds to abate. Four more boats joined us in the anchorage, all awaiting favourable winds. We soon settled into our familiar routine: mornings devoted to boat school, and afternoons to snorkelling and hiking. The highlight of boat school those days was the science fair Ben organized. For two days, the kids prepared science experiments, and on the third day, demonstrated them to their parents.

"A boat isn't a science lab," Pat warned as he watched Ben assemble vinegar and baking soda in the galley, and Liam retrieve matches from the nav station. In the end, the children were thrilled that their experiments unfolded as planned, and Pat was relieved there were no disasters.

Flamingo Cay yielded many surprises. We saw nurse sharks, manta rays and four-foot long sea snakes. But our most intriguing find was another Canadian family. Pat and the boys met them on the beach just as a squall was breaking overhead.

"Come for coffee tomorrow morning," Pat yelled as each family dashed to its dinghy.

After breakfast the next day, I found myself in a quandary. We had some fabulous Cuban coffee to serve our guests, but what kind of snack could I serve using pasta, rice and beans? I rummaged deep in one of the cubbies and pulled out a bag of hard seeds. Eureka! This wasn't dried peas or beans, but popcorn. I poured oil in a heavy saucepan, measured in a cup of kernels, and began sliding it back and forth on the propane burner. Soon a toasty aroma and the muffled sound of successive explosions filled the boat.

"What are you doing, Mom?" the kids asked. Their life experience thus far taught them that popcorn was made not on a stove, but in a microwave oven.

The Van Den Brink family arrived at our stern mid-morning bearing hostess gifts.

"Back home we would've brought you wine or chocolates," Dan laughed. "Out here we thought you might appreciate fresh water and energy bars!"

He was right. We gratefully accepted the five-gallon jug and box of goodies.

"And here are some shells from Haiti for the kids," Inger added.

"Have you been cruising in Haiti?" Pat asked. An extremely impoverished and war-torn country, Haiti wasn't known for its cruising grounds.

"Well, not exactly cruising," Dan replied. "We're outreach missionaries. We bring food, equipment and supplies from North American donors to Haiti every spring. We work at the missions in three different villages for six months, then cruise back through the Bahamas to Florida, and begin all over again. This is our fourth year of mission work."

Pat and I stared, stunned. They looked so normal, so very unlike the pale and pious prototype we had preconceived missionaries to be. With his grey beard, blue eyes and smooth tanned face, Dan could pass as Pat's brother. With her blond bob, dimpled smile, and coordinating shorts and golf shirt, Inger would fit in with the neighbourhood moms back in Edmonton. Ten-year-old Kirsten and nine-year-old Jason looked sturdy, sun-kissed and energetic, just like our kids. I couldn't help but regret my own petty misery just a few days previous when I saw the extraordinary thing this ordinary family was doing.

"What kind of boat do you have?" Pat asked.

Dan pointed to a huge steel vessel on the horizon.

"That's *The Tyrene Navigator*," he said proudly. "It's a retired Canadian navy ship, seventy-five feet long. We've got it loaded down with all kinds of donations for the Haitians – five thousand pounds of rice, two tons of double-treated lumber, a well-digging rig in pieces, a new refrigerator, power generators, lots of medicine, bags and bags of clothes – plus a year's worth of provisions for the family."

Pat wondered how much repair and upkeep was required on a vessel of that size.

"I bet Inger and I spend at least two hours every single day on maintenance," Dan replied.

"What did you do in Canada, before this mission work?" I asked.

"I was a bank manager in Vernon, B.C.," Dan said. "When our church began fundraising for this Haitian mission, it occurred to me that we might be able to do more than just give money. Now several Canadian churches fundraise for us. We use the money to buy supplies."

"Some suppliers throw in cash, too," Inger added. "Every year the project gets bigger."

"Your work must be so gratifying," I said. "How long will you keep doing this?"

"We don't really know," Dan said. "So far we're thriving on it. The kids love it. We'll know when it's time to go back to Canada. God will tell us."

"Where the Lord guides, He provides," Inger added. She said this in a refreshingly off-hand way, simply and without preaching. This was her truth, and I recognized the message. It was only another way of expressing the idea to not worry, but be happy.

The Van Den Brink children were very sociable. Kirsten joined our girls in Erin's stateroom, where they wove friendship bracelets, while Jason and our boys played a board game in the salon. I kept busy, dashing between the cockpit and the galley, preparing coffee and popcorn. Erin sliced the energy bars into small pieces and served them on a plate, presenting them as the special treats they were to our crew at that time.

"Hey look, you have more visitors," Dan said. Another catamaran, *Silverdust*, had just anchored nearby, and now its crew, a good-looking young couple, approached our stern by dinghy.

"We brought you a present," the woman called with a flash of smile, her brown eyes sparkling. She held it up high. We'd come to expect unexpected gifts, but this was new. It was a dog.

"It's Jib!" Inger squealed, pulling the wet fur ball into her lap. "Where did you find him?"

"He was swimming as fast as his little paws could paddle when we pulled into the anchorage," the pretty woman said. "Since he was headed toward *Cool Breezes*, we thought he must belong here."

"No, he belongs to us," Dan explained. "We left him chained to the deck when we left *Tyrene*. He must have wriggled out of his collar and dove overboard to find us."

"Good thing we picked him up when we did," the

woman continued. "Right behind him was a shark."

The cruisers we met loved to peek into the homes and lives of fellow sailors. Since the *Tyrenes* and the *Silverdusts* had already seen *Cool Breezes,* they invited us to tour their boats. Pat, Meara and I dinghied to *Tyrene.* We began our tour in the spacious and well-equipped pilothouse, then descended through two floors of labyrinthine metal hallways coated with thick yellow paint that led to rooms filled to high ceilings with cargo. Then, for a counterpoint lifestyle, we toured the interior of *Silverdust.* Sleek and gleaming, white with light teak trim, she was well appointed yet streamlined.

That evening, the crews of all five boats in the anchorage motored to the beach, our dinghies full of garbage. The anchorage community had planned a bonfire fuelled by trash. Garbage disposal on the Jumentos, as on all of the Bahamas Islands, was a huge and sensitive issue. Landfills were scarce. Since none of us would dream of throwing our garbage overboard, we'd stow it on board until we found the next garbage can or bonfire.

The six kids helped us build the fire, then hiked up to the Haitian grave markers with their dogs and their flashlights. Once they returned to the fire pit, a cantankerous old single-hander thrilled them with ghost stories. Meara pressed herself deeper in my lap.

Close to midnight, the party broke up. All of us had listened to weather reports and would weigh anchor the next morning. *Cool Breezes* would head to George Town, but the others planned different destinations. It was a typical cruisers' leave-taking; all of us hugging like long-lost friends, sad we'd never see each other again even though we'd just met. We put out the fire and boarded our dinghies.

The bobbing mast light atop *Cool Breezes* beckoned us home.

"I'll never forget this night," Erin sighed with a smile, tying the dinghy to the stern.

"Or the crew of *The Tyrene Navigator*," Pat added.

Nor would I. They were living that Caribbean mantra: Don't worry, be happy.

From:	The Kirwin crew
To:	Kith and Kin
Subject:	**Greetings from** *Cool Breezes*: **George Town at Last**

As I begin this missive, it's April 8, the day Pat and I finally deliver on our promise to the kids. Today *Cool Breezes* will ferry us from Flamingo Cay to George Town, that social Mecca where hundreds of boats and dozens of cruising families congregate each March for a cruiser's regatta.

"The regatta was almost a month ago, Mom," Erin reminds me.

"Heck, a month behind schedule is nothing for us sailors," I reply.

"All the girls my age will be gone by now," she frets.

"Hey, we're in the Bahamas, mon," I say. "Don' worry, be happy!"

This morning's weather report on the SSB predicts winds from the northeast, exactly the direction we're headed. That's been the forecast for the last four days. Today, however, the winds have diminished by five knots, so we can make forward progress. We'll beat hard, as usual, but we're used to that. The number of downwind sails we've enjoyed on this year's boat trip could be counted on the fingers of one hand.

Pat and the boys raise the jib. The white sail snaps in the brisk wind. Like a penned mare, she tosses her mane, eager to fly. Pat fires up the diesel engines and prepares to weigh anchor. Wait a minute – our friends aboard *The Tyrene Navigator* are heading straight for us. They're about to "buzz" us, Pat yells. Buzzing among boaters, like little boys teasing girls, is a fun way to show friendship. Here comes that massive steel prow, bearing down on our feeble Fiberglas, about to execute a last-minute swerve. Whoa, that was close!

April 2001, the Exumas archipelago,
The Commonwealth of the Bahamas.

Our passage to George Town will be challenging, even without a headwind. First we sail to Water Cay. Then we turn north toward Hog's Cay Cut, one of the trickiest slices of water among the Bahamas islands. At low tide, a scant three feet of water flows with a strong tidal current over a hard coral bar. The draft of our twin hulls measures only two feet, two inches, so the cut is passable for our catamaran, but just barely. Once through, we turn northwest, past Little Exuma and toward Great Exuma Island. George Town is at the south end of Great Exuma.

Right now we're bouncing vigorously against the wind, our bows bucking the swells.

"The water's not the only green thing around here, Liam," Ben teases.

"Oh man," Liam groans. "How come we never get a downwind sail?"

Pat breaks into song.

"O Lord, won't you give us a sail downwind!"

"What's that you're singing?" Erin asks.

I know what it is. Pat's adapting that old Janis Joplin tune, the one about the Mercedes Benz. I grab a pen and paper. Soon we've got our own lyrics all worked out:

O Lord, won't you give us a sail downwind,
We've been sailing this boat now for months on end,
We're tired of beating, again and again,
O Lord, won't you give us a sail downwind.

O Lord, won't you give us a wind from behind,
Our bows keep on pounding, time after time,
A wind on our stern please, if you don't mind,
O Lord, won't you give us a wind from behind.

> O Lord, won't you give us a sea smooth as glass
> With a wind that will make us go really fast
> With no real big waves, and the wind at our back,
> O Lord, won't you give us a sea smooth as glass.

"While we're at it, we might as well ask for the other things we want," says Erin.

"Yeah!" the other kids agree. They're full of beans, literally and figuratively. Pat stands at the helm grinning, while I scribble. We're all giddy, ready to poke fun at the pettiness of our wishes.

> O Lord, won't you give us a big bag of flour,
> A meal at a restaurant, and a nice long hot shower,
> To access our email, we just need an hour,
> O Lord, won't you give us a big bag of flour.

> O Lord, won't you give us a nice quiet berth,
> A still silent anchorage, away from the surf,
> Or else two feet firmly planted on good solid earth,
> O Lord, won't you give us a nice quiet berth.

A few hours pass. The wind and waves pick up. Some unexpected and menacing coral reefs near Water Cay bully us on a detour.

"It's taken more than an extra hour to skirt the reefs," says Pat. "Pretty soon the sun will set, and there won't be enough light to make it through Hog's Cay Cut. We'll anchor overnight and make a fresh start tomorrow."

"That means we won't get to George Town for another whole day," Erin complains.

"Sorry about that, honey," I reply, "but safety comes first. You know how it is at sea. Things don't usually work out exactly as planned."

It's 6:00 a.m., Monday the 9th. The sky is clear and bright. The SSB report says the weather will be grand today, especially for the northwest leg of our trip. Time to cook our morning bowls of white rice and marmalade. Just think, if we reach George Town today, we might actually get to buy yogurt and cereal for brekkie tomorrow!

We don't know the timing of today's high and low tides at Hog's Cay Cut, but we'll attempt it nonetheless. Even at three feet low tide, says Pat, we've got ten inches to spare.

Two hours later, we approach Hog's Cay Cut. The tide is at low ebb. The depth sounder flashes between two and three feet, so there's little room to spare beneath our hulls. I hold the helm, my breath as shallow as the water, while Pat stands on the foredecks, reading the water's depth ahead. The daggerboards are pulled up high; the jib is furled for maximum visibility. We use the same system of hand signals as when we anchor. I slow the engines to a mere throb, focus my gaze on Pat's every subtle gesture, and respond instantly with the slightest movement of the wheel. We weave through the crystal clear water among the sandbars and coral heads with the supple grace of a water eel. Adjust and adapt, adapt and adjust, just as the cruising guide advises. A half-hour later, we're through, unscathed. Ben and Liam whoop their relief.

"Let's anchor here for lunch," says Pat. I agree. If the passage through this cut doesn't take your breath away, the waterscape surely will. Erin sighs impatiently.

"I know you're in a hurry to get to George Town," I say, "but take a look around. The water here is so tranquil and clear, it feels like we're hydroplaning, like we're suspended above a dry ocean floor." I lead her to the trampoline at the bows, and we hang our heads over the edge. We can see every ripple in the sand below us, every tiny pink shell. We discern that the water isn't truly clear, but rather the palest shimmer of turquoise. "The sun is shining just for us," I say. "The sky is blue just for you. And soon we'll turn the corner and receive God's answer to our prayer – a downwind sail."

Just after 5:00 p.m., we tie up at the Exuma Docks in George Town. When we hail the local customs and immigration office by VHF radio, they say it's too late to check in.

"Jes' enjoy yesself in town tonight and show up at deh office in deh morning," they radio back.

We hustle off for our anticipated hot showers only to be disappointed: the water's merely lukewarm, and a huge cockroach carcass lies near the shower drain.

"Oh well," shrugs little Meara with a smile. "At least we're fresh-water clean!"

An hour later, we arrive at Eddie's Edgewater, our first George Town dining experience.

"Hey Erin," I say, nodding toward some other patrons. "Wouldn't you say those two families look like sailors?"

"How can you tell?" she responds with a sceptical glance at our neighbours.

"Just look at their wrinkled clothes, that sun-bleached hair, those peeling pink noses," I point out. "Well anyways, look, both families have girls. And wouldn't you say they're close to twelve years old? You gotta agree, dear, we've delivered on our promise!"

It's dark now, and late, but I've got my glass of wine, my flickering candle, and my laptop. Tonight I can tap away to my heart's delight, because we're plugged into shore power. And tomorrow, after three months' dearth, we can send you patient readers a flurry of stored-up email.

God bless and fair winds,
Love PJ+crew

April 2001, Volleyball Beach on Stocking Island,
near George Town, the Bahamas.

Chapter **25**
Life's a Beach

When we desire nothing, we have all that we need.
— St. Bernadette Soubirous

We landed in George Town on April 9, and spent two weeks there. Although we did boat school and all the usual chores, that fortnight felt like a holiday. Collecting and stowing wheelbarrows full of groceries, doing mounds of laundry, cooking meals, and scouring and maintaining the boat consumed huge chunks of time, as faithfully recorded in my diary. Nevertheless, everything seemed so easy.

That sense of ease was partly due to simple convenience. Everything was accessible, especially when we were docked at the marina. The laundromat was just a few steps away, so we could wear clean clothes every day. Exuma Markets down the street carried almost as much variety as the average North American grocery store, so whenever we liked, we could buy bread and flour, breakfast cereal and yogurt, milk and wine, fresh fruit and veggies and meat. Right outside the market, Mom's Bakery van was parked, gleaming white and teeming with rum cakes and hugs from "Mom" herself. The marine hardware store was stocked to the ceiling, so Pat could browse to his heart's delight. A few hotels offered Internet access, so we could send email and bank online at will. We could even rent a video! All the amenities we took for granted back in the fall, when we cruised the American eastern seaboard, or at home in our prairie city, now presented themselves as gifts.

The biggest part of that holiday feeling, though, came from the good company we kept in George Town. We entered the fold of another cruising community, this one full of families. Our first new friends were the crew aboard *Catarina*. Originally from Vancouver, B.C., Jeff and Natalie lived in Freeport in the Bahamas for four years, then decided to spend a year cruising in a catamaran with their four children. We felt an instant connection with Joel and Donna and their pretty thirteen-year-old Jayne aboard *A Bientôt*. They were from Virginia but had just completed a two-year cruise across the Atlantic and back. We were pleasantly surprised to re-acquaint ourselves with the *Goldeneye* crew – Alicia and Mick and their three kids – with whom we'd climbed the sand cliffs back in North Carolina. And it was a treat to meet Daniel, Mary and their two teens from Wisconsin sailing *Calumet Dreams*. Like us, they were midway through a one year sabbatical aboard a cat. The members of all these seafaring families became daily companions.

Of the fourteen children in our company, ranging in age from four to fourteen years old, five were girls twelve and thirteen years old. Every morning, we tuned in to the "boater's net," a half-hour program of weather and announcements on VHF channel 68. Then, Erin and the four other girls would radio each other to switch channels and make plans. It was like a rural party line.

The kids aboard all five family boats did schoolwork every morning.

"We're all in the same boat as far as that goes," Ben punned.

The afternoons, however, held endless possibility.

Most days we dinghied across Elizabeth Harbour to Volleyball Beach on Stocking Island. There, at 1:00 p.m. each weekday, the boat kids converged for "kids' club," an afternoon recreation program run by a church group. After water sports and snacks, the children listened to Bible stories and made crafts. Once kids' club wrapped up, Meara and Maggie from *Goldeneye* played in the sand. One of the dads sometimes organized a volleyball game. Later, the older kids played capture the flag among the thickets. Often they climbed trees, and lingered in the branches for hours.

We parents were far less energetic. We relaxed in the shade of palms and casuarinas at Chat'n Chill, an open-air watering hole and grill with a thatched roof. We swapped stories – mostly about the crests and trenches of cruising with kids – and traded strategies for boat schooling and cooking aboard. We'd nibble on Chat'n Chill's infamous ribs and quaff bright wet bottles of beer, relishing the certain knowledge that life would never get better than this.

For the first five days at George Town, we tied up at Exuma Docks, the only marina. We replenished our fuel and water tanks, our battery charge, and our bilge pantries. Once Jasper's two-day quarantine ended and we were officially cleared into the country, we lowered our yellow Q-flag and raised the Bahamian courtesy flag. Then we began to prepare for Easter.

"Do you think the Easter Bunny will find us?" Meara asked with grave concern.

"Oh yes, I'm sure he will," Pat and I reassured her. Privately, though, we knew the Easter Bunny might not be as generous this year. The price of chocolate bunnies at Exuma Markets shocked us, so we knew the children would not be receiving their usual heaping baskets of saccharine. Then someone suggested we inform the kids that in the Bahamas, families put out a single big basket. The Easter Bunny fills it early Easter morning, and the children of the family share the candy when they wake.

"Hmm, I guess that would work," Meara nodded. The older three looked dubious.

Good Friday was a day of sobriety in the Bahamas. All businesses remained closed until 6:00 p.m. Promptly at that hour, they re-opened and the party began. The cruising families congregated at the Two Turtles Inn barbeque. Just like at large family gatherings at home, the kids sat together at one long table, while we adults gathered at a nearby round one, indulging in Bahama Mama rum punch and high-spirited conversation. When a live band cranked up, everyone spilled onto the small dance floor. I felt a rush of appreciation when Liam, the first of the younger set to find his dancing feet, asked me to dance. Soon all the boys were dancing with their mothers, and the girls with each other.

Easter Sunday was another memorable day. The mingled scents of baking Irish soda bread and brewed coffee greeted my waking family. Meara was the first to rise.

"Look!" she shouted, pointing at the overflowing basket sitting on the salon table. "The Easter Bunny did find us!"

The other three scrambled out of bed to see for themselves.

"Voot, voot!" Ben exclaimed. "Let's do the candy-divvy!"

Knowing we'd leave the marina that day, and to prepare for Easter Sunday Mass, we all took one last fresh water shower. Dressed in what passed for a sailor's Sunday best, we strolled toward Victoria Lake in the centre of town, where many tiny wooden churches were assembled. The staid Catholic church was readily distinguishable from its neighbours. When we crossed the church threshold to hear the usual sedate organ hymns, I saw Liam looking rather wistfully back at the Baptist church, where vibrant gospel music poured forth from open windows. Yet even the Catholic service held some cultural intrigues. After the pale and elderly priest read the Gospel in English, an expressive middle-aged woman read it in Creole. Our fellow worshippers were fascinating, too. The little girls looked especially striking, with their bright floral dresses, ornate hairdos and ribbons, white gloves and gleaming dark faces. The town matrons, decked out in their best spring hats, beamed proudly. I felt like a plain brown wren next to colourful birds of paradise.

After Mass, we joined the other cruising families hunting Easter eggs on Stocking Island. Later, we moved the boat to an isolated anchorage on the lee side of Sandollar Beach. Pat barbequed lamb chops, while I prepared tender baby potatoes with butter and pepper, and steamed fresh broccoli with cheese. Erin made a chocolate silk pie.

After our Easter feast, we dinghied to shore for a twilight walk. We found a trail cut through the lush greenery and the sand dunes to the windward side of the island. There, spread in a postcard vista before us, a brilliant white beach absorbed the rolling crash of navy blue breakers. Swaying palms rustled restively behind us. Beneath them lay a mastless weather-beaten boat hull, half-buried in dunes. The spectacle awed us. God's fierce unfathomable power and splendour were everywhere.

The next morning, we dinghied back to George Town and hopped on a school bus headed to nearby Williams Town. Along with the entire cruising community, we were invited to an Easter Monday "community lunch." It was an ideal opportunity to witness the jagged inland geography of Great Exuma, to meet islanders in a rural setting, and to taste a hearty Caribbean meal of ribs, steamed conch, Bahamian macaroni, coleslaw and rice and peas. Rice and peas, we learned, is the Bahamian counterpart to that Cuban staple, *arroz con gris*.

After lunch, we explored the village. Among the scattered houses and profusely blooming shrubs we found the ruins of an old plantation.

"It's hard to imagine people actually lived here," said Liam, as we poked among the rubble of the slaves' quarters, now inhabited by goats and chickens.

"Or how such thin soil on this coral rock supported any cultivation," said Pat.

The next eight days, from April 17 to April 24, we waited for weather. The skies were mostly blue, but the winds from the north were too strong for northward passage. No one complained, least of all the kids. One mother confessed her daughter was to blame for the steady winds and successive cold fronts: "Every night she prays for more of the same!"

During that time we moved *Cool Breezes* from Sandollar Beach to "Hole One," a well protected pocket of water off Volleyball Beach, where the rest of the cruising families were huddled. Although the kids' club program had officially finished by then, the group of cruising children grew increasingly tightly knit. Each afternoon they'd work on their fort, assembled from discarded wooden pallets and interlaced with fallen palm fronds. Soon they formed their own new club, called COSK, an acronym for Club of Sailing Kids. They designed their own COSK banner from someone's yellow Q-flag and flew it proudly off the fort. One afternoon, when a cold front blew through, the adults hurried back to their boats to batten the hatches, close the windows, whip laundry off the lifelines, and check their anchors. But where did the kids go? Instinctively, each of them beelined to the fort.

"We found out the fort can hold all fourteen of us kids!" Ben announced proudly.

Another afternoon, Erin organized a book swap. During the announcements segment of the VHF boaters' net one morning, she suggested all interested readers meet on Volleyball Beach at a given date and time. Although originally conceived as a kids' book swap, it expanded to include adults. Dozens of people dinghied to the beach, bagsful of books in tow, and swarmed the picnic tables on Volleyball Beach. Erin smiled as she surveyed the success of her initiative. People of all shapes, sizes, colours and ages thronged the tables. For all our diversity, sailors have in common a voracious appetite for the printed word, and a willingness to try just about any genre.

"I'm beginning to realize that there's a whole world of cruisers out there," Erin said.

"Eureka!" Pat replied. "That was one of the main points to this sailboat trip, to show you kids there's a world of ways to live a life."

During that week, we received an email from Gary, one of our very best friends from our Varadero days, the writer aboard *Randy G.* He said his piece about our family would appear in the next issue of *Living Aboard* magazine. He also told me the editor would love to receive submissions from me on the topics of boat schooling and cooking aboard for a large family crew. That slight encouragement was all I needed. Each afternoon, after Pat and the kids dinghied to Volleyball Beach, I sequestered myself and wrote. I laboured over two articles, one entitled "Feeding Six (and a Dog) on a Cat," and the other entitled "St. Christopher's Boat School."

Each time I pulled out my papers and pen and began to rework the text, I remembered my late father, an engineer by profession and an artist by inclination. I pictured

Dad shaping a mound of clay into one of his perfect raku spheres. He'd make a ball, then smooth it, shape it, work it, and polish it until it was a gleaming thing, flawless from every angle. That's how I visualized the art of writing: a palpable work of shaping, smoothing and polishing, striving to truly represent from every perspective. How I longed for my dad!

In those days, our dinghy was indispensable. Ferrying kids to their various social engagements, and transporting laundry and groceries back and forth across Elizabeth Harbour to the George Town settlement, reminded me of the constant minivan trips of old. Instead of hopping into the upholstered driver's seat of my vehicle, however, I was now perched upon the centre passenger plank of our rubber tender, usually chauffeured by Liam, our able dinghy captain. Unlike the low hum of my efficient car engine, the dinghy outboard roared and whined. Rather than plot the quickest route through the windrows of winter snow or sloughs of spring slush, furtively checking my watch and anxiously sighing at every red light, I now braced myself for the next splash of seawater. Since the daily high winds whipped up sizeable waves in the harbour, we often arrived at our destinations thoroughly soaked. Our lifelines were constantly pegged with shorts fallen victim to "dinghy-butt."

Sometimes, for a change of scenery from Chat'n Chill, we adults would connect in the cockpit of one of our boats to enjoy sundowners and appetizers. One such afternoon, Joel and Donna arrived at the stern of our boat with extra wide smiles.

"Guess what?" Donna announced, climbing into the cockpit with a bottle of wine. "We just got an email from someone we both know. Guess who?"

Pat and I were stymied. It seemed unlikely that in this

setting, so far from home, we would know anyone in common with the *A Bientôts*.

"Jim and Edwina from *Jasper J!*" Donna exclaimed. "I used to work with Jim."

"Amazing," I replied. "They were just about our very first sailing friends."

"I know! I know!" Donna said. "They told us everything." The world was small, even at sea.

Tuesday, April 24 dawned with an especially auspicious glow. The weather report that morning promised a break in the northerlies a day earlier than expected. All of the cooped-up cruisers in Hole One could set sail the next day, instead of on Thursday or, heaven forbid, on a Friday. The weather news prompted onward plans and a spate of VHF communications among the cruising families. *Goldeneye* and *Calumet Dreams* were headed in other directions, but *Catalina, A Bientôt,* and *Cool Breezes* would buddy-boat northwards.

"If we're leaving tomorrow, we'll have to get fuel, water, food, laundry and email today," I said to the kids. "Sorry, but that means no boat school this morning."

Meara pouted, but the others cheered. After innumerable dinghy trips running errands back and forth across the harbour, our crew set about getting the boat shipshape. Pat changed the engine filters and tinkered with the temperamental refrigerator thermostat. The kids helped change the bedding, air the duvet covers, and stow fresh laundry. To guard against cockroach infestation, we stripped the packaging from the food we'd purchased, sealed it in plastic zipper bags, and stored it in the bilge pantries or fridge. We swept and swabbed, then jumped overboard for sea baths. By mid-afternoon our work was done.

"Let's go to the fort one last time!" the kids shouted. The kids from *Catarina* pulled alongside in their dinghy to pick them up, clearly with the same intention, so Pat and I dinghied to *Catarina* to get Jeff and Natalie. Less than a half-hour later we were settled in the shade on the deck of Chat'n Chill in the company of Joel and Donna and Mick and Alicia. Dinghy after dinghy of sailors pulled up on the beach right after us, all headed for the bar. In the distance, we saw a dozen Bahamian sloops with their distinctive homemade sails converging for a race.

"Today's the first day of the Family Islands Regatta," Jeff explained.

"Yes, and dat why we be havin' a rum Happy Hour," added the grouchy proprietor of Chat'n Chill, impatient for our order.

The rum drinks must have been stronger that day, because everything seemed brighter, crisper and funnier. Before we knew it, the kitchen at Chat'n Chill had closed.

"I've got a really nice pasta sauce started," Donna volunteered. "I could stretch it to feed the adults at least."

"And I just bought a beautiful rum cake from Mom's Bakery van," Natalie added.

"Great," said Pat, always eager to get a party going. "We'll herd the kids aboard *Cool Breezes* for hot dogs and movies, while we adults enjoy a civilized dinner aboard one of your boats."

"Come over to *Catarina*," Greg offered. "We can seat eight at our cockpit table."

It was a great night for everyone. The fourteen children hung out aboard our modest catamaran, watching *Maverick*. By then our kids knew the lines by heart. Meanwhile, we adults dined in much more sophisticated style aboard Jeff and Nicole's luxury cat. Since everyone had been to town that day to stock up on supplies, the wine flowed freely, and so did the conversation and laughter. Joel, especially, was in fine form that evening.

"After a night like this, it's gonna be hard to return to the 'Muggle world'," he said.

"The 'Muggle world'?" we asked. As parents of children who adored J.K. Rowling's *Harry Potter*, we were familiar with his allusion to the humdrum world of non-magic people, yet we couldn't quite grasp the analogy.

"Yes, the world of non-cruisers, the ordinary world to which we'll all return this summer," Joel replied.

Each of us looked round the table at our companions. Here we were, thrown together from points all over North America by sheer circumstance at this magical moment in time and place. All of us would be immersed in the quotidian come fall.

Less than four months remained in our year's journey. I felt a hint of nostalgia already.

April 2002, the Exumas, the Bahamas.
A wild pig swims alongside our dinghy.

Chapter 26
Aground Again

*There are many advantages to sea voyaging, but
security is not one of them.*
— *Edward Emerson*, English Tracts

The infamous morning-after-the-night-before
dawned all too early for Pat and me. We were still
asleep when Jeff of *Catarina* knocked on our stern
at 7:30 a.m.

"We're about to pull up anchor," he shouted from his
dinghy. "*A Bientôt* has already left."

"Okay, we'll radio you later," Pat yelled back.

A moment later, Mick from *Goldeneye* showed up at
our stern to return our dinghy, borrowed the night before.

"Wow," I muttered to Pat. "Our friends are made of
sterner stuff than we."

When I rolled out of bed to the full morning light in
the salon, I discovered the damage from the children's
party aboard *Cool Breezes*. Chocolate cake crumbs, popcorn bits, and dirty dishes were scattered everywhere. I
knew I shouldn't be surprised – a party of fourteen children would leave its mark even in the spaciousness of our
landlubber house, never mind a thirty-seven-by-seven-
teen-foot vessel – yet that didn't lessen my irritation.

Our young crew took a few hours to get the boat shipshape. At 10:00 a.m., we weighed anchor, ready to follow

in the wake of our buddy boats, *Catarina* and *A Bientôt*.
By then, the day's Family Islands Regatta events had
begun. Out on the water, we enjoyed an unparalleled vantage point of the races. The low-slung and beamy hulls
and telltale excess fabric of the homemade sails distinguished the race boats from every other seagoing craft.
Unlike the cruisers' regatta held in March, the Family
Islands Regatta race rules required all vessels to be
designed and built in the Bahamas, and owned and sailed
by Bahamians. Even the type of materials allowed on
board was restricted. The sight of all those masts bristling
up out of the blueness and those dozens of hulls heeling
hard into the wind was dazzling. Yet the children had eyes
only for the receding horizon. I watched them gaze wistfully back at George Town as if it were a shimmering
mirage of Neverland.

"I'm really sad to leave," Erin sighed. "But it wouldn't
be the same without the people anyway." She was right.
The magic of the place lay mainly in the community that
defined it. Ben put his arm around Erin's shoulders.

"Just think, though, we get to buddy-boat with two of
the girls your age!"

Liam lifted his face upward to watch the wind vane at
the top of the mast.

"I'm just glad to be underway again," he said simply.

We turned our bows northward and enjoyed an easy
downwind sail. By late afternoon, we'd reached the
anchorage at Little Farmer's Cay, the appointed meeting
place with *Catarina* and *A Bientôt*. Neither boat was there.
Puzzled because both boats had a few hours' head start,
Pat radioed them.

"We're back at Musha Cay," they replied. We'd already
passed that island.

"Well, it makes no sense for us to turn around and sail

back toward them," Pat said. All of us felt weary from the previous night's parties, and it was nearly sundown. "We'll just anchor here and they can catch up with us tomorrow morning."

Pat dispatched the boys to the bows to watch the water's depth while he stood at the helm. Anchoring at sundown was always tricky because the sun's slanting rays concealed the water's depth. On this particular evening, though, when our crew was not in top form, we got caught. We ran aground. This time we scraped not sand, but diamond-sharp coral reef.

The scrape of jagged rock on our Fiberglas hulls made an excruciating shudder, like amplified fingernails on chalkboard. Pat's eyes hardened. I watched the anguish on the faces of my two young boys as they realized their part in this mishap.

The tension on board felt as oppressive as the humidity. The tide was at low ebb, so we'd have to wait a few hours before attempting to dislodge the boat from its razor-edged perch. Then along came a Jamaican canoe with a powerful outboard. Its friendly crew of two cheerily pulled us off. We limped off to find a deeper anchorage. This time Pat stood watch at the bows while I took the helm.

The evening was miserable. Our hulls were intact, but the port rudder had been pushed up into the hull. The boys seemed wretched, their father angry. Now he faced new major repair problems. Pat was, after all, the captain of the ship, the one ultimately responsible for the accident and its repair.

I tucked my boys into bed more tenderly than usual that night.

"I just wish it had been me, not you at the bows this afternoon," I whispered, feeling better able than they to bear the burden of our captain's disapproval. *How darkly this evening's mood contrasts with last night's,* I wrote in my diary.

The next morning, *Catarina* arrived at our anchorage. Jeff dinghied to our cockpit and reported on their own suffering aboard. Both he and Natalie had put out their backs, especially Natalie, who could barely get out of bed, on her birthday of all days! Fortunately for them, I had invested in a lifetime supply of ibuprofen tablets, so we poured out a zipper-lock bagful for them.

When the comely Natalie rallied later that afternoon, Jeff made dinner reservations over the VHF at Ocean Cabin, a restaurant on Little Farmer's Cay. When we approached the restaurant entrance at 6:00 p.m., we found a sign that read:

Our Hours – Most days about 9 or ten, occasionally as early as 7, but some days as late as 12 or 1. We close about 5 or 6, but maybe about 4 or 5. Some days or afternoons we aren't here at all and lately we've been here about all the time except when we're some place else, but we might be here then too.

We knew this was a parody of Bahamian business hours in general, yet felt grateful when despite the hour of our arrival, the chef produced a fine meal of grouper served with peas and rice, accompanied by a redolent bottle of Merlot.

The next morning, *Catarina* radioed bright and early to say she was headed for Staniel Cay. The crew of *A Bientôt* was already there, anchored off an island called Big Major's Spot in the company of their old cruising friends aboard *Firelight.*

"I'm not sure we're up to the journey with only one operational rudder," Pat radioed back. "But we'll give it a go!"

Out in the main, *Cool Breezes* revealed her incapacity. It was impossible to hold our course without our port rudder. Even with the wheel turned hard to port, the boat veered to starboard. Pat experimented with the mainsail and jib to see if either or both would help steady our course, to no avail. Then he shifted the port engine into neutral and pushed the starboard hard. Nothing. All the while, we drifted hazardously close to the coral reefs and *Catarina* steadily outdistanced us. In one last desperate attempt, Pat put the port into reverse, but nothing would compensate for the boat's strong list to starboard.

"*Catarina, Catarina,* this is *Cool Breezes,*" Pat radioed. "We're heading back. We need to fix the port rudder before we can go any further. Go ahead, though, and catch up to *A Bientôt.* We'll keep in touch."

"No, no, we'll turn back too," Jeff radioed back.

Once at anchor, Pat quickly set to work on our "bunged up" rudder. Jeff arrived to brainstorm solutions and pass tools, while Pat clambered in and out of the engine compartment and dove under the stern to check on the downward progression of the port rudder. When I noticed Jeff wincing with back pain, I joined the work party, too, passing ibuprofen and tools upon request. It was a long afternoon and for Pat, a wet one. Then at sundown, Pat burst out of the water with a big cheer.

"That's it!" he shouted. "We've got the rudder back down to where it belongs."

Just as we sat down in the cockpit to celebratory drinks, another cruiser in the anchorage pulled alongside in his dinghy.

"Would you like some fresh mahi-mahi fillets?" he asked. "Our fridge can't hold them and they must be eaten today."

"We'll gladly take them off your hands for you," Pat replied. Once again we fed the kids aboard *Cool Breezes,* while the adults dined aboard *Cat.* Natalie braised the fish

Bahamian-style, smothered under a topping of sautéed tomatoes, onions, black olives and sweet peppers. *Magnifique!*

The next morning, *Cool Breezes* and *Catarina* travelled northward to Black Point. With our newly repaired rudder and a fresh breeze, we flew there, topping eight knots under sail alone. The next morning, winds were again favourable for pressing northward, so we sailed toward Big Major's Spot near Staniel Cay. It was a long day on the water. The sailing was easy but our journey not so smooth; the starboard engine seized up completely. Pat worried that the enigmatic warranty period on the Cuban transmission repair had truly expired.

At the anchorage off Big Major's, we reunited with *A Bientôt* and met two new cruising families. The couple aboard *Firelight* had been cruising continuously for over nineteen years. During that time they produced two daughters, then fourteen and eleven years old. The girls didn't take to the family's only attempt a few years previous to return to life on the land, so they decided to live aboard indefinitely. The other new boat, *Sweet Thing*, was crewed by a family with two boys, ages eight and ten, and two Dalmatian dogs. Like us, they planned a detour from their land-based life, but they would cruise for two years.

The weather was fickle for the next five days. From April 29 to May 3, we were stalled by wet winds, squalls and even thunderstorms, punctuated by brief spells of sunshine. Instead of moving further northward, we spent our days puttering among the anchorages surrounding Staniel Cay. Our kids had plenty of playmates. Every day after boat school, Erin and Meara hooked up with Jayne from *A Bientôt* and the girls from *Catarina* and *Firelight* to play cards or weave friendship bracelets. I worked on successive drafts of my magazine articles, and Pat tinkered on deck or read. Meanwhile Ben and Liam dinghied off every afternoon with the *Cat* boys to explore sea caves. One day the boys returned to the stern breathless with excitement.

"Mom and Dad, you've just got to see the sea cave we found today!" they said. "It's got lots of bedrooms, a balcony, and even a doghouse!"

Their enthusiasm was so infectious that both families dinghied ashore for a tour. Considerable imagination was required to recognize the balcony and doghouse, but I was delighted the boys had that vision. When the rain began to fall again, we hopped back into our dinghies and headed to our anchorage.

"Look!" said Erin, pointing. "There's a wild pig on the beach!"

Liam switched the dinghy engine into neutral so we could see for ourselves. There stood a gigantic pink pig, watching us from shore. When it saw the two dinghies full of people, the pig plunged into the water.

"Look, it's swimming out to see us!" Meara squealed.

"I didn't know pigs can swim!" the boys shouted. "It's doing the dog-paddle!"

The pig swam up to our dinghy, affording us an excellent view of its long and spotted hairy snout, and dirty drooping ears. When no handouts appeared forthcoming, the pig swam back to shore and trotted back into the bushes.

During those wet and dreary days, Pat got sick. His aching head, congested sinuses, high fever and hacking cough drove him to bed. On one of those flu days, Pat roused himself to start the port engine to recharge our batteries, but the engine merely clattered and clanked. Its complaint reminded me of the noise made by the starboard transmission when it gave out back in Cuba, off

Cayo Romano. The children and I looked up anxiously from our books. We knew the starboard engine was still seized; were we now stranded?

"Was that the sound of the port engine coupling?" I asked in dismay.

"I don't think so, but let me check," Pat replied. Screwdriver in hand, he buried his head in the port engine compartment and made a minor adjustment. A moment later, when the port engine roared back to life, the kids and I began to applaud.

"How bad is it," Pat later confided to our anchorage neighbours, "when the kids cheer if something actually works properly?"

On May 2, another wet and windy day, Pat and I checked into the marina at Staniel Cay. There, said our cruising guide, we could enjoy a restaurant meal and fresh-water showers. More importantly, we could plug into shore power to replenish our batteries and access a mechanic to look at our seized starboard engine. Our friends aboard *Catarina* and *A Bientôt* anchored nearby. While Pat and the mechanic worked on the starboard engine, the rest of us explored the town. We found the local Batelco telephone office, where we could send and retrieve email.

"I might as well fire off the magazine articles I wrote," I said to Ben, who helped me with email. "What do you think?"

"Go for it, Mom," he urged, in an interesting role reversal.

We returned to the boat to find Pat jubilant. The mechanic had managed to free the seized starboard engine merely by loosening the crankshaft, a repair much simpler than Pat expected. He also reported the day's other big news: *Catarina* had decided to move on.

"Their cruising year ends in June, not August, so they're on a tighter schedule than we are," Pat said. "Besides, Natalie's back is still killing her. They want to get back to Freeport to see her chiropractor as soon as possible."

The couples from *Catarina* and *Cool Breezes* converged aboard *A Bientôt* that evening for one last round of sundowners in the cockpit. That was the last time we saw Jeff and Natalie's crew. Once back in Freeport, the family sold the boat and packed up their house. Later that summer, they moved back to Canada. They were the first of us to leave the aquamarine sphere of sailors for the greyer Muggle world outside.

May 2001, Warderick Wells, the Exumas, the Bahamas.

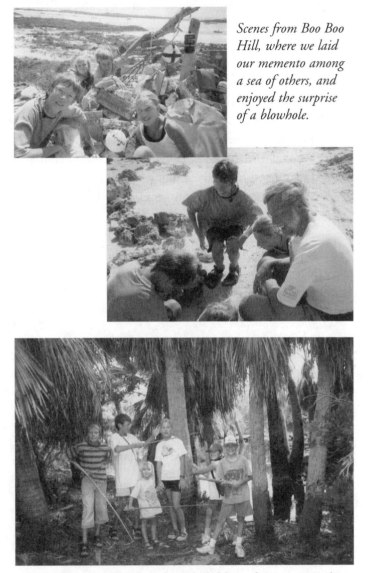

Scenes from Boo Boo Hill, where we laid our memento among a sea of others, and enjoyed the surprise of a blowhole.

The kids play pirate at the secluded lair of Captain Teach (a.k.a. Blackbeard).

From: The Kirwin crew
To: Kith and Kin
Subject: **Greetings from *Cool Breezes*:**
   Thunderball to Warderick Wells

George Town to Staniel Cay, Bahamas – Kids built fort and explored cool sea caves – adults enjoyed weeklong happy hour and ran boat into coral reef – Pat sobered up and fixed rudder – narrow dinghy escape from swimming pig.

That's an executive summary of my last group email, composed by my lawyer brother who's accustomed to reading law digests. I get the message. You readers want a change of pace, a report of something other than weather endured, repairs suffered, meals savoured, and drinks drunk. I'm not only happy but also able to oblige. At this very moment, we've just returned from a travel magazine adventure to Thunderball Cave, the famous and fabulous natural coral grotto featured in the namesake James Bond movie. Here's a synopsis:

The boat is anchored off Staniel Cay. The skies are cross. Grey clouds scurry southward in a fast-forward flee, but the rain stops long enough to allow us a dinghy ride to Thunderball Cay. Ten minutes later, we drop the dinghy anchor in sheltered water, surrounded by a dozen other tenders. The wind is so brisk and cool that many cruisers wear wetsuits. We hardier Canadians sport swimsuits beneath windbreakers and shorts.

The water is at high tide this morning. That means the cave entrance is below water.

"I'll stay back with Meara while the rest of you swim under," I offer. Pat and the three older kids strip their outer layers and dive overboard. Fifteen minutes later, they return.

"Mom, you gotta see it!" the boys exclaim.

"What about me?" Meara is a small and risk-averse child, not yet a good swimmer.

"To get to the cave, you have to swim underwater through a long tunnel, and the current is way too strong for you," Pat replies. "But I'll stay here with you while your mom takes a look."

My turn to take the plunge. My sons are eager to escort me. Pat's right: the tunnel is long enough to induce an ache for air in my lungs, and the current is stiff. Yet the reward for our efforts is glorious. We emerge from the tunnel into a high and airy limestone dome in the centre of the cay. There the dense and turquoise air is still, surreal. Through trellis holes in the grotto ceiling, streams of verdigris sunlight glint off shimmering water. As we tread water in the deep pool beneath the lattice, my sons look at me, expectant for my reaction. I feel breathless, and not just from the exertion required to arrive in this magnificent place.

"Etch this into your memory banks, boys." My voice echoes off the limestone walls.

The trip back out is a joy ride, rushing with the current to the greyness outside. When we rejoin the rest of the crew, we see Meara's little face pressed against the Plexiglas window in the floor of our dinghy.

"Look at all the fish!" she squeals. "Is this what it looks like when you snorkel?"

Today, May 5, the weather gods finally permit a substantial move northward. In the good company of our boat buddies, we enjoy a sweeping three-hour downwind sail, followed by an hour-long slog into the Emerald Rock anchorage.

"Hey, we can say we've been to Ireland," Ben quips. "You know, the 'emerald isle'!"

Emerald Rock is close to Warderick Wells Cay, the headquarters of the internationally acclaimed Exuma Cays Land and Sea Park. Supporters of the Sea Park include Hollywood actors, famous musicians and most notably, Prince Charles. Even some prominent Edmontonians are listed among its patrons. The snorkelling off this protected cay is spectacular, but Warderick Wells also boasts many land-based features. There's a pirate's lair here, once used by Edward Teach, also known as "Blackbeard," and the ruins of an old Loyalist plantation. We can climb a hilltop to see a cairn dedicated to some shipwrecked missionaries, and find blowholes, manhole sized openings in the limestone. Park wardens and volunteer cruisers have cut trails through the dense foliage leading to all of these attractions. It's too late for a hike this afternoon, so we'll begin exploring tomorrow.

It's May 6 today, blustery and cool but not raining. After boat school (marked by the incessant bickering of my two youngest students), we eat lunch. Then we dinghy to the beach where we can access the park warden's headquarters and the hilltop cairn.

The headquarters building, planted prominently atop Pepper Hill, is a spacious wooden two-storey structure lined with windows and wrapped by a veranda. Set squarely at its entrance is a bucket of water, along with a sign inviting us to rinse our feet before we enter; otherwise we visitors would deposit an overwhelming amount of sand on the floors in very short order. Not a bad idea, think I, the chief sweeper-upper aboard *Cool Breezes*! We meander the public display area, where copious information on coral reef preservation, weather monitoring, and flora and fauna is shown. Semi-domesticated lemon and nurse sharks, along with a barracuda, make their home in the placid anchorage off the beach, we learn. The wildlife specimens are fascinating, especially for Ben and Liam, my tactile learners.

We descend the wooden staircase from the headquarters building and follow the coral pathway down to the beach. There we find the reconfigured skeleton of a fifty-two foot sperm whale that washed ashore a few years ago.

"Incredible," Erin breathes. The sight is astonishing, but Meara runs right by it.

"Look, a playground!" she squeals. She hasn't seen equipment like this for months.

From the beach a path leads up to Boo Boo Hill, the site of the cairn dedicated to the doomed missionaries. Island lore claims that the missionaries' remains were buried on the hill long ago, and that their ghosts haunt the island. On moonlit nights, we are told, one can hear the sound of a congregation singing hymns, followed by its calling voices.

"Maybe that's why they call it *Boo-oo, Boo-oo,*" Ben speculates.

On this bright and breezy afternoon, ghost stories seem remote. Enroute to the cairn, we discover hundreds if not thousands of mementos left by visiting boaters. Each memento consists of a nautical artifact – a fishing float, a broken dinghy oar, even an old outboard motor – painted or carved with a boat name and date. I privately speculate the origin of this mariners' tradition. Perhaps because sailors are implicitly transient, we long to leave something permanent to mark our arrival at a certain place and time.

The kids are excited.

"We gotta leave a memento from *Cool Breezes*!"

At boat school this morning, we make our memento. We paint an old buoy with the words "*Cool Breezes* – Canada 2001" and attach it to a piece of driftwood. On the driftwood we glue a photo of our family, then shellac it. Tomorrow, when the paint and glue are dry, we'll hike up Boo Boo Hill and place our memento there. Today, we've invited Joel from *A Bientôt* and the two boys from *Sweet Thing* on a hike to Pirate's Lair.

The inland coral rock is rough and sharp, even along the cut trails. Meara soon tires. Pat hoists her on his shoulders. Sometimes I carry her on my hip. But the rest of the gang is full of vim and vigour. The prospect of touching history and discovering dark intrigue heightens the children's anticipation. We quickly discover that the younger boy from *Sweet Thing* is extremely accident-prone. Despite our admonitions to be careful, Calvin touches the leaves of poisonwood trees and falls twice, first scraping his knee and then cutting a large gash on his scalp.

"Oh, my goodness," I exclaim, trying to stem the profuse bleeding from Calvin's head. "What will your mother say when we return you to her with all your injuries?"

Calvin looks stunned, as if he's never before considered his mother's feelings, but his older brother just shrugs.

"Oh, don't worry, she's used to it," he replies.

First stop on our hike is at the ruins of the old Loyalist plantation, dating back to the late 1700s. All that remain are the walls of three buildings, made from rock and conch shell mortar. From there we hike a short trail lined with conch shells and palm fronds leading to the inland Pirates'

Lair. The pirates' meeting place is completely shrouded by bending palms and tall grasses, set beside a shady lagoon. The very air is eerie. The kids stand still, in awe, but only for a moment. The spell is broken when they notice a hammock strung between two tall tree trunks, and take turns dumping each other out of it.

Now it's May 8, another windy day, and we're still weathered in. After boat school, our crew heads back to Boo Boo Hill to memorialize our own presence at Warderick Wells.

On the way uphill we pass a blowhole, a large round hole that now, at low tide, provides a window to the sea below. We've read these holes are created by rain collecting in low spots in the limestone and eroding it.

"I wonder why they're called 'blow' holes," Liam muses aloud.

Just then, as if in answer, a huge whoosh of water spouts forth. The ground on which we're walking has become a shelf over the sea, allowing great gusts of air and volcanoes of water to burst through the hole.

The whole family gathers kneeling around the hole, eager to feel the next gush.

"Aagh!" we shout, when after a very short wait we are soaked with seaspray.

We continue our mount up Boo Boo Hill, looking for just the right place to park our own memento. I show Erin a memento marked *L'Alouette*.

"I bet Louise's family left it," Erin sighs, tears brimming over. "Let's put our memento right beside it." We take a photo of the two boats' mementos and walk slowly down the hill. "Sailing life sure does mean a lot of good-byes," Erin muses aloud.

Erin's observation prompts me to pose a question for suppertime discussion: "Now that we've been at sea for eight months, will you be glad to go home in August?" Here are the answers:

Meara: I'd be happy no matter if we stayed or went home. Whatever happens, I'll be happy!

Liam: It'll be good to be home, but I know I'll miss my boating life. In some ways I think I could always live on a boat, but it would be easier to live on a boat forever if you'd never lived on land. Then there wouldn't be people you missed back home.

Ben: There's a lot I miss on land, but a lot I'd miss on the boat. There are a lot of things I can't do if I'm living on a boat. So I'd gladly stay out one, two, even five years, but eventually I'd want to go back to land.

Erin: I'll be glad to go home in August, but I will really miss all this. Returning will be bittersweet.

Pat: I'll be happy to go home, but if we could, I'd gladly stretch out this year another long while. Eventually, though, I'd want to return to Edmonton to accomplish my goals.

Jeananne: I love my boat life most of the time, and could be happy living aboard quite a bit longer, but I'd need to know there was an eventual return date.

Won't it be interesting to see how we feel when August actually arrives?

God bless and fair winds,

Love PJ+crew

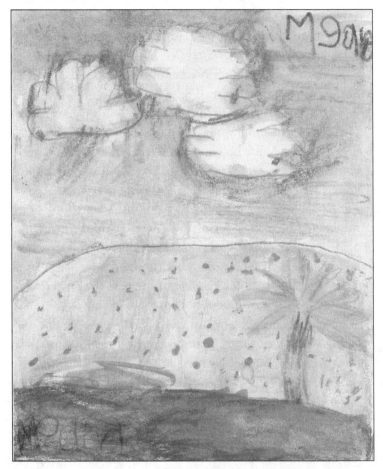

May 2001. A painting by Meara, inspired by the island anchorages of the Bahamas.

Chapter 27
More Tadpole than Frog

Time goes, you say? Ah, no. Alas, Time stays; we go.
  – Henry Austin Dobson, The Paradox of Time

Thirty-knot winds forced our stay in Warderick Wells a few days longer. Since the skies were sunny and stretched forever, we weren't confined to our cabin. After boat school mornings, we dinghied about the anchorage, hooked up with fellow cruisers, and returned with them to our favourite sites on the island.

I found dinghy rides a pleasure. Compared to the choppy waters of Elizabeth Harbour at George Town, the sea at Warderick Wells was placid. The sensory treats offered by dinghy travel offered delightful respite after an arduous morning at boat school, where the threat of class-room mutiny now overshadowed the joy of teaching. With Liam as capable pilot, and the drone of the engine muffling the children's chatter, I could simply shift my mind into neutral. I let the sun and the buzz transport me to another level, a level above the mundane and logical. There I offered my face to the wind. Through closed eye-lids, I soaked up the pink light and felt my soul recharge. Through open eyes, I took in the exquisite seascape: sandy islets with swaying palms, subtly spectacular gradations of watercolour, and unspoiled coral reefs lying just beneath a layer of liquid clarity. I squinted my eyes to blur my vision, a visual habit from travelling prairie highways. Instead of a ribbon of sky-blue and grain-yellow stripes, I now perceived a dappled mosaic of fluffy white and sandy fawn, watery turquoise and palmy mid-green. Beyond the perfect but immutable images of postcards, this vista not only spread itself before me but also flowed around me, shifting delightfully with our passage over time and distance. Just as I absorbed it, I was absorbed by it.

One afternoon, Joel of *A Bientôt* invited Liam aboard for a guitar jam session. Liam returned to *Cool Breezes* with a renewed enthusiasm for his instrument, and reams of new sheet music, including the chords for Pat's favourite, "Four Strong Winds." Another night, when Joel and Donna joined us for sundowners, they brought along a CD of Eileen Quinn songs. Her lyrics, often hilarious, sometimes poignant, were truly in key with our own nautical experience. We listened to it several times.

The morning of May 9, the winds slackened.

"A perfect travel day!" Pat said, clapping his hands with enthusiasm, once he'd heard the weather report.

A Bientôt radioed over.

"We're heading north with *Firelight* this morning," said Joel. "Got 'marshmallow' plans to anchor out near Shroud Cay."

"We're not ready to pull up the anchor yet, but we'll follow and keep in touch," Pat replied.

One of the reasons we weren't yet ready was that all of us were at various stages of our sea baths. The children's skin was becoming mottled, and I knew it needed a good sloughing. A seawater scrub and thorough terry-towel rub would take care of that.

Mottled or not, our children looked terrific. All of them appeared strong, confident and healthy. Gone were the round shoulders and pale skins of those who spent too little

time outdoors and too much time gazing at screens instead
of horizons. Erin was blossoming before our eyes, a lithe and
athletic girl with long legs and hair. She was almost as tall as
I. Ben, meanwhile, had long ago overtaken me in height, if
not weight. His lanky brown arms and legs had acquired a
definite muscle tone, and his blue eyes appeared startlingly
light against his smooth tanned cheeks. Liam, who tended to
be husky, now sported a trim and muscular bronze torso,
and his brown hair had acquired an even layer of golden
streaks. Meara's light and wispy hair had bleached out almost
white. Constantly slathered in sunscreen, her skin hadn't
developed more than a golden glow, but her chubby cheeks
were rosy and her little legs had grown sturdy. None of them
had been sick for even a day – not counting seasickness –
since Christmas.

And what about Pat and me? We too had developed
muscle tone and lost many sedentary ripples over the last
several months. We too were sun-kissed. Unlike our bodies, though, our hair had suffered this journey. Mine,
chemically highlighted for years, was now long and blond,
but shapeless and frazzled. Most days I gathered it in a
ponytail. Pat's grey beard was seriously overgrown, and his
thick silver mop curled below his ears. In short, we looked
healthy but poorly groomed, like almost every other cruising couple we'd met.

"All aboard that's coming aboard!" I shouted. The kids
piled wet and glistening into the cockpit, spanking clean
and ready for the voyage north. Jasper stood squarely in
the middle of the cockpit, her long pink tongue hanging
out, grinning in anticipation.

Pat switched on the twin ignitions. The port engine
caught but the starboard merely groaned. And so did Pat.

"It's seized up again," he said, "and I don't have a crescent wrench big enough to release the crankshaft again.

Let's set out with just one engine. Heaven knows we've done that before."

I took the helm while Pat weighed anchor. From the foredecks, Pat gestured me to steer toward the passageway out of our anchorage. Yet when I turned the wheel in that direction, the boat didn't respond.

"Jake!" Pat yelled. "What's going on?"

"The boat won't turn!" I called back. Pat darted to the cockpit and yanked the wheel. Nothing happened. Then he looked up, saw we were drifting dangerously close to the coral reef off Emerald Rock, and dashed back to the foredecks to drop the anchor.

"Something's wrong with the rudder," he announced. He stripped to the waist and dove overboard. A moment later his head emerged from the water.

"Port rudder's gone," he sputtered.

Sailing to Shroud Cay that day would be impossible. Not only was the starboard engine seized, the jury-rigged rudder had dropped out of the port hull and sunk to the sea floor. Luckily, the rudder was red, so we could see it nearby. At low tide, the water was only eight or ten feet deep.

"Ben and Liam, lower the dinghy," Pat ordered. "Let's go get our rudder."

Liam dinghied Pat to the spot above the red rudder. The rest of us watched from the cockpit. Pat dove down to the seabed, retrieved the wayward rudder and hauled it out of the water and into the dinghy. *Phenomenal!* I wrote in my diary that evening. I felt like Jane marvelling at Tarzan, Lois in awe of Superman.

That was the first step. The second was to find tools to make our numerous repairs. Pat radioed the Warderick Wells park warden, who agreed to loan Pat a number of tools: the correct crescent wrench to release the starboard engine crankshaft, a vice and sledge hammer to pound out the bend in the rudder shaft, and a drill to enlarge the original holes in the rudder so that a longer and stronger bolt could fit through the shaft.

While Pat toiled away at boat repairs, the kids and I worked at boat school. That afternoon, Ben and Erin donned snorkelling gear and dove below to help Pat replace the rudder. Their industry was infectious. Unable to sit idly in the cockpit, I polished the Plexiglas and scrubbed the mildew that sprouted during the recent wet spell. Liam swabbed the decks, and Meara swept the cockpit. By mid-afternoon our boat was shipshape, not just inside and outside, but also underneath.

"Given that mechanical breakdowns and boat repairs are a fact of cruising life, we've been pretty lucky," Pat mused, pulling on the last of our Mayabe beer from Cuba. "Lucky in that the damage arises at generally workable times and places. Take today, for example. What if we hadn't had the warden's tool supply to call upon?"

Liam, the master of "what-if," chimed in.

"And what if the rudder fell off while we were underway, with twenty-five feet of water below us?"

As the shadow of our mast lengthened on the water, we realized we wouldn't likely see *A Bientôt* again. Erin was tearful to think she'd seen Jayne for the last time, yet hadn't said goodbye. I too was melancholy, knowing how much I'd miss Donna's kindred spirit and Joel's euphemisms. They too are now well settled in the Muggle world, with a house, real jobs, land-based school and, perhaps, marshmallow plans to take *A Bientôt* on another long cruise.

Bright sunshine and brisk breezes the next morning inspired us to venture north with *Sweet Thing* to Shroud Cay. Among the many delights of this small island, we read, were its tidal lakes and meandering creeks, and a rustic encampment called Driftwood, touted as a replica of the setting for *Robinson Crusoe*. We anchored in the early afternoon. By then the tide was at low ebb, preventing us from exploring the myriad rivulet passages into the island. Instead, Meara and the boys played board games with the boys from *Sweet Thing*, while Drew and Pat took Erin and the three dogs ashore for a beach romp.

That left Betsy and I alone in the cockpit of *Sweet Thing*. Betsy brewed a pot of tea. We'd met only recently, but in the typical manner of socially starved sailing matrons, Betsy and I quickly dispensed with the pleasantries and bared our inner thoughts.

"I don't know about you, but I'm about ready to bury the anchor," Betsy confessed with a Southern drawl and a toss of reddish blond curls.

"How long have you been cruising?" I asked.

"Already a year, with a year left to go," she answered. "I don't know if I can take it, but I don't know how to tell Drew. He absolutely loves the cruising life, and so do the boys. So I just keep my mouth shut, just grin and bear it, and try to be thankful."

"I know, sometimes I have to remind myself to be thankful, too," I said aloud. Inwardly, though, I realized that lately, gratefulness came easier.

"I know it sounds selfish, but it's really how I feel," Betsy continued. "This lifestyle ain't what I signed up for. The weather is dreadful more than half the time. The boys and I are often seasick. The boat is too small for all of us, and most of the time it looks like a disaster area. Dog hair and sand get into everything. It's hard to get supplies and decent food around here. And something on the boat is always broken. If it's not one thing, it's another, and we're always trying to find a repairman. Drew's hopeless at fixing things."

"I know what you mean," I replied. I knew the timing was not right to expound on the virtues of my ever-resourceful and mechanical husband. Yet much of Betsy's complaint rang true. She articulated thoughts I'd sometimes harboured, grievances shared by many live-aboard women. Marinas along the southeastern American seaboard were well stocked with boats for sale, the outcome of many couples' dreams-come-true-gone-sour. A husband's heaven-on-earth was often a wife's private hell.

"Even bigger than all these physical problems is the loneliness," Betsy sighed. "On the one hand, too much togetherness with my husband and kids, and on the other, not enough social outlet with other women. I need to hear from someone else that she's tired of taking orders from her husband the captain, or she's in tears because she feels incompetent, or she's going crazy 'cause she hasn't showered for five days."

"Okay, you heard it from me," I laughed. "Yes, I'm tired of taking orders, yes, I'm terribly incompetent, and yes, my scalp drives me crazy if I don't take a real shower!" Then, more soberly, I added, "It's true. Once in a while I find myself thinking the bloom is off the rose. But then I remember what it's like back home, all that rushing around, all that stress related to time. It seems that the busier we are, the more important others judge us to be. And then I remember that this boat trip is the time of our life, it's like time out of our life. When I think of that, all those annoying things begin to matter less. Instead of wishing for time to pass, I worry that it's passing too quickly."

"So what would you do if you were me, with a year left to go?" Betsy asked.

"I'd tell Drew you need to regroup," I answered. "Maybe your next stop could be on an island with a decent hotel where you could hole up alone for a few days. Somewhere you could take a daily shower, eat restaurant meals, and not worry about anything breaking."

"Maybe even dress up for dinner!" Betsy added.

That evening I dealt myself a game of solitaire, pondering my heart-to-heart with Betsy. It seemed serendipitous that we'd been placed in each other's path. Each of us had needed a sounding board; Betsy to speak the unspeakable, and I to give voice to lessons unwittingly learned. I now consciously acknowledged how precious, how sacred, I'd come to regard the remaining time of our year away. I had the same threshold feeling I'd noticed on the brink of a short holiday, the sense that the short space of time ahead of me glistened like an iridescent bubble. That sense of delicious reprieve always elicited a smiling sigh of well-being, a heightened appreciation for the gift of the present moment. It didn't matter so much whether the weather was good, or what exactly we did with our time. This was it, the time of my life for which I'd ache once it had passed.

We rose early the next morning, in time to catch the rising tide at Shroud Cay. Along with the crew of *Sweet Thing*, we navigated the islet's winding alleys toward Camp Driftwood. We discovered Shroud Cay is more a mangrove jungle stretching across rocks and coral reefs than a single island. The route was often shallow and shoaled. We raised the dinghy engine and picked our way along by paddling or pulling the dinghy.

"Too bad our dinghy isn't lighter," Liam said. "We could've portaged like the Canadian voyageurs!"

After hauling the dinghies for more than an hour, and climbing the steep hand-hewn steps through a tangle of brush, our arrival at Camp Driftwood was anticlimactic. Originally a resting place of driftwood furniture adorned with sea treasures, the camp had deteriorated since a German hermit built it in the 1960s. Now it was nothing but a collection of weathered trash.

That afternoon the two boats set out for Highborne Cay, about twenty nautical miles from Shroud. Highborne was a small, H-shaped island with an excellent marina, a catering service, some rental cottages, and several curving beaches. For the crew of *Cool Breezes,* the main amenities were access to fresh water, diesel fuel, and telephones. Mother's Day was approaching, and both Pat and I knew we could give no better gift to our mothers than to call home. We'd leave the next day. But for the crew of *Sweet Thing,* the agenda was different.

"We're gonna take a break and regroup," Drew told us. "Get some laundry done, take some real showers, stuff like that." I hoped Betsy would rent a cottage for a few days, order catered meals, and dine in her best sundress. We never did see the crew of *Sweet Thing* again, nor did we get their email or street addresses. I've always wondered how the second year of cruising unfolded, and where the family is now.

On the morning of Saturday, May 12, the SSB weather report forecast ideal sailing conditions.

"Let's get to Nassau," said Pat when I relayed the good news.

Nassau was only a half-day sail away. Pat was eager to find a good mechanic, and had started a list of repairs to be made and parts to be bought. I too had a list, a litany of chores like "get a decent haircut," "do laundry," "buy groceries" (with its own separate list attached), and "send mail." We'd collected a pile of snail mail, including some homemade Mother's Day cards and letters for the kids' grandmothers and godmothers, and accumulated a stash of unsent email messages. There was no denying that once in a while, we had no choice but to hook in to civilization. Yet it held little appeal. By then, eight months out, we had become truly immersed in our world of wind and water and islands, where time and we could amble instead of rush. Still amphibious, we were nonetheless more tadpole than frog.

From: The Kirwin crew
To: Kith and Kin
Subject: **Greetings from *Cool Breezes***: **News
                from Nassau**

It's Saturday morning, May 12. We're headed to Nassau.
What a glorious sail we're having, exactly what rekindles
the magic of sailing! The wind blows briskly to starboard,
and the sails are set to a comfortable beam reach. We're
making good time, seven knots says the captain. Even better, the skies are a lofty light blue, and the seas a gorgeous
aquamarine, shading to royal then indigo as the depths
plunge. Those who favour blue – and that would be all
four kids and me – revel in the visual treat. Best of all,
both engines are working and the rudder hasn't fallen off.
Hallelujah!

Just past noon, we putter into Nassau Harbour. I've
just cleared in with Nassau Harbour Control over the
VHF, as per directions in our cruising guide; a minor
inconvenience compared to the rigors of the Guarda
Frontera back in Cuba. The older three are sprawled on
the trampoline, eager to capture their first impression of
the capital city and commercial hub of the Bahamas. Only
twenty-one miles long and seven miles wide, New
Providence is one of the smallest of the inhabited Bahamas
Islands. Yet because of its population concentration in
Nassau – upwards of two hundred thousand – and the
newly built Atlantis attraction, New Providence is the centre of Bahamian economic and social life.

The anchorages in this area are poor. The bottom is
muddy, making for unreliable holding, and heavy traffic
plying the waters makes for a rolly resting place.
Nevertheless, we'll spend the night here; the marinas are
all full. A glut of boats in this area await the arrival of

May 2001.
The writer and her faithful diary, at rest on the foredeck.

either a weather window to cross the Gulf Stream to Florida, or else boat parts to arrive for nautical repairs.

As soon as we drop anchor, the kids and I dinghy ashore to search out email access, a post office, and a grocery store. Pat, who could use some solitude, offers to make *paella* for supper. After tying our dinghy to one of the marina piers, we take in the sights, sounds and smells of the city. Palm trees and modern shops line Bay Street, the main shoreline artery. A variety of picturesque restaurants and historic residences face the shoreline drive, some recently refurbished and painted in pastel colours, others in disrepair, with sunken rooflines and overgrown foliage. The briny scent of seawater, the sharp tang of fresh fish, the sweet pungency of brilliantly blooming shrubs, and the acrid fumes of diesel fuel and car exhaust all hang together in humid mellow air. The constant shriek of rubber tires along the main drag, the oppressive thrum of unmuffled car engines and atonal rap music, and the appearance of a dead rat on the sidewalk remind us that along with its amenities, this urban centre has its drawbacks.

Back on board, our catamaran wallows in the wake of the raucous "Booze-and-Cruise" party boats streaming by. Pat is reading a book, trying to distract himself from the bad news: his discovery just this evening that the bottom four feet of our port daggerboard shredded and fell off, probably when we ran aground on coral back near Little Farmer's Cay.

This repair isn't just another to add to Pat's to-do list. This is a big headache. Pat can fix small Fiberglas dents and scratches, but this damage requires the skill of a tradesman.

Happy Mother's Day, all you mothers out there! What a sweet day it's been for me! Knowing I'll get breakfast in bed, I simply stay there upon waking. Pat makes coffee, and Ben and Erin cook blueberry pancakes and fried Spam for breakfast. Then, still in bed, I receive love poems and drawings from my children and husband. Erin gives me a homemade shell and bead necklace, and Ben a wooden fish he carved. Now these are gifts a Cuban might give!

Following the morning's festivities, one of the marinas hails us by VHF to say a berth has opened up. Hurray! Mother's Day will now include hot showers! We might even download email! And we can empty our stinky lockers of all that accumulated garbage!

Once we've cleaned both our boat and ourselves, we stroll eastward along Bay Street. There we find a shopping mall with a grocery store, bank, pharmacy, hardware store, liquor store, beauty salon and travel agency. We're proud – and amused – to find the windows of the travel agency covered with Canadian tourism posters, featuring our own spectacular Rocky Mountains. On a Sunday, most of the shops are closed, but the Dairy Queen is blessedly open. We treat ourselves to one of my all-time favourites, chocolate-dipped soft cones. Now that's a first in many moons! We're reminded of that Eileen Quinn song about food cravings, yearnings for culinary delights unavailable aboard typical sailboats: "Oh I want ice cream/French fries and ice cream/sweet and frozen, crispy golden/ice cream…" The ditty runs through my head all day.

Back at the marina, we learn the office will let us download email. Ben and I pack the laptop into its waterproof case and trot down the dock to mine our treasure chest, our email inbox. Your email, dear kith and kin, is truly a lifeline for us. You've no idea! After the download, we hurry back to the boat to pore over every word. The kids crowd around the screen on the salon table, mesmerized.

"Wow! Over thirty messages!" Erin squeals. One by one, they read each missive.

Suddenly Liam shouts out, "Hurray! Nanny and Shelby and Auntie Barbara are coming to Nassau!" General cheering and leaping about ensue.

"This I gotta read for myself," I say, sliding into the bench seat. "They fly to Nassau June first, just in time to celebrate the girls' birthdays!"

Late in the afternoon Pat and I enjoy sundowners in the cockpit, toasting to our good health, our safety, our fine and happy young foursome, and our bulging bank of lifetime memories. Problems that yesterday loomed so large, like the shredded daggerboard and cantankerous starboard transmission, lack of solitude and shortage of supplies, seem to vanish like the sinking sun into the watery horizon.

"Let's go out to dinner tonight," Pat says. "There's a decent restaurant just down the end of the dock."

I need no convincing. The marina is gated and guarded, so we leave Erin in charge and Jasper on guard. From our table at the Poop Deck, on a balcony overlooking the marina, we watch the moon rise above the bristly brush of boat masts reflected on the tranquil sea. We dine on shrimp and lobster and the fullness of the moment.

Ah yes! That was then and this is now: Monday morning. Jasper and I just returned from a run along Bay Street. I'm determined to polish off this email and launch it into cyberspace before boat school begins and the to-do lists loom.

God bless and fair winds,
Love PJ+crew

May 2001.
Artwork by Meara, inspired by the weather proverb,
"Red skies at night, sailor's delight."

Chapter **28**
Marooned

What is a ship but a prison?
   – *Robert Burton,* The Anatomy of Melancholy

From May 14 through May 21, we remained docked at Nassau Yacht Haven, awaiting boat repairs. That first scorching Monday morning, while Pat scouted for mechanics to repair the starboard engine, I trotted back and forth between boat school on board and the laundry room down the dock. On one of these runs, I noticed a small wiry man with safety glasses pulled over his dreadlocks, working in the cockpit of his boat. The acrid stench of Fiberglas filled the air.

"Hello," I shouted down at him. "Do you do Fiberglas repair work?"

The man must have thought I was daft; he was clearly in the middle of such work.

"Our daggerboard needs repair," I added quickly. "Would you come look at it?"

"Later, mon, later," he replied, turning back to his work.

That evening, the taciturn Albert arrived dockside to appraise the daggerboard damage. He and Pat negotiated a price of US$700 for the repair, to be completed by the weekend. Albert, a man of few words and curt gestures, handily hoisted the long and heavy daggerboard remnant over his shoulder, waving off all offers of help. We were grateful Albert was exactly where and when we needed him. Pat was relieved that this major burden was lifted, and I glad to be the agent.

In the meantime, Pat found diesel mechanics to repair our starboard engine. The mechanics said the Cubans had produced very good replacement parts for those damaged by the original misalignment. Yet like their Virginia predecessors, they'd failed to position them properly, resulting in continued rattles and seizures. We could choose either to import replacements for the damaged parts, or hire the mechanics to re-machine them. The decision for us was easy. Unwilling to join the ranks of cruisers stuck for up to five weeks awaiting customs clearance and the installation of foreign parts, we chose the second option. The mechanics said they'd charge about US$1000, and complete the work by the weekend.

Hard work was in store for all. Pat devoted his energy to changing and buying engine filters, shopping at marine supply stores, banking, and puttering about the decks. He filled all the tanks, including our stove propane and dinghy gasoline tanks. He also volunteered to help fellow cruisers with their own breakdown problems.

One morning, for instance, Pat and Erin used the dinghy to pull a sailboat into the main channel of Nassau Harbour. Her crew, utterly discouraged when the part it had imported didn't fit, decided not to wait another four weeks but to venture across the Gulf Stream completely bereft of auxiliary engine power.

"Talk about desperate to get home!" I remarked.

"Well, as the captain points out, he's got a sailboat, not a motorboat," Pat replied.

Another day, Pat helped the owners of a neighbouring boat repair its fallen rudder.

"In this I have experience," he assured the crew, much to their amusement.

"As they say, misery loves company," Liam quipped.

My days, too, were filled with chores. In addition to seven loads of laundry and three major hauls of groceries, I had ten rolls of film developed, bought new clothes, and got haircuts for Meara and me. Several inches of bleached blond straw were chopped off both our heads. My main work, though, was as schoolmistress. I knew that this week, holed up at a marina, would be ideal for working on our lessons.

"You don't want to do boat school when Shelby arrives on June first," I reasoned with my students. "Let's aim to finish off all our school work by the end of May."

"Yeah, that sounds good," they nodded.

The children's acquiescence was good only in theory. In practice, they were loath to do schoolwork. For one thing, the weather was too summery. By 9:30 each morning, the thermometer rose to over eighty degrees Fahrenheit, and by noon it was unbearably hot below decks. Back home, we sometimes endured snowfall in May, not full-fledged summer and its embedded association with school holidays. But the main reason for the kids' reluctance was boredom with their lessons. They'd finished every major subject except French, and were aghast when I insisted upon completing their curriculum.

"Aw, Mom, our teachers never make us finish the whole French book," Erin wailed.

"Sorry," I sighed. "Your regular teachers know what must be done, but I don't."

I devised a new strategy for the school day, an adaptation of Erin's learning stations concept. Every morning, after our Bible reading – we were close to the end of the

New Testament – Pat taught Meara math and reading. While I practiced French conversation with one of the older three, the other two worked on written French exercises and daily journals.

Every afternoon, the kids and I took a social studies field trip. Remaining aboard in the still and sweltering cabin was out of the question. At first, any place with air conditioning counted as a field trip. Once the thrill of visiting a Bahamian bank or grocery store wore off, more adventuresome trips were required. One day the kids and I walked all the way down Bay Street to downtown Nassau. The neighbourhoods along the way were noisy, dirty and run-down. Sidewalks often dwindled completely, and so we walked on the roads, inches away from the squealing tires of passing cars. Then suddenly, as if we crossed a border, we came upon the Disney-like tourist quarter, where immaculate streets lined with swaying palms, luxury hotels, and duty-free shops lured cruise boat tourists. We stopped at a gift shop, where the boys bought a board game called Pirateer.

"Hey look, there's the hotel where Shelby will stay," said Ben, pointing to the British Colonial Hilton, a pale yellow building with white trim and extravagant wrought iron railings. We walked through the elegant hotel foyer with its gently wafting fans, past the patio bar and freshwater swimming pool, and down to the striped umbrellas and lawn chairs of the freshly raked beach. It was grand.

"Wow, classy," sighed Erin longingly. "What if they won't want to leave the hotel to come sailing with us?"

"I wouldn't worry," Liam replied. "Shelby will definitely want to sail with us instead of staying at such a fancy pants place."

Perhaps Shelby and I could switch berths for a night, I mused. Like Pat, who often stayed back when the kids and I took our field trips, I knew I needed a break.

"Sometimes I feel this boat is getting smaller," Pat once observed. I understood exactly.

That was Thursday. We expected our starboard engine would be re-assembled and our reconstructed daggerboard delivered the next day. Late Friday afternoon, though, Albert and the mechanics were still working on repairs.

"That means we're here for another whole weekend, at least," Pat said. The kids' faces grew glum. All of us longed to loosen the docklines.

"Then let's go see Atlantis tomorrow," I suggested. We'd originally planned to postpone our visit to the theme park until Shelby's arrival, but our crew deserved a treat. "We've all been working hard."

The next morning was bright and brisk, perfect for the forty-minute walk to Atlantis. We crossed the sixty-five-foot-high arched bridge spanning Nassau Harbour to Paradise Island. The cay was green and manicured, with sweeping palm-lined asphalt roads and mansions with red tile roofs. Our first destination was a folk art centre. There we watched an artist render an acrylic painting and a jeweller produce intricate beadwork. We bought a brightly painted sisal mask. From the art centre we walked to the theme park, a modern incarnation of the legendary lost Mayan city sunk beneath the Atlantic. Atlantis was full of waterslides and amusement rides, but for us its main attractions were the gigantic aquariums and waterways filled with varieties of sharks, rays, groupers, turtles and exotic fish. We stared wide-eyed and grinning, enthralled by this light-through-water fantasy world. Even the hotel was a spectacle, featuring a casino, an archaeological dig, terraced waterfalls, and a huge domed ceiling decorated with an intricate mural.

The next morning, the kids and I took another social studies field trip, this time to Mass at the only Bahamian cathedral, St. Francis Xavier. The joy on the children's faces as they seated themselves in their pew might have impressed me, had I not known they were merely thankful for rest after walking almost an hour in the unmitigated hot sun.

Later that afternoon, a short and bare-chested man stopped by to introduce himself, not only as a fellow Canadian, but also a retired Montréal Canadien. Mario was clearly proud of his physique and Liam, who played hockey, was enthralled to meet an NHL player.

"A toned body is the sign of a disciplined mind!" Mario advised. "I will return first thing tomorrow morning to show you my exercise regimen."

Liam and I looked forward to learning how to obtain Mario's muscular abdomen, and were disappointed when the athlete failed to appear as promised. Pat just smirked.

"Even the most disciplined mind sometimes lacks muscle tone," he observed.

Instead, Albert arrived, bearing the newly repaired daggerboard. It was now ten feet long, and fit smoothly in its shaft. A few hours later, the mechanics began installing the repaired transmission parts. By 4:00 p.m., they finished. The starboard engine sputtered to life like a suddenly woken snorer, then purred rhythmically. Pat rubbed his hands in delight; our major repairs had coincided beautifully.

Early next morning, we motored into Nassau Harbour, bound for Rose Island. This island was to Nassau as Cayo Blanco was to Varadero: a tiny key northeast of a busy tourist destination. Both islands were popular with tour operators who ferried day catamarans stuffed to the gills with tourists each morning, and hauled them back to the city in the late afternoon. Reluctant to join the throngs on the beach, we puttered northward at a leisurely pace, testing the boat's newly repaired equipment, and trolling for grouper enroute. The starboard engine co-operated, but the grouper did not! Every time we hauled in the line after a promising tug, we found it had snapped, and our lure disappeared.

The morning of May 23 was brilliant, full of promise. We rose late in our Rose Island anchorage. What a joy to waken floating on the hook, listening to birdcalls and the rhythmic lick of waves on our hulls, instead of the jarring shriek of car tires! Pat and Meara cooked brunch while the older three and I worked on our *français*. Sated with pancakes and verb conjugations, we piled into the dinghy with our snorkelling gear and headed toward the famed coral reefs described in our cruising guide.

Our crew knew a lot about reefs. Beautiful but fragile underwater habitats, coral reefs are called the rainforests of the sea. They are home to more than a quarter of the world's species of marine animals and seaweeds, despite the fact that they occupy less than 1.2 percent of the ocean floor. Yet even that meagre area is diminishing. In the last few decades more than thirty-five million acres of coral reefs have been destroyed, a rate of destruction so precipitous that it threatens to reduce seventy percent of the world's reefs within our lifetimes. Human activity, not surprisingly, accounts for most of the destruction. Most boaters were well aware of our impact on the marine ecosystem. We recycled used motor oil and diesel wherever possible, and disposed of it properly the rest of the time. We burned our garbage instead of throwing it overboard. We swam over the reefs without setting foot on them, and we raised our dinghy outboards high out of the water as we approached. The morning boater's net in George Town was vigilant about spreading the word, with almost daily admonishments of how our every small action had an impact on the delicate ecosystem. Those lessons were reinforced not only at the Exuma Cays Land and Sea Park, but also by our own underwater experience. The more we explored reefs, especially the dark ones where bright fish darted among dying polyps, the more awed and respectful we became.

Two sea gardens lay beneath us in the Rose Island harbour.

"Voot, voot!" Ben shouted. We pulled our snorkelling tubes over our faces, and rolled over the rounded edge of the rubber dinghy. Wearing a life vest and hitched to Pat's waist by a boat line, Meara explored the underwater world with goggled eyes big as sand dollars. Inspired by the view through the Plexiglas bottom of our dinghy, she taught herself to snorkel.

In the brief moment it took for us to plunge through air into water, the environment was transformed. The world above with its inexorable sun and wind seemed stark, harsh compared to the gently swaying rainbow world below, thriving with fish of endless sizes, colours and varieties. The coral reef was an unrivalled escape.

That evening, peace lay muffled about the boat like a light grey scarf. Liam took a solo jaunt in the kayak. Pat and the others played cribbage, while I secluded myself in my stateroom to write in my diary. *If I were home right now,* I scribbled, *I'd be standing at a soccer field, getting eaten alive by mosquitoes. Worse, I'd be driving like a maniac from one soccer game to another.*

The next day, steady rain fell from morning to night. After reading from the Gospel of St. John, I introduced the substitute teacher.

"I have a new learning program for you kids," Pat said. "It's called 'captain-for-a-day.' I'll teach you how to plan a passage completely on your own. Then when you feel ready, you'll each get to be skipper for a day."

"You mean we'd get to call the shots all day?" Erin asked.

"And order everyone around?" asked Liam.

"Yep," said Pat.

"Now this is what I call real boat school!" Ben quipped.

Pat and the older three spent the rest of the day engrossed in nautical schooling, poring over charts, calculating tide changes, discussing the effects of wind direction, tuning in to weather reports over the SSB, entering waypoints onto the GPS, and planning sail sets. Their first assignment was to jointly plan a passage from Rose Island to Eleuthera.

Meanwhile, I ached to get away. I took Meara and Jasper to shore. There the drizzle fell as a delicate mist. While the others combed the beach – Meara for shells, Jasper for smells – I wandered listlessly, then sat down on a rock to work things out with my diary. I struggled with my inward mutiny. *I need off,* I wrote. I recognized my yearning as a big step backward from the progress I'd felt talking to Betsy. I too felt cabin fever.

The sunset, glowing through the grey haze, tinted the clouds a deep maroon. I'm marooned, I thought, unmoored. Just then Jasper came bounding toward me, a stick in her mouth, her tail wagging joyously. Meara ran to show me a treasure clutched in her hand.

Red at night, sailor's delight, I reminded myself. Tomorrow's another day.

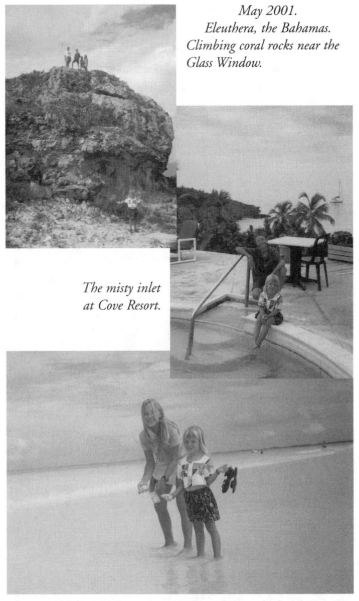

May 2001.
Eleuthera, the Bahamas.
Climbing coral rocks near the
Glass Window.

The misty inlet
at Cove Resort.

Erin and Meara scoop pink sand from the beach
at Harbour Island.

From: The Kirwin crew
To: Kith and Kin
Subject: **Greetings from *Cool Breezes*: Elegy to Eleuthera**

Pat and I wake at 7:30 this morning, hoping for an early departure from our Rose Island anchorage. The drench of rain doesn't bode well for sailing. Rain pelts our canvas dodger and drips onto our berths through cracks in the stateroom window seals. Within the hour, however, the heavy clouds scud away. Pat consults with his captains in training, and they decide to weigh anchor. *Cool Breezes* motors through dense warm air toward Eleuthera.

Eleuthera is a slender island, ninety miles long and no more than three miles across at its widest point. It lies east of Nassau and Rose Island in a curved embryonic shape, its head and feet reclining roughly north to south. The serene waters of the Bight of Eleuthera lap its soft underbelly, the concave western shoreline. The Atlantic surf pounds against its curved back, the convex eastern banks. Northeast of Eleuthera lies Harbour Island with its fabled pink sand beach, a favourite escape of the famous elite.

Shallows and reefs litter the Bight, and a ridge of coral heads known as The Devil's Backbone fends off the north ends of Eleuthera and Harbour Islands. The anchorages on the lee side of Eleuthera must therefore be accessed by an indirect route. Our guidebook outlines a northeasterly course, skirting the Bight, then turning sharply south to navigate one of a few narrow passages, or cuts. We follow that course, aiming for Current Cut, a tidal sluice between the tips of Eleuthera and Current Islands. We arrive there mid-afternoon to find the tide rushing toward us.

"What do you think, captains-in-training?" Pat asks.

"It would be dangerous to try crossing the cut right now," Erin replies.

"We should wait until tomorrow morning when the tide is slack," Liam opines.

"Good plan," Pat agrees. "What should we do now, then?"

"Find a good place near the cut to drop the hook," says Ben.

Liam takes the helm, my usual post. Pat stands at the forestay, helping Ben and Erin read the water. He demonstrates the hand gestures I know so well to guide the pilot to the chosen spot in the anchorage. Ben and Erin stoop near the bows, ready to unhitch the anchor and unwind the heavy clanking chain. Ben is so thin that crouched on his haunches, his limbs remind me of a folded lawn chair.

"Wow!" exclaims Erin, pointing at the crystalline water under the trampoline. "Hundreds of starfish are right beneath us!"

The children retrieve a sea star for each of our imminent visitors. Erin leads the way, diving the deepest. Liam is almost as intrepid. Ben, though, is the bravest: this is his first dive of more than six feet, a plunge of faith. Of the seven they harvest, the kids select the three most brilliantly coloured sea stars in that cruel but traditional process of elimination known as the beauty contest. In an ironic twist, it is the lucky less beautiful that are thrown back to sea, and the unfortunate most purple and orange that are gutted and dried.

Meanwhile, I gaze longingly at the island of Eleuthera, enshrouded in mist. Without having yet set foot on the place, I've fallen in love with it. Its name alone enthrals me, evocative of Elysium, a place of peace and bliss, but in fact it derives from the Greek word for freedom. The island was settled in 1649 as the first true democracy in the Western world by a band of one hundred known as the Eleutherian Adventurers. The Adventurers' life may have been free, but it was by no means Elysian. They sowed the seeds of their agricultural economy on thin virgin soil in the visually compelling yet challenging countryside of rolling hills and valleys, tranquil lakes and woodlands, steep cliffs and stunning beaches. They also contended with Spanish depredations and the unwelcome attention of pirates.

A hazy greyness lingers at sea level. Murmurous wavelets caress our hulls. I suspend myself above life aboard, allowing myself to hover over the emotional turmoil of living so closely with others. I immerse myself in the elements. The twilight mood to which I've succumbed, the ambience I've conjured, contributes to my perception of the island as evanescent and enigmatic.

"It's so, so – Eleuthera!" I breathe softly, rolling the "r."

The children look up, puzzled. Pat just rolls his eyes.

Today is May 26. The crew rises at 6:30 a.m. We hope to pass through Current Cut at 7:00 a.m. when the tide is slack. But the heavens pour forth their woes upon us and trap us at anchor. Our boat tugs at its tether.

"Ah, elusive Eleuthera!" I sigh.

By 8:00 a.m. the skies are clear, but the tide has begun to flow through the cut.

"At least the tide is running in the same direction we're headed," Ben observes.

"As a captain-in-training, I say let's give it a go!" says Liam.

"Yes, let's," Pat nods. "It will be tricky, though, so I want you, Jake, at the helm. Ben, come up to the bows with me to watch for coral heads. Erin and Liam, I want one of you watching on starboard, the other on port. I know there's a reef on the other side of the cut to avoid, but who knows what lies in between."

To steer the boat's seventeen-foot beam through this real-life rock and a hard place is a test not only of skill but also concentration. It's a thrill to feel the vessel beneath my feet become caught in the sweep of the current's swell, to sense it rush forward with the water, and then, under my hand, to veer sharply, jarringly, to starboard to avoid the coral snare.

From the morning's rush, the day winds down to an easy pace. We enjoy a serene motorsail toward the small settlement of Governor's Harbour, about five hours away. Approaching the inlet, I become mesmerized by the tranquil seascape. The muted sun shines through vapour hanging along the broad shoreline. Bordering the still and clear emerald bay curves a beach marked by dense casuarina trees and sparsely dotted pastel-coloured buildings. At the south end of the settlement lies a causeway leading to Cupid Cay.

The kids and I dinghy Jasper to shore. We buy groceries and find a car to rent. Our errands accomplished, we climb the steep streets of the quiet town, up the hill to the Batelco telephone tower. From there we can see *Cool Breezes* swaying gently at anchor, her lifelines pegged with lightly wafting towels and sheets. Back on board, Pat lights the barbeque, Erin bakes a chocolate dessert, and I cook potatoes and sauté vegetables. After a seemingly effortless dinner, we lounge about the foredecks, reading our books. Erin sits with her sketchbook and pastels, and captures the island's dreamlike haze. Somnolence sets in.

"Ah, ethereal Eleuthera," I whisper.

Unmarked time elapses. Again I am suspended. Then a brass band strikes up in the main settlement, marching toward Cupid Cay. Through binoculars we read their banner, "National Youth Awareness Week." Trumpets blast and drums thump, yet the sound is muffled. Our ears seem stuffed with felt. Only when mosquitoes swarm aboard at sunset do we shake off our lassitude, zip up the mosquito nets and retire.

It's the 27th, the day we tour the island in our rented car. Conditions are ideal: the sky is lightly veiled with cloud, the air warm and slightly breezy. Governor's Harbour is located midway between the north and south points of Eleuthera, so we could turn either direction. Pat shrugs and turns south into the right lane of the Queen's Highway.

Then he slams on the brakes.

"Whoa!" he shouts. Although we're in the right-hand lane, a vehicle heads straight toward us. Pat swerves left. A taxi roars by on our passenger side. The nasal blare of its horn disappears into the distance. Vehicles may be North American, with steering wheels on the left, but thoroughfares are British, geared to driving in the left lanes.

Our first stop is at Tarpum Bay, set in a quiet inlet on the Bight. Once the centre of the island's prosperous pineapple trade, it is now a drowsy settlement, best known as an artists' haven. We follow the signs directing us to the studio of artist Al Sanders. An affable Humpty-Dumpty shaped man with dyed black hair, Al doesn't fit my preconceived idea of an Eleutherian artist. His studio, however, is everything I imagined an artistic hideaway to be: a low-slung whitewashed building with large shuttered windows, shaded by palms and filled with easels, paints and artwork at various stages of completion. Erin and I each buy a driftwood seascape.

From Tarpum Bay we turn north, following the two-lane highway through several picturesque villages perched on cliffs or facing coves on the Bight side of the island, places with names like Alice Town and Gregory Town. On this sleepy Sunday, most islanders sit in the shade or walk along the road wearing black suits with crisp white shirts, or floral dresses and fancy hats. Our guidebook lists numerous eateries, but none are open on the Sabbath. Hungry and ever hopeful, we press on.

"The crew is growing mutinous," I observe.

"There's a resort up ahead," Pat points out. "Surely its restaurant is open."

He's right. We follow the palm-lined road to the Cove Resort. There we're served drinks and sandwiches poolside. Ben and Meara and I dip our bare legs into the pool. From there we feast our eyes on the vista, a misty inlet merging with a glossy gossamer sky.

"Ah, exquisite Eleuthera," I murmur.

Our sated crew clambers into the car and heads northward. We drive to the peak of Sugar Loaf Hill. From there the land falls abruptly away, nearly touching the sea. The road narrows to become a one-lane causeway built on a skinny strip of rock. To the right, we see the open and restless sapphire blue Atlantic. Shifting our eyes slightly left, across the causeway, we see the tranquil turquoise waters of the Bight of Eleuthera. This place is called the Glass Window, named for an arched piece of coral rock that once framed the view. A hurricane shattered the coral arch in 1923. It's only a matter of time, I've read, until the elements erode the rock under the causeway. Then the Atlantic Ocean and the Bight of Eleuthera will meet, and the island of Eleuthera will be cut in two.

North of the Glass Window we park the car and take a water taxi to Harbour Island. We land at genteel Dunmore Town, and step through a time portal to the 1800s. A row of miniature wooden clapboard shops faces the water. Behind them, lying parallel north to south, narrow cobblestone streets run up and down the hilly terrain. Each brightly painted Victorian cottage lining the streets bears a unique and carefully lettered name plaque. Tiny, tidy yards are bound by white picket fences, their slats entwined with florid bougainvillea. Shady sand paths cross the lanes and lead eastward over the crest of the island to the ocean. That's where we hike, and that's where we first see the rose-coloured beach, its three-mile length fanned out before us like a peacock's tail.

"The sand really is pink!" Meara and Erin gush, and rush headlong down the hill. I join them, laughing, scooping handfuls of suede granules tinted pink from particles of coral. Spray from the ocean mingles with showers from the sky.

After a long and blissfully aimless stroll along the ocean, we catch a water taxi to our car, and drive back to Governor's Harbour. There waits our dinghy, and not far beyond that, our faithful dog and boat.

It's Monday morning. We wake to gentle rain.

"Let's stay here another day. It's only the twenty-eighth," the kids beg.

"Why not?" says Pat.

"Fine with me!" say I, eager to stretch this elastic Eleutherian time, to remain enraptured here. I spend an hour with each of the older three, speaking *français*. When the sky clears, Erin and I head to shore. Everywhere I look,

"Property for Sale" signs beckon me. I realize I seek escape. Enthralling Eleuthera has become my Elysian field. Here, I'm free, in my element, one with the elements.

"When I die, cremate my remains and sprinkle them here," I tell my daughter.

This morning, the 29th, dawns still and humid. The weather forecast is good. We retrace our route through Current Cut, thrill ride and all, and anchor in the same place we took four days ago, between Current and Eleuthera. Pat and I dinghy to Current Island with Jasper. It's rare for us to be alone, good to have time off the boat. Pat takes my hand. I gaze wistfully at the island across the water, to the place whose spell has taught me to rise above the pettiness of sometimes cloying family life, to achieve the solitude I crave.

"Ah, Eleuthera," I sigh. "Ephemeral, ineffable Eleuthera."

God bless and fair winds,

PJ+crew

Chapter 29
New Crew in Nassau

Listen where thou art sitting
Under the glassy, cool, translucent wave...
– John Milton, Comus, Song

The last few days of May, we sailed toward Nassau in gradual increments. We anchored off Current Cut one night, Rose Island the next two. For Meara, these were exciting times aboard *Cool Breezes*. Each morning she announced the countdown: the number of sleeps until our guests' arrival (June 1), her fifth birthday (June 3), and Erin's thirteenth (June 8). Then Liam would gleefully add the number of days left of boat school.

"I don't wanna think about that," Meara would pout. "I wish boat school would last forever."

The morning of May 30, the older three passed their last written and oral French quizzes and packed their schoolbooks for good. On May 31, St. Christopher's Boat School gathered one last time. We read from the Bible and shared a daily reflection. Then I passed out my students' elaborately festooned report cards, and watched with pleasure the proud expressions spreading across their faces. Naturally, each had received straight As.

"Well, this is my best-ever report card," Erin grinned.

"Me, too," Meara giggled. "And my first-ever!"

The bubble burst when Liam peeked over Ben's shoulder.

*June 2001,
Nassau and
Rose Island,
the Bahamas.*

*Eldean, Barbara
and Shelby join
us aboard* Cool
Breezes.

*Snorkelling in the
turquoise blue
water off Rose
Island.*

*Relaxing
immersed in Rose
Island salt water.*

*Erin's thirteenth
birthday at
a Nassau
restaurant.*

"Hey Mom, you gave all of us the same marks!" he grumbled.

"Of course I did," I laughed. "I may be biased, but at least I'm fair about it."

"Can you imagine how unbearable it would be if one of us got better marks than the rest?" Ben grinned. Liam just grunted and shrugged. Then he brightened.

"And now we get to party!"

Teachers back home let their students drink pop, eat snacks, and watch a movie on the last day of school. My plan was to do the same, modified to reflect the fact we lacked shore power. Lukewarm Goombay Punch would be drunk without ice, popcorn would be popped the old-fashioned way, and to conserve battery power, the video we watched would be short. While I shook the popping pot on the stove, the kids plugged in a video we received from the Volleyball Beach missionaries, a half-hour feature aimed at ages five to fifteen.

"Hip-hip-hip-hippo-pot-a-mus! Hip-hip-hooray, God made all of us!" chorused the audio track.

"Oh, man," groaned Erin and Ben.

"This is for little kids, Mom!" wailed Liam.

"You don't have to watch it if you don't want to," I said calmly, placing the bowl of hot popcorn on the table. So starved were my kids for technological entertainment, however, that they watched every second, and even rewound the hippopotamus song so they could memorize it. By then they decided it was hilarious.

On June 1, we weighed anchor and motored into Nassau Harbour. This time we tucked into a berth at Nassau Harbour Club, a marina with a swimming pool. The afternoon was hot and sticky, but a bright breeze blew and the palm fronds swayed. There's nothing like the prospect of guests to prompt a flurry of cleaning, whether in a house or on a boat. I scoured the oven and stove while the kids attacked the mildew and scrubbed the salon seat cushions. Meara swept the interior teak floors while Pat swabbed the decks and polished the windows. Once the boat was shipshape and the crew showered, we hopped in a cab and headed west on Bay to the British Colonial Hilton.

"There they are!" Liam yelled. He pointed to the check-in desk, where three of my very favourite people were huddled with their luggage. There was Eldean, her face wan but happy, Barbara, an athletic woman with short blond hair, and Shelby, her only child, a skinny and tow-headed nine-year-old with social skills to burn. Hugging them all, I burst into tears.

Big-hearted Barb dabbed at the corner of her own eye.

"Look at you," she laughed, pointing at my sandaled feet. "Even the skin between your toes is tanned!"

That was a reference to our 1984 trip to Greece, when the darker our tan, the better we thought we looked. Isn't family grand, I thought, isn't it terrific to share a happy memory bank with someone, and aren't I lucky to share it with someone as wonderful as Barbara? And now history was repeating itself: Pat and I were making deposits into our own children's memory banks.

"Come up to our room with us!" Barb and Shelby urged. The nine of us crowded into the plush elevator, and bustled down the hushed hallway.

"Wow, look at your room!" Erin gawked, as Barbara unlocked and opened the door.

"Wow, look at your TV!" the boys added. Compared to the eight-inch box aboard *Cool Breezes*, this screen was gigantic. While the kids watched television, we adults slipped downstairs to the patio bar for sundowners. Eldean produced photos of her visit with us in Cuba, the most recent issue of the *Globe & Mail* for Pat, and copies of the *Living Aboard* issue that contained Gary's article about our crew.

"Look, he wrote we're 'obviously in love'," I read to Pat.

"Just proves you can't always believe what you read," he smirked.

While our guests caught up on their sleep the next morning at the Hilton, we swabbies did laundry and laid in provisions. The thermometer soared into the nineties well before noon.

"It's getting too hot for this beard," Pat mused. "I think I'll shave it off today."

"No, Dad, no!" Meara squealed, throwing herself in his lap. She'd never seen her father without a beard. I myself had never known him without at least a moustache. But Pat was determined. He returned from his shower bereft of facial hair.

Meara was distraught, but I was smitten. I couldn't take my eyes off this strangely familiar, incredibly attractive man, especially his newly unveiled, well-defined philtrum. After enduring all my affections, Pat likely wished he'd kept his beard.

How strange, I wrote in my diary that night. *How many times have I looked at Pat and wondered, who is this stranger I married? Well, today it truly felt like I was flirting with a new man. My mind said it's okay; he's the same man, only younger and cuter, less gruff and grizzly. But my heart felt as if it was falling in love again.*

After lunch we taxied to the Hilton to pick up Eldean, Barb and Shelby. From there, the group of us walked east toward the marina, stopping enroute to shop at duty-free jewellery stores and visit the intriguing piracy museum. Back at the boat, Liam led our guests on a tour, this one very thorough and detailed.

"And this is the head," he said. "To use the toilet, first you gotta turn this lever," he demonstrated. "After you're done, you grab this handle and pump it. Ten or twenty pumps, for sure. Then you push the lever down. Otherwise, water will fill the basin and overflow, and the boat could sink. And don't forget this sign: 'If it's yellow, let it mellow/If it's brown, flush it down.' Get it?"

"Yes, I get it!" Shelby sniggered.

"I'm not sure I get it," I overheard my sister tell my mother. "Sink the boat? I think I'd rather just hold it in."

I baked ham and my amateur version of Bahamian macaroni while the rest of the gang cooled off in the marina pool. That night, Shelby slept in Erin's berth, and Erin took his hotel room bed, the first of many sleepovers.

The morning of June 3, Meara proclaimed the joyous news.

"Today I am five!"

I produced her favourite breakfast, peach cobbler, and her first present, a twirly-skirted blue dress from Eleuthera. Once the hotel crowd arrived, we set sail for Rose Island.

Our new passengers proved seaworthy, even though the morning was windy and showery, and the water rough in spots. As soon as we laid our anchor, the sun emerged. The water beckoned, warm and clear, saturated with a translucent turquoise blue.

"Let's dinghy out to the best snorkelling grounds," Erin suggested. Shelby was excited.

"I've never snorkelled before," he said.

"It's easy," chirped Meara, as if she'd been snorkelling forever.

The snorkelling expedition returned effusive, and ravenous to devour Meara's birthday lunch. The frosting on Meara's lemon cake had visually deteriorated in the hot sun, but no one cared. Of greater interest were the manta rays and grouper circling our boat, angling for a free lunch.

After lunch, we dinghied to the shore of Rose Island in two shifts. The day cats had already dropped their tourist cargo, so the beach was crowded, throbbing with tuneless rap music.

"Sorry about this," we apologized to our landlubber guests.

"Sorry about what?" they asked.

"I guess we cruisers are a bit spoiled by our unspoiled beaches," Ben smirked.

Later that afternoon, we motored back to Nassau, and dropped our hook in the anchorage off the Hilton beach-front. Eldean treated all of us to Chinese food for Meara's birthday, and invited Meara to a sleepover at the hotel.

"This was my best birthday ever," she waved, carried off in Auntie Barbara's arms.

I loved our Hilton anchorage. From there we could see the huge cruise ships docked at Prince George Wharf, and watch them manoeuvre the deeply dredged turning basin right before our twin bows. We could easily dinghy back and forth from boat to shore, bringing our crew to the Hilton beach or picking up visitors. Each evening, we left behind a kid or two for a hotel sleepover.

Change is as good as a rest, they say. Pat was growing restless, I could see; he particularly disliked travelling in packs, and now there were nine of us. Moreover, it was time for me to take a dose of my own medicine: to follow the advice I'd given to Betsy.

"Let's mix things up a bit," I suggested. "Tomorrow, let's have a girls' day/boys' day. The girls stay at the hotel, go shopping, eat out, and visit Paradise Island, while the guys take *Cool Breezes* on an overnight cruise. You boys

could fish, snorkel, race around in the dinghy, play
Pirateer, and make all the rude noises you want. How
would you like that?"

"What's not to like?" Liam replied, amid general
cheers and whoops. "Jasper comes with us, though, even
though she's female."

I glanced at Pat. He was grinning.

We females enjoyed a perfect holiday together.
We shopped all morning at the two-storey, open-air straw
market, and returned to the hotel room with many treasures. We lunched at a funky café, then spent the afternoon
poolside, swimming, snoozing and reading in the sun. My
girls and I checked into our own hotel room for a real
shower. After almost ten months aboard a small boat, the
sense of luxury in our suite was tangible. Dove-grey walls
soared to high white ceilings. The bed sheets were smooth
and heavy, the carpets and towels lofty and thick. The
bathroom was spacious, and best of all, private.

Next morning I woke disoriented, startled by the huge
expanse of space above my head. Barb and I took an early
run, before the heat set in. We five then walked across the
long arched bridge to Paradise Island. My girls eagerly led
Eldean and Barbara on a tour of the Atlantis theme park,
beginning with the cave aquariums and the predators'
lagoon, and finishing in the hotel's fabulous lobby. It was
already noon, and Meara's short legs were weary, so we
agreed to catch a cab to the hotel. Just then the driver of a
navy blue limousine approached us.

"I kin drive you for deh sem price as a taxi cab," he
offered. My girls' eyes sparkled. What a grand finale to
girls' day!

The next day was Erin's birthday.

"How is it possible we're parents to a teenager?" Pat
asked. I knew what he meant.

"I find this birthday to be one of the hardest ever, and it's not even mine!"

Although she slept late, true to the teen stereotype, Erin woke happy. She chose to spend her birthday the same way Meara had: playing on the Rose Island beach, and dining out in Nassau.

The Rose Island shoreline was blessedly empty of tourists that day. It was far too hot to lie on towels on the beach. Instead, Barbara and Meara and I reclined on the ribbed sand under a few inches of water, and dabbled in the lapping crystal waves. From that vantage point, at sea level, our eyes followed the long fetch of blue. The wind rippled the liquid surface. Now and then, Barb and I would murmur a word or two, but mostly we felt content to simply listen to the music of the water and the tinkle of Meara's cheerful chatter. I felt so blessed to be in the company of my good and smiling sun-kissed sister, immersed to her shoulders in seawater, appearing at peace after her week away from the North American tumult. I felt so glad she'd come. How I missed the camaraderie of intimate female company!

Late in the afternoon we weighed anchor and turned our bows toward Nassau. The breeze freshened at our stern, so we cut the engines and cruised gently under sail to the hotel anchorage.

An hour later we gathered at a trendy downtown restaurant. I whispered to our waitress that it was Erin's thirteenth birthday. She passed the word to the lead singer of the band, who called Erin onstage. After singing a reggae rendition of "Happy Birthday" to her, he persuaded Erin to dance the Macarena by herself before all the restaurant patrons. She acted mortified, but danced anyway, her face beaming.

After dinner we shuffled back to the hotel, reluctant to part ways. Good night would be goodbye this time; our guests were flying out early the next morning. In one short week, they'd become an integral part of our daily life and adventures. They were crew, and we'd miss them.

The morning of June 9, we puttered out of our Hilton Hotel anchorage, headed for Nassau Yacht Haven marina. There we'd clean up, re-stock our bilge pantries and regroup before embarking on our next voyage. When we radioed the marina to announce our arrival, however, the dockmaster told us our reserved slip was still occupied.

"I guess we'll drop the hook for a few hours while we wait," Pat grumbled, and steered the boat to a crowded anchorage in Nassau Harbour.

As she ate a sandwich in the cockpit, Erin noticed that the boat anchored next to us also had children aboard, including two girls her own age.

"Let's invite them over!"

"*Anna Ray, Anna Ray*, this is *Cool Breezes*," I called on the VHF. "Care to visit another boatful of kids right next to you?"

"Sure, why not? The kids and I will be right over," replied a female voice. "My husband won't come, though. He's suffering a severe case of boat repair blues."

Pat grabbed the VHF handset.

"Tell him to come on over and commiserate with me. Wait till he hears what we've been through!"

Moments later we heard the drone of an approaching dinghy, the sputter of the engine as it was cut, and the cacophony of several voices as its passengers tied up at our stern. That's how we sound wherever we go, I thought. Out of the dinghy and into our cockpit spilled a family of six: two girls, fourteen and twelve years old, two boys, ten and nine, and two harried looking parents. Our young crew was delighted. Ben and Liam quickly hustled their counterparts off to their stateroom to play Pirateer, while Erin ushered the two visiting girls into the salon, where they traded bead-work skills. Meara hung out at the fringes, trying to fit in. Meanwhile, in the cockpit, we parents shared our tales of woe over lukewarm Kalik beer. What is it about human-ity that attracts us to stories of misfortune, our inclination to *schadenfreude*, the pleasure we take in the misery of oth-ers? Receiving sympathy for our own mishaps and finding we don't suffer alone does wonders to restore our spirits. Dennis and Danielle recounted their streak of bad luck, beginning with a house robbery the week before their departure date. Only one month into their cruise, we heard, they were stuck in Nassau, awaiting delivery of an engine part from Florida. We listened with empathy, and then described our own travails. Pat and I were the seasoned ones for once, passing along the wisdom of hard-won cruising experience: boat repairs were inevitable. Soon everyone, even Dennis, was laughing.

"Now we know why we were delayed getting into that marina," I said to Pat once our guests had left. "We were destined on a heaven-sent mission of mercy!"

With the passage of those few hours, our marina slip became available. We checked in and set about the usual tasks, including laundry.

"The Poop Deck is just upstairs from the laundry room," Pat pointed out. "We could fit in one last visit while our clothes spin around in the washing machines downstairs."

"Great idea," I replied. "That's about as close to multi-tasking as we cruisers would ever want to get."

From our balcony table overlooking the marina and the sunset, we toasted to Nassau, the hub of our excur-sions for almost a month. Then we unfolded our charts and planned the next stage of our travels: a northward cruise of the Abacos archipelago.

June 2001.
Artwork by Erin, inspired by the different shapes of catamarans.
Cool Breezes *is to the left.*

Chapter 30
Marshmallow Plans

For my part, I travel not to go anywhere, but to go.
I travel for travel's sake. The great affair is to move.
– Robert Louis Stevenson, Travels with a
Donkey

Our route from Nassau northward to the Abacos was indirect. Our first destination was Rose Island. From Rose we'd head north-northeast across to Royal Island, one of the little islands close to Eleuthera. From Royal we'd sail north-northwest to Little Harbour, a small settlement at the southernmost tip of Great Abaco Island. And from Little Harbour, we'd gunkhole northward among the Abacos cays, eventually reaching our jumping off point to Florida, and the end of our journey by sail.

By this time in our travels, we knew that all routes lead to surprises, and all plans must be marshmallow. If it's not weather that deters a sailor from the plan, it's happenstance: reluctance to depart from a particularly ambient place at a particularly magical point in time; or, perhaps, a chance meeting with a congenial soul; or, heaven forbid, boat repairs. All these things conspired to lead *Cool Breezes* on a number of detours on her route.

Anchored off Rose Island the evening of June 10, we lingered in the cockpit to watch an unusual sunset. The

languid orange sun dipped toward an imperceptible horizon between the fluid grey of water and an identical grey
haze of sky. Only the disappearance of the sun as it slid
lower revealed the earth's edge. If I squinted, it seemed as
if an enormous orange sphere, suspended in a grey universe, was being swallowed up.

Once the last tip of orange disappeared, the greyness
plunged to black. We retired to our berths. I revived our
nightly routine of reading aloud. As the kids lay sprawled
atop their beds, much too hot even for duvet covers, I sat
in the salon and read to them by candlelight.

Next day we got underway by 9:00 a.m., headed for
Royal Island. It was a six-hour voyage, a long passage
between islands by Bahamian standards, over deep and
inky purple waters. Flying fish broke the sea's surface and
launched forward on flashing fins. Around 3:00 p.m. we
idled into a small green harbour in the middle of Royal
Island. The heat was stifling. The moment the anchor was
set, we dove overboard for wet relief.

"Wow, the water here is barely cooler than the air,"
said Erin.

"Yeah, it feels like a hot tub," Liam complained, pulling
himself up on the swim ladder. The rest of us soon followed.

"Let's check out the island ruins," I suggested. I'd read
that the remains of a grand plantation, built in the 1930s
to produce pineapple and citrus fruit, were worthwhile
exploring. We dinghied to the wrecked stone dock and
landed in a jungle. Exotic foliage encroached on the moul-
dering stone walls, but we could still see traces of intricate
tile work, huge fireplaces, and stone pathways. Despite the
intrigue of the place, and although there was shade, we
were ready to leave within an hour. It was simply too hot,
humid and sticky for us Canadians. When Liam admitted
to feeling nauseous, we headed to the dock.

That's where we bumped into Billy Eamon. When he glimpsed the ribbon of red maple leaves trimming Meara's sunhat, he stopped to introduce himself.

"I'm Canadian too," he announced proudly. "Been puttering around Florida and the Bahamas in my trimaran for the last few years."

Pat replied with a brief outline of our background and onward plans.

"Ever been to Spanish Wells?" Billy asked.

"No, we haven't," Pat replied.

"You gotta!" Billy called over the din of our outboard. "I'm headed there myself."

"Spanish Wells," Pat mused, reading aloud from the cruising guide later that evening. "A small settlement on St. George's Cay, off Eleuthera. Sounds interesting. Wanna go?"

"Sure, why not?" I replied.

We set out the next day. It was a short journey, less than two hours. Erin took the helm the whole distance.

"I would have steered except I'm feeling only ninety-five percent better," said Liam, ever ready to quantify everything. We took a mooring and dinghied to shore, eager to explore the town.

Spanish Wells had an unreal air to it. Neat rows of modest, uniform and well-maintained homes with manicured yards revealed the settlement's orderliness. The abundance of late model pickup trucks and satellite dishes told me it was prosperous. But these qualities didn't define this town's uniqueness. The fact that Spanish Wells was "dry" – no alcohol was sold or served there – distinguished it from other communities, yet this distinction wasn't visible. Perhaps, I thought, the absence of shade trees and the resulting stark shadows in the midday sun set it apart. Then I realized the biggest difference was the town's homogeneity.

Everyone was white. After months in Cuba and the Bahamas, we weren't used to that. Our guidebooks reported that the fifteen hundred residents of Spanish Wells descended from American Loyalists and Eleutherian Adventurers, but didn't say why no blacks lived there.

The other unique aspect of Spanish Wellsians was their accent. To our Canadian ears, it sounded like a delightful cross between British and Bostonian. We found the townspeople unfailingly friendly and polite. They were also notoriously self-sufficient. Most were born, raised, married and buried in Spanish Wells, and most lived off the sea. Every business was locally owned, even the power company. Gazing behind us as we dinghied back to our mooring, I felt we'd just visited a societal time warp, a place untouched, where despite technological advance, a way of life stands still.

Back on board, Ben cranked his wind-up radio and tuned in to a Spanish Wells station.

"I just heard it's ninety-four degrees out here!" he shouted down the companionway.

"Well if it's ninety-four degrees outside, it's a hundred and four below decks," Pat said. "Let's rig up some kind of a canopy over the boat."

He and Ben strung a canvas tarp that formed a tent over the dodger of our cockpit. The canopy not only created shade but also caught and magnified every whiff of breeze that blew by. Soon all the kids camped out beneath it, playing cards and listening to the radio.

Another way to get respite from the heat was to eat at an air-conditioned restaurant. Billy came up with the same coping strategy. He joined us for dinner.

"I thought I might find you here," he said. "I brought you some mangoes and wine from Eleuthera. Speaking of Eleuthera, you gotta see Ridley's Head. You been there?"

"No, we haven't," I replied.

"Well, you gotta," Billy replied. "It's got the most beautiful beach I've ever seen."

"Ridley's Head," Pat mused aloud, reading from the cruising guide later that evening. "The only thing the guides say is that the channel leading to it is treacherous. That means it's probably one of those drop-dead gorgeous, off-the-beaten-path kind of places. Billy was right about Spanish Wells – you wouldn't want to miss it. Wanna go to Ridley's Head?"

"Sure, why not?" I replied. "I'm only too happy to spend another day at ethereal, ephemeral Eleuthera. Ah, Ridley's Head on Eleuthera…" I added, rolling all the "r"s.

"No Mom, no!" moaned the kids. They were still recovering from my earlier infatuation with all things Eleutherian.

The next morning, we motored slowly down the dredged and well-marked channel out of Spanish Wells. From there we turned hard to port, toward Harbour Island Channel and the tail end of The Devil's Backbone. It was a mere half-hour sail to Ridley's Head from there, but time crept. We wove our careful way under a brilliant morning sun through submerged coral heads, our dagger-boards pulled high out of harm's way.

Billy was right again. Ridley's Head was stunning. As we turned the corner at Gun Point, we beheld a spectacular sweep of pink sand. Breakers crashed on the deserted crescent beach, and swaying palms fringed it. We anchored at a respectful distance, and dinghied to shore with our lunch, sand toys, towels, and a tarp. There we found the coastline strewn with sand dollars and a million pastel shells.

Jasper was the first to leap into the surf. It was pure joy to watch her dash up and down the long beach, pawing at the sand, prancing in the shallows near the shore. Within an hour, we white-skins developed heat rash, so we propped up an improvised tent using the tarp and some poles and stakes gleaned from the beach. We felt like survivors on a reality television show. Later that afternoon, the rustic imagery was shattered when a group of boys from Spanish Wells invaded our refuge, racing parallel to shore on their Seadoos, water-skis, sea biscuits and race boats. That's when I decided to swim back to the mother ship for a sea bath. I felt small as a speck, but hoped I appeared larger, as I crossed the whizzing traffic lanes and the rolling wakes.

Once the crowds roared off, the anchorage became still. Billy rowed to our cockpit for sundowners, bearing more mangoes and wine.

"I don't usually like to hang around with cruisers," Billy confessed, "but you guys seem different than most. I guess I'm a bit of a single-hander in everything I do."

He told us of his tree-farming business in Ontario, his house renovation work in Key West, his many sea adventures, and his failed romances. A lean and curly-haired thirty-something, earnest and intelligent, with an easy and self-deprecating laugh, he was certainly attractive. What doomed his business and romantic ventures, I figured, was his zest for travel, his yearning for the sea. He was the consummate sailor, kin to the water and keen for adventure. Not too many long-term relationships can survive that.

"If I ever settle down, it'll be on Eleuthera," Billy told us. "I got my eye on a place in Tarpum Bay, got the money set aside. But how long would I last there, looking out on the water every day, longing to be off, alone in my trimaran, just me and the sea?"

That was the last time we saw Billy, but we did receive a long letter from him when we returned to Alberta.

"I got over buying a house in Eleuthera, or anywhere," he wrote. "Every time I rowed back to my trimaran from shore, I realized the beauty of living aboard. No bugs, breezes galore, privacy, quiet, amazing stars. Well, you know what I mean."

Pat and I rose at 6:15 a.m. on June 14, eager for an early start to our seven-hour voyage to Little Harbour. The children were still asleep as we navigated the tight channel running northwest off Ridley's Head toward Great Abaco Island. Sunken coral reefs lay both to port and to starboard, threatening to shred our Fiberglas hulls.

"Attempt this channel only in good light conditions with an experienced pilot to guide you," our guidebook cautioned in italic letters. Perhaps inspired by intrepid Billy, Pat felt confident. He stood on the bows, reading the water, and I at the helm, following his every slightest hand gesture. We couldn't stray off course to any degree. So concentrated was our effort that I couldn't say whether it took a half-hour or half-day to get through, but get through we did. Despite occasional strife and chafing, I realized that Pat and I made a good team.

We approached Little Harbour in the mid-afternoon, full of expectation. We weren't disappointed. It was a small settlement built around a well-protected horseshoe inlet. Most of the shoreline was rimmed with a white sand beach. High and rocky cliffs bordered the rest, dotted with yawning caves. The anchorage waters were still and green, an ideal haven for the colony of turtles that thrived there. Ben, who loved turtles, was excited to see dozens of them swimming alongside our hulls.

"I love it here!" he shouted.

All of us did. We anchored off the sandy beach, and dinghied to shore. There we found unusual beachside attractions: a foundry, gallery and artist's studio, all established in the 1950s by Randolph and Margaret Johnston. A bronze sculptor and ceramic artist, respectively, they left England to pursue their artistic vision at Little Harbour. As homesteaders, they paid for their land by planting coconut trees, and lived in caves until they could build a home. After they died in the 1990s, their son Pete maintained the studio, foundry and gallery. An artist in his own right, a goldsmith and sculptor, he also founded Pete's Pub, an open-air beach bar.

After touring the beachside gallery, I took Jasper on a gentle run up the hills behind the Johnston businesses. There, along shady and fragrant village lanes, private homes sat high on the hills, with windows that overlooked the tranquil harbour from the back, and the tumultuous sea from the front.

The next morning, our family explored the area by dinghy and snorkelled the coral reefs in the channel. The underwater world beckoned us with its undulating versi-coloured fronds, waving in the surge. Then we poked along Little Harbour Creek, where dozens of cays, beaches, and shady lagoons lay scattered.

Later that afternoon, Pat and I dinghied ashore to visit Pete's Pub. Business was brisk. A clutch of islanders, lined up in what were clearly customary chairs, sat on one side of the bar, while we newcomers, the cruisers, sat on benches on the other. We could easily see our boat (and crew) from there. Brad the bartender didn't need much prodding to regale us with stories of Hurricane Floyd, the storm that hit the Abacos islands in September 1999.

"This pub was submerged in five feet of water," he told us. His voice was theatrical, his gestures well rehearsed. "The foundry was totally devastated. It took twenty-one months to rebuild it. It only just re-opened a month ago. Twenty of Pete's most loyal clients helped by pre-paying for their copies of his limited edition sculpture, 'The Bahamian Boat Builder.' He just finished pouring the bronze for those sculptures. And see that trawler grounded at the top of the hill behind us?" We cruisers turned our heads. Brad continued. "Well, Floyd washed it up there. At one point, winds that had blown up to a hundred and fifty and two hundred miles an hour dropped to ten or fifteen. The eye of the storm was right over us for two hours. The air was like soup, full of dust. We wondered if it was all over. Then the eye was gone, and Floyd was unleashed on us again."

I wanted to learn more about the Johnston pioneers.

"You can visit the caves they lived in if you like," he offered. "Just pull your dinghy up to the docks by the cliffs. The sign says 'private' but don't worry, the owners won't mind."

The next morning, we set out to look for the Johnstons' caves. As soon as we secured our dinghy to the dock and began climbing its ladder, a red-faced man screamed at us from his home across the bay.

"Can't you read? That dock is private!" he shrieked.

"Oh," said Pat. "Brad said it was okay to use it."

"Well it's not okay. You're trespassers!"

We climbed down the ladder and untied the dinghy painter. A speedboat roared up. At the helm stood the same furious man, his blue eyes bulging. Shaking his fist, he shouted swear words and character aspersions, despite our children's presence. Our adrenaline began pumping, and with it the fight-or-flight mechanism. Flight, I felt; fight, felt Pat.

"He's not worth your trouble," I urged, when Pat shouted back. "Let's just leave."

The altercation dramatized a classic tension between islanders and boaters. Some, like the Johnstons who thrive

on the business brought by cruisers, welcomed us with
open arms. Others, like the furious landowner we'd just
encountered, considered gunkholers to be a nuisance. To
them we were polluters, freeloaders, poachers and trespassers.

Shaken, we retreated. We beached the dinghy on a
patch of sand on the other side of the caves, and scrabbled
up the cliff to explore.

"These caves aren't all that great," Liam said, "not like
the ones off Big Major's Spot." He was right. The adventure proved anticlimactic. That old maxim, that travelling
is all about the people, had a flip side to it.

We weighed anchor that afternoon and moved north
toward Sandy Cay. This island was peaceful and secluded,
part of a protected national park. We anchored in what
felt like the middle of nowhere. The kids begged to go off
on their own in the dinghy to snorkel.

"Well, alright," Pat agreed, "but you must stay within
eyesight of the boat."

"Yippee!" they shouted. Pat and Meara and I watched
the dinghy recede in the distance. Suddenly we heard a
shout.

"Shark!" they yelled. We saw them scramble into the
dinghy and beeline to the boat.

The next day was Father's Day. We were headed to
Marsh Harbour that afternoon, but took the morning to
celebrate Pat. The kids and I rose early to prepare his breakfast. Erin and Ben fried slices of ham, and made blueberry
and strawberry pancakes from muffin mixes. I made coffee
and served it to him in the cockpit. How Pat loved his
golden anchorage mornings! The only thing he lacked was
a newspaper. Instead, he read homemade poems and cards.

"Thanks for taking us on this trip of a lifetime," Liam
wrote. "Thanks for letting us live your dream."

Chapter **31**
Onward!

For me, my craft is sailing on,
Through mists today, clear seas anon.
Whate'er the final harbour be,
'Tis good to sail upon the sea!
    – John Kendrick Bangs, The Voyage

For a month beginning mid-June, Marsh Harbour was home base to *Cool Breezes*. This town was established in the late 1700s. A hundred years later, it prospered as a sponging and shipbuilding centre. By 2001, its commercial centre had diminished. Yet to the cruiser in need of regrouping, it had everything: a spacious anchorage, several marinas, lumber and propane supplies, a post office and telephone station, banks, laundromats, drugstores, medical and dental offices, mechanical and welding services, and a wide range of shops and restaurants. It was to the Abacos what George Town was to the Exumas: a cruiser's Mecca. It was the birthplace, in fact, of the daily morning cruisers' net on VHF Channel 68, with which we'd become acquainted in George Town. Within a day of our arrival, we'd already tuned in to the 8:15 a.m. net and to Marsh Harbour life in general.

Our list of chores to accomplish in Marsh Harbour was long. At the top was to re-stock our fridge and bilge pantries. Ironically, the black clouds of smoke billowing

June 2001,
the Abacos islands, the Bahamas.
Standing on the trampoline at the bows, Pat anticipates
yet another summer squall.

from shore when we approached the harbour on June 17 came from the highly esteemed Golden Harvest market. It burned to the ground. Two local grocery wholesalers stepped into the breach, however, allowing individuals to purchase reasonable quantities. We made several re-provisioning trips, and on one of them, bought the kids a new kite to fly off our stern.

Another one of our major goals was to arrange electronic repairs of our finicky autohelm and battery charger. Fixing the battery charger had become especially important, since without a consistent charge, the electrical system couldn't maintain a low fridge temperature. The red LED display on the outside of the fridge, where its internal temperature was shown, had crept from twenty-eight to thirty, then to thirty-three degrees. One day it soared to forty-three degrees. At that point, the red display developed its own perverse sense of humour, mocking its failure with the flashing message "HA! 44! HA! 44!"

Pat dismantled both the autohelm and the battery charger, and brought them to a repair shop. Its dusty shelves were lined with parts from defunct electronics, all victims of the harsh marine environment. A day later the repairman radioed us by VHF to say he could fix our autohelm, but must order a new part for the battery charger from Florida.

Another important task was to take Jasper to a veterinarian for her annual check-up, immunizations, and health certificate. Without the latter, she wouldn't be permitted to enter either the U.S. or Canada. The earliest appointment we could get was almost a month ahead, on July 12. Booking an appointment so far into the future signalled to me the fact that we were beginning the transition back to life on land. I resented that. Our days of sailing at a whim were numbered, and we knew it.

Getting a vet's certificate was straightforward compared to the other major decisions we had yet to make, such as how to get our selves and our gear back home, and where to leave the boat. We made a few enquiries about airfares and motor home rentals, and then, tired of being leashed ashore, weary of the unrelenting heat and humidity in town, we motored to Great Guana Island to ponder our decisions. Like Scarlet O'Hara, we decided to think about it tomorrow, and then we were gone with the wind.

Our short voyage to Great Guana was brilliant. The sun gleamed in its azure setting, streaked with high white horsetail clouds. The wind wafted lightly at our stern.

"C'mon kids, let's put up the spinnaker!" Pat said.

A spinnaker, a three-cornered sail of light, colourful fabric rigged to the bow, was used in light aft winds. Ours was striped the colours of the rainbow. Filled with air, it looked like a giant beach ball, but it flew and fluttered like a butterfly. Our spirits soared with it.

Pat cut the twin engines. A whoosh of silence greeted us, and we revelled in the moment. Our moods lifted as if on a spring breeze blowing after a long stale winter.

"Let's have a party!" I called out. A downwind sail was cause to celebrate.

Ben fetched pop and chips, while Liam popped in a CD by local Bahamians Stevie S. and the Calypsonians. The kids and I danced in the cockpit, singing the lyrics by heart, while Pat filmed us on the camcorder. Then Liam pulled out his guitar and strummed us a tune while we glided along, pulled by the spinnaker.

"Wouldn't it be fantastic if all our sails were like this?" Erin smiled, her face turned to the sun.

When we arrived at Baker's Bay, an inlet off Great Guana Cay, we doused the spinnaker and set the anchor. Beneath our hulls lay a constellation of sea stars, their five points shimmering in the pellucid water. When the wind rose later that afternoon, the kids assembled their new kite and flew it off the stern.

When we dinghied Jasper to shore that evening, we discovered a clutch of cruisers on the beach, relaxing with a glass of wine after their potluck dinner. They called us to join them. When the sand flies and no-see-ums began biting, we waded out on the firm and sandy ocean floor and sat down to watch the sunset, immersed chest-high in the gently lapping water, our wineglasses held high.

"Wouldn't it be fantastic if all of our days ended like this?" I murmured to Pat.

The next day, Pat raised the ugly subject.

"Well, what do you think?" I stirred from my reverie to listen. "What should we do from here? When should we return to Florida? Should we fly home or drive a motor home? Do we stay here in the Bahamas or do we go somewhere else before we head north?"

I tossed out some thoughts but they were vague. Such questions seemed too big. *Having just nicely learned to wallow in the present, I resist looking to the future,* I wrote in my diary. *To make a grocery list is daunting enough; a long-term plan is downright frightening.*

The next morning, we returned to Marsh Harbour so we could check in with the electronics repairman, and check out the Goombay festival to be held in town that night. Enroute to our anchorage, the clouds knit themselves into a big grey snarl.

"Looks like one of those summer squalls we've read about," Pat fretted. "We'd better tuck into Fisher's Bay till it clears off."

Not a minute after we'd lowered the sails and anchored, the clouds exploded.

"Time for a freshwater shower!" Pat roared. The kids

squealed with glee to see their father lather up in the cockpit and then, amid bluster and thunder and high waves, rinse himself off in the furling drapery of rain at the foredecks.

"Hurry back!" I shouted. "What if there's lightning?"

That evening we dinghied to shore and followed our noses to the Goombay festival. We soon found a wide street lined with booths selling Bahamian fare. We tasted here and sampled there as we moved along the tables. Then a sweet young girl ran after Meara and held out a fresh mango. The two little girls, both clinging to their mothers, smiled coyly at each other, the Canadian with her wispy white-blond hair and wide blue eyes, and the Bahamian with her glossy chocolate skin and cornrow plaits. Meara accepted the mango with whispered thanks. Their exchange was tender enough to undo the most intransigent racist.

I turned to pay the child's mother for the mango.

"No, no, jes' keep it," she laughed. "Dere be way too many, plen'y for everyone." She was right. On our walk through the streets, I'd noticed the trees were literally dripping with the heavy and juicy ripe fruit.

A live band set up at the end of the street burst to life with the runaway Bahamian hit, "Who Let the Dogs Out," followed by those ever-present Stevie S. tunes. After the "native" fashion show – little more than a strut of bathing beauties – came a Junkanoo parade complete with horns, drums and colourful masks. Then the dance contests began.

"You!" someone shouted, tapping my shoulder. "And you!" he said, tapping Erin's. "You be in deh 'shake-it-up' ladies' dancin' contest."

Erin and I stared at each other, laughed, and shrugged our shoulders.

"Why not?" I mouthed to her above the infectious

drumbeat. After a few dances, I got "picked off" – eliminated from the contest – while Erin competed with three other girls in the semi-finals.

Pat and I watched our daughter shake it up. She was beautiful. More than that, she was radiant, glowing with the gyrating joy of rhythmic movement, her exuberance still innocent. I remembered when I was Erin's age, or perhaps a little older, when I realized I'd grown more attractive than my mother. I always wondered how she felt about that, and now I knew: she felt wistful at the passage of her own physical prime, yet proud of her healthy and appealing young daughter. Mostly she felt grateful that unlike her daughter, she'd already survived the tumultuous teens and twenties.

Erin didn't win the dancing contest, but she walked away from the Goombay Festival with a one-of-a-kind T-shirt, and a one-of-a-kind story to tell her friends.

The next morning Pat connected with the electronics repairman.

"The new parts for our battery charger won't be here for a week," Pat reported. "We might as well gunkhole till then."

"Let's go to Great Guana," I suggested.

After lunch, we headed out. We planned to pick up a mooring off the beach of Guana Seaside Village, where there was a pool and an upscale restaurant. Mid-afternoon, another summer squall arose, and we got caught out in the open. This one was fierce; there would be no showers on the foredecks this time.

"Meara, get below decks!" Pat hollered. She fled. Jasper had already found her hidey-hole under the salon table. Ben and Erin scurried below, battening the hatches, locking the companionway, and chinking in the Plexiglas windowpanes.

Meanwhile, Pat and Liam and I toiled on deck. The weather grew wilder. The wind screamed higher, reaching a pitch of sixty knots. The rain pelted our skin. The wind snatched our beloved Canadian flag and flung it to the churning blue sea. The winch handle broke off and flew away, splitting off a piece of the winch moulding. Lightning blazed and thunder blasted. Liam's eyes filled with fear, but he persevered. I found the storm refreshing, even exhilarating, but not scary. I was drenched in the moment. Taking the helm, I strained to hold the boat directly into the wind. Bending my neck upwards, I fixed my eyes on the arrow-shaped wind vane at the top of the mast. If it pointed straight ahead, that meant the bows were aimed straight into the wind, and Pat and Liam could lower the jib. If the boat strayed to either direction, the sail would flap about wildly. Father and son struggled with the copious folds of sailcloth, a rough and deafening chore. At last they lowered the jib, but not before it ripped along the foot, and before Pat's hands were bruised and bleeding.

An hour later, the blistering squall passed overhead. We limped into the anchorage off Guana Seaside Village, and secured the boat to one of the mooring balls. That's when another even more violent squall hit us. This time, though, we were tied up and battened down. Enduring that second squall only reinforced our sense that we were completely safe, cocooned within our beloved *Cool Breezes*, cozy as if at home in a raging blizzard. Down in the galley, ensconced within our flat-floating catamaran in the middle of a storm, Meara and I turned out a big meal: chicken pieces marinated in Italian sauce, pasta, sautéed green beans, apricot matrimonial cake and a pot of hot tea.

It was a relief, when the storm abated at midnight, to open the companionway and let the fresh breeze flow through. That's when Pat discovered our mast light was damaged.

"Yet another thing to get fixed," he sighed, setting up an alternate light source to alert passersby of our presence in the black night. I soothed him to sleep with a back rub. The next morning dawned incongruously clear and bright. We hung our wet clothes and blankets on the lifelines, and listened to the net. One by one, cruisers checked in to report the damage they'd suffered through the two squalls. Swim ladders and dinghies had been torn away. Anchor lines had snapped, leaving boats to rollick aimlessly. At Baker's Bay, we heard, five anchors were uprooted by the winds and five boats collided into each other. And over at Treasure Cay, one boat's mast was struck by lightning and all of her electronics were fried. We felt lucky to have escaped so lightly from nature's wrath.

"Let's treat ourselves to a day at Guana Seaside Village," Pat suggested.

We dinghied to shore to find a little piece of paradise. While the kids leapt into the freshwater pool, a welcome novelty for them, Pat and I sidled up to the open-air bar and indulged in another rare delight, bottles of ice-cold beer. I clinked my Kalik with Pat's.

"Here's to doing what our friends and family imagine we do every day!"

"I know what you mean," laughed the barkeep. Gerry was a petite and energetic woman with a silver-tipped pixie cut and a wide smile. "Bob and I were sailors ourselves. We lived in Maine, but our hearts were back in the Bahamas. One day we figured out we could do anything we liked. Our kids were grown. So we sold everything and bought this resort."

"See that boat over there?" asked Bob. He had a gruff voice, and a white beard that set off a tanned and weathered face. He pointed to a pretty little sloop bobbing on a mooring ball. "That's our *Clementine*. We sail her whenever we like. We're living the dream."

The willingness to risk, to dare to live the dream, was a common thread binding the disparate crowd of cruisers we'd met along our ten-month journey.

We swam and lounged poolside, then lunched on burgers at the restaurant. There we met Gerry's niece from Maine, who was painting a large seascape mural in the dining room. The kids watched her work as Pat and I sipped sundowners with Bob and Gerry.

When the sun sank, we dinghied back to our boat. The heat of the day had beat down on her. Down in the galley, the accumulated heat was stifling, so I called the kids to open the hatches and replace the Plexiglas windows with screens. No sooner had they accomplished the assignment than the sky darkened.

"Batten the hatches, chink in the windows!" Pat yelled. Another squall blew through. Within an hour, however, the rain let up, and Pat and the kids could play crib in the cockpit.

Yet another storm roused us next morning, but this one was just a little spitfire. Once it passed, we loosened the mooring line and pointed our bows toward Man o' War Cay, reputed to be one of the best boat-building centres in the hemisphere. We'd read in our cruising guide of a master sailmaker there, whom we hoped to hire to repair both jibs: not only the one that had just torn, but also the one blown out back in the Jumentos in March.

A short motorsail later, we navigated the narrow channel entrance to the settlement. From there the channel parts at right angles into two sheltered harbours, one north and the other south. I steered the helm hard to port. Pat picked up a mooring, and we tied up for lunch. Liam and I dinghied to shore to pay the mooring fee and find the famous sailmaker.

Man o' War was a charming settlement with tidy streets and well-kept homes freshly painted an array of pastel colours. The townsfolk were friendly but conservative, and overwhelmingly white. Like Spanish Wells, Man o' War was dry. Unlike Spanish Wells, however, it was hilly and lush. Coconut palms, orange trees, sea grapes and multi-coloured hibiscus lined the narrow streets. Near the small playground of the marina we visited, a large cork tree spread its branches, offering shady refuge. In addition to all the usual boating businesses, we found unique gift and clothing boutiques, restaurants and ice cream parlours. But when we found the sailmaker, and learned he was about to depart for a three-week vacation, we decided we'd leave Man o' War too.

We really enjoyed our family stroll through the quiet streets tonight, I wrote in my diary that evening. *Children laughing, riding bikes, choir music wafting out church windows. Returned to the boat to sip coffee liqueur with Pat in the cockpit (is that allowed in this dry community?) and to ponder that irksome question: how and when are we going to get home? Still no answers. I fear my brain is addled. I can't seem to focus on anything but the next day's journey.*

The next morning, when we tuned in to the cruiser's net, Pat radioed a request for leads on sailmakers. Several listeners responded. One suggested a certain boater docked in Marsh Harbour, who was always eager to supplement her cruising kitty. A little later in the program, Gerry from Guana Seaside Village spoke up.

"I'd just like to say we really enjoyed the company of a wonderful family the other day, the crew of *Cool Breezes,*" she effused. "Their four children are about the happiest and best-behaved I've ever met."

Pat and I stared at each other, stunned. Could she possibly be referring to our kids?

"Happy and well-behaved children?" replied the net anchorwoman. "Isn't that an oxymoron?"

We returned to Marsh Harbour later that day. We docked at the same marina as the cruiser who repaired sails, and hired her to repair our jibs. The days slipped by. Although we continued to await replacement parts for our battery charger, and coped with a fifty-degree fridge, other repairs got done. The tears in our two jibs were sewn, our autohelm was fixed and re-installed, and the mast light replaced. Pat managed to get the air conditioning going. It was noisy but essential, especially when the thermometer climbed to almost one hundred degrees Fahrenheit. The day the temperature reached one hundred and one, Pat and the kids went shopping for the latest in heat-beating devices: personal fans hanging from cords around their necks. When Ben's fan broke a few days later, he and Liam constructed a "Frankenfan" using the same motor and tiny whirring fan blades, attached to the body of a burglar alarm.

Most afternoons, when the cabin grew oppressive and walking about town too hot to bear, we trundled down the road with our snorkelling gear to Mermaid Reef. The coral was dark and dying, but its polyps still supported a breathtaking variety of fish.

"As they say on the net, tension is water soluble," Liam observed.

Aside from the usual marina routine – shopping, showers, and doing laundry, email and repairs – our major goal in Marsh Harbour this time was to make onward plans, onward to the Muggle world. It was time to face the inevitable: we were heading home. Armed with prepaid phone cards and the Internet, we devoted hours every day to an earnest investigation of airfares and train tickets, motor home rental rates, and the cost of buying a mini-van. Many airlines, we found, wouldn't allow dogs to fly during the summer months. Canadian railway lines accepted dogs as passengers, but American lines did not. Although buying a minivan made sense, since we'd need a new vehicle upon our return to Canada, its luggage capacity was severely limited. And so far, we hadn't been able to find anyone who would lease a motor home for anything but a return trip excursion.

The morning of June 30, we found an American motor home agency that agreed to a one-way rental from Orlando, Florida to Calgary, Alberta. Even factoring in the drop-off fee, gas, campground fees, meals out and sightseeing, the cost would be lower than flying the seven of us home. Driving a motor home would also eliminate another headache: how to pack and ship, or else abandon, our many treasures. Our kayak, two dozen conch, helmet shells and sea stars, several boxes of small seashells, a guitar, snorkelling gear, fishing rods and tackle, charts and cruising guides, life vests and souvenirs – all of it could come home with us. We booked a thirty-foot motor home to be picked up on August 4, and delivered in Alberta two weeks later.

The other good thing about travelling in a motor home, I wrote in my diary, *is that it will allow for an easier transition to life back on land than flying home would. To wake in a berth on the water in the morning and go to bed at home on land that same night would feel too strange.*

"Let's celebrate at the marina bar," Pat said to me, the day we made the booking. "Do you realize I've never had a *piña colada?*"

"What's a *piña colada?*" asked Ben and Liam, our live-aboard mixology students.

"A frothy drink made in a blender out of fruit juice, ice and rum," I replied.

"Hmm, that's a little beyond *Cool Breezes*," Ben said. "We usually have rum, and occasionally fruit juice, but we rarely have ice, and never a blender."

"Even if we had a blender, we don't often have electricity to run it!" added Liam.

I smiled. My sons might soon return to life as landlubbers, but for now they were thoroughly sailors.

From: The Kirwin crew
To: Kith and Kin
Subject: **Greetings from *Cool Breezes*:**
                 Celebrations

Ahoy there, ye landlubbers! It's June 30, and we're sailing
the cobalt sea enroute from Marsh Harbour to Treasure
Cay. The sky is clear, the water deep, and the route direct,
perfect conditions for putting Otto, our newly repaired
helmsman, to work. Seated in the sun-filled cockpit, we
dine on potato salad. Liam pops in the Stevie S. CD, ideal
for dancing and singing along. All this sunshine and cheer
is good for the soul!

Three hours later, we arrive at Treasure Cay. Despite its
name, it isn't truly a separate island, but a resort built on a
small peninsula of Great Abaco Island. The marina here is
filled with sport fishermen, but we can pick up a mooring
offshore for US$8 a night, and still take advantage of the
marina's amenities like the freshwater pool and showers.
We dinghy to shore and poke around the settlement.

"Look, a bakery that's actually open!" Ben exclaims. He's
been on the hunt for a pie for months. We pick up a key lime
pie from Rosie's Bakery and head back to the boat.

"And look, a library!" Erin shouts. We haven't set foot
in such an establishment since October. The doors are
closed today, but we can visit tomorrow.

"It's Canada Day!" I announce, as each child emerges
from his or her berth. "Back home we'd go on a family
outing. What should we do this year?"

"Go to the beach!" two of them shout. Treasure Cay is
famous for its spectacular, three-and-a half-mile beach.

July 2001, the Abacos islands, the Bahamas.

The kids enjoy the marina pool at Treasure Cay.

The boys relax poolside at Nippers club on Great Guana.

Cool Breezes *is immortalized on a mural at Guana Seaside Village.*

"Go to the pool!" shout the other two. The marina's curvaceous pool with its colourful deck chairs lures us, too.

We end up doing both. In the morning, we putter to shore with our towels and shovels, pails and paperbacks, sunscreen and water bottles, and trundle down the jutting peninsula to the beach. Not only is it deserted – no one else celebrates Canada's birthday, it seems – it's breathtaking. A long ribbon of white velvet sand is arranged in a crescent shape. The tranquil sea is aquamarine, a meeting place of blue and green. White sails and butterfly spinnakers dot the water, and whispering palms and yellow umbrellas fleck the beach. Behind all this soars a relentless turquoise sky. Our cruising guide says Treasure Cay beach is rated one of the world's top ten, and we believe it.

We plunge into the surf. Then Pat settles in with his novel, the boys and Meara build sand forts and holding tanks, and Erin and I walk Jasper the entire length of the beach.

After a light lunch on board, we shake the talc sand from our towels, and dinghy to the marina pool. There we spend the afternoon, reading in the shade and dipping in the pool when we get too hot. After a freshwater shower, my skin feels positively luminous.

Late in the day we walk to the town library. What a treat for the whole crew! Being transient, we can't borrow anything, but we buy books from the cast-off bin.

A marvellous Canada Day, from start to finish.

Today's July 3, my forty-third birthday, the last family birthday to be celebrated aboard *Cool Breezes*. This isn't a morning to rise early, set the coffee to brew, and sweep out the cockpit. This isn't a day to start breakfast, then tip each child's toothbrush with a minty squirt, so I can tell later whose teeth have been brushed. This isn't the time to slip silently from my berth and hunker down with my novel in progress, scribbling furiously in the salon until I hear the first stirrings in the staterooms. This is a day to lie in bed, and let my family come to me.

Meara is the first to wake. She crawls into bed with me and Pat for a giggly snuggle. Soon Ben and Erin appear with a plate of blueberry pancakes and cup of hot coffee. When I finally manage to get my lazy (old) bones out of my berth and into the cockpit, the children bring me birthday gifts. Ben gives me a shapely dolphin carving, and the girls each present me with a piece of embroidery. Liam, not known for his fine motor skills, has prepared a homemade booklet of coupons for back-rubs and other treats.

"Look, here's a coupon entitling me to steal any of the coupons Dad got for Father's Day!" I laugh.

Pat's gifts of perfume and jewellery are classic, yet unique: a delightful scent called Bahamas, contained in a glass seashell, and an exquisite silver sea star bracelet.

"This is the bracelet I wanted, from the shop back in Marsh Harbour," I exclaim.

"Yes, I did manage to catch your very broad hints," Pat responds.

By now it's mid-morning, time to cast off the mooring line and head to Great Guana Cay, where the family will dine out in honour of this last live-aboard birthday. The wind is up and the seas are rollicking. Cloud tufts speckle the light blue sky. Liam and I enjoy one-on-one time at the bows, he with his pensive pencil, and I with my diary. I feel the fullness of the moment. I am all here, right now.

Instead of mooring off the Guana Seaside resort, we pick up a mooring ball in the town anchorage so we can better access Guana settlement. Ashore we discover a picturesque hamlet. The winding narrow paths and boardwalks are lined with coconut palms and casuarina trees. It's almost one hundred degrees today, and muggy. We see a supermarket and a liquor store, conch fritter and hamburger stands, beach bars and T-shirt shops. Strolling the beach, we find Nippers, the hottest Abaco nightclub. It's decked out today in red, white and blue streamers and balloons, ready for Fourth of July celebrations tomorrow when the Abaco Regatta makes its stop here in Guana. Many cruisers follow the regatta from island to island, we're told, whether they're racing or not, just to join the relay party. The anchorage will be packed with boats like a *guagua* full of Cubans, and the pubs even more tightly.

Late that afternoon, Bob picks us up in his Jeep to take us to Guana Seaside Village for dinner. The roads are almost impassable, reminiscent of Cuba's *pasos malos*. A half-hour later, we arrive at the resort.

"We had no idea the trip would be so difficult," I tell Bob. "Today's my birthday, though, and we really wanted to have dinner here. We really enjoyed ourselves with you and Gerry last week."

"We did, too," Bob replies. "Wait till you see the surprise we have in store for you."

We hop from the Jeep and hurry into the lobby. Gerry greets us, beaming.

"Remember the mural my niece was painting when you were here? Well, she finished it. Come see."

Beneath whirling white fans a large seascape is painted. Only two boats bob in the water. One of them is *Clementine*, Bob and Gerry's sloop. The other is *Cool Breezes*.

"We're immortalized!" says Ben.

The children are thrilled. My eyes glisten, overwhelmed at the honour.

Today is the Fourth of July. American boats stream into the anchorage, filling it to capacity. The Abaco Regatta has moved to Great Guana today, and with it, throngs of cruisers. The weather is cloudy and blustery. We see no reason to go ashore. Instead, we curl up in our berths with our new library books. Although it can be fun to be in the midst of a party, we're averse to crowds today. As it turns out, our disinclination is provident.

Propped on a pillow facing the stateroom windows, Pat notices something amiss. Suddenly he sits bolt upright, then leaps off the berth, up the stairs and into the cockpit. The kids and I follow close at his heels.

"What's going on?" I ask.

"The boat in front of us is dragging anchor. It's about to hit us!"

Pat fires up the twin engines, unties our bowline from the big red mooring ball, and motors away. We tie up to another mooring ball, out of harm's way, and watch, astonished, as *Shannon* plows right over the mooring we've just left.

"*Shannon, Shannon!*" I call on the VHF. There's no answer.

Shannon drags toward the next target, a boat named *Conch Fritter*.

"*Conch Fritter, Conch Fritter!*" I call on the VHF. "*Shannon, Shannon!*"

Still no reply. The two boats are due to collide at any moment.

"I bet the crews aren't even on board," Pat thinks aloud. "I bet they're out drinking."

I radio the settlement's various drinking establishments. All of them are equipped with VHF.

"Please page your guests," I ask each barkeep.

A few moments later, the owner of *Conch Fritter* calls us back.

"A boat dragging in the anchorage is headed straight for you," I say.

"Really," the owner replies in a gravely Southern drawl. We can almost smell the bourbon on his breath. "I think I'll just wait and see what happens."

Pat grabs the VHF handset from me.

"What'll happen is you'll be hit!"

"Well, thanky sir for watching my boat. Bye-bye now!"

We stare, stunned, at the VHF.

"Well, I can't just stand by and watch," Pat says. "C'mon Liam! We're off to another boat rescue!" The two of them hop into the dinghy. "Let's try to use the inflatable to keep the two boats apart." Off they roar.

Just then the owner of *Shannon* calls back on the VHF. When I tell him what's happening, he's frantic.

"I'll be right there!" he replies.

By now the two boats are mere feet apart. Pat and Liam arrive in time to fend off the worst of the collision, but the stern of *Shannon* hits the bow pulpit of *Conch Fritter*. I hail the bar at which the *Conch Fritter* owner imbibes.

"The two boats just collided," I report.

"Well, I guess I'll have to come on over," comes the laconic reply.

The owners of *Shannon* arrive by dinghy and take control of their boat. Their thanks are profuse. But the owner of *Conch Fritter* isn't so gracious.

"So you're the frogs who kept calling us on the VHF!" he snorts as he pulls his dinghy alongside *Cool Breezes*. He gestures to our stern flag.

"Do you mean Canadians?" Pat asks.

"Well, yeah, whatever you call yourselves," the fellow replies with an arrogant snigger. A fat cigar dangles from his mouth, dusting his inflatable with hot ashes. He guns his outboard and takes off into the dark without a word of thanks. We begin to appreciate why that hotheaded landowner back in Little Harbour hates cruisers so much.

Close to midnight, a fireworks display crackles and sparkles overhead.

"Let's sing *O Canada!*" I rally the kids. We burst out in loud anthem. Our anchorage neighbours respond with applause, followed by a ringing rendition of *The Star-Spangled Banner.*

The skies are clear this morning, the 5th. Pat and I take Jasper ashore for her morning jaunt. On the leeside beach we lay side by side in a hammock, facing each other with mugs of coffee.

"Let's go to the ocean beach today," I suggest. "It faces the third largest barrier reef on the planet. I bet there's terrific snorkelling there. And then we could take the kids to Nippers. It's got a two-tiered swimming pool with a waterfall cascade."

"Sure," Pat agrees. "But tomorrow the battery charger will be repaired, so we gotta get back to Marsh Harbour."

The seashore is grand today, but the water is too rough for Meara to snorkel. She and I sit in our own private pool, a small water-filled depression in the coral. Each time a wave crashes, the water spills over us. When the others return from their snorkel, we walk to Nippers. Pat and I find a table overlooking the bi-level pool, where the boys and Meara play. We can also see the stage, where a guitarist strums mellow tunes, and the hair-braiding station, where Erin is having beaded cornrows plaited into her long blond hair. Two cold Kaliks sweat on our table.

"It feels like we've got a wealth of time left on our journey," I muse aloud. "On one hand, our year is almost up. On the other, now that we've made onward plans, we know we have a whole month ahead of us. That's longer than most people's summer holidays."

Pat clinks his bottle to mine. "Here's to our last month!" he says.

God bless and fair winds,

Love PJ+crew

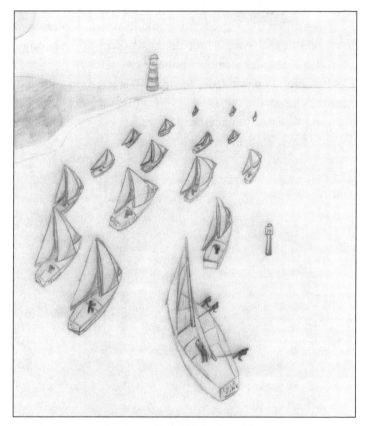

July 2001, the Abacos, the Bahamas.
Artwork by Ben, inspired by Hope Town.

Chapter 32
Gunkholing in the Abacos

*They that go down to the sea in ships, … these see
the works of the Lord, and his wonders in the deep.*
— Old Testament, Psalms 107: 23-24

At dawn July 6, we picked our cautious way among
the boats and mooring balls crowding the Great
Guana anchorage, our bows aimed at Marsh
Harbour. There we'd accomplish the usual boat-keeping
chores, plus two other important tasks: retrieving our
repaired battery charger, and sending email inquiries to
sailboat brokers.

"If I'm very very good, can we keep the boat?" Meara
begged when she heard Pat and I discuss selling *Cool
Breezes.*

We laughed.

"You're always a very good girl," I replied. "We still
might not keep the boat, though."

Pat and I knew that once back home, family excur-
sions to Florida to sail our seafaring catamaran would be
infrequent. A huge financial investment was tied up in
Cool Breezes, a chunk of money we could use. Much as we
wanted to keep our boat, we knew we should try to sell
her.

A harbinger of life in Alberta appeared while we were
docked in Marsh Harbour. Pat and I sat at a restaurant

down the dock from our boat, listening to the live band. A vocalist on guitar played with a musician on the saw. Holding an ordinary carpenter's saw under his chin like a fiddle, he produced a warbling rhythmic sound.

"Can he ever make that saw sing!" we heard from the table behind me. Then I felt the back of my chair being bumped.

"Oh, pardon me," came the same voice. I turned to see a pretty, diminutive woman of eighty years, dressed in fuchsia.

"No problem," I turned to reply. The lady seized the chance to introduce herself.

"Hello, how are you? I'm Zetta from Alberta, Canada. Where are you from?"

"We're from Alberta, too!" I replied.

"Incredible!" Zetta exclaimed. She told us she was a widow with numerous children and grandchildren. Every summer for the past fifteen years, she'd brought one of her grandchildren with her on a holiday to her timeshare condo in Marsh Harbour. This year she'd brought Jennifer, a curvaceous young woman who was bopping on the dance floor.

"Jennifer says she's ditching me this evening," Zetta laughed. "Mind if I join you?"

"Not at all," we replied. Before Pat could rise to help her, Zetta dragged her chair to our table and engaged us in a long chinwag that eventually revealed the amazing coincidence that her niece was married to my uncle.

The more she talked, the more Zetta reminded me of my beloved grandmother Eugenie, a warm and charming person who had passed away seven years previous. I was enchanted, and so was Pat. On and on Zetta chirped, broken only by flights to the dance floor. She'd break off mid-sentence, rise from her chair and begin twitching on thin legs to the beat of the music. One of the gentlemen from the bar would jump up, take her hand, and lead her off to dance. Close to midnight, Pat and I escorted Zetta home. She led us down the street, around the corner, and up at least fifty steps, chatting all the way.

A few nights later, we decided to take the kids out to the popular "rib night" at the Jib Room restaurant. On a whim, I telephoned Zetta to join us. She was out when I called, so I left a voice message giving her the details. Just as our family was being seated in the restaurant, Zetta appeared at the threshold, brightly plumed again, her pert eyes scanning the crowd. I hurried to greet her.

"Well, hello Zetta," I said.

"Oh, that's who you are," she replied. "I couldn't understand the message on my answering machine, and didn't know who called me. All I heard was Jib Room at six. So I decided I'd just take a taxi down here and find out."

Zetta nestled in among our children at the bench seat, and spent the next few hours chatting with them.

"Meara, you've won my heart," she confided, tucking her beneath her wing. The feeling was mutual. Meara's tears flowed when Zetta hopped in a cab to go home.

That was Saturday, July 7. By then our chores were done. The morning of July 8, Ben sat at the salon table poring over charts, and entering waypoints into the GPS. He would take the first turn as captain-for-a-day, and planned a short journey of eight nautical miles to Hope Town on nearby Elbow Cay.

At noon we threw off the docklines.

"Dad, you take the helm," Ben ordered. "Take us out of the marina. Meara, take Jasper and keep her in the salon. Liam, stand at the bows and watch for shallow water. Erin, tidy up the lines. Mom, make lunch."

Ben clearly relished his role. Everyone performed the

same tasks as usual, but Ben got to issue the orders to do it.

Two sunny hours later, we arrived in Hope Town harbour. Above waving palm fronds towered the fabled red-and-white lighthouse, a Bahamian national symbol. The Hope Town lighthouse is said to be the most often photographed in the Bahamas.

"I think we're going to like this place, skipper," I remarked to Ben. "Good job."

We docked smoothly at the Club Soleil marina mid-afternoon, and coiled our docklines. Erin and I took Jasper for a short run in the hot sun to the lighthouse and back, and returned for a plunge in the marina's freshwater pool.

That pool was a Godsend during our Hope Town sojourn. The weather was sweltering, but the village was enchanting. Across the water from the marina, we found a clutch of quaint and well-kept cottages and shops. Most of them lined a slender road that faced the sheltered harbour and backed onto the roaring Atlantic. The lane was so narrow that we had to squeeze over if a golf-cart overtook us. The days slipped by. We read, kayaked around the anchorage, swam in the pool, cooked and cleaned, bought groceries and souvenirs, and, since we were plugged into shore power, borrowed videos from the marina.

One of the videos we watched was *Captain Ron*, a comedy about a family of novice sailors. Just as the family's journey is about to end, and their sailboat approaches the Florida dock where it will be put up for sale, the family decides to abandon its life on land. They turn the bow about and sail, quite literally, into the sunset.

"Do you think we'll do that, too?" Meara asked wistfully, her little voice quavering.

One day, we hiked to the hundred-year-old candy cane lighthouse, and climbed its one hundred and one steps to the top. From there we soaked up the spectacular seascape, in which every imaginable shade of blue sparkled, and the white sails of regatta boats fluttered. We also met the lightkeeper, whose job it was to wind the rotating mechanism operating the bulls-eye lens every hour and a half.

"This light can be seen from twenty miles offshore," he boasted.

Another day, we visited the miniature town museum, crammed with memorabilia. There, tucked among its many antiques, weathered photographs and bits of recovered ship's treasure, we found a compellingly written history of The Commonwealth of the Bahamas. We learned that the Bahamas' first inhabitants were the Lucayans, or "island peoples," relatives to the Arawak natives of Haiti and Cuba. The words hammock, maize, potato, tobacco, hurricane and cay all have Arawak roots. The gentle and generous Lucayans welcomed Christopher Columbus and his Spanish crew when they landed in the Bahamas in 1492. Yet within thirty years, the Spaniards enslaved and sold them all, and eventually, the Lucayan population was decimated.

The next people to inhabit the Bahamian islands were the Eleutherian Adventurers, religious freedom seekers who landed on ephemeral Eleuthera in the 1600s. An influx of American Loyalists followed in 1785. Plantation owners brought their black slaves, who later gained freedom and whose descendants now form a majority of the Bahamian population. The industries of wrecking, or salvaging shipwrecks (from 1648 to 1863), blockade running (1862 to 1865), sponging and boat building (1800s and early 1900s), and rum running (1920 to 1933), once fuelled the Bahamian economy. Now, we read, tourism dominates.

Last but not least in any historical account of the Bahamas is the weather's effect on the economy.

"The many moods of Mother Nature are strongly felt here," read the museum mural. Hurricanes wreaked havoc upon the islands every few years, most recently in 1999.

Bahamians celebrate their independence July 10. Our family joined in festivities marking the nation's twenty-eighth anniversary at Hope Town Harbour Lodge, an upscale hotel across the harbour. We dinghied there in our best dress to attend the "luau" celebration. Despite the Hawaiian theme, we found huge buffet tables laden with typical Bahamian cuisine, live Bahamian music playing on an outdoor dance floor overlooking the ocean, and limbo contests. Of our family, Liam was the best limbo dancer.

We motorsailed back to Marsh Harbour on July 12, the day of Jasper's veterinarian appointment. We anchored, and dinghied to shore. While Pat downloaded email and phoned a Florida sailboat broker, the kids and I walked to the vet. It was one hundred and one degrees Fahrenheit in town that day, so we were delighted to wait in the vet's air-conditioned office. The vet found Jasper to be healthy and fit. He administered the vaccinations and issued the necessary certificate of good health. He also weighed her.

"She's only seventy-three pounds, five pounds lighter than a year ago," Erin noted.

"Don't I know it," I replied. "She lost five pounds just from shedding hair!"

Next morning we departed for Baker's Bay. It was Erin's turn to be captain-for-a-day.

"I don't care if it's Friday the thirteenth!" she said. Erin was well prepared, and managed the journey beautifully. We enjoyed a fabulous sail on a brisk beam reach. The only glitch arose when a huge sport fishing boat roared within twenty feet of us without breaking an iota of its speed. *Cool Breezes* rollicked in the huge wake that followed, sending all of her crew and much of her contents lurching off balance.

"Liam, grab the binocs, tell me the name of that boat," Pat roared.

Liam read the name aloud, then added with a glower, "And everyone on board is pointing and laughing at us."

"Stink-potters," Pat muttered. The tension between sailors and sport fishermen could be obvious.

At lunchtime we anchored near Spoil Bank Cay, a tiny islet off Great Guana Cay. We spent the whole afternoon beachcombing. Erin found the best specimen: the delicate lavender shell of a sea urchin. But Meara made the best discovery: that she could swim!

Just after our expedition to shore the next morning, dark clouds gathered and a northerly wind rose. A big squall was on its way. I ran to the lifelines to gather towels and swimsuits. Hustling below decks clutching my bundle, I looked up to see the catamaran anchored next to us pass behind our stern. A curious time to head out to sea, I thought. Then I did a double take. All of the six or eight adults standing on deck were naked.

"Did you see what I saw?" I called out to Pat in the cockpit.

"No, but what I do see ain't good," he replied. "Quick! Hand me the engine keys!"

"What is it?" I asked. "Is the boat at our stern dragging? Should I radio its crew?"

"No!" Pat yelled, firing up the engines. "We're the ones who are dragging!"

To move our boat and re-set her two anchors amid a squall was rough. Gusts of wind howled and swoops of rain assailed us. Pat struggled with the two anchor lines while I stood at the helm, craning to see the wind vane, straining to hold the bows into the wind. At last the anchors were set, but the roaring wind and heaving seas tossed us about for the rest of the day. Peering out the companionway at sundown, both Erin and Liam squawked.

"Our new Canadian flag is ripped to shreds!" Erin shouted.

"And the tiller of the dinghy outboard is gone!" Liam added.

Pat dashed out to the cockpit to see for himself.

"The wind pushed the dinghy right between the hulls," he reported. "I can tell from the black marks it left under the bridge deck. I can't see the tiller anywhere."

His face bore that stiff expression I knew spelled stress. Without an operating outboard engine, the dinghy would have to be rowed, and Pat would be chief rower.

Liam's reaction was much more turbulent. He burst into tears, heartbroken that his beloved dinghy was impaired. He shut himself, hotheaded and tear-streaked, in his stateroom. Even when I initiated his favourite card game – poker – he refused to emerge.

"What a romance that would be, if Liam ever loves a woman as fiercely as he loves the dinghy!" I said to Pat.

The storm continued unabated. The mood aboard was sombre. I cooked an early dinner. To conserve battery power, we turned out the lights and retired early to berths damp from seeping window seals.

The next day dawned dry but grey, foreboding more rain. We moved the boat to a more protected anchorage, as close as possible to shore to minimize the dinghy ride. The skies began to pour forth once again. The boat began to rock and roll, inducing an afternoon nap for the whole crew. When we awoke, the sky was clear.

"Time for sea baths, everyone!" I announced.

The boys heaved their obligatory sighs, but in fact, everyone was happy to emerge from our cooped quarters. As we towelled off in the cockpit, a dinghy arrived at our stern.

"Hi there!" called a young curly-haired woman at the tiller. "I'm Cheryl from *Serifa*. My son Mikey noticed you have kids aboard and wants to meet them."

Young Mikey, only four years old, shrank close to his mother. It became quickly clear that it was not he but Cheryl who wanted to make acquaintance. We invited them aboard for cookies and tea.

"Man, oh man, it's so good to get off the boat," Cheryl confided a moment later. "My husband is seasick and the nineteen-year-old has mutinied. Both of them hate the cruising lifestyle, and both are mad at me for making them go on this trip," she went on. "I thought cruising would be a great way to bond our blended family. We sold everything we owned to buy the boat, but now everything is turning sour."

"How long have you been out?" I asked.

"Only nine months," Cheryl lamented. "I love it, but the guys want to return to land. We planned to live aboard indefinitely, but now I'm not so sure we're cut out for it."

"Had you ever sailed before?" Pat asked.

"No, never," Cheryl replied, a tear welling in the corner of her pale blue eye. And Tevi thought we were audacious, I thought. Our faces must have shown our astonishment.

"I know, I know," Cheryl shrugged, the tears now spilling down her cheeks. "I should've figured out we needed more experience. At first, we'd never leave the marinas, because neither of us knew how to lay an anchor, but also because my husband worried he'd get seasick."

"Well obviously you've learned by now how to anchor

and you got yourselves this far," said Pat, his voice encouraging.

The situation reminded me of my time with *Sweet Thing*, when Betsy spilled her woes to me after a very short acquaintance. In that case, it was she, and not her husband, who was intensely dissatisfied with the cruising lifestyle. Yet both situations had the same thing in common: the harder decision wasn't to cash in and go to sea, but to admit defeat and return to land.

When the wind and rain began to rise, Cheryl and Mikey left. We endured yet another rolly night, heaving with the water's turmoil, buffeted by the troubled wind.

The next morning, I woke to relative calm. The crew was asleep. I slipped out of bed and trod barefoot upon smooth polished teak toward the head. I gathered the accumulated wet towels and clothes from the last few leaky, dripping days and hung them on the lifelines. Then I sat in the cockpit with my diary.

All shall be well, and all shall be well, and all manner of things shall be well. All is well. It's a gorgeous anchorage morning. The water and wind have made sweet peace. The breeze wafts lightly, the water twinkles back. They're flirting with each other. The fronds of palm skirts sway and whisper. Even the air smells delicious, I wrote. *Sweeter than the morning is my solitude. Sweetest of all is feeling grateful. We are so lucky to have no tracks to retrace, no heavy soul-searching to guide us to the right decision. We'd set a time limit on our travels, and now our challenge is facing the fact that the end is looming.*

My eyes lifted from the page to gaze at Spoil Bank Cay. Jasper slumped at my feet. She too looked longingly ashore, but for a different reason. As Pat's footsteps approached, my suspended moment dissolved, and I sighed. Yes, our gunkholing days were numbered.

Chapter 33

All I Longed for I Found by the Water

Lord, as I drift on the waters,
Be the resting place of my restless heart . . .
. . . All I longed for I have found by the water . . .
— Cesáreo Gabaráin

The sparkling morning of July 17, Pat joined me on the cockpit cushions.

"Wouldn't it be grand to stay another day in this paradise?" I sighed, gazing round.

"Yep, but we can't," Pat said. "Gotta get to Green Turtle Cay. The outboard dealer there might be able to replace the broken tiller on our dinghy engine. Rowing the seven of us to shore is getting a tad tiresome."

I steered the boat out of Baker's Bay. Three hours later, Green Turtle Cay came in sight. As we approached the anchorage, Pat radioed the local outboard dealer.

"Sorry," the dealer replied. "I'd have to order in a new tiller from Florida. It would take three or four weeks to get here."

"By then, we'll be off the boat and back on land," Liam commented.

"We might even be home," I added.

The kids looked at me, startled. Meara looked as if she might cry.

We decided to dock at one of the Green Turtle mari-

*July 2001,
the Abacos
islands, the
Bahamas.*

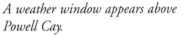

*A weather window appears above
Powell Cay.*

*Erin catches
a baby sand shark
off Great Sale Cay.*

*Our messages-in-bottles await our
last crossing of the Gulf Stream.*

*A moment
suspended at
Double Breasted Cays.*

nas rather than anchor out, for both Pat's and Jasper's convenience.

"It smells really good here," Erin observed. "Like flowers." She and I took Jasper on a short walk to the settlement of New Plymouth.

"Look at that sign, Mom," said Erin. "Down on the dock there."

"'Remember these shores'," I read aloud.

We found a small grocery store, a tiny historical museum, a secluded Loyalist Memorial garden, and numerous territorial brown dogs. Unlike his cousins, one mutt stood still, allowing Jasper to come close for a sniff. Then he bit her hindquarters.

"Thank goodness you just got your rabies shot," Erin crooned, hugging her pet's neck while I stroked her back. Jasper just wagged her tail.

Weary of the angry barking chorus that followed us about town, Erin and I headed back to the marina. There we found Pat and sons had jury-rigged a flexible rubber handle that, together with a hand grip to help steer, accomplished the task of the broken tiller.

"Now we can anchor out on our way north," Pat said.

"You amaze me," I said, full of admiration.

"As they say, necessity is the mother of invention," said Liam.

We spent a full day at the Green Turtle marina, doing laundry – not too much though, at US$16 a load – and downloading email.

"Guess what, Mom!" Erin shouted out, skimming the latest harvest of messages. "*Living Aboard* magazine accepted your articles!"

I felt ecstatic. Was this an omen that my dream of success at writing might come true? To celebrate, the family dined on seafood sandwiches, ice cream desserts and chilled drinks at Wrecker's restaurant in town.

Later, Liam and Pat sat down at the salon table with charts and the GPS, plotting waypoints to Powell Cay. Liam took his imminent role of captain-for-a-day very seriously. I took a pensive walk along the shady lanes between our marina and the settlement, letting my thoughts meander with my feet. In those days I was wading through Stephen Hawking's *A Brief History of Time*, which addresses the concept of time running backwards. I'd be content if time merely stood still, I mused, and reclined in a canvas hammock suspended between two palms near the docks. I felt acutely aware that all too soon, this gentle swinging moment would become but the glimmer of a memory.

"C'mon Mom, we're gonna play charades!" Ben called from the boat.

My gaze shifted. I glanced up to see that the kids had zippered in the cockpit screen and lit a citronella candle to fend off mosquitoes and no-see-ums. In my immersion in the moment, I'd failed to notice I was being eaten alive.

I sat up late that night, tapping reply messages on the laptop. New Plymouth was the last email link on our route northward through the Abacos. I knew the email I polished off would be one of the last few of the year's journey.

"We can tangibly feel the winding-down tempo of our travels," I wrote in closing.

The next morning, July 20, we cast off the docklines and moved north to Powell Cay. Liam stood at the helm, barking orders. A huge grin spread across his face as we skirted all of the menacing clouds. *Liam makes for a very capable, conscientious and natural skipper,* I wrote in my diary that night. As soon as we dropped anchor, we jumped overboard to cool off.

The next day we explored Powell Cay. We dinghied to

the small beach facing the anchorage, where we found a path leading to the spectacular ocean shoreline. The bug juice we'd applied was no match for the ruthless swarm of mosquitoes that greeted us at the threshold of the jungle path. Once we reached the beach, we wasted no time admiring the view. We dove straight into the water for mosquito-bite relief.

Once in the water, it was easy to stay. We sat submerged to our shoulders, awash in the rolling waves. Then the boys splashed around with washed up pilings, and the girls and I went shelling. So bountiful were the shells that each of us chose to collect within a single colour scheme: shades of pink for Erin, an array of yellows for Meara, and black and white for me.

Meanwhile, Pat sat alone on the beach, staring pensively at the liquid horizon. The sky was grey and the air hot. Neither drop of rain nor riff of wind disturbed the surreal moment. As if to punctuate its poignancy, a patch of sun broke through the hazy skies.

"Look, a weather window!" Ben called out, pointing. The break in the clouds formed a nearly perfect rectangle.

July 22 dawned hazy and overcast, *like our moods*, I observed in my diary. I prepared a big fruit pancake to bake in the oven, while the four children took Jasper to poke about ashore. Pat and I listened to the weather report.

"The weather should be good for a few days," Pat said. "There's no point getting to Florida before the twenty-eighth, so let's check out the fancy marina at Spanish Cay."

The kids and dog returned.

"We found a plaque on the beach," Ben reported, "dedicated to the memory of a lady who died here in the anchorage."

"She was only twenty-seven," Erin said.

"Yeah, she died in a propane fire on board her sailboat," Liam added.

"I think I'll go check the propane tank," Pat responded. *I wonder how many accidents that simple plaque has prevented,* I later wrote in my diary.

We pulled up the hook and puttered north to Spanish Cay, a private island with a decidedly Florida feel. We docked amid the fluttering flags and spotless decks of American sport fishing yachts. Manicured lawns bordered by neat rows of cheerful flowers surrounded the turquoise pool. Ben and Liam spent the entire afternoon in the Jacuzzi. The rest of us settled into white chaise lounges beneath striped poolside umbrellas. Bright notes of Caribbean reggae floated on the breeze from the outdoor bar.

A jagged shard of lightning and fat splatters of rain shattered the idyll. The marina bartender, protected beneath his thatched roof, watched with mirth as dozens of chaise lounges suddenly emptied and swarms of boaters milled about the docks. So suddenly did these summer squalls arise that even experienced boaters were often caught off guard. Experience does, however, produce efficiency in battening the hatches; in no time we were shut in, cozy as Canadians by the fireplace in winter.

Later that evening, Pat and I poked our noses out the companionway. The rain had stopped, but the wind was up, and so was the tide. The new moon, combined with forty-knot breezes from an exposed direction, rendered the marina breakwater useless. Seawater washed over the dike of rock into the docking basin. The water level had increased so much that the waves licked the piers. Boats rollicked in their berths, their decks several feet higher than the docks. If the water rose any more, it would flood the docks, and boats would collide. Anxious boaters fiddled with spring lines and fussed with the rubber fenders buffering their boats from the pilings.

"It's an unusually high spring tide," said the guard on patrol. "It's happened before. It will be normal again by morning."

He was right. The next day was still and scorching. Jasper and I attempted a run of the three-mile length of the island under a blazing morning sun. When we arrived at our destination, the airstrip at the island's tip, we turned around and walked back.

"I can see why Jasper didn't run the whole way," Pat said, referring to the dog's thick red coat, "but what's your excuse?"

"I had to keep her company," I laughed.

That evening Pat and I left the kids on board to watch a rented video while we sauntered down the dock to the thatched roof bar. We'd just sidled up and ordered drinks when the bartender told us the fellow across from us had offered to pay our tab.

"I don't recognize him," Pat said. Nor did I. Pat beckoned the fellow to join us.

"Just wanted say thanks for helping me tie up today," said A.J., pulling up a barstool.

"It wasn't me who helped you!" Pat laughed. "That means the next drink is on me."

A.J. was a short stocky man of indeterminate age, with a yellow brush cut stiff as straw and skin like a leather baseball glove. He was a yacht captain by trade, hired at that time to bring an eighty-two foot yacht to the Bahamas. Like many boaters, A.J. loved to tell big fish stories; the size of his fish was extraordinary, though, and none of them got away.

"The expression 'three sheets to the wind' comes to mind," Pat whispered, leaning toward me. A.J. lit his Camel, preparing to spin another salty yarn.

"No small fry for my boss, no siree," A.J. drawled, pulling a deep draught of cigarette. "I'm talkin' eight hundred-pound marlins, a thousand-pound tuna. As soon as we land the big catch we radio to shore. By the time we're docked, Japanese buyers are lined up, ready to pay twenty-seven or twenty-eight dollars a pound."

Pat and I grinned sheepishly at each other. Neither of us was willing to admit that our fishing luck had been dismal for almost a whole year.

"Hey lookee there," A.J. grinned, nodding at a couple approaching the bar. "There's your twin brother."

The fellow walking toward us was the marina dockmaster. Like Pat, Maurice was tall, slim, spectacled and silver-haired; unlike Pat, it was his job to tie up newly arrived vessels. He and his wife Pauline were fellow Canadians, whose passion for recreational sailing became their livelihood.

"We met at a sailing course off the West Coast," Pauline explained, flipping her long brown ponytail over her shoulder. "We became instructors. Then we began crewing charters. When we landed in the Bahamas, we agreed to manage this marina for the owner."

"And who knows what we'll do next?" Maurice shrugged with a wide grin.

We checked out of our last Bahamian marina the next mid-morning, pointing our bows north toward Hawksbill Cay. By then it was July 25. The sun, seas, and breezes conspired so beautifully that afternoon that we sailed past Hawksbill to the anchorage off Great Sale Cay, a popular stopover for boats preparing to cross the Gulf Stream to Florida.

"*Cool Breezes, Cool Breezes,*" came voices in greeting over the VHF radio. Three crews with whom we'd become acquainted during our earlier Abacos travels were anchored there. All three awaited a weather window; hurricane season was fast approaching.

"What about us, Dad, are we going to Florida soon, too?" the kids asked.

"Yes," Pat replied. "But I think we have one more island left in our journey. I've heard rave reviews about Double Breasted Cays. Let's go there before we cross to Florida."

The kids cheered. They longed to go home, yet resisted the concept of leaving this halcyon life. Later that day, the kids stood at the bows with their fishing rods.

"I got one, I got one!" Erin yelled. She wound in the line only to find she'd hooked a baby nurse shark, all of one foot long. Its tiny jaws snapped in the air.

"Throw it back!" Ben urged. "Where there's a baby shark there's gonna be a mother."

I woke before dawn the next morning with a start, compelled to write. I dropped catlike out of our berth and slid into the bench seat at the salon table. Meara's face was pressed up against the netting alongside her berth. While everyone slumbered, I wrote some notes entitled "Vignettes from our Voyage." That piece, along with my regular emails home and faithfully kept diary, would become the basis of this book.

An hour later, Ben awoke in his typical fashion: by stretching his long arm through the window of his stateroom, groping for his glasses on the windowsill, and grabbing his book. Then I heard Pat clap his hands and rub them together with glee.

"Up and at it, crew! It's a boat fix-it day!" he announced. The kids moaned.

"If we're gonna sell the boat, she needs to be shipshape," he added cheerfully.

The kids groaned even more loudly. Pat hadn't given them the very best incentive.

Pat painted the porthole window frames while I mended tears in the mosquito nets. The kids polished the brightwork. We toiled away the morning. Afternoon visits from our friends in the anchorage and a trip to shore with Jasper provided welcome reprieves. Then the sudden rush of wind bearing sprinkles of rain signalled the onset of another squall.

The kids were about to chink in the Plexiglas windows when Pat bellowed.

"Stop! The paint is still wet!"

Once the squall passed there were big puddles to mop up. When a second angrier storm began to gather, Pat relented.

"Okay, okay, chink in the windows," he muttered.

"Carefully, kids, carefully," I added. Pat seemed testy those days; unwillingness to depart this lifestyle was stressful for everyone.

The morning of July 26, when we planned to sail to Double Breasted Cays, dawned rosy.

"As they say, red in the morning, sailor's warning," Liam observed.

"And the SSB weather report predicts a tropical depression this afternoon," Pat added. "Our destination is only eight miles away, but we'd better get going soon."

An hour and a half later, we arrived at Double Breasted Cays. A large sandy hill called Sand Cay was the centrepiece jewel in this necklace of islands. The islet was set between two low-lying islands shaped like parentheses, and surrounded by a scattering of smaller rocky cays that appeared and disappeared with the tides. Deep channels of water gleamed brilliantly as they flowed around flats, sandbanks and beaches. The sun beamed so brightly we could see shimmering spokes of light extend from it.

The same elements that caused the archipelago to be a

spectacle of colour and texture made anchoring there a trial. Sharp rock punctuated the deep channels. The current was stronger than the breeze. When Pat set two anchors – one up current, one down – both anchor lines stretched taut. In a typical anchorage, all boats point into the same direction: into the wind. Yet the bows of all seven boats anchored at Double Breasted Cays were oriented differently. *Cool Breezes* lay with her stern to the wind, so the breeze blew through the cockpit, down the companionway and into the staterooms.

Once anchored, we took Jasper to Sand Cay, the heart of Double Breasted Cays. We returned quickly, though, when the skies menaced. The wild confusing winds of the tropical depression blustered through, just as predicted. We retreated indoors. I produced five empty wine bottles and corks, one for each child and a fifth for Pat and me, and engaged the kids in one last Language Arts project.

"Let's write messages-in-a-bottle to throw into the Gulf Stream," I suggested. Boat school was dismissed, but my students set to work eagerly. After giving their names and home address, the kids wrote proudly of their family's year aboard.

"The waters of the Gulf Stream sweep northward all the way to the British Isles," Pat reminded the kids. "Your bottles could land anywhere."

That evening, at low tide, the boys took turns kayaking. The rest of us walked ashore. Since tidal variations at Double Breasted were so steep, many sea treasures were revealed at low tide. Erin, with the sharpest eyes, spotted several sand dollars as well as an elegant tulip shell, but Pat found the rarest specimen: an angular triton. When darkness tumbled down that evening, we all went straight to bed.

"Lights out!" Pat ordered.

"But first let's say nighttime prayers!" Meara insisted.

"Dear God," Erin prayed. "This is our last night in the Bahamas. Like the sign at New Plymouth says, let us remember these shores."

"And St. Christopher, keep us safe," Meara added.

We planned to set out for Triangle Rock the afternoon of July 27, anchor there until midnight, then embark in the wee hours of July 28 on a sixteen- to eighteen-hour sail across the Gulf Stream to Florida. We aimed to arrive at Fort Pierce, Florida about 5:00 p.m.

Before we embarked, we had a whole morning to enjoy. And she glowed. She spread her diaphanous wings and embraced us. When Pat announced he was bringing Jasper to shore, everyone clamoured to join him. This often tedious morning chore became a family outing. We swam to shore and meandered the sand spits left by the ebb tide. When the waxing tide returned, consuming the sand spits, we headed back to the mother ship.

I spent the rest of the morning in the galley, preparing meals for that day and the next, when we would be under way. Then, as I swept the floor, I suddenly stopped in my tracks. What am I doing? I chided myself. If ever there was a time to seize and savour, this was it. I flew from the galley, slipped into the kayak, and paddled away.

My kayak glided effortlessly. *Cool Breezes* was just a dot on the horizon when I slowed and paused. I sat level with the sea, one with it. It was so lovely and lonely there, just what I craved. My eyes drank in the shallows; clear water shading to palest chartreuse, seafoam green blending to turquoise, aquamarine deepening to ultramarine. I watched the sand spits vanish as the tide rolled in.

The tide rolled in and with it, a flood of memories. Those early days in Virginia, coping with a new lifestyle while Pat was away. The breast lump and the lesson it taught me. Those sparkling days in Washington, D.C. and Windmill Point. The rough weather, and occasional sweet still nights at anchor on the Chesapeake. So many long, wet and dreary days on the Intracoastal Waterway. Christmas in St. Petersburg, and that brilliant day sail with the dolphins on Tampa Bay. Our first overnight sail on a glorious velvet night. Sighting Cuba's beautiful and brooding shores. The motley crew of sailing friends at the Varadero marina. The artisans on Cayo Blanco. The inhospitable Cayo Romano and the hospitable Puerto Vita. Alba's small and worn brown hands, proffering a seed necklace. The beach at Guardalavaca. The grandeur of Santiago de Cuba. Our Québécois friends. Our crossing to the Bahamas, and meeting Leonard. The sailing community at Volleyball Beach. And Eleuthera, ah, the ephemeral, ethereal Eleuthera . . .

I sat poised, adrift, as the scenes unfurled. Then my mind's eye slowed and time stood still. I rested at the cusp of an experience of time. This very moment, a glittering crystal, enthralled me. All year I'd struggled to learn to live in the present. Now, on the brink of our return to life back on land, where my focus would certainly shift to the future, it seemed I'd stumbled upon the secret of being present. The gist of it was to turn my gaze around – not ahead or behind – and be still, a solitary island in the ebb and flow of life.

Uncounted moments passed. Everything I wanted was in them; God was all around. A spring tide of emotion engulfed me, and tears slid silently along the weather-wizened creases of my face. Then with a sigh, I picked up my paddle, and turned the kayak's prow toward the stern of *Cool Breezes*.

July 2001.
Our parting view of Double Breasted Cays, the Bahamas.

From: The Kirwin crew
To: Kith and Kin
Subject: **Greetings from *Cool Breezes*: Our Last Crossing**

It's the afternoon of July 27, the day we depart the Bahamas. Pat and Ben wrestle both anchors from the seabed. They stand at the bows scrutinizing the water, while I stand at the helm deciphering their hand signals. Together, we wend our cautious way along the deep, narrow channels carved through the shoals and shallows of Double Breasted Cays. The sun is high, the sky is clear, and the mosaic colours of sea, land and water are bright. Yet the mood aboard is solemn. This isn't just our last overnighter; it's also the beginning of the end of our boat trip.

"Where are you headed?" shouts a fellow cruiser from the cockpit of his boat.

Pat might have said, "To Triangle Rocks, then Fort Pierce." He might have said, "We're crossing the Gulf Stream to Florida."

His answer is shorter, yet larger: "Home to Canada."

Those three terse words trigger a swell of emotion on board. They give weight and finality to unspoken thoughts. Watching us dab at our eyes, the other sailor might think we dread going home. Truth is we're glad to be Canada-bound, but sorry to swallow the anchor.

Once past the threatening rocks and reef, we raise the sails and cut the engines. We flip on the autohelm and point our twin bows westward. The wind is at our stern, and the seas follow. Silently, swiftly, we are carried toward the sunset.

A half-hour passes almost wordlessly. Then Meara pipes up.

"Hey, this must be my turn to be captain-for-a-day!"

"You're absolutely right!" Pat agrees, hoisting her up onto the captain's chair.

"Look!" she shouts from her perch, pointing to the port of our gently cruising vessel. "A dolphin!" A moment later the entire pod, a dozen or more, join to play in our wake.

Erin sighs, "It's as if they're saying goodbye."

It's just past midnight, July 28. Pat and I rise after four hours' sleep, and prepare to leave the rollicking anchorage in the lee of Triangle Rocks.

"Didn't sleep well in these rolling waves," Pat says.

"Felt like we anchored in the middle of the ocean," I agree.

A half moon hangs at a rakish angle in the eastern sky, casting a long and luminous silver stripe on the steady following seas. The winds are light. I help Pat weigh anchor, raise the sails, and set up the radar and GPS. Then I drop back to sleep in my berth.

Pat wakes me at 3:00 a.m. for my watch, but he's not yet willing to relinquish the helm. The radar screen shows a large dark cloud chasing us! It feels like we're living a real-life video game, watching the big black blob with its amorphous edges closing in on the beeping fleck that represents our boat. It's inevitable: the cloud moves faster than our six or seven knots, and will soon overtake us.

"Batten the hatches, chink in the windows!" Pat hollers below. Ben staggers out of dreamland to help, then joins us in the cockpit. We three crowd around the radar screen to watch the blob overshadow the dot. We're lucky. Only the rainy fringe of the cloud sweeps over us, and all we feel is a brief shower.

As Pat retires for his two-hour portion of sleep, Erin arises.

"Look over there – shooting stars!" she says. Off our starboard, a meteor shower lights the sky. "I counted at least twenty," says Ben. "And look at the water." Foaming in our wake, millions of phosphorescent points of brightness provide another light show.

At 5:00 a.m., Pat and I trade places. He takes the helm, and I assume the warm spot in our gently swaying berth. Just as I'm about to drift away, Meara clambers in beside me. I adore her small and affectionate self, and hug her close. A few moments later, though, Meara begins to toss and kick in her sleep. After a half-hour pressed against the wall defending my diminishing territory of the bed, I stumble on deck to join Pat.

By 6:30 a.m., the entire crew is awake, gathered in the cockpit to witness the break of day on water. The sun soars in the Caribbean skies just as quickly as it plummets at nightfall.

The morning is mild. Light winds from the stern provide ideal conditions to fly the spinnaker, so Pat and the boys hoist it up. When the winds become too variable to sustain the rainbow balloon at our bows, it dances in the fickle breeze. Pat dances, too, manually tacking the sail back and forth from port to starboard, trying to keep it filled with air.

"Why don't you give up, Dad?" Liam asks.

"This might be our last chance to sail," Pat replies.

About noon, we enter the Gulf Stream, and throw our messages-in-bottles overboard. Who knows who might find them, and when? Then, to take full advantage of the Gulf Stream's rush, we point our bows twenty degrees north. *Cool Breezes* plunges like an eager porpoise into the current's surge. We watch giddily as the GPS speedometer leaps forward, from 6.6 knots to 9.9, and then to the yet uncharted realm of the double digits.

"Ten point three knots!" Meara calls out. A boisterous cheer flies into the wind. The spinnaker billows, full of air and glorious colour.

The rest of the warm and cloudless day passes quickly. In the late afternoon, the Florida shores appear on the horizon. Ben rounds us up into the cockpit for a last rendition of our family's favourite ballad:

Four strong winds that blow lonely,
Seven seas that run high,
All those things that don't change, come what may,
Our good times are all gone,
I'm bound for moving on,
I'll look for you if I'm ever back this way.
Think I'll go out to Alberta,
Weather's good there in the fall,
Got some friends that I can go to workin' for . . .

We finish singing and gaze resentfully at the approaching landfall. Meara turns her face in defiance.

"I'm not looking at this land," she announces, "because it means our sailboat trip is over."

"Remember back at Warderick Wells, when Erin said returning home would be bittersweet?" Liam asks. "Well, today all I feel is the bitter."

At 7:30 p.m., we drop anchor off the Florida coast. The Fort Pierce skyline looms. A sinking sense of anticlimax settles on board.

"Welcome back to the Muggle world," says Erin.

"You know that expression, 'This too shall pass'?" asks Liam. "Well it works both ways, you know."

"What do you mean?" Pat asks.

"We usually say it when things are bad," he says, "But good things too 'shall pass'."

After a cold supper of five-bean salad and homemade bread, Pat lowers the dinghy and takes Jasper to shore. From there he'll phone the U.S. Customs Office to announce our arrival. I stay back to tidy up on board and tuck the kids into their berths.

The children and I are so exhausted we're in tears. It's been a trying day, both physically and emotionally. Yet our crossing couldn't have gone better. At nighttime prayers tonight, each child expresses thanks for safety.

It's only 10:00 p.m., but I'm way past ready to turn in. The next few days will be busy and hectic – packing, cleaning, repairing, shopping and hauling – and then we'll head to Alberta in the rented motor home. In three short weeks we will be seeing many of you.

Since Internet access from the campgrounds enroute is unpredictable, this will be the last email update of our year's journey. Thanks to each of you kith and kin for your kind thoughts, wishes, prayers and emails these past twelve months. Your support was invaluable. It seems incredible that we six and our dog spent a year on a cat...

May all of your seas be following, and the wind be always at your back!

God bless and fair winds,
　　Love PJ+crew

Part Five: Ship to Shore

Edmonton

Cypress Hills

Billings · Little Bighorn

· Casper

Kirwin ·

N

Memphis · Lake Allatoona
· Atlanta

· Titusville
· Jensen
Beach

July 2001, Fort Pierce, Florida.

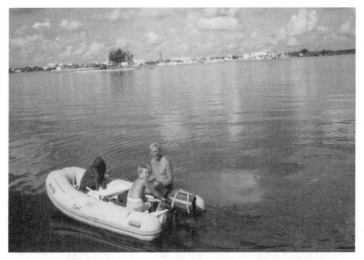

A typical morning trip to shore, with Liam as dinghy captain.

The day we bid goodbye to Cool Breezes.

Be careful how you think; your life is shaped by your
thoughts.
  – Old Testament, Proverbs 4:23

From our anchorage off Fort Pierce, we motored toward Jensen Beach on July 29. The waters of the Intracoastal Waterway were reassuringly familiar, yet busy on this particular sunny Sunday afternoon. Fleets of powerboats left unrelenting wakes.

"The water is rougher today on the ICW than it was in the Gulf Stream," said Ben.

Ben's observation was an apt metaphor for our ship-to-shore transition. Our passage to Florida was almost flawlessly smooth, but our shift to land was decidedly bumpy. Those transition days were ragged in many ways.

First, our clothes were tattered, worn by salt, sand and sun. Liam, for example, had only two pairs of shorts, only one of which was fit to be worn off the boat.

Second, we kept erratic hours, especially Pat and I, rising early and retiring late, to clean, pack, and repair.

And last but not least, we felt emotionally frayed. As we whittled away at the list of one zillion chores, I realized that in a way, we'd already returned. The year-old image in my mind's eye of an ever-scrolling to-do list became alarmingly recurrent. We were already living in the future, not the present. Our conversion to a lifestyle governed by clocks, plans and accomplishments was big and difficult. Threads of excitement, frustration, wistfulness and exhaustion grew tangled into a ragged knot within each of us.

The marina our broker found for us was only twenty-five miles from our anchorage off Fort Pierce. We radioed to the marina dockmaster when we arrived in the late afternoon, but there was no reply, so we anchored a short distance away on the broad St. Lucie River. I peered anxiously through binoculars at the run-down docks and weatherworn signage of the marina. A huge blue houseboat occupied half of the outside T-berth.

"I feel uneasy about the place," I said.

The next morning we resumed our VHF attempts to reach the marina dockmaster. Finally we received a response.

"The dockmaster isn't in," said a voice. "But I'm docked here, so I can give you directions to find the marina entrance."

An hour later, puttering along the marina laneways, we discovered that the only berth wide enough to accommodate our seventeen foot beam was on the outside T-dock, right across from the barge-like houseboat we'd seen from our anchorage. The dockmaster was still missing, but the friendly couple aboard the adjacent trawler helped us snug up.

"Things are pretty casual around here," said John, the voice who guided us in. "The showers are grungy, but the dockmaster lets you download email and make phone calls from his office."

"Plus the laundry is cheap," Anne added. "A dollar per wash, seventy-five cents for the dryer."

My eyes lit up at the latter bit of news. The last time I did laundry, it cost US$16 a load. While Pat left to pick up a rental minivan, Erin and I bundled up several sailbags of dirty clothes. Land life has its compensations, I thought, filling the washer with our first load.

When Pat returned to the marina with a late-model minivan, our culture shock began to manifest itself.

"We're going for a car ride!" Meara squealed. The kids scrambled into the air-conditioned interior. Outside, the air was humid and ninety-nine degrees Fahrenheit, but inside we sat cool, comfortable and content.

The vehicle rolled on smooth black asphalt over a long arch of bridge. Beneath us, the water lay glistening.

"This feels like a Disneyland ride!" Erin said.

Our first destination was the closest American immigration office, located at the airport an hour and a half away. Like the customs clerk who gave Pat a clearance number by telephone the evening we arrived, the immigration officer wasn't especially fastidious. She didn't bother even to check our dog, or the five of us waiting in the minivan. Jasper might have had rabies, or we might have harboured Cuban stowaways. She'd never have known.

"Isn't it incredible how indifferent the Americans are to our arrival, after all the fuss we endured in Cuba and the Bahamas," Pat said. No doubt, after September 11 that same year, the procedures became much more rigorous.

The next stop was at Publix, the local grocery store. Our minivan joyride over a soaring bridge was nothing compared to cruising with a grocery cart along the supermarket lanes. After hunting and gathering bits of food in small settlements for seven months, our kids were gleeful to see the cornucopia spread before them.

"Look at all the different kinds of apples we can buy!" Liam pointed.

"They've got bagels!" Ben shouted.

"And yogurt, all flavours!" Erin added.

The four children darted and skipped along the aisles dropping food into the cart. Even fresh vegetables warranted exclamations of sudden appreciation.

"Yes you can have apple juice, yes you can have salami, yes you can have a melon, yes we can make a salad tonight, yes, you can have pop," we laughed. "Yes, yes, yes!"

"Publix should film these poor deprived kids for a TV commercial," Pat said to me.

Compared to the cost of food in the Bahamas, grocery prices in Florida seemed ridiculously low. That shouldn't have been surprising in the case of fresh bread and produce, yet even a six-pack of Bahamian Kalik that cost US$12 in Nassau was only US$6 in Florida.

The morning of July 31 unfolded steamy with heat and mugginess. Pat took the boys with him on an errand run. The girls and I seized the opportunity of having three fewer bodies and heads of ideas on board to do a quick clean up, photo-shoot and video-clip of the boat's interior. We knew that from that moment forward, when we would begin packing things up, nothing aboard would be the same.

"Why don't you start packing your stateroom cubby-holes," I suggested to the girls, once we were done filming. "I'm going to phone the motor home agency." Pat and I hoped to pick up our motor home in Orlando a few days earlier than booked.

That's when we received our first nasty surprise.

"Your reservation has been deleted from our system," the clerk said. "One-way trips to Canadian destinations aren't allowed."

"The agent who booked it didn't tell us that rule three weeks ago," I complained.

"Well, she should have," the clerk replied.

"No one emailed us to tell us we've been deleted from the system," I went on.

"Well, that's not my problem," the clerk answered.

I paused to gather my thoughts. My uncle lived in Spokane, Washington, the closest American drop-off point to our Canadian home. Perhaps we could re-book our one-way trip to arrive there.

"Sorry, all our units are totally booked up by now," the clerk responded.

A hot and syrupy lump collected in my throat. We were stranded, I thought, stranded on the mainland, of all places. Choking back my emotion, I asked to speak to the woman's supervisor. The boss was out, so I left a detailed voicemail and fled back to the boat.

By then Pat had returned. His reaction to my news was swift and angry.

"I'll sue them if they don't find us a motor home!" he vowed. He strode to the marina office to call the rental agency. I tagged along, clutching my notepad with names and telephone numbers. Pat called the boss of the agent who had made the original booking, and threatened him with a lawsuit. I sat mutely praying, my adrenaline racing. Within an hour, the agent's boss located a motor home based at a sister office in Lake Worth. It would be available August 2, and be due three weeks later in Spokane.

"Wow, I'd never guess from that phone call that you'd been away for a year on a sailboat," said the laid-back dockmaster, who had overheard everything. Pat smirked. Yes, I thought, we're definitely back in the nerve-wracking mainstream.

The next day, August 1, was the official start of hurricane season. The day began with a clap of thunder and pounding hail, then continued with steady rain. The storm provided not only a welcome reprieve from the sticky high-nineties weather we'd endured, but also an excuse to remain below decks. Instead of exterior repairs and deck swabbing, we packed up the boat's contents in a systematic fashion. The work was tedious, the crew glum, and our living space much less home-like, but we weren't yet tearful.

The next day, we planned to drive to Lake Worth to pick up the motor home. We rose early to receive another unwelcome surprise: Hurricane Barry. The tail end of it lashed out at the Atlantic coast of Florida, packing winds topping sixty knots, and rainfall measuring ten to thirteen inches in less than two hours.

The crew of *Cool Breezes* was below decks when the hurricane hit. At the first sprinkle of rain, the kids sprang into storm mode. The whooshing sound of sealing hatches and the solid *kachunk* of wooden chinks against Plexiglas windows could barely be heard above the rising wind. When the starboard hull began pounding against the T-dock, there was nothing to be done. Feeling anxious and helpless, we gathered round the salon table. With every strike against the dock, our bodies flinched. Each whomp felt like a personal blow, especially to Pat. His face was contorted, his knuckles white. Meara gripped my hand with both of hers. I stroked her hair and silently prayed, "Please God, don't let our boat trip end this way." It felt as if our starboard hull would be destroyed.

Then we heard an ugly splitting sound and a huge splash. Pat and Liam poked their heads out of the companionway into the lashing storm. They saw the dinghy davits had snapped off at the base, causing the dinghy and solar panel to crash into the water. Now it was Liam's turn to be distraught. I decided to pray aloud.

"Dear Lord, please keep *Cool Breezes* safe," I said. The kids joined me in prayer.

"Please let this storm end soon." Holding hands and speaking aloud our fears, entrusting them to God, helped us cope.

An hour later, the rain slowed to a drizzle and the winds abated enough for us to leave the salon. We opened the companionway door to find the cockpit flooded. The deluge had overwhelmed the scuppers, and four inches of water waited to drain. Pat pulled the solar panel out of the water, and Liam scampered into the dinghy to bail it out. That's when we noticed that the houseboat across from us had moved at least three feet closer to our stern. The common piling to which both vessels were tied had shifted due to the weight of the houseboat and the force of the winds. That shift caused our spring lines to became lax. Since the lines no longer controlled our boat's movement, the starboard hull had banged against the dock during the storm.

Despite everything, though, the hull was miraculously unharmed.

"It's clear we can't leave *Cool Breezes* here," Pat said. "That storm was only the tail end of a hurricane, not a full-fledged one. We can't leave her tied to the same piling as the big barge, and that's the only berth at this marina wide enough for her. We'll have to find another marina. Even if it's more expensive, at least I can sleep at night knowing *Cool Breezes* is safe."

The highway to Lake Worth was closed that day due to hurricane flooding, so we picked up the motor home a day late, on August 3. The kids were delighted with their newest travelling home, but Pat and I were less impressed with it: the rental agency's logo and phone number were plastered across the exterior.

"Great, we get to drive across the continent advertising the rental company," Pat grumbled.

"You're right, Dad," said Liam. "They should pay us to drive it, not charge us."

We parked the motor home in the lot at the end of the marina docks, and began to unload our boat. Moving our sea treasures, nautical gear, and the trappings of our boat trip onto the motor home was a two-day operation. We had a system. I packed and cleaned the interior, while processing countless loads of laundry. Pat emptied the cavernous bow and stern lockers. The boys carted endless boxes and bags down the docks to the motor home. Erin received the boys' packages and stowed them away. While she waited for the next load, she made beds, stowed cutlery and kitchenware into cupboards, and prepared sandwiches. Meara's contribution came in the form of encouragement; she made dozens of cheerful notes and drawings and picked samples of local wildflowers for everyone. The pages of my diary from those days are well decorated.

As for Jasper, she noticed the steady stream of worldly possessions making their way off the boat and onto the motor home. Humans go where the stuff is, she might have articulated. Perhaps recalling the time she was left behind on the docks of the Seven Seas marina, she parked herself at the threshold of the motor home, and wouldn't budge. Even when the rest of the crew slept aboard *Cool Breezes,* Jasper slept on the dirt outside the motor home door, determined never to be stranded again.

Those days were drizzly, dreary, wet and sweaty. One day was even bloody. Pat ran into the pointed edge of an overhead cupboard door left open in the motor home, and cut a big gash on his forehead.

"Isn't is ironic that the only time we used the first aid kit this entire year away, it was to treat an injury that happened on land," I said. Our last night aboard *Cool Breezes* was marked not with a bang, but a ragged sigh.

On Sunday, August 5, we took our last trip aboard *Cool Breezes*. We brought her from the marina on St. Lucie River to a more sheltered one in Manatee Pocket, a nearby "hurricane hole." Our departure from the dock against the strong river current was difficult.

"You boys should know by now how to fend the boat off the docks," Pat shouted.

Their faces fell. We sat glumly in the cockpit, but not for long. Erin popped in a CD. Soon we were singing along. The sun shone. Then we noticed how frisky *Cool Breezes* felt, emptied of her over-brimming bilges and lockers. When we arrived at the marina in Manatee Pocket, Pat steered *Cool Breezes* into her slip. Ben tossed a bowline to Liam, I tossed a stern line to Erin, and the two on the dock secured her snugly. Meara kept Jasper safe in the salon. It was our last, perfect docking.

Now that the boat was empty, all that remained was the cleaning. *Cool Breezes* never looked better, inside and out, all at once. Considering her brand new engines, the new upholstery in the salon, new custom-made cockpit cushions, our thorough cleaning, and Pat's meticulous maintenance, *Cool Breezes* was actually in better condition after our year aboard than when we bought her. Pat sighed as he handed the boat keys to our broker.

"It's my mind that's selling her, not my heart," he said.

That night we slept in the motor home in the marina parking lot. Our sleep was unsettled. Besides emotional turmoil, we contended with the security guard's all-night radio station, punctuated by the intermittent whistle of trains roaring by in the wee hours.

At sun-up, Pat and I abandoned all hope of sleep. We rose from our motor home beds and gravitated toward *Cool Breezes*. The kids soon followed. We took one last walk and look around, one last photo shoot. The many frustrations and difficulties we'd encountered in Florida eased the sweet sorrow of parting with *Cool Breezes,* yet our leave-taking was hard. To bid her goodbye meant saying farewell to our journey, our lifestyle. The girls and I wept. The boys and Pat stood silent, sombre. And Jasper, wagging her tail, looked puzzled.

"We all knew it was going to happen one day," Erin mused, "and now it actually, finally, has." She stooped down to pick up a familiar piece of yarn on the docks.

"Dad," she said. "The friendship bracelet I made for your ankle back in Virginia just fell off. That means you get to make a wish!"

"I wish for a safe trip home," Pat said.

We trudged to the motor home and closed the door. A week and a day after landing in Florida, we drove away.

Chapter **35**
Alberta Bound

We shall not cease from exploration
And the end of all our exploring
Will be to arrive where we started
And know the place for the first time.
   – *T.S. Eliot,* Little Gidding

At noon on August 6, we embarked on our diagonal road trip from Stuart, Florida, to Edmonton, Alberta. That first day we drove only as far as Titusville, where we parked in a lush campground shaded by palm trees and fern fronds, close to the Kennedy Space Centre at Cape Canaveral. After a delicious sleep and hearty bacon-and-egg breakfast the next morning, we dropped Jasper off at a day kennel near the campground, and drove to NASA. Following our recent adventures and misadventures, we felt more than ready for a day of passive tourism.

The children loved the Kennedy Space Centre and soaked up loads of information. I felt benign, almost philosophical, viewing the exhibits as if from afar, from space. The sense that we feel gazing at the Milky Way with its astonishing multitude of stars, the reassuring awareness that we are, after all, very small peons in the Creator's grand scheme, overwhelmed me. When I read T.S. Eliot's observation about the end of explorations, placed along-

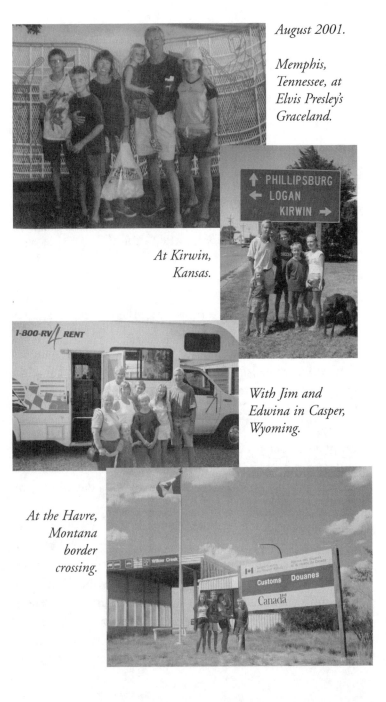

August 2001.

Memphis, Tennessee, at Elvis Presley's Graceland.

At Kirwin, Kansas.

With Jim and Edwina in Casper, Wyoming.

At the Havre, Montana border crossing.

side a photograph of our planet Earth, I pulled out my coiled notebook and scribbled it down. That's what we were doing, in our own small way: returning to the place we began, after a year of exploring.

From Cape Canaveral we drove northwest toward the Georgia state line. We parked for the night at a campground near the Suwanee River and a little town called Jasper.

The next day, August 8, we rose before 7:00 a.m. and crossed into Georgia. Pat was eager to pass through Atlanta's legendary traffic gridlock before rush hour. We arrived at noon upon the city's threshold. There the highway expanded from six to twelve lanes, all running through the metropolitan core. Our passage through Atlanta was much quicker than expected. By mid-afternoon we arrived at McKinney campground on beautiful Lake Allatoona, Georgia, where we'd arranged to meet some transplanted Edmonton friends.

"Now this is what a campground should look like!" my boys exclaimed as we entered it. The ferns and palms of Florida had given way to pine and oak. Later that evening, our friends Donny and Joanne pulled into the site next to us. Once the children were in bed, we four adults sat at the campfire on the shore of the placid lake. Light breezes and campfire smoke kept the mosquitoes at bay. Crickets chirped and tree frogs sang. Donny and Joanne, recipients of my regular group emails, admitted their regret that our travel year was over.

"We lived vicariously through you," Joanne said. "And now we'll have no more adventures."

"You're not alone," Pat laughed. "Our friend Val begged us not to return for the same reason! We promised to keep her updated with detailed accounts of minivan travels chauffeuring kids, school events and work details, but that didn't seem to cut it."

I smiled, recalling Val's email, received a week after I sent my last travel update.

"There were a lot more than six and a dog on your cat for the last year," Val had responded. "You have no idea how many of us lived aboard with you."

The next morning, Donny took us for a spin in his twenty foot Sea Ray, a speedboat packing a one hundred and eighty horsepower punch. Compared to *Cool Breezes*, whose twin diesels boasted a mere twenty-six horsepower, the Sea Ray was fast. Liam, especially, enjoyed his turn at the helm.

"You're creating the same kind of wakes we sailors used to curse," Pat pointed out.

"Yeah, but there are no sailboats on the water right now!" Liam yelled back.

Halfway through the outing, we cut the engine and dropped anchor in a secluded cove. The clear water lay whispering still. A patch of sunshine broke through overcast skies. We took a dip in the fresh water, so cool and silky compared with the salty Caribbean seas from which we'd just emerged.

The morning of August 10, we set out on an ambitious day of travel. We were due home on August 18, because the kids had emailed invitations to their friends to visit us at home that day.

"No more marshmallow plans," I quipped.

"It's a year to the day that Ben and I flew out to Washington to buy *Cool Breezes*," Pat mused as we crossed the Tennessee state line at Chattanooga. The countryside was hilly, peaking at Lookout Mountain from which an ambitious hiker might see four states: Tennessee, Georgia, Alabama, and North Carolina.

The weather grew drizzly and grey. We drove the scenic secondary route for a while, alongside leafy vines enveloping overhanging trees and oddly misshapen bushes. The landscape flattened as we turned onto the Davy Crockett Highway and passed David Crockett State Park. My boys burst into that Disney song about the legendary Crockett. We had to agree with the lyrics: Tennessee was mighty pretty. We carried on due west, arriving at the eastern outskirts of Memphis, Tennessee, by sundown.

Memphis was the home of Elvis Presley. We decided to tour his estate, Graceland, the morning of August 11. That day just happened to be the Saturday of Elvis Memorial Week, drawing dozens of Elvis impersonators to the venue. Our half-day tour was corny, but thoroughly entertaining. From Memphis we crossed the mighty Mississippi River, and travelled the broken-down highways of Arkansas. The scenery was forgettable, improving as we veered north and saw the blue-green Ozark Mountains from a distance.

The next few days we burned up the highways by day and camped by night. No matter where we parked, train tracks were nearby. We became quickly accustomed to the long and lonely train whistles and thunderous rumblings through the night. The nights became much cooler; we slept under covers for the first time in months. The morning air was crisp and clear when Jasper and I took our daily runs. Pat did most of the driving. The boys read books. Meara and Erin sat chatting and weaving friendship bracelets. I spent my hours reading roadmaps, fixing meals, assembling photos in albums, and simply gazing out the window. While Pat seemed tense those days, I felt weepy. The kids did very well, navigating the tentative territory between their two emotional parents.

From Arkansas we crossed into Missouri, and from there to Kansas. The Ozark Mountains gave way to fields of sunflowers, corn and wheat. The highlight of our Kansas travels was visiting the tiny hamlet of Kirwin, population two hundred and thirty, lying only thirty-six miles west of the geographical centre of the contiguous United States.

"Talk about 'the American heartland'!" Ben grinned.

As we approached the little town on August 13, we could see the Kirwin Wildlife Preserve and reservoir and hear the honking Canada geese. Then we saw the sign: Kirwin, the Goose Capital of Kansas. I couldn't resist ribbing my silly goose Kirwins.

Down the quiet and dusty main road we drove, past the disused clapboard schoolhouse, the out-of-business corner store, and the two-storey brick library and municipal building optimistically called "City Hall." We pulled up to the only open business: the Hill Billy Inn. The frizzy-haired proprietor had heard of no Kirwins and had no idea why the town bore that name. Nor did our perusal of her phone book reveal a listing for Kirwin.

"Come back tomorrow when the library is open," she told us. "The librarian knows everything about everyone!"

That evening we checked into the nearest campground, a rustic place on the edge of the reservoir in the wildlife preserve. When Pat remarked to the park warden his surprise that so many residents had rifle racks in the back of their pickup trucks, the warden laughed.

"You must be Canadian," the warden laughed. "Out here we think 'preserve' means preserved for us to hunt."

Early the next bright morning, we visited the library. While our children devoured books, Pat and I chatted with Helga, the librarian, a slight woman with a long grey ponytail.

"You can photocopy my historical file if you like," she offered. We learned that Fort Kirwin, now submerged under the reservoir, was named after Colonel John S. Kirwin who was commissioned in 1869 to defend the territory from "hostile Indians." Our family was disappointed to hear of the town's politically incorrect origins, but pleased to learn that Colonel Kirwin relocated from the area when he discovered there were very few settlers to defend, and virtually no hostilities in the area.

"Do you have any artifacts about the town?" Pat asked Helga. She paused to think.

"Well, we do have some memorabilia from the hundred and twenty-fifth anniversary we celebrated a few years ago. Would you like to see that?" Pat nodded eagerly. The town's small cache of leftover belt buckles, plates and mugs was soon stashed aboard the motor home.

From Kirwin in the northwest corner of Kansas, we travelled through Nebraska along the famous Platte River, then northwest through Cheyenne toward Casper, Wyoming. The prairie landscape reminded us of home: flat and yellow, with a huge blue dome of sky, and hoodoos like those in Drumheller, Alberta. As we neared Casper, a grand vista sprang up. Foothills lay spread in a circle around us. Unlike those approaching the Alberta Rockies, these foothills had stunted flat tops, as if they were cropped off midway to becoming mountains. The sun was setting and a thunderstorm brewed on the horizon as we drove on the highway cresting a plateau.

"Isn't this an amazing world?" Erin wondered, gazing at the dramatic view. "From coral reefs in the Bahamas to sunsets in the hills of Wyoming," she trailed off.

The morning of August 15, we reunited with the crew of *Jasper J* at a diner in Casper. Jim and Edwina were visiting their family in Wyoming, but by fall, they'd be back aboard for their annual cruise to the Exumas. I found myself wistful to hear their sailing plans, yet not poignantly so. By then, our break from beloved *Cool Breezes* and our cruising lifestyle was complete. We were becoming land-based, eager to reach Edmonton. Like Dorothy in the colourful land of Oz, we felt reluctant to leave, yet drawn toward our duller but predictable home.

"It's all about the people," my friend Lorraine had emailed me. Her remark referred to the joy of travel, but was equally true about returning to kith and kin.

We crossed from Wyoming into Montana at the Little Bighorn Battlefield National Monument. We paused there to listen to a park ranger – a native Crow woman – deliver a stirring retelling of the story of Custer's last stand. We could envision the legendary battle unfold in the yellow canyon at our feet.

That evening, our last in the United States, we camped in Billings, Montana. We strolled beneath shade trees bordering the banks of the Yellowstone River while our laundry churned away in the campground machines. We had just downloaded email.

"This last dose of email really drives home the fact that we're returning to our old reality," I told Pat. "I had to dig up a calendar to record all the commitments we've made."

"Really?" Pat asked. He skipped a stone in the river. "Like what?"

"Well, just in the first three weeks after we return, we have Liam's hockey camp in Calgary, a welcome home party, a dinner club evening, my brother's wedding, a fundraiser cocktail party, my high school reunion, a camping weekend with cousins, and a canning bee with my aunts. Plus there's back-to-school shopping, doctor and dental appointments," I said. "It's all good – I'm not complaining – but I do feel intimidated."

Pat fell silent. We knew from the previous experience of some friends, another travelling family who returned to

Edmonton after four months in Africa, that it would be impossible to bow out of the North American pace of life. Despite our intention to emulate the slower, easier rhythm of life we'd just experienced, we knew we were about to resume our busyness. It was sobering to watch, as squares on the calendar filled up, how very quickly blocks of time were disappearing. A crowded calendar, the visual symbol of many future plans, seems synonymous with our urban lifestyle.

On August 16, we rose at 6:00 a.m. and drove north to Havre, Montana, where we'd cross into Saskatchewan. I spent most of the four-hour trip making a list of acquisitions to present to the Canadian Customs officer. How much detail need be reported by a family of six that had been away for a whole year, in what seemed to be a whole other world? While some of our foreign purchases were truly souvenirs, others were merely accoutrements of living. Must we declare, for example, the purchase of Liam's now worn-out shorts?

The Havre border crossing consisted of a humble set of buildings set in a flat and lonely farmer's field. The air was dry, and the sky enormous. Just as Pat unrolled his window to speak to the Canadian customs officer, Ben and Liam bolted from their seats and burst out the side door of the motor home.

"We're home, we're in Canada!" they shouted.

"Whoa there! Not so fast, you boys!" the officer snapped, and ordered them back inside. Upon reviewing my elaborate list of acquisitions, however, he seemed to relax. He admitted us without requiring an inspection or payment of duty.

Not until we were waved through did we realize how anxious we'd felt about dealing with Canadian customs after such a long absence. Pat laughed aloud when I wiped my brow with exaggerated relief. As soon as we drove over the fictional line in the grass, Pat parked the motor home. We clambered out and stepped ceremoniously on Canadian soil.

"Man, oh man, it feels good to be back in our native land!" I grinned. I hugged my children as we posed for a photo beside the Welcome to Canada sign.

From the border we drove north to Cypress Hills Provincial Park, Saskatchewan, where the scenery exuded Canada. The terrain was hilly and green, with dancing clear water and stark stands of lodgepole pines. The air was thin and clean, the sunshine brilliant, and the pure scent invigorating.

"It looks just like the Canadian travel posters we saw in the windows of the Nassau travel agency!" Erin exclaimed.

That evening we spent at the Cypress Hills cabin of our Edmonton friends, Fred and Eileen.

"Do you feel ready to go home tomorrow?" Eileen asked.

"Both very ready and yet unready," I replied. How could the portion of a year pass so quickly? As I tucked Meara into bed that night, she sighed with deep satisfaction. She folded her hands, closed her eyes and prayed.

"Only one more sleep till we're home, God!"

The next morning, August 17, Pat and I woke at dawn, full of anticipation, unable to sleep. The kids rose shortly afterward. We feasted on a big pancake breakfast, took a walk around the lake, and toured the provincial park. The highlight of our excursion was Lookout Point. From there, Fred said, we could see a hundred miles. My gaze fell northward.

After lunch we set out on the last leg of our travels. It was a pleasant seven-hour drive on Alberta's excellent highways, yet we were not relaxed. The excitement began to build as we passed Red Deer, Alberta. When we reached the outskirts of Edmonton, the buzz in our vehicle was tangible. The city was especially fresh, clean and flowering following a recent spate of rain and the 2001 World Games it had just hosted. I pulled out the camcorder and recorded the frenzy within the motor home.

The children screamed as we drove north into the city, west onto Whitemud Freeway, then east to our home in leafy Capital Hill. By the time Pat turned onto our shady avenue and then our driveway, the kids and I were laughing and crying at once. We spilled out of the motor home, over the lawn, past the treehouse, and to the front doorstep. Jasper's tail wagged with such vigour that she could hardly propel herself toward the backyard gate.

"Someone left us hundreds of things!" Ben shouted. Bags and coolers full of pop, muffins, chips, juice, fruit and cake were lined up against the brick planters. A Welcome Home banner stretched across the entryway windows.

"Haven't used this key in quite a while," Pat smiled. He unlocked the front door.

The children laughed hysterically as they burst through the front door and ran all over the house. Pat and I beamed, thrilled to see their uncontained joy. We too felt overwhelmed to be back home. The tenants had kept the house clean, tidy, and in good repair. They'd left lasagne in the freezer, coffee in the cupboard, wine in the fridge, and a drawer full of plastic grocery bags neatly folded in perfect origami triangles.

"The house looks better than we left it," Pat remarked.

"And look at how big it is!" the kids chimed in.

Pat phoned one of his brothers, and I called Eldean, who was in Edmonton at the time, visiting her sister. All of them were eager to see us.

"Hey kids, quick!" I called throughout the house. "Let's say a prayer before our guests arrive."

We lit a candle in the living room, and came together for a prayer of gratitude. We took turns thanking God for an incredible year, our good health, a safe trip, and each other.

"I'm reminded of a quote I read at Cape Canaveral," said Liam when it was his turn, and recited verbatim the very same lines I had scribbled into my notebook. "Thank-you, God, for letting us get to know the place where we began for the first time."

Tears welled in my eyes. We turned to Pat, whose turn was next.

"What he said, God," Pat said, smiling with pride.

Our youngest completed the circle of prayer.

"Thanks for the boat trip, God. And St. Christopher, thank-you for keeping us safe."

Afterword
Back in the Mainstream

I see the dolphins leap from the clear, turquoise water of the
* Bahamas,*
And the ocean calls me.
I hear the lapping of the waves and the cries of the dolphins,
And the ocean calls me.
I smell the ocean air and the starfish fresh from the sea,
And the ocean calls me.
I taste the ocean salt and lobster from the fishermen,
And the ocean calls me.
I touch the smooth surface of the sea polished stones,
And the ocean calls me.
– Meara Kirwin, age 9, The Ocean Calls Me

Like a twig that has been meandering gently along a trickling stream, only to be pulled into the swift current of a mighty river, our family left off gunkholing in the Caribbean islands and was drawn into the maelstrom of the North American mainstream.

There's no doubt that during the first few weeks after our return, we were on a social high. It was thrilling to see everyone again and to feel how excited they were to see us. We noticed our kith and kin were curious about the same things. One night at the supper table, the kids said we should compile a FAQ list – a list of most frequently asked questions. I took notes:

Q: Did you ever go so far away from shore that you couldn't see land?

A: Yes, regularly.

Q: Did you ever get seasick?

A: Yes, except for Dad.

Q: Were you ever in any bad weather?

A: Yes, gales and squalls, and even the tail end of a hurricane. We avoided most storms by listening to weather reports.

Q: What's a sundowner?

A: Any drink consumed at sundown.

Q: How did you like your mom for a teacher?

A: It was cool (Erin). No homework (Ben). Fantastic (Liam). I loved it (Meara).

Q: What was the worst part of sailing?

A: No social life (Erin). No organized sports (Liam). Missing my friends (Ben). Getting seasick (Meara).

Q: What was the best part of sailing?

A: Living on a boat (Meara). Snorkelling and seeing new places (Erin). Dinghying super fast (Ben). The dinghy, period (Liam).

Q: How did Jasper "go"?

A: We'd dinghy her to shore. She never "went" on board.

Q: What was your favourite place?

A: George Town (Liam and Meara). George Town and Puerto Vita (Erin). Double Breasted Cays (Ben).

Q: If you had to sum up the year in one word, what would it be?

A: Mind-expanding (Erin). Exciting (Meara). Incredible (Liam). Eventful (Ben).

Q: In hindsight, would you still do the boat trip?

A: In a heartbeat.

Q: Would you do another trip like it?

A: Yes (Erin). Of course (Liam). Yes, but in a while (Meara and Ben).

Q: Are you glad to be home?
A: Yes!

Re-establishing ties with family and friends was easy, but re-connecting to technology was not. Reluctant to take that particular plunge, we dipped our toes in cautiously. Multi-tasking, even in its simplest form, was the biggest challenge. To hear the telephone ring while involved in another project, however mundane, was startling. We didn't reactivate our telephone answering service for more than two weeks, because it seemed far too onerous to not only answer but also return phone calls. Although we picked up the occasional newspaper, we didn't subscribe to daily delivery for months. I didn't replace our obsolete cell phone until October, and then only as a safety measure when the four kids and I took a highway trip without Pat.

Life aboard had been busy and challenging, but at least each day had a single focus, whether it was to deal with weather, arrive at a destination, or merely get groceries or do laundry. By contrast, each day in our new old life presented myriad goals. We now perceived that we urban North Americans absorb considerable stress and strain just getting through an average day of constant messaging, background noise, and distractions.

I must admit that at first, I revelled in the accessibility of grocery stores, and the availability of every conceivable consumer product, right here in my city of six hundred thousand. To run downstairs with a load or two of laundry whenever I liked was a treat. It did seem odd to run only one load at a time, instead of the multiple loads I juggled at the previous year's laundromats, but I didn't miss the tightly packed sailbags, wet dinghy rides to shore, scrounging for correct change, and line-ups.

Like every woman, I'd always taken pride in my ability to multi-task. It was therefore strange to find efficiently juggling chores and commitments to be one of the hardest ship-to-shore transitions. I could now see how multi-tasking, directed as it is to smoothing the transition to the future, saps the presentness from the moment. The boat trip had taught me the beautiful simplicity of doing just one thing at a time, really focussing on that one thing: flow. No matter the task at hand, performing it with single-minded grace can be calming and soothing, a way of recharging batteries and entering into the singularity of the moment. I'd learned aboard that the way to find peace was not to become more efficient, but to slow down. Living in urban North America doesn't reward that strategy, and so the lesson found on the water didn't always translate well into our land-based lifestyle.

For example, sometimes when I prepared supper in the kitchen while Meara sat chattering at the table, I became irritated. At first I was peeved to be distracted; I was under pressure to produce a meal on a schedule. Then I became frustrated with myself. I realized I'd drifted off from Meara's soliloquy into my own thoughts, and should re-focus or, better yet, stop what I was doing, sit down at the table, and truly be with her. If *carpe diem* – seize the day – was too much to ask, I could simply seize the moment! Often I did pause, but sometimes I simply snapped to attention and continued my chore. I didn't have the luxury of time – or felt that I didn't – to indulge in the moment. The way I handled this situation after the boat trip, compared to how I approached it before, was therefore not so different, except in two respects: I was now aware of what was happening, and sometimes I actually did something about it. More often after than before the boat trip, I sat down with Meara and really listened.

All of us became more fiercely Canadian. I often remarked on how blessed we are in every way, so much so that Pat rolled his eyes whenever I broached the subject. Our winters may be deep and long, but there is nothing like a brilliant, crisp Alberta day in the snow. Cold and dark as our winter days may be, our summer days are suffused with long and lilting light. And, after a year battling the critters that proliferate in a temperate climate, the fact that Canada's harsh climate can be inhospitable is something to appreciate.

"The sunsets are pretty amazing here in Alberta, too," became my shorthand expression for recognizing the beauty at home.

Pat returned to the office right away with renewed vigour. Meanwhile, before resuming my practice, I pursued my writing for a few months. I wrote sample chapters of this book, and sent proposals to prospective publishers. I entered writing contests and took writing courses. I joined the Writers' Guild of Alberta, and through it, three writing groups.

"I'm not a struggling writer," I'd quip, "but struggling to be a writer!"

Writing is for me one guaranteed avenue for escape to the present; time flows when I write.

The kids are all thriving. Meara, age nine, is a Grade Four student attending the neighbourhood elementary school. She has proven to be a gifted thinker and prize-winning Irish dancer, and she still sleeps with Dolphy! She and Pat take piano lessons. Liam, fourteen, is in Grade Nine at an academic junior high, plays hockey and soccer, takes tae kwon do, and excels at music. He plays the piano, guitar, tuba, French horn, and drums, and even composes songs. Ben, sixteen, in Grade Eleven at an academic high school, now stands 6'3" tall. He plays basketball, soccer, guitar, and hackey-sack, and loves parkour, or free-running. By the time the boys returned, they'd changed their minds about sharing a bedroom and setting up a lab in the spare room. Erin is now seventeen, in Grade Twelve at an arts magnet school. Musical drama is her main passion, but she also sings in a choir, takes voice lessons, directs drama productions, works at a coffee shop, and plays soccer year-round. She and Louise from *L'Alouette* did fulfill their dream of exchange visits the summer of 2002!

The kids' return to mainstream schooling was effortless. That first fall, however, I confessed that as schoolmistress of St. Christopher's, I was as nervous as the kids to receive their report cards.

"No, you're not," Erin retorted. "You're even more anxious!" To my relief, their report cards were excellent. They're all strong students.

Jasper, now ten, is somewhat arthritic, but essentially healthy and fit. Of all of us, she adapted best to our new old life. She has always lived in the moment, no matter where she is. And *Cool Breezes?* Just as I finished writing this book, almost four years after our return, we sold her. We had talked of reclaiming her, taking her north to the Great Lakes, or south to Cuba. The reality is, though, the children have physically outgrown her. Ben and Liam could no longer share a berth, or Meara sleep on a shelf. Her new owners think Witness catamarans are the best in the world, so we know *Cool Breezes* is in good hands. Nevertheless, we long for her, grateful for the chance she gave us to move over to life's slow lane and savour each day. I feel sure there is another boat trip in our future.

Mementos from the boat trip fill our house. Sea stars hang on walls, and clear jars brimming with seashells adorn counters and shelves. The finest conch and helmet shells sit on bookshelves. The beauty contest winners, our best coral specimens and shells, are displayed on black suede under the glass of our living room coffee table. Artwork from Cuba hangs in the living room. The boat trip photo albums are also stowed there, always within easy reach. The sailboat duvet covers returned too worn and weather-beaten to be used, so I've begun dismantling the squares and reassembling the best ones as wall hangings for the children.

Even more important than the tangible mementos are our memories. Very quickly after we returned, our time away took on a faraway quality. Within three months, we found ourselves telling friends that the boat trip seemed like a lifetime ago. The photographs, videos, journals and emails are all there, but they seem to come from a past more distant than they are. Even if remote, our boat trip memories remain vivid, and suffuse our family life. A whole year's accumulation of shared moments and memories, both dark and bright, forged an unbreakable family bond.

"Remember this golden moment," I often tell the kids. "Then if you're sad or hurt or stressed, you can conjure it up and escape in your memory." The boat trip provided a treasure trove of such moments upon which each of us can draw.

The boat trip also provided a touchstone in our family. We refer to events as either before or after the boat trip.

Besides the mementos and the memories, we gained the precious gift of a lifetime lesson: the importance of living in the present. I find myself actively seeking pockets of time within which to be truly single-minded, completely devoted to only one thing, a stowaway in the moment. I appreciate every golden reprieve, the beauty of my children growing before my eyes, God's many blessings, my husband's love, and every chance I get to write. As a full-fledged swimmer in the North American mainstream, not just immersed but sometimes struggling against the cur-

REETINGS FROM COOL BREEZES

rent, I cannot pretend to truly savour every moment. Yet at least I now know how. I can slip away to a side stream and dwell in the present, an island immobile amid the ebb and flow of life. We've returned to the place where we began, and we're coming to know it for the first time: moment by moment.

Gratitude

An African proverb teaches that it takes a village to raise a child. Likewise, it took a community to foster this book. The following people formed part of my community:

The members of my Writers' Guild of Alberta monthly critiquing group, in particular Wayne Arthurson, Juanita Krause, Dennis Lee, Sandra Konrad, Tony Capri, Michael Dean, Todd Babiak, Cameron Hoffman, and Tom Lincoln. The Guild's non-fiction women writer's group and Canadian Authors Association provided invaluable support during the latter portion of the writing process.

Writing instructors and writers-in-residence Thomas Wharton, Myrna Kostash, Shirley Serviss, Eunice Lynn Scarfe, Gloria Sawai, Curtis Gillespie, and Reinneke Lengelle, who gave generously of their time and advice.

The staff of Providence Renewal Centre, Star of the North Retreat House, and Banff Centre for Fine Arts, where I wrote much of my manuscript and did much of my thinking.

Michelle Wozny, Marie Tappin, and Brian Kathol, all of whom showed exemplary patience with me as they helped with technical aspects of assembling this manuscript.

My knowledgeable and personable editor and my congenial and visionary publishers. Professor Peggy Lynn Kelly had a clear vision of the shape of this book and helped me mould it, and Dr. Frank Tierney and the late Dr. Glenn Clever, Professors Emeritus of Canadian literature at

University of Ottawa, created a venue for new Canadian writers and believed that my project had a place there.

Our kith and kin: friends and family who emailed us regularly during our travels, and the fabulous community of sailors whom we encountered in our travels. All of these fine people supported us in myriad ways.

My friend Heather Birnie, who offered feedback on parts of this book and accommodated our dog Jasper during the transition period of our year's journey.

My aunt and uncle Peggy and Ab Kirdeikis, who hosted Pat and Jasper during the shift from shore to ship.

Fr. Jacques Johnson, O.M.I., whose weekly column "Missionary's Musings" inspired me to look beneath the surface of a thing to search for the profound.

My late father Bernie Kathol and my husband's late father Bill Kirwin, whose life stories inspired our journey, and in particular my father, whose example as an artist inspired me.

My husband's mother Mary and step-father George Kenny, who hosted us for Christmas our year aboard, and who kept us in their prayers while we were at sea.

My mother Eldean Kathol, who harboured my children and me the summer before we left, who visited us not once but twice during our travels, and who prayed for us.

My sister Barbara Kathol and nephew Shelby Goodwin, who joined our crew in the Bahamas. Their willingness to go the distance was an important part of our story.

Jasper, who slept at my feet nearly every moment this book was being written, and who epitomizes the goal of living in the moment.

My four incomparable children Erin, Ben, Liam and Meara, whose lives make my heart grow. They are the gifts to whom Matthew refers in 6:21: For where your treasure is, there your heart will be also. When I finished this manuscript, they prepared a congratulatory card that acknowledged my creation of "a fifth masterpiece." To my sons goes credit for preparing the maps that appear in this book.

Above all, my visionary husband Patrick, without whose dream this book, and the adventure itself, would not exist. To him I owe gratitude beyond telling. He not only suggested I write this book, but also offered helpful critique, gave me many golden opportunities to retreat from life and write, and made me laugh.

For more information about the author,
her family,
her other writing projects,
and the 2000-2001 sailing sabbatical,
please visit the website
www.JeananneKatholKirwin.ca

Glossary

adiós. Spanish word for goodbye.

agua. Spanish word for water.

amigo/amiga. Spanish word for friend.

anemometer. An instrument that measures wind velocity.

archipelago. A large group of islands.

armas. Spanish word for weapons.

arroz con gris. A popular Cuban dish, rice with black beans.

autohelm. An automated steering system connected to the boat's compass by which the boat is steered on a preset course, also referred to as autopilot, and often nicknamed "Otto."

autopista. Spanish word for highway.

avenida. Spanish word for avenue.

bahía. Spanish word for bay.

baño. Spanish word for washroom or bathroom.

beam reach. A point of sail in which the wind blows at right angles to the boat's lengthwise centre line.

beat. To sail against the wind. Often used in the expression "to beat hard."

Beaufort scale. An internationally recognized scale to measure the force of wind.

berth. A bed; also the slip in which a boat lies at dock; broadly speaking, a resting place.

bight. A bend in a shoreline.

bilge. The lowest point of a vessel's interior hull, the space under the floorboards.

blowhole. A naturally occurring sea cliff opening through which wind and water may suddenly blow.

boom. A spar used to hold the bottom length of a sail.

bosun's chair. A canvas seat used to hoist a person aloft to repair rigging.

buenos días/buenas tardes/buenas noches. Spanish greetings that mean good morning, good afternoon/ evening, goodnight.

bueno. Spanish word for good.

bulkhead. A transverse wall in the hull of a boat; bulkheads create the interior compartmentalization of a boat.

cabin. The interior of a boat.

calle. Spanish word for street.

camaróne. Spanish word for baby prawn.

castillo. Spanish word for castle.

catamaran. A boat with two hulls.

cayo. Spanish word for islet or cay.

cerveza. Spanish word for beer.

chart. A map used for seafaring that shows hazards, water depths, buoys, and other aids to navigation.

ciudad. Spanish word for town or city.

cleat. A fitting to which **lines**, sheets and **halyards** are temporarily secured.

cockpit. A recessed part of a boat deck, usually toward the stern, in which the crew may sit, and where the steering and other control mechanisms are located.

cold front. A meteorological term describing the meeting of a mass of cold air with warmer air; as warm air is forced upwards, heavy clouds are formed, bringing rain and strong winds.

companionway. An entrance from the cockpit to the **cabin** or interior of a boat.

concha. Cuban word for seashell.

¿cuánto cuestas? Spanish expression that means how much does it cost.

cuatro. Spanish word for the number four.

cubalibre. A Cuban term for a beverage made of rum and cola.

daggerboard. A board inserted and retracted vertically into a slot in the deck of a boat, used to control leeway or sideways movement.

davit. A support, usually at the stern of a boat, used to hoist and suspend a **dinghy**.

de nada. Spanish expression that means don't mention it, or you're welcome; *nada de nada* means it's nothing, nothing at all.

depth sounder. An electronic instrument that measures the depth of the water below a boat and displays the result.

despacho. A Spanish word for dispatch. In Cuba, the term for the navigational license issued by the Guarda Frontera permitting a foreign boat and crew to travel from port to port within Cuba.

dinghy. A small boat or tender accompanying a larger boat, used to transport people, gear and supplies back and forth from ship to shore.

dodger. A canvas and metal structure sheltering a **cockpit**.

douse. To quickly lower or drop a sail.

downwind sail. To sail with the wind.

draft. The vertical distance between the waterline and the lowest point of boat's hull, propellers, rudders, or keel, and thus the minimum depth of water in which the boat will float. A boat is said to draw a certain measurement of water.

dragging. The unintentional movement of a boat when its anchor is insecure and drags along the sea bottom.

entre. Spanish expression that means come in.

es muy caro. Spanish expression that means it's very expensive.

escuela. Spanish word for school.

estación. Spanish word for station.

fender. A cushioning device, usually made of rubber, hung between a boat and a dock.

following sea or **following waves**. Waves coming from astern.

frittata. A baked egg and vegetable dish.

galley. The kitchen aboard a boat.

GPS (Global Positioning System). A highly accurate worldwide radio navigational system based upon the coordinate positions of orbiting satellites.

gracias. Spanish word for thank-you.

grouper. A fish, namely a large and muscular reef predator.

guagua. A Cuban slang term for bus.

Guarda Frontera. The Cuban border (or coast) guard.

Gulf Stream. Best known of the ocean currents, the Gulf Stream originates in the Gulf of Mexico, passes through the Straits of Florida and then flows northeast parallel to the U.S. coast. Northward from there, it merges with the North Atlantic Drift. Its breadth is up to fifty statute miles across and its flow averages four miles per hour.

gunkhole. To meander from one secluded anchorage to another.

gusto. Spanish word for pleasure.

harina. Spanish word for flour.

halyard. A **line** used to hoist a sail aloft.

hasta la vista/hasta luego. Spanish expressions that mean goodbye, see you, or see you later.

hatch. A deck opening that provides access to the interior; sometimes also refers to the hinged or sliding fitted covering for a hatch.

haul-out. The removal of a boat from the water.

head. The toilet aboard a boat.

headwind. The wind that the bow of a boat heads into.

heel. To tip or lean to one side, usually from the force of the wind.

helado. Spanish word for ice cream.

helm. The tiller or wheel and other steering gear.

hola. Spanish greeting that means hello or hi.

holding tank. Storage tank for sewage, held until it can be pumped out.

Intracoastal Waterway (ICW). A succession of connected bays, rivers, sounds and canals that runs inland of the U.S. Atlantic coast, enabling travel sheltered from the open sea.

inukshuk. A Canadian Inuit term for a cairn in the shape of a person, often used as a landmark or guidepost.

jib. A triangular sail set ahead of the **mainsail.**

jibe (also gybe). To change course by passing the stern of the boat through the wind, so that the mainsail and jib move from one side of the boat to the other. An accidental jibe can be dangerous.

jinitero/jinitera. A Cuban term for a street hustler (male/female).

Kalik. The brand name for a Bahamian beer.

keel. The principal underwater structure running along the lengthwise centre line of a boat hull, necessary for steering stability and reducing leeway.

key lime pie. A pie made using the juice of island, or key, limes.

knot. A unit of speed, one nautical mile per hour, used to express both boat speed and wind velocity.

lee. The direction toward which the wind blows; **leeward** means toward the lee.

lifeline. A **line** usually made of wire and covered with plastic, strung along stanchions at the sides of a boat's deck to prevent the crew from falling overboard.

lifesaver. A life preserver shaped like a ring; a buoyant device designed to keep a person afloat in the water.

line. A rope used aboard a boat. Some specialized types of **line** are a sheet, used to control a sail's lateral movement; the mainsheet, used to control the **mainsail**; a **halyard**, used to hoist a sail aloft; and a dockline, used to secure a boat to a dock. One of the most important docklines is a spring line, used to control the forward and backward motion of a boat tied to a dock. Another type of dockline is a bowline, used to secure the bow of a boat, not to be confused with a type of knot by the same name.

locker. A storage space or closet.

maestra. Spanish word for teacher.

mainsail. The large sail hoisted on the stern side of the mast, pronounced "mains'l."

mañana. Spanish word for tomorrow.

marmalada. Cuban word for marmalade.

mogotes. A Cuban term for the misshapen green hills that erupt from the plains.

mojito. A Cuban term for a rum drink with lime juice, soda, and crushed fresh mint.

momento. Spanish word for moment.

monohull. A boat with one hull.

mooring. Permanent ground tackle to which a vessel may attach a line instead of anchoring.

motor-sail. To travel under simultaneous power of both the boat's engines and its sails.

motorsailer. A sailboat with an especially large engine and spacious accommodations.

mucho grande. Spanish expression loosely translated to mean much or very large.

muñeca. Spanish word for doll.

nautical mile. An international measure of distance, 1.852 kilometres. A nautical mile is approximately ten percent longer than a statute mile.

niño/niña. Spanish word for child (male/female).

no problema. Spanish expression that means no problem.

on the hard. An expression describing a boat and crew's position hoisted out of the water and onto the land.

on the hook. An expression describing a boat and crew's position at anchor.

painter. A towline or tie-up line for a dinghy or other small boat.

paella. Spanish word for a baked dish made of rice and meat or seafood.

paladero. A Cuban term for a restaurant in the dining room of a private home.

panadería. Spanish word for bakery.

pan jamón. A common Cuban sandwich, bread with ham.

paso malo. Spanish expression that means bad passage, or bad road.

Perfect Paul. Cruisers' nickname for the digital voice of the local weather announcer transmitted over the **VHF radio**.

perro/perra. Spanish word for dog (male/female).

por favor. Spanish expression that means please.

porthole. The window of a boat; not necessarily round.

protocolo. Cuban term for a type of hotel.

pulpit. The metal railing at the bow of a boat.

ranchito. A Spanish word for a small thatch-roofed hut.

regatta. A boat race event.

río. Spanish word for river.

rudder. The broad surface, usually at the stern and below the water, by which a boat is steered. It is connected to the tiller or wheel of a boat by means of a post or shaft.

salon. The living area of a boat, in which the seating for meals is located.

salud. Spanish greeting that means cheers, taken from the Spanish word for health.

schadenfreude. Pleasure derived from the misfortunes of others.

scuppers. Drain holes in the deck or cockpit of a boat.

sí. Spanish word for yes (*si* means if).

single sideband (SSB) radio. Radio equipment intended for reception and/or communication of signals over distances exceeding twenty-five nautical miles. Its name derives from the single sideband it uses adjacent to a carrier wave.

sole. The floor of the **cabin** or **cockpit**.

spinnaker. A three-cornered sail of light, often colourful fabric, used in downwind sailing.

sloop. A sailboat with one mast.

spring tide. A tide that occurs when there is a new moon in conjunction with the sun, or a full moon in opposition to the sun, resulting in a markedly wider tidal range.

stateroom. Sleeping quarters.

stay. Wire rigging used to support the masts of a boat and to carry certain types of sail, such as a **jib**. The stay at the bow of a boat is called a forestay.

sundowner. Any beverage enjoyed at sunset.

tack. To change course by passing the bow of the boat through the wind, so that the mainsail and jib move from one side of the boat to the other.

tapa. Spanish word for appetizer, snack, or *hors d'oeuvre*.

tender. A small boat accompanying a larger vessel, used to transport crew, gear, or supplies; a dinghy.

tienda. Spanish word for shop or store.

topping lift. A cable supporting the **boom**.

trampoline or **tramp**. The large net stretched between the twin bows of a **catamaran**.

tropical depression. A meteorological term describing a disturbance of tropical origin characterized by counter-clockwise winds of less than thirty-three knots. When the winds increase beyond thirty-three knots, it is a tropical storm. When the counter-clockwise circulation reaches sixty-four knots or more, it is a tropical typhoon, more popularly known as a hurricane.

underway. In motion, enroute; neither at anchor, nor aground, nor made fast to shore.

VHF (very high frequency) **radio**. Direct voice radio equipment intended for communication over short distances up to twenty-five nautical miles.

wake. The disturbance of the water resulting from the passage of a moving vessel, resembling twin furrows emanating from the hull of the boat.

weigh. To raise the anchor; to weigh anchor is to depart an anchorage.

y. Spanish word for and.

yerbabuena. Spanish word for the herb mint.

Acknowledgments and Permissions

Collecting quotations appeals to writers; the apt often appears with graceful synchronicity. I have drawn the epigraphs appearing at the top of every numbered chapter from a myriad of sources such as books (including books of quotations), newspaper and magazine articles, and even plaques in public places. A thorough search was conducted to determine whether previously published material included in this book requires permission to reprint. I apologize for, and promise to correct in a subsequent edition, any error or omission.

A word about privacy and anonymity is in order. Some of the sailor, sailboat, and other individual names contained in this book are pseudonyms, to protect privacy where I have been unable to contact the individuals in question, or they have indicated their preference for anonymity. Similarly, I have obtained consent from those individuals whom I have been able to reach for the use of their images in photographs.

All artwork and maps, most of the photographs, and some musical lyrics reproduced in this book are credited to the crew of *Cool Breezes*, with some exceptions. For example, willing and cheerful, but anonymous, passersby whom I am unable to locate took some of the photographs. Where other identifiable artists are the creators, I have sought permission to use their works. The authors, publishers, photographers, musical artists, and estates or agents who have graciously granted their permissions include the following:

Eileen Quinn granted permission to use lyrics from her musical compositions throughout this book. Her CDs may be obtained from her website www.eileenquinn.com or by calling 1-800-289-6923.

Jim Young took the cover photo, and permitted me use of it.

Susan Fryer was commissioned to take the author photo.

Ian Grant, Photohouse Studios Inc., was commissioned to take the family photo that appears on page 2.

Gary Graham allowed me to use excerpts from his article "If I'm Really, Really Good, Can We Keep the Boat?" on pp. 205 and 425. *Living Aboard* magazine, May/June 2001, Volume XXVIII, Number 3, pp. 27-29.

Sailing: A Lubber's Dictionary, copyright 2001 by Henry Beard and Roy McKie. Excerpt reprinted on page 41 by permission of Workman Publishing Co., Inc., New York. All rights reserved.

"Four Strong Winds," composed by Ian Tyson, copyright Slick Fork Music. Reprinted in part on page 494 with permission. All rights reserved.

"Little Gidding," from *Four Quartets,* copyright 1942 by T.S. Eliot and renewed 1970 by Esme Valerie Eliot. Reprinted on page 509 with permission by Harcourt, Inc.

"Pescador de Hombres" ("Lord You Have Come"), Spanish text and music copyright 1979 Cesáreo Gabaráin. English translation copyright 1987 by OCP Publications, Portland, Oregon. Excerpt used on page 477 with permission. All rights reserved.

The glossary was compiled with reference to numerous sources, among them *Chapman Piloting* (New York, New York: Hearst Marine Books, 61st ed., 1994), *Nelson Canadian Dictionary of the English Language* (Scarborough, Ontario: Thomson Canada Limited, 1997), *HarperCollins Spanish College Dictionary* (Glasgow, Great Britain: HarperCollins Publishers, 3rd ed., 1998), and the captain of *Cool Breezes,* Patrick Kirwin.

MEMBER OF SCABRINI GROUP

Québec, Canada
2005